"The House That Jack Built: Florence Maybrick & Jack the Ripper"

By

Kieran James*
University of the West of Scotland
Kieran.James@uws.ac.uk and
Kieran.James99@yahoo.co.uk

A revised form of this article was originally published as follows: James, K. (2017), "The Florence Maybrick Trial of 1889 and the need for courts of criminal appeal", *International Journal of Critical Accounting*, Vol. 9, No. 2, pp. 85-102.

*Address for Correspondence: Dr Kieran James, School of Business and Enterprise, University of the West of Scotland, Paisley campus, Paisley, Renfrewshire, Scotland PA1 2BE, tel: +44 (0)141 848 3350, e-mail: Kieran.James@uws.ac.uk and
Kieran.James99@yahoo.co.uk
Facebook: https://www.facebook.com/kieran.james.94©

© Copyright Kieran James 2017, Paisley, Renfrewshire, Scotland

Published by Kieran James, 2017.

ISBN 978-0-244-34638-6 (paperback version)

Author bio

Dr Kieran James is a Senior Lecturer in Accounting at the University of the West of Scotland, Paisley, Renfrewshire, Scotland. He was formerly the Accounting Professor at University of Fiji, Fiji Islands, from 2013-15. He has published scholarly articles in the following journals: *Accounting Forum*, *Critical Perspectives on Accounting*, *International Journal of Critical Accounting*, *International Journal of Social Economics*, *International Journal of Sport Management and Marketing*, *Musicology Australia*, *Pacific Accounting Review*, *Punk & Post Punk*, and *Sporting Traditions*. He runs a heavy-metal music website Busuk Chronicles which has had over 70,000 page-views as at 26 August 2017. He also founded and is the current manager of the Joo Chiat Road Online (Singapore politics); Nadi Legends Club (football); and WAFL Golden Era (Australian Rules football) websites.

The House That Jack Built:
Florence Maybrick & Jack the Ripper
Abstract

The criminal trial of Mrs Florence Maybrick, held in Liverpool, England during the height of the British Empire 1889, is widely regarded as one of the greatest travesties of justice in British legal history where even the judge at the end of the trial remarked "well, they can't convict her on that evidence" and the chief prosecutor nodded his head in agreement. Mrs Maybrick was tried for murdering her husband via arsenic poisoning. However, the trial became a morality trial when the learned judge, **Mr Justice James Fitzjames Stephen,** linked Mrs Maybrick's demonstrated adultery to her alleged desire to physically remove her husband by administering poison. The jury, which pronounced a guilty verdict, consisted of twelve untrained and unschooled men who were unable to grasp the technical evidence and were probably unduly influenced by the judge's summing-up and by the professional status of one of the medical witnesses for the prosecution. The case is a timely reminder today for an international audience of the fallibility and inherent weaknesses of the legal system and the desperate need to retain Courts of Criminal Appeal within the courts system.

Keywords: *Arsenic addiction, British History, Florence Maybrick, Legal History, Liverpool, Jack the Ripper, James Maybrick, Social History.*

Introduction

The criminal trial of Mrs Florence Maybrick, held in Liverpool, England during the height of the British Empire 1889, is widely regarded as one of the greatest travesties of justice in British legal history where even the judge at the end of the trial remarked "well, they can't convict her on that evidence" and the chief prosecutor nodded his head in agreement (as witnessed by a newspaper reporter and cited in Christie, 1968, p. 141). Mrs Maybrick was tried for murdering her husband via arsenic poisoning. However, the trial became a morality trial when the learned judge, **Mr Justice James Fitzjames Stephen,** linked Mrs Maybrick's demonstrated adultery to her alleged desire to physically remove her husband by administering poison. Mr Justice Stephen was wrong to attempt to, in the words of his brother Sir Leslie, turn his own criminal court into a "school of morality" (cited in Christie, 1968, p. 134). The jury, which pronounced a guilty verdict, consisted of twelve untrained and unschooled men who were unable to grasp the technical evidence and were probably unduly influenced by the judge's summing-up and by the professional status of one of the medical witnesses for the prosecution.

István Szijártó (2002, p. 212) writes that the advantages of microhistory such as the present paper are as follows: "...it can appeal to its readers by being interesting, it transmits lived experience, it stands on both feet on the ground of reality, and with all the lines branching out from the event, person or community in focus, it points towards the general". The case presented here is a timely reminder today for an international audience of the fallibility and inherent weaknesses of the legal system and the desperate need to retain Courts of Criminal Appeal within the courts system. It also suggests that senior judges aged over 55 years, and especially those who have suffered strokes or head injuries, need to be regularly evaluated by their peers or by other qualified persons. Mental decline can occur earlier than expected and can have disastrous consequences.

James and Florence Maybrick – the initial meeting and early married life

Mr James Maybrick, cotton merchant of Liverpool, was an eligible bachelor in his early-40s when he met the 17-year-old American Miss Florence "Florie" Elizabeth Chandler on board the steamer *SS Baltic* heading back from the USA to England which had departed from New York City on 11 March 1880 (Christie, 1968, p. 36; Feldman, 2007, pp. 75-6; Graham and Emmas, 1999, p. 28; Harrison, 2008, p. 219). Whilst gathered around the bar on the first evening offshore, Mr Maybrick was introduced by General J.G. Hazard of New Orleans to the Baroness von Roques and her daughter Florence (Christie, 1968, p. 37; Graham and Emmas, 1999, p. 28).[1] Mr Maybrick had been in the New World to attend to his cotton interests. Maybrick & Co. had opened an American office in the cotton-exporting port-city of Norfolk, Virginia in the late-1870s (Graham and Emmas, 1999, p. 31). Christie (1968, p. 37) was not over-exaggerating his point when he wrote that the introduction of James to Florence by General Hazard "set in motion a portentous train of events". To the surprise of many observers, James and Florence began a romance

---

[1] The population of Norfolk had been 21,966 in 1880, rising to 34,871 ten years later.

which had crystallized into a committed relationship by the time the ship arrived in Liverpool six days after its departure. When they left the ship it was decided that if they still felt the same way about each other in a year's time they would marry (Graham and Emmas, 1999, p. 32).[2] This criteria must have been fulfilled because the couple duly wed in St. James's Church (which still stands today) in London's Piccadilly on 27 July 1881 when Florence was only 18-years-old **(Christie, 1968, p. 38;** Feldman, 2007, p. 76; **Graham and Emmas, 1999, p. 34; Maybrick, 2012, p. 21). Christie (1968, p. 39) offers the following observations about the marriage which seemed to begin favourably but soon deteriorated amidst adultery and arsenic addiction:**

> "As events unfolded it is now clear that the marriage was founded in part on avarice and deception. While unquestionably sincere in his affections [how can Christie, from the vantage point of 1968, be so sure about this point?], James was intrigued by the Baroness's glib tales of a vast tract of Southern lands that would some day be inherited by her daughter. The mother, for her part, was nearing the end of her financial rope and envisioned a life of ease in her twilight years with the aid of a seemingly rich son-in-law. Genuinely in love for the first time [how can Christie, from the vantage point of 1968, be so sure about this point also?], Florie was an innocent pawn in the game – dominated by her mother, bedazzled by her bridegroom".

---

[2] However, Nigel Morland (1957), incorrectly it seems, dates the first meeting of the couple to a trip from the USA to England in 1881 not 1880. This is why he, also incorrectly, assumes that the marriage occurred almost immediately after disembarking the ship.

After briefly honeymooning in Bournemouth they lived in Norfolk for the next three years, spending about half their time in USA and the other half in Liverpool (Christie, 1968, p. 40). In 1884, James Maybrick was replaced by his brother Edwin as the buying agent for Maybrick & Co. in Norfolk, and James Maybrick's family returned to Liverpool (Christie, 1968, p. 40; Graham and Emmas, 1999, pp. 38-9). They first rented a house known as Beechville in the suburb of Grassendale Park North (Christie, 1968, p. 40; Graham and Emmas, 1999, p. 39). The family later took out a five-year lease on Battlecrease House in Aigburth, near the Mersey River, Liverpool, in February 1888 (Graham and Emmas, 1999, pp. 43-4). According to Christie (1968, p. 41), and there can be no dissenting opinions here, "it was [at Battlecrease House] that fate would strike". The couple brought with them to the ill-fated Battlecrease House (which still stands today on Riversdale Road) their two children the elder Master James Chandler Maybrick ("Bobo") (born 24 March 1882) (Christie, 1968, p. 41; Graham and Emmas, 1999, p. 39, note; Maybrick, 2012, p. 21) and the younger Miss Gladys Evelyn Maybrick (born 20 June 1886, according to

Maybrick, 2012, p. 21, and 21 June 1886, according to Graham and Emmas, 1999, p. 39).

Christie (1968, p. 42) comments that "[i]n an age dedicated to the worship of property and material things it is significant that Maybrick, despite his high position in the world of trade, never owned a home throughout his married life". The Maybricks were much like the "new money" Forsytes (although the Forsytes were richer than the Maybricks) in the novel *The Forsyte Saga*, always being concerned with the maintenance of the appearances befitting a family of high social standing. As Christie (1968, p. 42) commented: "From all appearances in the first years of their marriage the Maybricks were safely embarked on the conventional social life of Victorian England". An important reason for the Maybricks' endless whirl of dinner-parties was no doubt to impress their business and social acquaintances. Mr Maybrick's attitude towards his arsenic eating reflected the hypocrisies of the times, with him swinging from boasting about it to angrily denying it depending on the person he was talking to and the immediate context. For example, when Florie wrote to James' younger brother Michael in March 1889 to advise him that James was taking a "white powder" which might explain the pains in his head, James angrily responded to Michael's questioning about the powder with: "Whoever told you that? It is a damned lie" (cited in Christie 1968, pp. 48-9).

Mr and Mrs Maybrick's marital relationship worsened during their time at Battlecrease House when it was put under considerable strain by Mr Maybrick's financial problems, his arsenic habits, his infidelity (Edwards, 2007, p. 54), his aloofness, the couple's spending habits, and Mrs Maybrick's personal debts. Sometime during 1887 Florie discovered that James was regularly seeing and maintaining a mistress and it was from this point onwards that the Maybricks slept in separate beds (Christie, 1968, p. 45).

Mr Maybrick almost certainly had an arsenic addiction; the eating of arsenic by middle-class men as a medicinal or sexual tonic seems to have been a 19th century phenomenon. A brief, signed by Charles Russell QC, I. Fletcher Moulton QC, Harry Bookin Poland QC, and Reginald Smith QC, at Lincoln's Inn on 12 April 1892, and prepared by Messrs. Lumley & Lumley presents evidence that a Mr Valentine Charles Blake signed a statutory declaration to the effect that he had procured for Mr

Maybrick 150 grains of arsenic around two months before his (Maybrick's) death (cited in Maybrick, 2012, pp. 278, footnote, pp. 312-3). Mary Howard of Norfolk, Virginia, the madam of a brothel Mr Maybrick patronized at least three times a week for several years prior to his marriage, spoke as follows about Mr Maybrick's arsenic eating: "I saw him frequently in his different moods and fancies". He took arsenic two or three times each evening, she swore, and she was afraid that he would die on the premises and "some of us [the house girls] would be suspected of his murder" (cited in Christie, 1968, p. 36). Thomas Stansell, a black servant of Maybrick's from his bachelor days in Norfolk (1878-80), also testified to Maybrick's arsenic habit but it seems that this witness failed to receive the respect he deserved in court perhaps for race-related reasons. Stansell testified that, in his first year of service, he was asked three or four times to go the drug-store and buy arsenic for Maybrick without a prescription (Christie, 1968, p. 119).

Mr Maybrick's health progressively deteriorated in late April 1889 and his death on 11 May 1889 of exhaustion caused by gastro-enteritis (**Graham and Emmas, 1999, p. 173;** Lumley & Lumley-prepared brief cited in Maybrick,

2012, pp. 268, 309, 335) could have been influenced by the effects of arsenic withdrawal. The quantity of arsenic found in his body post-mortem, one-tenth of a grain total in the liver, kidney, and intestines, was consistent with an arsenic eater who had left off the habit for some time perhaps even for a couple of months (Christie, 1968, p. 70; Feldman, 1997; Lumley & Lumley-prepared brief cited in Maybrick, 2012, p. 336). The gastro-enteritis which killed Mr Maybrick was probably caused by bad food or drink or by excessive consumption of the same or by Mr Maybrick's distressing experience of being soaked wet on the day of the Wirral Races, 27 April 1889 (**Graham and Emmas, 1999, p. 173;** Lumley & Lumley-prepared brief cited in Maybrick, 2012, pp. 266, 268, 309). The effects of arsenic withdrawal may well have been a factor in his death (Christie, 1968, p. 167). In fact, Christie (1968, p. 167) calls this the "most sensible theory" yet advanced about the cause of death.

Key participants at the Florence Maybrick trial

For the first nine decades of the 20th century James and Florence Maybrick were remembered because of the notorious 1889 criminal trial of the American Florence when she was convicted of murdering her older English husband James by arsenic poisoning (Schoettler, 1993). During the trial the jury and court reflected on the salacious details of her affair with Alfred Brierley and the trial was widely regarded as a trial of Mrs Maybrick's morality. Consistent with the ethos of Victorian times Mr Maybrick's extra-marital relationships (Edwards, 2007, p. 54) were glossed over while those of his wife's were viewed as unforgivable (Christie, 1968, pp. 126-7; Graham and Emmas, 1999, p. 7). It was easy for many people of the era to believe that a woman capable of committing adultery was easily capable of committing murder as well. In fact, the aging Mr Justice James Fitzjames Stephen (born 3 March 1829 – died 11 March 1894) (father of "Jack-the-Ripper" serial-murder suspect James Kenneth Stephen, 25 February 1859 – 3 February 1892) presented the case to the jury specifically as a *morality trial* (as we shall see). Generally it is perceived that the defence erred in not asking for the trial to be moved away from Liverpool

(Graham and Emmas, 1999, p. 156), as Mrs Maybrick had requested in a letter to her mother from Walton Jail (dated 28 June 1889) (Maybrick, 2012, p. 51). However, Mrs Maybrick herself suggested in her 1904 book *My Fifteen Lost Years* that the reason had been a funding shortfall (Graham and Emmas, 1999, pp. 157-8; Maybrick, 2012, p. 51).

Charles Russell (10 November 1832 – 10 August 1900) (later Baron Russell of Killowen and Lord Chief Justice of England) was Mrs Maybrick's famed defence lawyer and a strong supporter of her innocence (although at the time this was denied by certain commentators belonging to the anti-Florence Maybrick camp including Lord Hugh Cecil (Maybrick, 2012, pp. 144, 255)). Christie (1968, p. 72) remarks that Sir Charles: "was regarded by most authorities as the most brilliant advocate of his day". Confirming this assertion, he rose to the pinnacle of the English legal system, the Lord Chief Justice of England. However, Sir Charles performed only moderately well in defence of Mrs Maybrick. The reason for this was that he was mentally exhausted following his important role in the earlier Parnell Commission hearings which had included his finest hour, a six-day defence speech (Christie, 1968,

p. 111; Graham and Emmas, 1999, p. 161). His biographer R. Barry O'Brien (1901, p. 259) wrote that: "To dwell on any of Russell's cases after the Parnell Commission would be an anti-climax" but he does spend five pages at this juncture on the Maybrick trial. Mrs Maybrick was later to call Sir Charles, who visited her in Aylesbury Prison, "the noblest, truest friend that woman ever had"; "the champion of the weak and the oppressed"; and "the brave upholder of justice and law in the face of prejudice and public hostility" (Maybrick, 2012, pp. 143-4). Sir Charles' direct opponent at the Florence Maybrick trial was Mr John Edmund Wentworth Addison QC MP (5 November 1838 – 22 April 1907).

Mr Justice Stephen exhibited signs of approaching insanity during the trial and he was widely regarded as being only a shadow of his former self (Graham and Emmas, 1999, p. 193; Maybrick, 2012, pp. 237, 393). He was forced to resign in April 1891 (Christie, 1968, p. 145; Graham and Emmas, 1999, p. 193; Maybrick, 2012, p. 393) and he died on 11 March 1894 in a private lunatic asylum in Ipswich (so clearly Mrs Maybrick (2012, p. 237) was wrong when she wrote in 1904 that he died "a year" after her trial) (Christie, 1968, p. 145; Graham and Emmas,

1999, p. 193). He was called "the great mad judge" in the Liverpool *Daily Post* of 13 August 1900 (cited in Maybrick, 2012, p. 238). This *Daily Post* article concluded that "[i]t was shocking to think that a human life depended upon the direction of this wreck of what was once a great judge" (cited in Maybrick, 2012, p. 239). In the 1890 second edition of his book *A General View of the Criminal Law of England* Mr Justice Stephen was to write that the Florence Maybrick case was the only case out of the 979 he had tried between January 1885 and September 1889 where "there could be any doubt about the facts" (Stephen, 1890, p. 174, cited in Christie, 1968, p. 145 and Maybrick, 2012, p. 394).

Mr Justice Stephen's closing address in the Florence Maybrick trial was an oddity in that he was favourable to Mrs Maybrick on the first afternoon but inexplicably changed his tone when he began again the next morning (Christie, 1968, pp. 19, 137; Graham and Emmas, 1999, p. 5; Lumley & Lumley-prepared brief cited in Maybrick, 2012, p. 364; Maybrick, 2012, p. 393). It was the closing day section of Mr Justice Stephen's address which was ultimately the one factor which was crucial in the failure of Sir Charles to secure his client's acquittal (Edwards,

2007, p. 54). Ultimately Mrs Maybrick was found guilty based on nothing more than "the mere gossip of servants" (Maybrick, 2012, p. 41). Christie (1968, pp. 56, 57) concludes as follows about the shadowy coalition below-stairs who were waiting for Mrs Maybrick to trip up so that they might conspire to do her harm:

> "It is undoubtedly true, however, that an amorphous, loosely organized cabal was operating at Battlecrease House to snare Florie in some misdeed that would break up her marriage and deprive her of her children; but, whatever its objective, it was certainly not to hound her to the gallows. ... Over the span of fifteen days from Saturday, April 27th [1889] to Saturday May 11th, this deadly cabal did its work at Battlecrease House".

Christie (1968, p. 56) lists Mrs Briggs, "abetted by her married and unmarried sisters", a group of women who had earlier held romantic aspirations in relation to both James and Alfred Brierley but who had remained friends of the family and were frequent visitors to Battlecrease. The aptly-named Miss Alice Yapp was also named by Christie, a nosy domestic-servant who opened a letter of Mrs Maybrick's she had been given for the purpose of posting it to Brierley on the pretext that three-year-old Gladys had dropped it in the mud. Alice Yapp was arguably bitter after suffering a recent relationship breakup of her own. Miss Yap brought the letter to Edwin Maybrick who telegraphed his brother Michael with instructions to come to the house straight away from London (Christie 1968, p. 61). Miss Yapp was also the one who reported to Mrs Briggs seeing flypapers in the bathroom and these were later tested for arsenic. In a recent murder trial in Liverpool two working-class women had been convicted for murder by obtaining arsenic from flypaper. On the same day as the two previously mentioned events, Miss Yap telegraphed Michael Maybrick with the message: "Come at once strange things going on here" (cited in Christie 1968, p. 61).

Drs Carter and Humphreys were ready and willing to write out "acute inflammation of the stomach" on the death certificate but only decided not to do so after a discussion with Michael where Mrs Maybrick was implicated (Christie, 1968, pp. 70, 99-101). We then had the strange situation of a musical composer advising two medical practitioners as to the cause of death (letter from family friend Charles Ratcliff to John Aunspaugh, May / June 1889, cited in Christie, 1968, pp. 63-4). After the cross-examination of Dr Humphreys at the trial, Christie (1968, p. 100) remarks that "[t]here were strong doubts [among those assembled in the courtroom] as to how far Michael Maybrick and his suspicions had swayed the doctor in withholding a certificate of death". At Michael's insistence, James' body was exhumed two weeks after its burial but, as mentioned earlier, only one-tenth of a grain was found in the kidney, liver, and intestines and none in the rest of the body (Christie, 1968, p. 70).

My analysis of the Florence Maybrick trial

Mrs Maybrick was found guilty largely based on the flypaper containing arsenic (Edwards, 2007, p. 54). She claimed that she was using this recipe as a facial treatment (Schoettler, 1993). Lumley & Lumley noted that: "[t]he purchase and soaking of fly-papers is the only direct evidence of the possession of arsenic in any form by Mrs. Maybrick" (cited in Maybrick, 2012, p. 269). After she was imprisoned her mother found such a fly-paper recipe dated 1878 inside Mrs Maybrick's family Bible, which was cited by the Lumley & Lumley-prepared brief (cited in Maybrick, 2012, pp. 347-8) as additional evidence in favour of her innocence. This prescription for face-wash containing arsenic was signed by a Dr Bay of New York City (Christie, 1968, pp. 216-7; Maybrick, 2012, p. 348). It was duly made up by a French chemist in Paris on 17 July 1878 (Christie, 1968, pp. 216-7; Maybrick, 2012, p. 348). Unfortunately this information was received far too late for the original trial and the authorities consistently rejected appeals for a new trial. Other evidence unfavourable to Florence included: the finding of arsenic in meat juice (half a grain); on a handkerchief; on a dressing-gown; in a bottle; and in a package labelled "Arsenic: Poison for Cats" (Christie,

1968, p. 102). The handkerchief; dressing-gown; bottle; and package were all found in the defendant's bedroom (Christie, 1968, p. 102). The amounts ranged from a fraction of a grain to 65 grains (Christie, 1968, p. 102), but are also consistent with self-medication of arsenic by James. The ridiculous inscription on the package "Arsenic: Poison for Cats" strongly suggests a sick joke and possible malicious intent on the part of the domestic servants.

The following somewhat strange statement by the Home Secretary, Mr Henry Matthews (13 January 1826 - 3 April 1913), was the ground for the 1889 decision to spare Mrs Maybrick the death penalty and reduce her sentence to life imprisonment:

> "After the fullest consideration, and after taking the best medical and legal advice that could be obtained, the Home Secretary [H.M.] advised Her Majesty [Queen Victoria] to respite the capital punishment of Florence Elizabeth Maybrick and to commute the punishment to penal servitude for life; inasmuch as, although the evidence leads to the conclusion that the prisoner administered and attempted to administer arsenic to her husband with intent to murder him, yet it does not wholly exclude a reasonable doubt *whether his death was in fact caused by the administration of arsenic*" [cited in Maybrick, 2012, pp. 226-7, emphasis original].

As Maybrick (2012) explains, there are a number of major problems raised by this statement. Firstly, if there was indeed "reasonable doubt" (a legal term) whether James

Maybrick's death *"was in fact caused by the administration of arsenic"* then the prisoner Mrs Maybrick should have been found "not guilty" by the jury and should have been immediately set free rather than simply have had her sentence reduced to life imprisonment (Henry W. Lucy, *The Strand Magazine*, London, November 1900, cited in Maybrick, 2012, p. 253). Henry Matthews was indeed trying to claim some totally untenable middle ground. For the jury to have found Mrs Maybrick guilty, all of the following pre-conditions should have been satisfied: (a) that Mr Maybrick's death was caused by arsenic poisoning; (b) that Mrs Maybrick administered the fatal dose of arsenic; and (c) that the arsenic was administered by Mrs Maybrick with the intent to kill (Christie, 1968, p. 113).

If only pre-conditions (a) and (b) were present then Mrs Maybrick could have been convicted on a lesser charge but not on the charge of murder. In fact, there were serious doubts associated with each of the three necessary pre-conditions and it can well be argued that none of the three pre-conditions, even taken as individual propositions, were ever proved beyond reasonable doubt. In regards pre-condition (a), taken by itself, if over 65 grains of arsenic was found in the house how can we explain why such a tiny quantity of arsenic was found in the body of the deceased? **Even if the Home Office's statement that "although the evidence leads to the conclusion that the prisoner administered and attempted to administer arsenic to her husband with intent to murder him" was valid (which it wasn't (**Lumley & Lumley-prepared brief **cited in Maybrick, 2012, p. 296)) this should not have been enough to have sustained a murder charge because the death had not been proven beyond reasonable doubt to have been caused by arsenic poisoning (Maybrick, 2012, p. 244). Even Mr Justice Stephen, although on the whole a poor performer at the trial, had told the members of the jury that "[i]t is** *essential* **to this charge** *that the man died of arsenic*" **(cited in Maybrick, 2012, p. 227, emphasis original).**

Secondly, Mrs Maybrick was never tried at court for "administering and attempting to administer arsenic ... with intent to murder" her husband (Lumley & Lumley-prepared brief cited in Maybrick, 2012, p. 365) so she could not and should not have been found guilty of such a charge (Christie, 1968, p. 170; Maybrick, 2012, p. 228). This was the charge which the Home Office perhaps wished or imagined that Mrs Maybrick had been charged with.

The medical evidence made it clear that the quantity of arsenic contained in Mr Maybrick's body – one-tenth of a grain – was insufficient to have caused death (Maybrick, 2012, p. 235; Lumley & Lumley-prepared brief cited in Maybrick, 2012, pp. 313-4). Mr Davies found 0.02 of a grain in the liver and Dr Stevenson found 0.076 of a grain in the liver and 0.015 in the intestines making the total amount found by both doctors combined around one-tenth of a grain (Graham and Emmas, 1999, p. 173; Lumley & Lumley-prepared brief cited in Maybrick, 2012, p. 311). The smallest quantity of arsenic previously found to have caused a victim's death had been two grains and this was with respect to a woman who had not been an arsenic eater during life (Lumley & Lumley-prepared brief cited in Maybrick, 2012, p. 311). The experienced doctors for the defence (with the exception of Dr Stevenson) were of the opinion that the low quantity of arsenic found in Mr Maybrick's body was consistent with "administration in medicinal doses, and [the arsenic] might have been introduced a considerable time before [death]" (Maybrick, 2012, p. 235 and see also Lumley & Lumley-prepared brief cited in Maybrick, 2012, p. 313). In other words, the evidence merely showed that Mr Maybrick had been self-administering arsenic and that he may have stopped doing so (with disastrous consequences) some time prior to his eventual demise.

We should now briefly refer to the sub-standard responses from the star expert witness for the prosecution, Dr Thomas Stevenson (a lecturer on forensic medicine and chemistry at Guy's Hospital (Christie, 1968, p. 107)), under cross-examination in the courtroom. The evidence also shows how deeply divided the doctors on this case were. In response to a question from QC Addison for the prosecution, the witness answered as follows: "I have no doubts that this man died from the effects of arsenic" (cited in Christie, 1968, p. 108). It is worth following the cross-examination responses closely. When he was then asked about the fatal dose of arsenic needed to kill an adult he responded: "Two grains or thereabouts" (cited in Christie, 1968, p. 108). Then it was Sir Charles' turn to cross-examine. Christie (1986, p. 109) remarks that: "Sir Charles realized he had a formidable witness on his hands", but the reference to "formidable" should be held to refer to his overall self-confident presence rather than to the quality of his answers. Sir Charles asked whether there is any "distinct symptom" of arsenic poisoning which distinguishes it from gastroenteritis caused by other factors. Dr Stevenson was snide and over-confident when he replied: "There is no distinctive diagnostic symptom of arsenical poisoning: the diagnostic thing is finding the arsenic". We see here the doctor falling into the careful trap laid by the expert defence counsel. Sir Charles let his case rest when he then got Dr Stevenson to confess that 0.076 of a grain of arsenic was found in the liver and 0.015 of a grain in the intestines, totalling 0.091 of a grain. Clearly then, given that "*the diagnostic thing is finding the arsenic*", there was no evidence at all that Mr Maybrick died from arsenic poisoning. As Christie (1968, p. 110) concludes: "If two grains of the poison is a fatal dose on the average, as the witness had testified, it is not surprising that many in the court felt that such minute traces of arsenic represented rather feeble evidence on which to base the doctor's opinion as to the cause of death". Sir Charles could be forgiven if he believed that this time he had landed the case's decisive blow. In contrast to the testimony of Dr Stevenson, Dr Charles Tidy of the London Hospital (who held a position comparable to Dr Stevenson's at Guy's (Christie, 1968, p. 115)) and Dr Frank T. Paul, medical authority at University College, Liverpool and Victoria University, Manchester, both argued that it was *not* a case of arsenic poisoning; Dr Tidy said the case "absolutely points away from arsenic as the cause of death" while Dr Paul testified that "[t]he post-mortem appearances do not show that it was set up by arsenic" (cited in Christie, 1968, p. 117).

On the second and concluding day of his summing-up, Mr Justice Stephen told the jury as follows:

> "You must consider the case as *a mere medical case*, in which you are to decide whether the man did or did not die of arsenic according to the medical evidence. You must not consider it as *a mere chemical case*, in which you decide whether the man died from arsenic which was discovered as the result of a chemical analysis. You must decide it *as a great, high, and important case*, involving in itself not only medical and chemical questions, but embodying in itself *a most highly important moral question* – and by that term, moral question, I do not mean a question of what is right and wrong in a moral point of view, but questions in which human nature enters and in which *you must rely on your knowledge of human nature* in determining the resolution you arrive at.
>
> "I could say a good many other things about the awful nature of the charge, but I do not think it will be necessary to do any one thing. Your own hearts must tell you what it is for a person *to go on administering poison* to a helpless, sick man, upon whom she has already inflicted a dreadful injury – an injury fatal to married life; the person who could do such a thing as that must be destitute of the least trace of human feeling. ... We have to consider this not in an unfeeling spirit – far from it – but

> in the spirit of people resolved to solve *by intellectual means an intellectual problem of great difficulty* [cited in Maybrick, 2012, pp. 319-21, emphasis original].

This extraordinarily incoherent, muddled, and problematic set of statements, which was very influential in determining Mrs Maybrick's eventual fate, deserves careful study. In the first sentence the statement appears to begin well but it immediately deteriorates in quality from that point onwards, and doubles back to contradict itself. Instead of the above incoherent statements, the judge instead should have asked the jurors to reflect upon three straight-forward questions and three straight-forward questions only (Lumley & Lumley-prepared brief cited in Maybrick, 2012, p. 321): (a) did Mr Maybrick die of arsenic poisoning; (b) did Mrs Maybrick administer arsenic to Mr Maybrick; and (c) did she do so with the intent to kill? Mr Justice Stephen's last-quoted statement that the members of the jury must "solve *by intellectual means an intellectual problem of great difficulty*" (emphasis original) seems faintly ridiculous given that the medical evidence clearly indicated that Mr Maybrick's body contained around one-tenth of a grain of arsenic and the smallest quantity ever known to have killed someone was two grains (or twenty times as much). It hardly seems an intellectual feat of staggering proportions for someone to conclude that there was reasonable doubt that Mr Maybrick did *not* die of arsenic poisoning.

What is especially interesting in Mr Justice Stephen's statements is that he directly informed the uneducated laymen of the jury to disregard the expert medical testimony of the experienced doctors for the defence including Dr Tidy and Dr Paul. This is the interpretation which I give to the following sentence: "You must not consider it as *a mere chemical case*, in which you decide whether the man died from arsenic which was discovered as the result of a chemical analysis" (emphasis original). When this sentence is taken out of the convoluted paragraph in which it first appears its inappropriateness is even starker. Instead of giving due weight to the medical evidence, Mr Justice Stephen instead referred the members of the jury to "*a most highly important moral question*" (emphasis original) where they must "*rely on your [their] knowledge of human nature*". In other words, Mr Justice Stephen set this case up *as a trial of the morality of Mrs Maybrick*. He then stated that "she has already inflicted a dreadful injury – an injury fatal to married life" upon Mr Maybrick. He was thus explicitly encouraging the jurors to regard Mrs Maybrick's adultery and her husband's strange death while she was nursing him as connected sordid pieces of the same morality play. The adultery was specifically portrayed as relevant. By encouraging the jurors to *"rely on your [their] knowledge of human nature"* (emphasis original) Mr Justice Stephen appeared to be implying that the "human nature" of someone who had inflicted the injury of adultery upon her husband would incline that same person to want to remove her husband's presence physically so as to begin a new life with her lover. However, Mr. Justice Stephen ignored the facts that the Brierley affair had long since ended and that Mrs Maybrick could simply have divorced her husband and in fact had already taken some steps in that direction (Maybrick, 2012, p. 365). QC Addison, on behalf of the prosecution, had earlier set the deadly wheels in motion when he had (reprehensibly) claimed that Mrs Maybrick "had so interwoven her adultery with her conduct that it was impossible to treat it as an ordinary case of adultery and not treat it as having any actual connection with the alleged crime" (cited in Christie, 1968, p. 131).

Mr Justice Stephen was clearly on a dangerous course when he instructed the jurors to listen to "[y]our [their] own hearts [which] must tell you [them] what it is for a person *to go on administering poison* to a helpless, sick man, upon whom she has already inflicted a dreadful injury" (emphasis original). Given that it was an all-male jury (Graham and Emmas, 1999) (women jurors were first used in England in 1920) the appeal for them to effectively listen to their emotions was clearly inflammatory and most prejudicial to Mrs Maybrick's cause. Mr Justice Stephen was effectively asking the jurors to put themselves in Mr Maybrick's shoes, imagine that it was their wives who had betrayed them personally, and then to feel the full gamut of emotions which such circumstances would engender. Clearly, in such a context, a man's own adultery would not be relevant and Mr Justice Stephen in the above quoted statements did not refer to it. Mrs Maybrick (2012, p. 236) wrote that "[t]he jury belonged to a class of men who were not competent to weigh technical evidence", and so direct pleas by Mr Justice Stephen to the emotions of the jurors would most likely have been powerfully effective.[3] Despite the case

---

[3] The jury consisted of three plumbers, two farmers, one milliner, one wood-turner, one provision dealer, one grocer, one ironmonger, one house-

producing nearly 800,000 words of testimony it took the jurors only 38 minutes to reach their guilty verdict (Christie, 1968, p. 20). Another basic factual error made by Mr Justice Stephen was to say "you have been convicted by a jury of this city" (cited in Christie, 1968, p. 20). The jury members were from Lancashire County but not from the city of Liverpool. One of the judge's more serious factual errors, which even the Crown counsel was forced to correct him on, was to state that the reconciliation between husband and wife had taken place before (rather than after) Florence's overnight tryst with Brierley at Flatman's Hotel in London (Christie, 1968, p. 139).

Lastly, there was no evidence presented at the trial which conclusively proved that Mrs Maybrick had administered arsenic or any other poison to her late husband, and Mr Justice Stephen clearly erred by suggesting that such evidence had been presented. The statement "the person who could do such a thing as that must be destitute of the least trace of human feeling" clearly suggests a morality trial where the judge had already found the prisoner guilty before the jurors had even left the courtroom to begin their deliberations. It

---

painter, and one baker (Christie, 1968, p. 79; Graham and Emmas, 1999, p. 164; Maybrick, 2012, p. 236 footnote).

seems that Mrs Maybrick was found guilty by the judge of harbouring a certain state of alleged inner wickedness rather than because of actual proven actions or actual physical evidence. There is also an obvious ambiguity in that the judge's statement that "the person who could do such a thing as that" could reasonably be held to be referring back to *either* the adultery of Mrs Maybrick or to her alleged administration of poison to her late husband. The ambiguity suggests that both the adultery and the alleged administration of poison were both seen by the judge as consistent with and indicative of the certain state of alleged wickedness which I claim the judge was imputing to Mrs Maybrick. Mr Justice Stephen's brother Sir Leslie, in his biography of his brother, remarked that James (Stephen) was a "moralist in the old-fashioned sense" and that "he took advantage of his strength to carry out his own ideals of a criminal court as a school of morality" (cited in Christie, 1968, p. 134).

Mr Justice Stephen also mentioned a dog that had apparently died of arsenic poisoning, although there was no trace of arsenic in its body post-mortem, either not realizing or not caring that arsenic would work its way through a dog's system much quicker than it would a man's (Lumley & Lumley-prepared brief cited in Maybrick, 2012, p. 323). The judge turned himself into an impromptu witness for the prosecution during his closing address; his ill-advised statements were of such a nature that any defence lawyer would have torn them to shreds. However, Sir Charles was not given this opportunity. The judge at the end of the trial remarked: "well, they can't convict her on that evidence" and the chief prosecutor, QC Addison, nodded his head to agree (as allegedly witnessed by a newspaper reporter and cited in Christie, 1968, p. 141). At the end of the trial Sir Charles was overheard saying to his fellow barristers in the corridors of St. George's Hall: "Mark what I say, it is the most dangerous verdict that has ever been recorded in my experience" (cited in Graham and Emmas, 1999, p. 9). Within half an hour of the trial ending, a petition against the verdict was signed by every junior barrister and by every Queen's Counsel present at the Assize Courts that day (Graham and Emmas, 1999, p. 9).

Although many informed commentators at the time, including Sir Charles, and afterwards suggested that Mrs Maybrick had been wrongly convicted (Beadle, 2005a; Maybrick, 2012, p. 225) there was no Court of Criminal

Appeal at that time. Mrs Maybrick (2012, p. 89) wrote in 1904 that "[t]he supineness of Parliament in not establishing a court of criminal appeal fastens a dark blot upon the judicature of England, and is inconsistent with the innate love of justice and fair play of its people". Other notable advocates for a Court of Criminal Appeal were Lord Esher in *The Times* of 17 August 1889 and *The Times* newspaper itself of the same date (Maybrick, 2012, p. 260). A Court of Criminal Appeal was eventually established by the *Criminal Appeal Act 1907* (Christie, 1968, p. 266). The Florence Maybrick case is a timely reminder today for an international audience of the fallibility and inherent weaknesses of the legal system and the desperate need to retain Courts of Criminal Appeal within the courts system.

Later life of Mrs Maybrick

As mentioned, Mrs Maybrick's death sentence was nearly immediately reduced to life imprisonment on the directions of the Home Office (Adamson, 1993, p. 6; Edwards, 2007, p. 54; Maybrick, 2012, p. 60; O'Brien, 1901, p. 259). Sir Charles continued to lobby the Home Office for Florence's release up until his death in 1900. As O'Brien (1901, p. 263) wrote: "And so, to the end, the fate of this unhappy woman occupied his thoughts, and he never ceased, either in private or officially, to say that there had been a grave miscarriage of justice in the case, and that Florence Maybrick "ought to be allowed to go free"". Mrs Maybrick was transferred from Woking Prison to Aylesbury Prison on 4 November 1896 (Christie, 1968, p. 181; Maybrick, 2012, pp. 127-32) when the former institution was reassigned to be used for military purposes (Maybrick, 2012, p. 132). In the end she was released after having served just fifteen years (Beadle, 2005a; Edwards, 2007, p. 54). At the date of her departure she was the only prisoner left at Aylesbury Prison who had also been a prisoner at Woking Prison (Maybrick, 2012, p. 194). However, her final release was not a special dispensation (Maybrick, 2012, p. 251) but was the result of a review which was accorded to all "life" prisoners after 20 years or somewhere between 15 and 20 years when there had been good behaviour (Maybrick, 2012, p. 211). It does appear that Queen Victoria had an ill opinion of Mrs Maybrick and, because of this, Mrs Maybrick's release was only possible after the Queen's death on 22 January 1901. The Queen had convicted Mrs Maybrick for immorality in her own mind and was hostile to reversing that decision (Christie, 1968, pp. 224-5). This was finally confirmed as proven fact in 1930 when George Earle Buckle published an edition of the Queen's letters (Christie, 1968, p. 224).

Mrs Maybrick was 41-years-old when she was released at 6.45am on Monday 25 January 1904 (Christie, 1968, p. 227; Maybrick, 2012, p. 217). She spent the last six months of her sentence recuperating at Home of the Community of the Epiphany in Truro, Cornwall, from which she was released on 20 July 1904 (Maybrick, 2012, p. 218-9). About her time spent in Truro, Florence commented: "I look back upon the six months spent within those sacred walls as the most peaceful and happiest – in the true sense – of my life". After staying with her devoted mother in Rouen, France for three weeks (Maybrick, 2012, pp. 11, 220), Mrs Maybrick boarded the Red Star Line steamship

Vaderland at Antwerp, Belgium bound for New York City (Christie, 1968, p. 229; Maybrick, 2012, p. 221) and "the sacred soil of my [her] native land" (Maybrick, 2012, p. 222). Her name was entered on the ship's passenger list as Rose Ingraham "that I [she] might secure more quiet and privacy" (Maybrick, 2012, p. 221). The ship arrived in New York Harbour on 23 August 1904 (Christie, 1968, p. 230; Maybrick, 2012, p. 222).

After being an itinerant speaker about prison conditions for some years, Mrs Maybrick passed away on 23 October 1941 (Adamson, 1993, p. 6). She never remarried. For over a decade before her death she had been living as a recluse with her cats in the rolling hills of the Connecticut countryside near Gaylordsville, South Kent (Christie, 1968, Chapter 15). She was described by Colin Adamson in *The Evening Standard* newspaper (now renamed *The London Evening Standard*) of 22 April 1993 as having "died penniless and in squalor in America" (Adamson, 1993, p. 6). She had befriended the local school staff and was a well-known local eccentric in the community and at the school. Mrs Maybrick never again got to see her own children ("the children to whom I am dead" (Maybrick, 2012, p. 223)), Bobo and Gladys, after they were forcibly removed from her, at the orders of Mr Maybrick's domineering younger brother Michael (Graham and Emmas, 1999, p. 125; Maybrick, 2012, p. 25), in May 1889 (Maybrick, 2012, pp. 25, 223 footnote). According to Michael Maybrick, Bobo, who had been made acquainted with the anti-Florence Maybrick version of his mother's trial, "did not wish either his own or his sister's photograph to be sent to me [Florence]" in prison which up until then had been the annual practice (Maybrick, 2012, p. 223 footnote). For a family which was apparently never too far removed from tragedy, it is perhaps not surprising that Bobo was killed in a bizarre mining accident in Canada in April 1911, aged 29, when he drank a tube of cyanide believing it to be water (Christie, 1968, pp. 245-6). He left his sister Gladys a sizeable estate of £4,755 (Christie, 1968, p. 246). For her part, Gladys married in 1912 and died in South Wales in 1971 aged 85.

With very little supporting evidence Paul Feldman (2007, pp. 181-3) concludes that Florence had an illegitimate son, William Graham (Billy Graham's father / author Anne Graham's grandfather), born in Hartlepool, England in January 1879 when she was 16-years-old (see also Beadle, 2005a; Graham and Emmas, 1999, p. xxi).

Feldman (2007) surmises that this child's existence explains why Florence hoped to see "them" (plural) (*Sunday News*, 1 May 1927, cited in Feldman, 2007, pp. 181-2), meaning "her children" (plural), in a last visit to England in 1927 when she already knew that her son Bobo had died in the 1911 mining accident and Gladys was her only other child with James (Feldman, 2007, p. 183).

Recent developments: the "Jack-the-Ripper" diary

The discovery of the alleged "Jack the Ripper" diary was made in May 1991 (Beadle, 2005a; Begg, 2005, p. 369; Skinner, 1999, p. x), when a Liverpudlian unemployed scrap-metal merchant Michael Barrett was allegedly handed the diary by his drinking friend the late Tony Devereux **(Whitehead and Rivett, 2012, p. 124)**, a retired printer (Knightley, 1993; **Schoettler, 1993**), in Liverpool pub The Saddle Inn[4] (Begg, 2005, p. 369; Knightley, 1993). The diary (hereafter referred to as "the Diary") claims internally to be authored by the 19th century Liverpool cotton merchant James Maybrick (25 October 1838 – 11 May 1889) (Adamson, 1993, p. 6; Edwards, 2007, p. 54; Gowers, 1995; Harrison, 2008, p. 215; Skinner, 1999, p. x) and also to be the diary of the never apprehended Whitechapel serial-killer "Jack the Ripper" of 1888 (Adamson, 1993, p. 6; Beadle, 2005a; Edwards, 2007, p. 54; Feldman, 2007; Harrison, 2008, p. 215; Knightley, 1993; Linder et al., 2003; **Schoettler, 1993**).

Noted Jack the Ripper author Keith Skinner (1999, p. ix) writes that: "The alleged 'Diary of Jack the Ripper' has

---

[4] This Saddle Inn (located at 86 Fountains Road) is about equidistant from Anfield and Goodison Park football stadiums and should not be confused with The Saddle Inn at 13 Dale Street (in the Liverpool city-centre).

always been shrouded in controversy, ever since it first came into the public domain back in 1992". Before the discovery of the Diary, which has somewhat dubious "provenance" (Beadle, 2005b; Begg, 2005, p. 369; George, 2006; Knightley, 1993), no writer on the Jack the Ripper murders of 1888 had ever nominated James Maybrick as a plausible suspect **(Harrison, 2008, p. 214; May, 2007)**.[5] It was the internal Diary references to "Battlecrease House", in Riversdale Road, Liverpool, which led Michael Barrett, in his follow-up private research, to conclude that the Diary's author was clearly presenting himself to the world as being James Maybrick (Harrison, 2008, p. 214).

Tony May (2007) from Hastings, East Sussex comments as follows: "He [Maybrick] was not connected to the enquiry at the time, and had not even been thought of as a suspect until the diary came to light so, in fairness to him, [i]f we believe the diary to be a fake I think we

---

[5] I use the term "Jack the Ripper murders" rather than the more genteel "Whitechapel murders" not to shock but because the latter term includes all murders committed in the Whitechapel region during the period 1888-91 which were not obviously domestics or gangland killings. These include the "torso murders" which experts agree are unlikely to be by the same hand as the murders committed by the serial killer Jack the Ripper (Evans and Skinner, 2000, p. 480; Rumbelow, 2013, p. 135). The Jack the Ripper murders are generally thought to include: Mary Ann "Polly" Nichols, Annie Chapman; Elizabeth Stride; Catharine Eddowes; and Mary Jane Kelly (all 1888); as well as possibly Martha "Maggie" Tabram (1888); Alice MacKenzie (1889); and Frances Coles (1891).

should all acknowledge his innocence". However, despite voluminous debate amongst Ripperologists (students of the Jack the Ripper murders) over the past 20 years and numerous forensic tests of ink, phraseology, and handwriting, the possibility that the Diary is in fact genuine has not been conclusively disproved (Edwards, 2007, p. 54; George, 2007).[6] Christopher T. George (2007), the Editor of *Ripperologist* magazine, writes as follows: "the Diary has not been conclusively proven to be a hoax because no one has been proven conclusively to have forged it". The fact that forgery has not been proven (Harrison, 2008, p. 230) is itself significant given that the "Hitler diaries", for which the *Sunday Times* paid £1 million in 1983 (Schoettler, 1993), were exposed as fraudulent within a relatively short space of time (Knightley, 1993; Schoettler, 1993). In fact, a leading history professor has stated that the Diary is "probably genuine" or it would have been proven to be a forgery by now. Harrison (2008, p. 230) observes that: "[The Diary] has survived possibly the most

---

[6] For space reasons I forego in this paper any extended discussion of the debates about the Diary's authenticity. Interested readers are referred to the debates for and against the Diary on the Yoliverpool.com forum at: http://www.yoliverpool.com/forum/showthread.php?2439-James-Maybrick [accessed 18 June 2013].

rigorous investigation of any manuscript this [twentieth] century".

A more satisfactory provenance was later given the Diary when Michael Barrett's ex-wife Anne Graham claimed that her late father Billy had been bequeathed the Diary among the possessions of his grandmother Elizabeth Formby (Beadle, 2005a) before World War II; had first seen it when he came home on leave from the army in 1943; and had finally taken possession of it in 1950 (Begg, 2005, p. 371). Ms Graham gave the Diary to Tony Devereux, so that he would give it to her then husband Barrett. Ms Graham was hoping that her then unemployed husband would use it to write a novel; she did not give it to him personally because she was worried he would bother her aging father with endless questions about it (Beadle, 2005a; Begg, 2005, p. 372). If this story is to be believed it points in favour of the Diary's authenticity since there are facts in the Diary which were not made public until 1987 (Knightley, 1993). It follows unarguably, from the internal text of the Diary, that James Maybrick and Jack the Ripper are one and the same person (Harrison, 2008, p. 215). Given the fact that forgery has *not* been proven (Harrison, 2008, p. 230), it is certainly not impossible that it is in fact a genuine document. The possible origins of the Diary are as follows: (a) it is a modern forgery; (b) it is an old forgery written for unknown reasons but perhaps to benefit Florence during the trial; (c) it was written by James Maybrick but the events described are pure fantasy; and (d) James Maybrick really was Jack the Ripper.

According to the Diary, Mrs Maybrick's infidelity (the Diary refers to her as "the whore" and "the whoring mother" (Beadle, 2005a; Graham and Emmas, 1999, p. 64)) in turn led her husband James into a period of mental anguish (mixed with sexual excitement (Begg, 2005, p. 370; Graham and Emmas, 1999, p. 71)). This prolonged intense emotional state then led to the series of Jack the Ripper murders where the casual prostitutes of the East End of London literally stood in as "scapegoat[s]" (Graham and Emmas, 1999, p. 53) for the "whoring" Florence.

My concluding comments about the Diary are as follows: The Jack-the-Ripper Diary, incriminating James Maybrick, is an interesting modern development which has not yet been conclusively proven or disproven although it is regarded as suspect by most Jack-the-Ripper scholars. If the Diary's internal claim is valid,

James Maybrick confessed his crimes to his wife prior to his death but this was not mentioned in court for fear that it would grant Florence an additional "motive" for murder. However, the importance of the Florence Maybrick case today in no way stands or falls on the validity of the Diary. For one hundred years the Jack-the-Ripper case and the Florence Maybrick poison case were linked only by their closeness in time.

Conclusion

The criminal trial of Mrs Florence Maybrick, held in Liverpool, England during the height of the British Empire 1889, is widely regarded as one of the greatest travesties of justice in British legal history where even the judge at the end of the trial remarked "well, they can't convict her on that evidence" and the chief prosecutor nodded his head in agreement. Mrs Maybrick was tried for murdering her husband via arsenic poisoning. However, the trial became a morality trial when the presiding judge, **Mr Justice Stephen,** linked Mrs Maybrick's demonstrated adultery to her alleged desire to physically remove her husband by administering poison. Mr Justice Stephen was wrong to attempt to, in the words of his brother Sir Leslie, turn his own criminal court into a "school of morality". The Jack-the-Ripper Diary, incriminating James Maybrick, is an interesting modern development which has not yet been conclusively proven or disproven. However, the importance of the Florence Maybrick case today in no way stands or falls on the validity of the Diary.

Szijártó (2002, p. 211, emphasis added) writes that microhistory can usefully, when "contextualiz[ed] as full[y] as possible, put the stress on the *ramifications* of *the single case*". The Florence Maybrick trial of 1889 remains today a timely reminder for an international audience of the fallibility and inherent weaknesses of the legal system and the desperate need to retain Courts of Criminal Appeal within the courts system. Following **Szijártó (2002, p. 211)**, "**[we must] step beyond the individual case and proceed towards the general**". I was lecturing in the Fiji Islands at the time this paper was written (2013-2015). It is fortunate that Fiji has a Court of Appeal enshrined in the new 2013 *Constitution*[7] (Section 99(1)-(5), Government of Fiji, 2013, p. 57). However, I humbly suggest that there should be a splitting up of this court into a Court of Criminal Appeal and a Court of Appeal for civil (non-criminal) cases. The Maybrick case also suggests that senior judges aged over 55 years, and especially those who have suffered strokes or head injuries, need to be regularly evaluated by their peers or by other qualified persons. Mental decline can occur earlier than expected and can have devastating consequences. The Maybrick case also highlights the weakness of the English jury system where uneducated people are asked to pass judgement on what must appear to them to be complex

---

[7] This *Constitution* was issued by the government of Frank Bainimarama in September 2013 prior to the 2014 General Election which was won by his Fiji First party.

medical evidence. Christie (1968, pp. 78-9) commented that the jurors lacked "the technical training to cope with the complex medical and legal testimony". In the Florence Maybrick trial the jurors were overly impressed by the bearing, reputation, and social standing of the judge and of the star medical practitioner witness, Dr Stevenson, who testified in a manner prejudicial to the interests of the accused.

References

Adamson, Colin (1993), "Is this the face of Jack the Ripper?" *Evening Standard [UK]*, 22 April, p. 6.

Beadle, William (2005a), "Revisiting the *Maybrick 'Diary'* – *Part One*", available online at: http://www.jamesmaybrick.org/pdf%20files/Diary%20(William%20Beadle%20article).pdf [accessed 18 June 2013].

Beadle, William (2005b), "Revisiting the *Maybrick 'Diary'* – *Part Two*", available online at: http://www.jamesmaybrick.org/pdf%20files/Diary%20(William%20Beadle%20article).pdf [accessed 18 June 2013].

Begg, Paul (2005), *Jack the Ripper: the Definitive History*, revised paperback edition (Harlow: Pearson Education).

Christie, Trevor L. (1968), *Etched in Arsenic* (Philadelphia, PA: Philadelphia Lippincott).

Edwards, Martin (2007), *Mind to Kill* (Hoo, Kent: Grange Books).

Evans, Stewart P. and Skinner, Keith (2000), *The Ultimate Jack the Ripper Sourcebook: An Illustrated Encyclopedia* (London: Constable and Robinson).

Feldman, Paul (2007), *Jack the Ripper: the Final Chapter*, paperback edition (London: Virgin Books).

George, Christopher T. (2006), "Untitled forum post", Yoliverpool.com, 11 August, available online at http://www.yoliverpool.com/forum/showthread.php?2439-James-Maybrick, [accessed 26 June 2013].

George, Christopher T. (2007), "Untitled forum post", Yoliverpool.com, 2 May, available online at http://www.yoliverpool.com/forum/showthread.php?2439-James-Maybrick/page3, [accessed 26 June 2013].

Government of Fiji (2013), *Constitution of the Republic of Fiji*, available online at: http://www.paclii.org/fj/Fiji-Constitution-English-2013.pdf [accessed 24 June 2016].

Gowers, Rebecca (1995), "At each others' throats over Jack the Ripper", 31 August, *The Independent [UK]*, available online at: http://www.independent.co.uk/news/at-each-others-throats-over-jack-the-ripper-1598714.html [accessed 28 August 2013].

Graham, Anne E. and Emmas, Carol (1999), *The Last Victim: the Extraordinary Life of Florence Maybrick, the Wife of Jack the Ripper* (London: Headline Book Publishing).

Harrison, Shirley (2008). "The Diary of Jack the Ripper", in: M. Jakubowski and N. Braund (eds.), *The Mammoth Book of Jack the Ripper*, American edition (Philadelphia, PA: Running Press Book Publishers), pp. 213-236.

Knightley, Phillip (1993), "Is this man Jack the Ripper?: Certainly a lot of money is being spent trying to tell you so", *The Independent [UK]*, 29 August, available online at: http://www.independent.co.uk/news/uk/is-this-man-jack-the-ripper-certainly-a-lot-of-money-is-being-spent-trying-to-tell-you-so-phillip-knightley-a-veteran-of-publishing-hoaxes-untangles-the-evidence--and-feels-he-has-been-here-before-1464073.html [accessed 14 June 2013]

Linder, Seth, Morris, Caroline and Skinner, Keith (2003), *Ripper Diary: the Inside Story* (London: Sutton Publishing).

May, Tony (2007), "Untitled forum post", Yoliverpool.com, 2 November, available online at http://www.yoliverpool.com/forum/showthread.php?2439-James-Maybrick/page4, [accessed 26 June 2013].

Maybrick, Florence (2012), *Mrs. Maybrick's Own Story: My Fifteen Lost Years* (New York, NY: Forgotten Books) [originally published 1904].

Morland, Nigel (1957), *This Friendless Lady* (London: Frederick Muller).

O'Brien, R. Barry (1901), *Life of Lord Russell of Killowen* (London: Smith, Elder and Co).

Rumbelow, Donald (2013), *The Complete Jack the Ripper: Fully Revised and Updated* (London: Virgin Books).

Schoettler, Carl (1993), "The Ripper's 'diary,' not yet published, is being slashed to pieces", *The Baltimore Sun [USA]*, 23 September, available online at: http://articles.baltimoresun.com/1993-09-

23/features/1993266235_1_jack-the-ripper-diary-gryphon [accessed 18 June 2013].

Skinner, Keith (1999), "Foreword", in *The Last Victim: The Extraordinary Life of Florence Maybrick, the Wife of Jack the Ripper* (London: Headline Book Publishing), pp. ix-xv.

Stephen, James F. (1890), *A General View of the Criminal Law of England*, 2nd edition (London and New York, NY: Macmillan) [reproduced from the original copy held at Harvard Law School Library as part of the *Gale Making of the Modern Law: Legal Treatises, 1800-1926* series].

Szijártó, István (2002), "Four Arguments for Microhistory", *Rethinking History*, Vol. 6, No. 2, pp. 209-215.

Whitehead, Mark and Rivett, Miriam (2012), *Jack the Ripper* (Harpenden, Hertfordshire: Pocket Essentials).

Lightning Source UK Ltd.
Milton Keynes UK
UKHW011829030622
403957UK00001B/112

BORDER LINES

ACKNOWLEDGEMENTS

I would like to thank the following people who read the manuscript at varying stages and gave me their most helpful opinions: Lisa Frank, James Martyn Joyce, Amanda Driscoll, Annegret Walsh, Susan Millar DuMars and Des Kenny.

My thanks also to Marilyn Gaughan and Breda Cunningham at the County Galway Arts Office for their support and the publication award for this book.

A slim-lined version of 'New Year's Day' was short-listed and highly commended in the 2011 Over the Edge New Writer of the Year competition.

'The Way Things Happen' written by Lisa Frank and John Walsh.

CONTENTS

A Day Like Today	11
Jimi	19
The Trumpet in the Towel	21
Such a Good Invention	34
A Different Story	39
A Beautiful Day	42
Border Lines	46
You're Never Alone	58
Hawk	64
Winter Sun	70
Sand	74
Yesterday's News	81
New Year's Day	88

This Could be Heaven	101
The Way Things Happen	108
My Perfect Uncle	116
Author Biography	127

dedication

to lisa

i dedicate this poem to   you
with no because
it is reason enough
that it is   written

to pluck the nerve-ends of this day
as we reach   out
for its goodness

on some border line   we   cross
leave no tracks
no sense of   us

while you still pick   up
the frequency of my   thoughts

i dedicate this poem to   you
this is   all   that   matters

A DAY LIKE TODAY

'You're scared, you're scared!' My Uncle Roy taunted me from the garden below. He had just jumped off Tierney's wall, landed soundly on his two feet. I hovered above him, nervous, unsure. 'You're a coward if you don't jump.'

'I'm not a coward,' I shouted and jumped. I heard the sharp crack of my leg under me as I landed, an arrowhead of pain pulsed up my thigh.

Uncle Roy rushed toward me. 'You did it!'

'My leg's broke. I can't get up.' I tried not to whine. I was feeling sickish. The pain spread in waves.

'Fuck!' He bent over me, all Brylcreem smell, and made to straighten my leg.

'Don't!' I squealed.

'Put your arm over me. I'll shoulder you out.'

I looked at him and I looked at the steps up out of Tierney's. 'No way,' I said. 'You'll have to go for help.' Tierney's was abandoned. The big house was ready to fall down.

'Jay-sus.' Uncle Roy wiped his hands on his trousers as he stood looking at me. 'How's the pain?'

'Hurry up,' I mumbled.

After that I was on crutches for two months. The day they cut the cast open, my left leg lay on the white sheet of the hospital trolley, confused.

Uncle Roy worked as a chippie along with his father. Not a good match. He was trying to get his father to start their own business. 'But he won't go for it,' he complained to me as we walked along the docks past the empty clapboard warehouses. We rarely saw a ship being unloaded, a few dockers now and again hanging around. 'He's afraid of the risk, sure what's the risk? There's loads of work for good chippies, we could be building the houses ourselves, raking the money in.'

Uncle Roy always talked to me as if I was much older and knew about these things. Or maybe it was because I listened to him. We crossed the Strand Road and went up the stairs to the snooker hall. I couldn't get the hang of snooker, the right tilt of the cue, so we always lost. Still he took me along and teamed up with me. We stood in the line waiting for a table. Uncle Roy pulled out a packet of Woodbine. 'Here, you have to start some time.' I twiddled the thin, tight cigarette between my fingers and waited for him to light it. After the first puffs I broke into a fit of coughing. 'Fair enough,' Uncle Roy said. 'You're not ready for it yet. Save your money.'

At weekends we went on cycle trips together. Grianan and Hegarty's Rock, the far-away ones, were my favourites. Father Hegarty had jumped off the rock to escape the soldiers but wasn't able to swim across. The English cut his head off. People said cracks in the face of the big rock joined up to make a cross.

'I'm thinkin' of packing it in with my da.' We were lying on the grass near Fr. Hegarty's grave. Everything was peaceful. 'I've put my name down for Tillies. Just waitin' to get the shout.'

'What will Granddad say?' I'd only once seen my grandfather lose his temper. It had frightened me because he turned into someone I didn't know.

'My da can say what he likes. If he wants to be a stick-in-the-mud, that's up to him. I'm not goin' to be workin' for other people the rest of my life.' He got to his feet and started stripping off. 'C'mon, let's jump!'

'Are you crazy? You could kill yourself.' He was already down to his underpants.

'C'mon, it's only water,' he shouted back at me as he ran to the edge of the rock. 'If Father Hegarty could jump, so can we.'

'But they cut his head off,' I mumbled to myself as I got to my feet and followed him. Below us the waves were scary. 'You're mad if you jump.'

'Try an' stop me.' He threw himself out over the edge. 'Here goes nothing!' I watched him sail out and splash into the water below. 'C'mon Neph. It's fuckin' freezin' but it's great. Jump!'

'No way,' I shouted back at him. 'I ain't doin' it.'

Not long after that Uncle Roy was taken on in the carpenter's shop in Tillies. Tillies shirt factory was all women and girls, but not in the carpentry shop. The mechanics, carpenters and painters all got together there. 'It's a doddle. An' better money than me and my da ever made,' Uncle Roy told me. When he started making his own guitar, bigger and better than any he could afford to buy, the other men kept watch for him.

Two evenings a week he played in a pub-band, mostly Jim Reeves' songs. Any chance I got, I sat listening to him practice in the front room of my granny's house in The Wells.

'You're only wasting your time with that nonsense.' My grandfather stood at the door for a minute watching the two of us, didn't say anymore. Then he disappeared. I didn't understand. I thought Roy was good, as good as Pat Boone. When he strummed and crooned 'Love

Letters in the Sand', his hair licked back in a wave and shine, I thought he looked just like Pat Boone.

Outside the house Uncle Roy was a big hit. Girlfriends came and went like dandelions, he never seemed to want to hold on to the same one for long. I had my exams and the Young Nationalists. We were Big Eddie supporters and we wanted a university for Derry. But dropping leaflets door-to-door with Joan McMahon, my first steady girlfriend, was a much more real issue. I wanted to hold onto her for as long as I could.

'Your Uncle Roy's goin' off to London.' My mother and me were in the kitchen, doing the dishes. Her arms were scalded and covered in suds.

'He's leavin' Derry?'

'He's got a bee in his bonnet. He can't stick at anything for long.'

'I thought he liked it in Tillies.'

'Didn't we all, but you know your Uncle Roy. He has his own ideas about things.' My mother was protective and fond of her younger brother because he was the baby. 'Your granny and granddad aren't goin' to like it one bit. He hasn't breathed a word to them yet. Thinks I'll break the news to them, but he has another think coming.'

I knew there would be trouble but I was too caught up with my exams. And my mother did her best to keep me out of it. She wanted me to do well, 'to make something of myself'. In her mind that meant not turning out like my uncle.

On the Saturday afternoon Uncle Roy called for me. 'Where's the scholar? C'mon, take a break, everybody needs a break. Let your brain cool off.'

We took the usual route around the town, ended up outside Phillips' window, eyeing the latest singles and LPs. It was all about The Beatles now. No one talked about Pat Boone anymore.

'I s'pose you heard,' he finally said.

'Of course I have. I'm not deaf.'

'Don't jump down my throat!'

I pulled away from the window. 'Let's go. I hate talking to my reflection.' We walked up Shipquay Street, winding in and out between all the other window-gazers. 'When are you going?'

'Not sure yet. But it won't be long.'

'And why? I thought you'd found your feet in Tillies. You were happy where you are.'

'Tillies is alright, but there's a big world out there. Do you want to be stuck here the rest of your life?'

I tried to find an answer for him. I wasn't stuck. Everything I had was here. 'Won't you miss everybody? Granny, Granddad and us all?'

'You have to cut the apron strings some day, Neph. Take on the world on your own. Maybe you're still too young to understand that yet.'

'I'm not a baby,' I hissed. 'I understand enough.'

'Okay, okay, keep your hair on.'

We crossed The Diamond and sat down on one of the benches under the war memorial. I looked up at Austin's copper dome, at a seagull perched on top of its small spire calmly watching all the people hurrying around below. We were probably like ants to it, I thought. As seemingly clueless as ants were to us.

Uncle Roy hung out of the compartment window waving at my mother and me until the Belfast train took the curve and twisted out of sight.

'We won't be seein' him for a while, that's for sure,' my mother said as we turned back along the platform. 'We'll miss him, you and me, won't we?'

I could hear the tears and I wanted to say something to comfort her, but the tight knot in my stomach wouldn't let me. I reached for her hand and held it. Of course we would miss him, everybody in their own way would miss him. He knew that, but the big world out there was what he wanted.

Uncle Roy left me his old guitar and a book of chord shapes. Along with them a note: *Get practicing, Neph. When I get back, you and me are going to have our own band. We got to think of a good name for ourselves. See ya!*

That summer I picked out 'Day Tripper' and played it until the skin on my fingertips was burning. Pep told me to rub methylated spirits into the tips before playing. 'They harden more quickly then. But the pain is part of it,' he said. 'It goes away when you practice every day.'

'Groovy Kind of Love' was number two in the charts. I twisted and stretched my fingers along the fretboard until I had the lead part off. After that my fingertips felt nothing anymore.

I kept asking if there was any word of Uncle Roy coming back, excited to show him how much I had learned. 'The Journeymen' was the name I came up with for our band. Uncle Roy would like that, I was certain.

But he never came back. Granddad stopped talking about him, Granny talked only when we were alone. We got postcards, love and best wishes, no word of a visit. For a while I covered my bedroom wall with the cards, as if they were some kind of litany that would lead to something good. Then one day I ripped them all down. I began to understand that there were reasons for his going away, things he hadn't told me, things no one was telling me.

Pep and I formed our own band. Pep was a crossover between George and Paul. I was John. 'This Boy' was our big number and it was Joan's favourite. I stretched for the high notes while Pep mastered all the harmonies. With that and 'Groovy' we won the talent show in the Embassy, but Ferris cheated us. 'No money,' he lied. 'But you's can get in free from now on.' That's how we got to see Them, every time they played. We were stationed at the edge of the stage, our necks aching as we stared up at Van. His face would turn blue, the way he sang. We were afraid he was going to have a heart attack.

Then, one by one we all left, just as the marches began. In the following years car bombs shattered the big window of Phillips' shop. Nothing was spared.

*

On a Tuesday evening in September, Amy and I are trying to decipher the board menu outside Zona Verde in Mogan. It has been so hot all day, I am glad we have found somewhere we can cool off and eat.

'Are you sure we want to go in here?' Amy gives me that look of hers, the one that always leads to trouble.

'It's the sun,' I say. 'It makes the paint peel.' It also makes me more irritable, I could add. But when we walk through to the beach-garden, she relaxes.

We find a table under the mango trees and order the freshly-grilled prawn kebabs. The smell of them on the open log barbecue is good. Maybe it will take a while but we are in no hurry. I sip the house red and look around. There is a guy dressed in white flannels and a straw hat walking across the garden. He is carrying an expensive-looking guitar case. At the other end of the garden I notice a small stage that he walks straight towards.

'I don't believe it,' I say. 'I just don't believe it.'

'Don't believe what? What are you on about?' Amy squints at me.

'It's my Uncle Roy, over there. He's the band.' Uncle Roy bends over the mixer with his back to us, setting the switches. 'I haven't seen him in over thirty years.'

'Your uncle who?'

'Roy. I've never told you about him. He went off to London, never came back.' Amy turns around to get a look at him. He's taking the guitar out of the case. 'We were going to have our own group together. That's why he left me his old guitar.'

'Thirty years, god! Are you sure it's him?'

'Of course I am.' Flashbacks of Uncle Roy jumping off Hegarty's Rock are coming back to me. It was a lifetime ago. 'He hasn't changed that much.'

'Well, aren't you going to go over and talk to him?' Amy looks at me, questions all over her face.

'In a minute. I want to watch first. I want to hear him play. Can you believe this?' I reach for the wine. 'Want some more?' She nods and laughs.

Uncle Roy leans forward to the mike. 'Hello everybody. My name's Roy McCloon and I'm going to play a few songs for you right now. Here's one you all know.'

From the opening bars I know it is 'Hotel California'. He can't go wrong with that. It is hard to tell what's backing-track and what's Uncle Roy. It sounds like he has The Eagles on stage with him. Except I can still hear a faint Pat Boone croon in his voice.

'He's good, your Uncle Roy's pretty good.' Amy smiles at me.

'He always was,' I say, thinking of my granny's front room, the lick and wave in Uncle Roy's hair. The last notes of 'California' trail off and the small crowd applauds.

'Well thank you. Thank you very much.' Uncle Roy beams at his audience and goes straight into 'Wonderful Tonight'.

'He's sure-fire,' Amy says.

'I know.' I have to laugh. 'He was born with it.'

JIMI

My father was not normally a violent man. Still, he had an undercurrent of bitterness in him that came out in bursts. The day I came home after the Hendrix concert he had to be pulled off me. My mother was screaming. 'Stop him! He'll kill him. Stop him!'

Of course I stood up to him. 'Go on, hit me again.'

It took him a long time to forgive himself. But we let it pass and eventually restored the closeness between us. The thing was, for Jimi I would have done the same again. I can still hear Redding's high-pitched voice in the dark outside: 'Where are the girls? Where are the girls?' I can still see Jimi slouched in his chair across the room from me, his lips kissing a litre bottle of vodka. He was exhausted but on a high. I stood there, only half-believing I was in the same room as Jimi Hendrix.

That morning I had been stuck in the senior study, making out shapes in the clouds above in the big windows, wondering what I was going to do. The Experience at Rag Week. How many times had the Hendrix quotes in my books got me into trouble? *Not just stone but beautiful*. That's what I thought he was singing. It was poetry. *Excuse me while I kiss the sky*. Or was it *this guy*? It didn't matter. Everything Jimi said made sense. Jimi followed his own creed, backed it up with the irrefutable logic of his guitar.

I told Tony I was hitching to Belfast. Somehow I would manage to get there and find a way in to see The Experience. He'd tell my parents where I was, he said. No problem. Tony lived in one of the better houses on the corner of our street.

When I got to Queen's, Macker and Johnson were the most unlikely stewards on the door. They stuck a badge on me and hauled me in. We were three crazy Hendrix fans, watching Jimi do the plucking-with-his-teeth, his Foxy-Lady tongue-tease, the guitar-on-fire ritual. Everything I had heard and read about. Jimi reinvented the thunderstorm, gave it a new definition.

After the concert it was only me and Jimi in the Blue Room for a few minutes. He didn't seem to be the giant who had towered over us before. Vodka bottle to his lips he laughed at me, amused by my hanging dumbstruck at the door.

'Where are the girls? Where are the girls?' The limos pulled up, the girls bundled in on either side of Mitch and Noel. Jimi, before he walked out the door, turned and smiled at me, a full-blown Hendrix smile.

The fists came first. Then the questions. What had I been thinking of? My mother had been worried sick. They hadn't slept all night. They were about to go to the police. I tried to explain but then I realised Tony hadn't told them. About Jimi. About The Experience. You see, my father was not normally a violent man.

THE TRUMPET IN THE TOWEL

Outside BusÁras I watched the dip of the driver's arse and the white band of his y-fronts as he crawled into the luggage compartment of the six o'clock express. Onboard people were trying to get comfortable, hoping to catch some sleep, others struggled with evening newspapers. The engine pumped out waves of heat that would gradually turn the bus into a stifling capsule chugging into the dark of the November evening.

So far the seat beside me remained empty. But a few minutes before six Raymond swung onto the bus and came heading toward it.

'Holding it for someone?'

'You're okay.' Reluctantly I got up and dumped my things in the overhead rack.

'Heading for Derry?' he asked and dropped into the seat beside me.

'Yeah.'

'Me too. I'm Raymond.'

'Ian.' I hadn't wanted company or conversation on the journey but now, as the bus pulled out of BusÁras into the lines of evening traffic on

Amiens Street, there was no way to avoid it.

'Been in Dublin long?' Raymond asked.

'Two years, university.'

'Ah! I'm a musician. Came down here to try my luck in the clubs. Not much of a scene here anymore. I'm heading off to London soon.'

I took a quick look at him. He was a few years older than me, eyes packed with energy in the outline of a lean face. There was a bit of a resemblance to an uncle of mine who had ended up in Australia.

'Have to say my farewells to the folks before I go,' Raymond told me, as if I had asked a question.

'Everyone seems to be going to London. I prefer Dublin. London makes me feel out of my depth.' I wondered why I was telling him this. 'You going on your own?'

'My girlfriend, Nadja, she's Spanish, is going over with me. She prefers Dublin too, but not without me.'

The bus was making its slow trek through the Northside.

'All my family are showband,' Raymond went on. 'Music and drink, and people actually enjoying life. We weren't supposed to enjoy ourselves, were we? Even in the swinging sixties, real living wasn't on for us.'

'I know what you mean,' I said.

'Eventually I followed my old man into the showband scene, got sucked in. "Do the Hucklebuck" in haysheds they called ballrooms, with the owners screwing us for as much as they could. "It was Fun while it Lasted". Now there's a good title for a song.'

'Think it's been done,' I said and he laughed. 'So what kind of stuff do you play?'

'Jazz. Jazz trumpet. That's the reason. There's not much work around Dublin for a jazz trumpet.'

I remembered I had a Count Basie LP. I wasn't sure if that was the kind of jazz he meant.

'Call me when you get back to Dublin,' Raymond said when we arrived in Derry. He scribbled a phone number on a scrap of paper. 'Be good to meet up again before I leave. It's a coin-box in the hall. Let it ring. Someone will answer it.'

I stuffed the piece of paper into my pocket as we were jostled by people trying to get at their luggage. There was a car waiting for him on the other side of the road. 'Enjoy your farewells then,' I said. 'See you in Dublin.' He dashed across and waved back at me before getting into the car.

Back in Dublin I phoned Raymond a few times. No one answered. I was about to throw away the piece of paper but something prompted me to give it one last try. This time Raymond was there, glad to hear from me. 'Let's meet up. And bring someone with you,' he said. 'I'll be with Nadja. I told you she's Spanish. Her English isn't great.'

A few days later I bumped into Nola at the lights outside The Green. She hugged me in the arms of her short Afghan, all fur and perfume. I listened to her reel off the stories of her German summer. Lashings of sun and bronze admirers, everything she missed at home. As she shook her black curls, I remembered she was doing Spanish as well as German.

'You speak Spanish, don't you?'

'Enough to get by. What's up, amigo?'

'This guy I met a couple of weeks ago, Raymond. His girlfriend is Spanish. We're meeting up again before they go off to London. Would you like to come along? Practice a bit?' The rest I left unsaid.

Nola bit her lower lip, the way she did when she was thinking something over. 'Sure, why not.'

'He's a musician, jazz.'

'Oh, I love jazz.'

I looked at her. Cohen and Dylan was as far as Nola and I had got. Birds on wires and loves speaking like something I couldn't remember anymore. They just spoke. I went back through The Green, by the lake picked up a few left-over crumbs and threw them at the ducks.

We met at the Arch. Nola was wearing a maxi-coat, her long legs revealed in one of her micro mini-skirts. She linked my arm as we crossed into Grafton Street, and snuggled up. I silently cautioned myself. I was playing Kiro in Dramasoc's *Narrow Road*. Every evening I had to do a hari-kari. It took a lot out of me.

We reached The Bailey in time to get one of the last free tables. Nola threw her heavy coat over the seats, lapping up the attention she was attracting.

'Gin and tonic?' I asked. Nola smiled. On my way to the bar I saw Raymond and Nadja edging through the crowd. We waved at each other but it seemed to take ages for them to get close.

'You made it. Good to see you again. This is Nadja.' Raymond stepped back to let Nadja and I brush cheeks continental-style. 'You alone?'

'No, Nola's holding the table over there.' Nola gave a big wave. 'What are you two having?'

'A pint and a vodka and lime for Nadja.'

By the time I got back with the drinks, Nola and Nadja were giggling.

'I'm afraid my Spanish is not up to it,' Nola said. 'I should have gone to Spain instead.'

'And miss all those bronze admirers?' I teased her. In reply Nola faked a smile at me.

'You're better than I am,' Raymond told her.

'It is not hard to be better than he.' Nadja leaned across the table towards us. 'He not speak because he afraid to say wrong things.'

'She's been trying to teach me the basics. But every time I say something, she bursts out laughing. Try learning with someone like that!'

'It is not so. I only laugh when he say bad things to me.'

'Didn't you do Latin?' I asked.

'Don't embarrass me. School wasn't my forte.'

'And what is your forte?' Nola put in, adding that special Nola touch. I could see she was taking to Raymond.

'I like to think it's my music.' The note of seriousness in Raymond's voice would have slowed down anyone but Nola.

'What kind of music?' she fired at him again.

'Jazz.'

'Oh, I love jazz.'

Suddenly Raymond disappeared under the table and started groping around. Nola looked at me with too much innocence. Nadja laughed. When he resurfaced, Raymond was holding something wrapped in a towel.

'What is it?' Nola screeched.

Without answering, Raymond opened the towel and brought out a trumpet.

'What's the towel for?' I asked.

'Tell you later.' He wrapped the trumpet back in the towel and placed it on his lap.

'Sabes?' Nola drew closer to Nadja.

'No puedo decir. How you say: my lips are sealed?' We all laughed.

'Anything lined up in London yet?'

'A few addresses where we can crash for a while. But there should be no trouble finding work. Just don't want to end up doing the same thing as here.'

'What's so terrible about here?' Nola almost jumped on Raymond. 'Are the other musicians so bad?'

'No way. Some of the guys here are amazing, believe me. But they never get the chance to show it. They have to play the same old tripe day-in, day-out. That's soul-destroying.' He stared for a moment at Nola and then went on. 'You see, jazz is different. You can't lash it out. You have to put more of yourself into it. And if at the end of it, all you get is more stupid requests for the same old crap, then ...'

'You leave for London.' It was her way to be Nola. The way Raymond stared at her I wondered what he was going to reply. Nadja was watching them both.

'You leave for anywhere. Sooner or later you have to draw the line. London simply happens to be the next place on my list.' Nadja's hand closed over Raymond's as she leaned forward to kiss him. I raised my glass to Nola, who gave me a nasty smile before swinging round to gaze off into the crowd.

'Anyone on for some music?' Raymond asked. 'I know a place not far from here. We can walk. We'll just be in time.'

We headed across the river and through the narrow streets on the other side. Raymond stopped at a pub on a corner, then went ahead of us up the stairs. In the semi-darkness of the upstairs bar we found our way to a candle-lit table.

'It's my round. They'll be playing in a minute.' Raymond was gone before anyone could say otherwise.

'Are you happy to go away?' Nola asked.

'I do not know. I am happy here. London is very big. Dublin is right size. I get scared. But we are together happy. Raymond say he need me; I him too. We belong together, to each other.'

My eyes fell onto Raymond's chair and the trumpet. 'Tell us what the towel means. We won't tell Raymond.'

She looked around to make sure Raymond wasn't coming. 'He tell me it mean he want people to ask him to play. He like to play but only when they ask it. It is a thing for musicians.' Nola and I nodded as if we understood.

At the far end of the room the musicians were coming on stage. Raymond arrived with a tray of drinks. He set the tray on the table. 'Be back later. Got to talk to some people.'

'He is so. Always here, there, away. He do everything at same time.'

Then the band started up. Around the bar people became silent, drawn into the feel of the music. One musician after the other took on a solo, handing over to the next in a burst of applause. After the solos the whole band took up the theme again. At the close we all applauded,

Nadja at the same time searching the room for Raymond. The second set was slow, the Count Basie style I was familiar with. Raymond returned and without a word slipped in beside Nadja, who leaned her head back onto his shoulder. I took the chance to slip my arm around Nola and draw her close to me. She turned around and pecked me on the cheek, then lay back warmly against me. It felt like the kind of setting I had always imagined for Count Basie music. No one talking, just the touch of Nola's curls on my cheek. The applause broke the spell. Nola jumped away from me and turned to Raymond. 'When are you going to join them?'

'Later, maybe. They're doing all right, aren't they?'

'Yes, but we want to hear you.' Nola shook her curls in mock anger and fell back with a thud against my shoulder. 'He doesn't want to play for us.'

'He will,' I said. 'Give him time.' But he stayed with Nadja, smooching while they listened to the music. In the break there was a rush to the bar. Nola and Nadja went to the ladies' together.

Raymond propped his elbows on the table and stared straight at me. 'What do you think?'

I needed a moment to come up with an answer. 'She's pretty crazy about you.'

'I know. And I'm crazy about her. But it's me who wants to get away. Nadja would be happier to stay here. It kind of worries me.'

'Why should it?' I remembered what Nadja had said earlier.

'What if things go wrong? If the whole thing backfires? It's alright if it's only me. But I couldn't forgive myself if anything happened to Nadja.'

His doubts confused me. I wanted to hear from him that he knew it would all work out. But it was as if he needed me to encourage him. Raymond moved his glass around on the table, focusing his thoughts. 'Maybe I should go on my own first and then bring Nadja over when I get set up.'

'But would she want you to go without her?'

'I don't know. I don't think so. No, I know she wouldn't. It's ironic really. Just when I think I'm setting myself free, I go off and fall in love and tie myself down again.' He broke off and looked around, then turned back to me. 'It's not meant to be as cold and calculated as it sounds.'

'I didn't think it was,' I said. 'I don't have the feeling that you're that type.'

'Thanks.' He reached across the table and squeezed my hand. 'That's enough of the soul-searching for now. Too much of it is not a good thing. Anyway, the two Ns are coming back.'

I laughed at the way he said *the two Ns* but underneath I was left with my own doubts.

Halfway through the second half of the evening, the bandleader approached the microphone. 'We'd like to call on someone who will be leaving us very soon. We don't want to let him go but we've run out of good reasons for him to stay. So maybe this is our last chance for a long time to hear him. Please welcome onstage Mister Raymond Coyle.'

Raymond was already on his feet with the trumpet, letting the towel slip back under the table. He kissed Nadja on the forehead. 'I'll be back in a minute,' he told us.

We watched him make his way around the tables and step onto the small stage. The band shifted into a different tempo, building up to Raymond's cue. He stood fingering the keys of the trumpet. When he joined in, the rhythm picked up. His body moved and swayed. The musicians played off each other, topping solos in a seemingly endless progression. Raymond's trumpet led for a time, then fell back in again with the band, creating a different kind of jazz, a different drive. In the gleam of a spotlight his face almost shone. When the music came to a powerful finale, the applause was thundering. The other musicians were smiling at each other. The bandleader called out: 'On trumpet, Mr Raymond Coyle!' Then they swung back into a mellower rhythm.

'Wow! I didn't know the trumpet could be played like that!' Nola's jazz expertise had its limits.

'He is genius. He put everything into his playing, his heart, his soul, his whole life. He live for his music. His trumpet is his real love. I only come somewhere far, far …' Nadja ran out of words.

'No, no, no!' Nola reached across and caught Nadja's hand. 'You are his muse, you inspire him. He loves you very much.'

'But I not want to go away. I want us to be here, with people we know, with you. You are friends. In London I know no friends. I afraid we lose everything, we lose each other. Maybe the big break, as he say, will come. Or maybe it will be the big break for us. Sometimes I afraid. I wish he is happy here. He is so good; he play so good with the band.'

Before either Nola or I could say anything, Raymond was back. Nadja jumped up and threw her arms around him, laughing and kissing his cheeks.

'It's her fiery Mediterranean blood.' Raymond was trying to get her to sit while she continued to hug him.

'You were brilliant,' Nola insisted.

'We were good, weren't we? You think you've given your all and then somebody takes you onto a new level.' Raymond was drying the trumpet and tucking it away in the towel again. A round of drinks arrived from the bar. 'On the house,' the waiter said.

The evening mellowed into a haze of music and drink. Raymond came and went, arriving with more drinks, then wandering off. We laughed, then fell silent when nothing came into our minds. Nothing but desire. Nola's body lay heavy against me, rekindling nuances. Without drawing attention, I eased my hand under her blouse, just enough to send little ripples along her back.

In the early hours of the morning, we made our way into the outside world again.

'We'll get a cab back to the flat for a nightcap.' At the corner of O'Connell Street Raymond flagged down a taxi and we all piled in. Raymond kept up a conversation with the driver until the taxi pulled up outside a row of houses with flights of steps leading up to massive

Georgian doors. We tumbled out and set about managing the steps.

'For god's sake shut up the lot of you. If you wake everybody up, we'll all be in trouble.' But Raymond was as giggly as the rest of us as we watched Nadja and Nola in their attempts to get up the steps. Fortunately his flat was on the ground floor. He turned the key and ushered us out of the hall into a large, high-ceilinged room with a bay window niche. 'The bathroom's in the hall if anyone needs it. Throw your things anywhere.'

I noticed the large trombone that stood in the corner of the bay window, larger than any I'd ever seen. 'Can you play that?'

'Not at two o'clock in the morning. Good one isn't it? Picked it up at the Rathmines market. Give you a blast some other time. Anyway, who's for a brandy?'

'I shouldn't,' Nola said. 'I've had so much already. I have to get home soon.'

Raymond was already pouring the brandy into large glasses. 'You can stay here if you like. There's a bed in the alcove.' He handed round the glasses of brandy before we could say anymore. Nola and I looked at each other, then at the alcove. She shrugged her shoulders, 'Why not.'

'Good, then that's all settled.' Raymond gave me a knowing look. 'Why is everybody standing?' Raymond and Nadja took the couch. Nola tugged at her miniskirt as she sat on my lap in the armchair.

'Here's to a great evening,' Raymond toasted.

'No, no!' Nola objected. 'Here's to your playing.'

'Okay.'

The brandy sent a burn curling into my stomach. 'Neat,' I said with a voice of experience.

'My favourite.' Raymond held up his glass and let the brandy swirl round. 'After a gig it helps me come down nice and slow again. That's the nature of this game, you spend half the night playing and then the other half drinking. Or drugging.'

'You seem to be able to handle things okay.'

'I'm lucky. Nadja keeps me clean. She's my beautiful dark Spanish watchdog, aren't you?' She snuggled up to him, silent and tired. 'I'll miss this place. I like living here. I love the park outside. I can sit for hours at the window looking out into the park, daydreaming. I'm a dreamer. Deep down that's what I am.'

'There's a bit of the dreamer in us all,' Nola said softly. 'It's good for you.'

'Yeah, but making the dreams come true is hard work.'

'It ain't meant to be easy.' Nola reached into the depths of her wisdom.

'How true,' Raymond said, putting his glass down. 'Even at this time of the morning. But everyone's beat. We'd better get to bed. We can delve deeper another time.' He and Nadja rose from the couch. 'The bed's a bit narrow. You'll have to snuggle up. We'll see you in the morning, some time.'

When they left, Nola and I got close on the couch. She lay back as I undid the buttons of her blouse and reached round to unclasp her bra. My hand slipped under her skirt.

'Wait, wait. Not here. They might come in again. Let's go to the bed.'

The sheets on the narrow bed were cold. Nola clung to me for warmth. 'You'll have to be careful. It's not a good time.' I made noises that I would, not knowing exactly how. I didn't want to stop now. I eased myself on top, ready and excited. But suddenly Nola pulled away and pushed me off. 'I can't. Don't. I can't.' She struggled to get out of the bed. 'I need the bathroom. Where is it? I'm going to be sick.' She threw off the bedclothes and ran out naked into the hall.

I stumbled out of bed and pulled on my trousers. Grabbing a blanket, I hurried after her.

'Go away! I don't want you here.' She fought me off as I wrapped the blanket around her. 'Please, go away!'

I went back into the room, still fumbling at my trousers. The light was on, Raymond and Nadja were there.

'We heard all the commotion,' Raymond said. 'Is she alright?'

'She's sick. But she doesn't want me near her.'

'I'll go,' Nadja said.

The two of us were left standing in the room, listening to the sounds of Nola being sick. 'I'm sorry,' I said. 'I'm sorry it had to end like this. I feel like a fool.'

'I'm the fool for forcing more drink on people. We'd all had enough.'

He didn't understand and I couldn't tell him that I felt like a fool because of myself. 'It's spoilt everything,' was all I managed to say.

'Don't talk rubbish. As long as she's okay. We can all go back to bed. Things will look different in the morning. It's nearly morning anyway.'

There were things I wanted to say, about him and me. About how in such a short time something had happened between us and how his leaving would just as quickly erase it. But before I could even try to put all this into words, Nola returned, looking frail, runs of mascara under her eyes.

'I'm sorry. Can we call a taxi?' She pulled the blanket tight around her.

'Are you sure?' Raymond asked. 'Why don't you get some sleep? You'll feel better for it.'

'No!' Nola snapped. 'Sorry. I'd rather go home.'

'Okay, I'll call a taxi,' Raymond relented.

We could hear the coins dropping into the coin-box. Nadja brought Nola a cup of coffee but she refused it. She wiped the mascara from under her eyes.

'About ten minutes,' Raymond said. 'You're looking better already.'

'I feel like shit. Sorry.'

'Everybody round here wants to be sorry. But listen, I'm really the one to blame. I shouldn't have forced brandy on you. So sorry-time is over for everybody right now, okay?'

Nola smiled wearily at him. 'Are you coming?' she asked me.

'Of course I am.' She nodded and gave me a faint smile. At some traffic lights I'd leave the taxi, let Nola go on. I knew neither of us would mention this again. I turned to Raymond. 'No chance of seeing you again before you leave?'

'We leave on Wednesday. We've already given up the flat. You can have it if you like. They haven't found anyone yet. I'll throw in the trombone.'

'A place like this? Couldn't afford it. But I'll come over to London when you get settled in.'

'Good idea,' he said.

I heard the news about Raymond in my final year. I was hitching to Derry and near Monaghan got a lift from a musician. He was telling me stories of the antics that Horslips got up to. It was fun to listen to him, then a thought came into my mind.

'Maybe you know a guy called Raymond Coyle. He plays trumpet. Jazz trumpet. He went over to London about two years ago.'

The way he looked at me, I knew there was something wrong. 'I knew him alright. Don't you know?'

'Know what?'

He briefly took his eyes off the road. 'He was found dead in his flat about a year ago.'

Raymond dead? How could he be dead? The trumpet in the towel, the dreams? 'What happened?'

'I don't know for sure. There was some talk about heart problems. But I don't want to say anything wrong. Things didn't work out for Raymond the way he expected them to.'

'And his girlfriend, Nadja, what happened to her? She was crazy about him.'

'She cracked up completely. As far as I know, she was the one who found him. She had to go back to Spain.' He looked at me. 'We all liked Raymond but he was a bit of a loner. He wasn't easy to get close to. We didn't understand really what he wanted. I wonder if he knew himself.'

I stared out at the long stretch of road in front of us. It didn't make sense to me. It just didn't make sense.

SUCH A GOOD INVENTION

Ian was on the sun terrace that overlooked the bay. It was the last day of his holiday and he was all set to make the most of it. The bubbles in his sparkling wine rose with precision and fanned out to the sides of the glass. The base of the glass's long stem was blue, a shade deeper than the blue of the ocean. There was a slight breeze curling the leaves of the palm trees. His plan was a walk along the beach to the Grand Café, where he would order his coffee, write some postcards. Then, when the beach had emptied, he'd go for a late dip.

A line of geese crossed the sky, heading south-west. Out of habit he counted them as they passed overhead. There were exactly fourteen, moving in silent formation, gradually disappearing behind the cypress tree that shaded the terrace. Make a wish he told himself. A double wish. He thought of people who would have told him to do so. 'And don't tell me!'

He hesitated. Right now he could think of very little to wish for. When he got back, it would be different. He reached for his glass, took a sip, closed his eyes and made his wish. Then on second thoughts he reformulated his wish. Just in case. At that moment a cloud passed across the sun. He looked up at it disapprovingly. A wisp of cloud, in a moment it would be gone. He stared out at the ocean that moved so effortlessly. A seagull was circling the bay. A small fishing boat was poised equidistant between the lighthouse and Cap del Pinar.

Back in London the smog irritated his skin, made him feel ill-at-ease. Every morning he took the Circle Line train to Context, where he spent the day in front of his screen, doing translations. It started out as a summer job but after the summer they offered him a decent hike in salary to stay on. His boss told him to work on his accent, get rid of the moccasins and never to contradict him. Ian put up with him, knowing it would only be a matter of time before one of them moved on. It was a job. Back home there were no jobs.

Then one sunny day there was Deborah, crouched Buddha-like on Holland Road, a sketch pad resting on her lap. She looked up from the sketch and smiled at him. Her black hair cropped, her skin so Californian. He smiled back and hunkered down beside her to take a look.

'Hey, I like.'

'Thanks. It's not finished. I always tell myself I'll get round to finishing them later.' She looked over at him. 'Mostly they end up in my grand collection of unfinished masterpieces.'

'Seems a pity. Not that I'm an expert or anything. You an art student?'

'No, this I do on holiday. Other people have their expensive cameras; I have my sketch pad. In real life I'm a seamstress. You know? I sew things. Exciting stuff.'

'Never met a seamstress before. Suppose you've done Carnaby Street an' all that?'

'First day. It's our Mecca.'

Returning office-workers hurried past them, some glancing at the two figures huddled over the sketchbook. Deborah showed him her charcoal sketches of people caught like snapshots, buildings that seemed to hover in mid-air. There was a sketch of a line of geese. He counted five. 'Where was this?'

'The Lake District. I'm big into Wordsworth. All those lakes. I promised myself.'

'An' was it worth it?'

'Every minute.' She let her eyes rest on his.

'Pity there weren't seven, you could have made a wish.'

'Seven?'

'Seven geese.' He pointed at the sketch.

'Oh that. I'm not superstitious. I don't believe in those things, I just liked the way they flapped across the sky. And it kind of made me think of myself wandering around Europe all on my own. You know geese always seem to be together. I don't think I've ever seen one on its own. Have you?'

His mind lingered on her word 'superstitious'. He'd never thought of it like that. It had more to do with luck, good things happening to you. 'I guess not.'

'So what did you wish for with your last seven?'

'I saw fourteen actually. A double wish. But you're not supposed to tell.'

'Hey, you are superstitious. That's cute.'

She had a room in a nearby hotel. 'It's so small, there's nowhere to sit except on the bed. But it's enough for me for a couple of nights.' She laughed at herself the way he already liked about her.

'I need to wash,' she told him when they got there. 'You get real sticky in London. Help me.'

Ian undid the buttons on the back of her calico blouse and slipped his hands in around her breasts. He cupped them lightly, enjoying their weight.

'Do they pass the test?' She pulled away from him and removed the blouse. Then she undid her jeans.

'Certainement.' He watched the slight arch of her back as she worked the zip. She wriggled out of the tight jeans and eased her panties down over the whites of her buttocks. At the washbasin she splashed cold water on herself. Easy, natural. Then she came over and handed him the towel. 'Over to you.' He dabbed at the pearls dripping over her brownness, chasing them down the length of her back and thighs.

'C'mon, we've got to get you out of your protective clothing.' She climbed onto the bed. 'Now the sun's gone, I need you to warm me.' She tugged at his tie and threw it onto the floor, then undid his shirt and wrapped it back over his shoulders. He went to open his belt but she stopped him. 'Let me.'

In the morning Deborah lay with the wrinkled sheet pulled up to her shoulders, watching Ian dress. 'His shining armour glistens as he prepares himself for battle.'

'More like he throws on his sweaty shirt for yet another day. Hoping no one comes too close. Then again, no one ever does.'

'Oh, that sounds so sad. You want me to feel all sorry for you?'

'Well, if you find the time, why not. But don't overdo it.'

'I have a busy day ahead. I'll see if I can fit you in.'

'Talking of which, what time this evening?' He was taking it as a given, hoping she would too. 'What time and where?'

Her eyes met his. 'Let's not. It wouldn't be the same.'

He stared at her, propped up against the pillows on the tousled bed, so within reach but trying to close herself away. An inner voice told him to argue with her, to persuade her. But he didn't.

'Let's keep it as it was,' she insisted. 'Not complicate it. Anyway, I have to pack. I'm leaving for Scotland tomorrow, I'm visiting some people in the Borders. I'll write you, I promise. Who knows, I might run into a few more geese, maybe get a wish too. I hope you got yours.'

Ian leaned over and kissed her. 'No worries about that. But remember mine was a double wish.'

'You're greedy. All men are. Don't try to get me to change my mind. Please. It's better this way.'

He wondered what made it better this way. All day he could be looking forward to coming back, counting down the hours till they met again. But it seemed that without knowing it she was superstitious after all.

'I have to go. Enjoy Scotland. People there are more friendly than here.'

'Hey, that sounds promising. Does that ex - or include you?' She was smiling at him, the way she had the day before when she looked up from her sketchbook.

'You know what I mean. Think of me when you see those geese.' What a crap exit line he thought as he opened the door. But he didn't have time to come up with a better one. The door shut behind him and he walked down the corridor past all the other closed doors.

On the tube Ian studied the blur of his reflection, trying to decipher if something was different. It was impossible to make out any change. There was nothing anyone would notice. But who was there to notice, he asked himself. It triggered other questions. How much longer would he stick the job? How many more times would he make the same ride there and back? How many more Deborahs would it take before ... Ian stared at his reflection and wondered what it was he was trying to tell himself.

A week later Deborah's card arrived.

A promise is a promise, and I said I would write. In case you're wondering, it's bloody cold up here. It's been raining for days. I haven't finished the sketch yet. Sunshine was such a good invention.

A DIFFERENT STORY

I had never touched another man's penis before. But I had no choice. The man beside me driving the car expected me to do it. We were on the M25 heading south. Ten minutes earlier he had stopped to pick me up. Said he could take me as far as Maidstone. That's where this was happening.

'Your whole body gets so tense, stuck in the car all day.' It sounded like a harmless comment. How it came with the job, on the road from customer to customer. Smooth shirt, loose tie, jacket laid out neatly on the back seat. 'Have a feel,' he said, kept his eyes fixed on the road ahead, his body primed as he gauged my reaction. My instinct warned me not to let him see this was scary. I was locked in his car. Right now letting me out wasn't what was on his mind.

I reached my hand over. His trousers were silky and cold. I could feel the fat bulge of his cock. It was brutal. 'Yes,' I said. 'I can feel it.' I took my hand away again, carefully.

'You want to do something for me. You want to help me relax.' These weren't questions, he wasn't giving me options. 'You know what I mean.'

I looked at the round face, the sleek features of a man who knew how to get what he wanted, a man who knew he was the one in control. 'Yes,' I told him, and fed his words back to him. 'I know what you mean.'

He eased back into the seat as I reached over again and unzipped his fly. I tugged the flap of his trousers and let my hand slip in and close around his penis, suppressing an impulse to pull my hand away again.

He sighed at the touch of my fingers. 'That's good. That feels good what you're doing.'

'Good,' I said and rubbed in circular movements. His hands were tight on the steering wheel, his attention on the traffic, as if what was happening was happening to someone else.

'Take me out.' His voice was sharp, insistent. I hesitated. I wondered if passing drivers would notice what was going on. Or lorry drivers high above in their cabs. But I knew it didn't matter to him. This was a routine. The way he locked my bag into the boot. How he told me he was glad of a break in the monotony, someone to talk to. He could take me as far as Maidstone he said, when I told him I had to make the ferry out of Dover.

I could have refused. I could have told him to let me out. But it felt safer to go along with what he wanted, get it over and done with.

His penis stood up naked and awkward, the dark purple veins etched along its length. I gripped my hand around it and began rubbing.

'Not too tight.' He clenched his teeth, leaned forward to the wheel, then fell back again into his seat. 'Easy does it.'

I loosened my grip and stroked more gently. 'Is this alright?'

'Don't ask questions. Just go on.'

The juices started to spill as my hand moved up and down along the shaft. I could feel the moment coming closer, his body tense.

'Open the glove compartment, get the tissues. I'm nearly there. Don't let any get on my trousers.'

I took out the packet of tissues and fumbled one out with my free hand.

'Get ready,' he said.

I held the tissue closer and kept rubbing. A milky cream oozed over the inside of my hand. Then his hold on the wheel tightened again. I caught the tip of his penis in the tissue as he moaned and came. I waited till the throbbing stopped, conscious of the smell of him on my hand.

'Get rid of it!'

I rolled down the window beside me and flung the soiled tissue out. I saw it flutter for a moment, then it was carried away on a gust of wind. He ignored me as he slipped his penis back into his pants and did up the zip. 'Do you feel better?' I asked in an attempt to cut through the uncomfortable silence. He shot a cold look at me but didn't answer. I waited. The tension grew. I wondered what was going to happen. At the next services he pulled in and stopped the car.

'Get out!'

I unhooked the belt and opened the door. 'My bag.'

He popped the boot and let me get my bag out. Then he drove away.

I watched his car drive down the slip-road, filter back into the flow of traffic and vanish. I stood there a long time, mesmerized by the constant line of cars. Then I turned away and forced myself to walk over to the picnic area. I sat down on a bench, stared at the people filing out of and into the Welcome Break. Normal people doing normal things in a seemingly meaningful and harmless routine. All the time it had been happening, I had not wanted to admit I was afraid. Most of all, I had not wanted him to know that I was. Now I could feel the fear shiver through my body. I looked around to reassure myself he had definitely gone. Then I picked up my bag and walked over to the main building to find the restroom.

As I lathered the soap onto my hands, washing his smell off me, wiping the image of his round face out of my mind, I stared at myself in the mirror. Part of me wondered how I had done it. And part of me knew that if I hadn't, this could have been a different story.

A BEAUTIFUL DAY

It was madness, sheer madness. Any sane person would have been out of there, downing a pint in some nearby pub or tucked up at home in front of a good soccer match. But here we were at the old power station across the border, arse-deep in a river, the rain lashing down on us. Fishing. I had never done it before. The cast and spin, the trail and flick. I hadn't a clue. And the patience it took. Nothing was happening. Nothing. Everything around me seemed to have a negative mindset. The river, the rain, the wind in the drenched trees, the fish, if there were any. Part of me knew that if I could see myself from the road, I would be thinking, 'What a nutter!' I'd always thought that about men I saw fishing, especially ones arse-deep in the middle of a river in the lashing rain.

Another part of me was beginning to get into it. The rain ran off my bulging cape, the waders kept me dry. I still had my problems with the casting, but slowly I was acquiring a kind of technique. My younger brother Jim was the expert; Danny was his side-kick. Jim showed me five minutes of the basics, then said he'd leave me to get the hang of it. He kept an eye on me, shouting bits of advice across at me. Most of what he shouted got carried away with the rain. But being with the two of them began to feel good. Each one of us covered our own stretch of the river, still somehow connected like a set of navigation points.

When I got a bite, Jim rushed over. 'Hold tight. Bring her in nice and easy now.' He stayed with me until I had it in the net, then waded out into the river again. Getting the barb out wasn't as bad as I thought it would be. I tried to twist it out humanely at first. But no way. Then I ripped it out. I didn't look at what I was doing. Just did it. The fish still jiggled a bit until I used the stone.

But Danny's salmon was the real thing; landing her lasted about half an hour.

'Don't let her break away!' Jim screamed. 'She'll snap the line. Hold on to her.' He kept his eyes on the way the fish was manoeuvring, the way she played the line. 'Let her have plenty of slack, Danny. Jesus, she's a big one. Let her run with it.'

Jim was beating through the water; Danny did his best to do what he was told. They'd been friends for years, fixed up cars together. And women. That's why they understood each other better than Jim and I ever would

'I think she got away, Jim. She's not pulling anymore.'

'She's a clever one, Danny. She's still there alright. Hold on to her. She'll be back in a minute. There she goes!'

I could hear the jerk that went through Danny's rod, thought it would snap in two as a bright flash shot out over the grey of the river. Something inside me wanted the line to break. This fish deserved to live. But no way was I going to say that.

'Tire her out, Danny! She's giving you a run for your money.'

The tail of the fish was kicking in the water as she hit out at whatever was holding her back. I could feel the energy in her, defiance in the way she struggled.

'Okay, Danny. Wind her in. Nice and slow now.' The fish bolted at the first tug of the line and shot off. The reel whirred loudly as the fish drew the line with it into deeper water. Then something jammed.

'Fuck it, Jim!'

'Hold on, Danny!'

Danny's rod looked as if it wouldn't hold out much longer. Jim waded through the water and belted the locked reel with the side of his fist. It must have hurt, but the line was freed.

'Wind her in again now, Danny. She must be nearly beat.'

This time my younger brother was wrong. As if she had heard him, as if the only thing she wanted now was to prove how wrong he was, the fish took off again. Danny was splashing after her, trying to keep up.

'She's a good one.' Jim rushed behind him, laughing. 'She had us good'n fooled that time.'

She didn't want to be caught. Every fibre inside her was primed against it. But each time she pulled on the line, the barb lodged itself deeper in the roof of her mouth. That was how it worked. Even I understood that now. If she hadn't managed to snap the line when her energy was at its peak, now that she was tiring, her chances of getting away were gone. All Danny had to do was let her flag herself out and then wind her in. Eventually he got her into shallow water again and Jim heaved her out.

Her tail still flapped. She was a magnificent creature, dappled and shimmering with lost life.

'Jesus, there's some weight in her. I can hardly hold her. You got yourself a whopper of a one there, Danny.'

Jim cradled the salmon in his arms while Danny worked at the barb. There was no way it would come out easily. She flailed and twitched as Danny's hands worked at her mouth.

'Fuck this, Jim,' Danny said.

'Give it a good hard jerk,' Jim told him.

The shock kicked through the fish's body, then it lay motionless.

'Some prize for a day's fishing.' Jim held out his arms full of fish.

'You're a lucky fucker, Danny Gilmore.'

A year later Danny was shot in the back by the Paratroopers. He was running away from them. Everybody was running away, trying to get behind something solid. The bullet went in one side and out the other. Danny gasped and toppled forward. A priest, waving a white handkerchief, crawled over to him to give him the last rites.

After Danny's burial, they would find his mother in the middle of the night with a blanket over his grave, trying to keep the cold off him.

BORDER LINES

Lyn and I grew up together. Same street, same constellation of kids, and parents who didn't need to see too much of us. We spent a lot of our teens in Fiorentini's, sharing straws, feeding the jukebox. In those days 'We're All Going on a Summer Holiday' sounded wild to us.

I don't know why it never happened with Lyn and me. Sometimes I think there was a side to Lyn that got a kick out of keeping me hanging on, like the song said. Boyfriends were easy-come-by. After each break-up she came looking for me again. I was always there. On the other hand, maybe it had to do with me. Maybe I needed it that way.

When I came back from college, I landed a job as a junior partner in a solicitor's office. Normally it would have been boring but The Troubles changed that, kept us on our toes. Mike was my senior partner. The Monsignor, Mike's father, had built up the practice. He had a lot of church dealings going on, hence the name I suppose. He liked to get his picture in the newspaper, that sort of thing. There was an only sister, a nun, over in Africa. She was allowed a home-visit once every seven years. Mike had a picture of her on his desk. She looked very young in her nun's habit, surrounded by a group of Nigerian children with flawless white teeth.

Lyn came to me after her crash. She was up for drink-driving. I managed to get her off with a large fine, a brief suspension. She was impressed and said we'd celebrate. The day I closed Lyn's case, Mike and I went for lunch in The Castle.

'You handled it well, Stephen. With anyone else on the case, she would have come out of it a lot worse.' We picked up soup and sandwiches at the deli-counter. Mike made a big deal about paying. There was a free table in the corner. 'I hope she knows how to thank you.'

I had an idea what Mike was getting at.

'They say she'd ride anything.' Mike was stirring his soup. Then he looked up at me. 'I wouldn't mind a go at her myself.' *How many fingers?* That was always the first question. Mike was bringing it all back. 'You're old friends, aren't you?'

'We grew up together.' I bit into my chicken sandwich.

'Was she always a wild one?'

'She was like the rest of us,' I told him. I didn't have any other answer.

Lyn and I arranged to have dinner in The Roadhouse. It probably had a reputation. I didn't want to phone, so I drove across the day before and booked a room. People did it all the time. I told Lyn about the table reservation. I didn't mention the room. My plan was we'd drink enough. That was all.

Seven-thirty Friday evening when I picked her up, I knew the buzz between us was different. From her red high-heels to the faint quiver of her plucked eyebrows, Lyn was sexy. She slipped into the seat beside me with a swish of nylon and a tug at her miniskirt, the fragrance of Chanel or Dior. There was sweat on my fingers as I held the steering-wheel.

That night we danced to the beat from the downstairs disco. We collapsed onto the bed and rolled over into each other's arms.

'I won't tell, if you don't tell,' Lyn said. 'Promise?'

'Promise.' I pulled her close. Lyn's lips were soft, softer than I could have imagined. I melted into them. We told ourselves we deserved this. Then we made the most of it.

'Will you set me up with her?' Mike had just come off the phone. The incessant rain wasn't doing anything for my mood.

'With whom?'

'With your friend Lyn.'

I was about to say she wasn't my friend but stopped myself. 'You're a big boy. Why would you need me to set you up with anyone?'

'C'mon Stephen, you could make it a whole lot easier for me. Just point us in the right direction.' Mike was already dialling the next number.

That weekend something made me mention it to Lyn. We had got a green light at the checkpoint. Lyn rolled the window down as we drove through.

'Where are they? Do they really exist?' She stuck her head out to get a look.

'Don't make a scene. They scan the reg. They know who we all are.'

'But it's not my car. I could be anybody.'

'You're alright, you're with me.' Lyn settled down as the checkpoint disappeared behind us.

'You never ever got involved, did you, Stephen?'

'We were kept from getting involved. My parents saw to that. They didn't want any dead heroes or martyrs in the family. That's why they were happy when Ian went away, one less to worry about. Our job is to help the guys who get involved. That's where we come in useful.'

'You and Michael. You two are good together, aren't you? Have you met The Monsignor?'

'A few times. He's from a different era, still goes to mass every day.'

Then I told her about Mike.

'What's his interest in me?' Lyn asked as if the question was relevant.

'Purely carnal I would think. When you get that part sorted out, I suppose you can move on to the rest.'

'You don't seem too worried about it.'

'Me? I'm just the messenger boy. Like always. Nothing has changed, has it?' I thought she was going to reply but she went quiet on me instead. I would have preferred her to say something. There was a checkpoint on the Strand Road, the police this time, but they waved us through.

'Are you coming in?'

My fingers hesitated on the keys in the ignition. 'I won't.'

'Oh Stephen, don't be a baby! You always come in. What's wrong with you?'

'Nothing.' It was stupid but I wasn't in the mood. 'It's late and I don't want to run into anymore checkpoints.'

'Okay. So when are we going to meet again?'

'You pick a date,' I said. 'Ring me. I'll arrange something.'

'No, let me arrange next time. I have an idea.'

'Sounds good. You want to tell me?'

'No, it's a surprise. Anyway, I'm not sure yet. I'll ring you.' She swung round and reached for her bag in the back. Then leaned across and kissed me. 'Thanks for the weekend. I enjoyed it.'

I drove off, aware that neither of us had mentioned Mike again.

Mike and I had to put up with a lot in court. We grilled the detectives on the nitty-gritty of their evidence. They made it up as they went along. Each charge we got dismissed meant more resentment. Mike took the brunt of it. They liked to make sarky remarks, out of earshot of the judge, usually about The Monsignor. A few times Mike flinched. I could see the effort he was making not to rise to the bait. But they were clever enough not to say anything we could nail them on.

'Nigger-uncle,' a plainclothes-man called him one day as we entered the chamber. It sounded so absurd I expected him to laugh it off. He froze on the spot, his face crimson. I thought he was going to lose it.

'Take it easy, Mike. Don't let him get to you. That's all they want.' I touched his arm. 'Walk with me.'

The plainclothes-man was ready for more but I managed to get Mike to move away. We were called to order before anything else could happen.

Later in the Castle Mike was still fuming. 'They know everything, the bastards. It's a dirty fuckin' war alright. Just in case we might have any illusions to the contrary. They know where to dig out the dirt.'

I let him take a gulp of his pint. 'Do you want to tell me what this is about? If you don't, it's alright. I don't need to know.'

'If these guys know it won't be much of a secret for long. You might as well hear it from me.' He glanced around the bar. The Castle was pretty quiet around this time. We didn't have to worry. 'My little sister, the holy one, when she got settled in her out-of-Africa, she discovered she wasn't into all this holy stuff as much as she thought she was.' He straightened up to take a drink. 'Are you starting to get the picture?'

'Kind of. I presume there's more.'

He leaned across the table. 'There's like three kids more, plus a Nigerian father, husband or man-friend, whatever it is she calls him.'

'Three kids?' I couldn't help it. 'How long have you known?'

'It's in vault number three-o-nine of the family secrets. When this gets out The Monsignor's holier-than-the-rest-of-thou-poor-suckers image will be blown. I hate to think how much he has already forked out to keep it under locks. What the fuck does it matter? Nobody gives a shit in this day and age. But my da likes to believe he has something to live up to. I worry about him.'

I was thinking of the sister. 'Will she ever come home?'

'Are you fuckin' mad? Not as long as The Monsignor is alive. He pays her to stay away. He takes good care of her, makes sure she doesn't want for anything. That's as good as his Christianity gets.'

Mid-week Lyn phoned and told me she would come by the office on Friday. 'Try to get away early,' she said. 'And be ready to hit the road.' I suggested we could meet up somewhere in town but she wanted me to introduce her to Mike. 'He did ask.'

It wasn't easy to fend off Mike's questions. He wouldn't believe I didn't know where we were spending the weekend. 'Hey, sounds kinky. You two into that kind of thing?'

'There's nothing kinky about it. I just don't know.' But his version made Lyn more interesting for him.

'Are you going to be mad at me when I cut in on you?'

'It's not like that.'

'Hey, c'mon Stevie, you're going off with this woman for a weekend, you don't know where. She's picking you up, looking after your every desire and whim, and dropping you back on your doorstep. And you say it's not like that. Get real, Stevie. What is it then?'

'Mike, she wants to meet you. She's coming by, specifically. Whatever you two do is your thing. I have no claims on Lyn. I never did.'

Mike looked at me as if I had said the weirdest thing he'd ever heard me say. 'I don't get you. Tell me to back off and I will. I'll leave you to it. She's all yours, if that's the way you want it.'

'You've got it all wrong. It's Lyn who always gets it the way she wants it. Not me. That's the way it works.'

That weekend we ended up in Edinburgh. Lyn had everything arranged. We spent Saturday morning doing the tourist thing, then Lyn headed for the boutiques around the Mile. I was reading the paper in the pub when the news came on. Back home all hell had broken loose again. It was like one of those bad dreams that were impossible to wake up from. There had been all night rioting, petrol bombs and CS gas after a Saracen had crushed someone against a wall. The dead man's name sounded familiar. From here it looked crazy, like on a different planet. I hated to think we were so close. I didn't say anything to Lyn when we met back at the hotel. Instead I offered to go for the gin and tonics.

'Do you like the place?' Lyn had chosen a Moroccan restaurant.

'It's fine,' I said. 'Kind of exotic. Now tell me what to order.'

'Take a risk, Stephen. Go for whatever sounds good to you. Here, try the mechoui of lamb.'

'You know me and risks.' If I hadn't said that, we might not have got into what followed.

'It's what life's about.' Lyn looked at me over the top of the menu.

'I take enough risks just getting out of bed in the morning.'

It didn't work. Lyn hung in there. 'You never did, Stephen. As long as I've known you you've always played it safe.'

'That's rubbish.' I was beginning to wonder if there was something else on her mind. 'I've taken enough risks in my life.'

'Name one.'

'So far my job is the biggest one.' At that point we were interrupted by the waiter. I ordered the lamb mechoui. Lyn went for daurade with couscous, something I'd never heard of before. We decided for red.

'You were saying,' Lyn continued when the waiter had gone.

'We don't exactly make ourselves very popular with what we do, Mike and I. The way it is, you always rub somebody up the wrong way. We get our fair share of threats, some pretty ridiculous ones, some we have to take more serious.'

'I didn't realize.'

'We try not to publicize it. The police warn us every now and then, even when the threats probably come from some of their own people. I won't bore you.'

'But I wasn't talking about that kind of risk. I mean risks like with me.'

'With you?'

'That's right Stephen, with me. Is that a little too obvious?'

'Tell me more.'

'What do I mean to you, Stephen? Have you ever thought about that?'

'As if I haven't.' Then I heard myself tell her about how I always felt taken-for-granted, how everybody else always seemed more special to her than me.

'Maybe when we were younger, things were a bit like that. We were always together, like brother and sister really. Then you went away.'

'So?'

'I missed you. When you weren't there anymore, I really missed you. You being there was important to me. When I heard you were back, I was glad. I've been trying to show you that, but you make it hard. You're very closed, Stephen. Like you are now. You still haven't answered my question. What do I mean to you?'

It was a relief that the waiter came. My brain was racing. Lyn kept her eyes on me as the waiter arranged the small plates on the table, his fingers moving with precision. The music in the background seemed to get louder.

'I'm not very good at this,' I said.

'You prefer being on the sidelines. It's safer, isn't it?'

'Yeah.'

'Comfort zone. Is that what you want?'

'Maybe. I'm not sure. It's what you're used to. You, as in all of us, I mean.'

'You, as in Stephen, need to think about that.' She flicked her words at me, then turned round, looking for the waiter. 'I'm going to order white. To hell with poverty.'

I could see Lyn fitting in perfectly with Mike's set-up. A big house poised on the edge of town, a few kids in the right schools, a ladies' golf club membership. Upwardly mobile, I imagined it was how she saw herself. Mike was the way to go. When she started seeing Mike, Lyn and I went on meeting, not as regular as before, but enough to make life complicated for the three of us. We had to give up our weekends. They were too risky. Lyn soon ran out of plausible excuses. I was edgy with Mike in the days around our meetings, afraid I might give something away.

The news about Mike's sister never really went anywhere. Mike said The Monsignor used his pull to keep it out of the local papers. I wondered how big of an effort it was. We all had enough other things to bother us. One evening my car was pulled over at the border. A tough regiment had been brought in, all set to shake things up. I tried to keep my cool as they took the car apart simply to annoy me. 'We'll be watching you, Stevie boy,' the officer in charge said in a heavy English accent as he threw my keys back. 'Mind how you go.'

I got in and drove out over the ramps, nervous and cursing. I knew anger was a trap. You wanted to hit back at them. That was all they were waiting for.

I got the marriage thing from both sides. Mike pushing for it, as if there was some urgency, Lyn stalling for her own reasons.

'I don't know what Mike's rush is,' she complained to me.

'It's part of the whole deal. He needs you to complete the picture.' I knew I wasn't being very sensitive, but I didn't see why I needed to be.

'I'm not a commodity, Stephen. Not something to be ticked off Mike's list.'

'Maybe he's afraid he'll lose you if he waits too long. Your track record isn't great.'

Lyn poured her glass of wine over me. It dribbled down onto the sheets. 'Ah fuck, Lyn. Lick it! Lick it off me now!'

'You deserve it.' She leaned over and curled her tongue across my chest. 'Stop saying things like that about me.'

I had to stop myself from thinking what went on between her and Mike. We never talked about it. I just knew that I would miss being with her.

I got back to the office one day in the middle of one of their calls.

'You can't do this, Lyn,' Mike was yelling. 'It's blackmail.' I wanted to leave again but he signalled me to stay. 'I've got to go. Let's meet this evening. We can talk about this then. But think about it. Think about it real careful.' He put down the phone. 'She's putting pressure on me.' I thought it best to wait for him to go on. 'She's insisting my little sister and her African combo be invited to the wedding. Otherwise she won't go ahead with it. What do you think of that?'

'Does she give a reason?' I couldn't think of anything else to say. I had to stop myself from laughing. I didn't know how she had come up with it, but it was genius.

'She doesn't want to be part of a cover-up. She wants me to stand up to The Monsignor. Says I never have. Now is the time to do it. Jesus wept!'

'She has you cornered.'

'Yeah. And it's all your fault. What am I going to do? My da will go bananas. After all he's done to keep it secret.'

'But everybody knows.'

'I know, I know. But he doesn't want to know that. He goes on pretending.'

'This is a weird country,' I said.

'Tell me about it.'

I knew Mike would ask me to talk sense to Lyn. But I didn't try. Anyway she was adamant about it. She wanted Mike to take his stand. She wasn't going to let The Monsignor dictate her life as well. I understood her. It was the way we grew up. With his background Mike would probably never understand it. They had serious arguments and at times I couldn't believe that Lyn would really push it. So much was at stake. But she gave no sign of backing down. The Monsignor dug his heels in. It wasn't an easy time for Mike.

On one of our evenings Lyn and I drove out to The Argony Pipe. They had a backroom there that gave people who needed it some privacy. Priests and lawyers were among their best customers.

'I'm going to call the whole thing off. Serious,' Lyn told me. 'Last thing I want is to be tied to a man who let's his father dictate his life.'

'Mike feels responsible for his father.'

'He's afraid his father will cut him out of his will. That's what he is.'

'You're very hard on him.'

'Not as hard as his father. You have no idea what goes on, what The Monsignor is capable of. It's not like where you and me come from, Stephen. Our mothers and fathers never had anything much to dangle in front of us. There's a lot more at stake for little Michael. If he doesn't toe-the-line he's going to have to pay for it.'

'And what about you? Why are you pushing him? Look what you stand to lose?'

'Lose? How can I lose what I haven't got? You think I'm after Mike's money? Oh Stephen, you're so fuckin' shallow. All this time and you still don't know me. It's not what Mike has that's important to me, it's who he is. He has to take the risk. He has to prove that at least I'm worth that much to him.'

But it never got that far. On the day of the explosion Mike phoned in to say he was running late. He had to drop his father off at the hospital for his check-up.

'I won't make it back to the office in time. The Conway files are on my desk. Do me a favour, Stephen, can you bring them in? Meet me at the courthouse at eleven. I'm on at eleven-twenty.'

I waited in the hall outside the courtroom, the minutes ticking by, the files under my arm getting heavier. The judge agreed to a fifteen minute postponement, then rescheduled. We never let it happen to us before. I knew something serious was wrong. Outside on the steps I heard the sirens in the distance.

'Must be a bomb,' a court clerk said.

Mike and his father were killed outright. The full force of the blast rebounded off a bread van pulled up beside them. The driver was delivering across the road. There were no passers-by. The one comfort Lyn and I have is that Mike didn't know about us. Not that it matters anymore.

I helped Lyn with the funeral arrangements. She insisted everything be delayed until the sister and her husband arrived. I offered to pick them up at Aldergrove. They looked so incongruous, this small thin woman and her tall African, a lawyer. In an ironic way it made sense. She hadn't been home for such a long time, it seemed like a different country to her. I looked in the rear mirror. I could have said that nothing was really different. That this was the way things always were. As long as I could remember. But there was little comfort for her in that. She was very brave. She shook hands with everyone at the graveside.

Lyn's plan is to get away. Canada or Australia, wherever is the quickest. She wants me to follow her out as soon as I can. I could be next she says. I need time. There are so many things to be taken care of. Theko needs to be shown the ropes before I can leave him on his own. They're waiting to carve him up between them. But where he's come from, it will take better men than they are.

YOU'RE NEVER ALONE

The chances of running into another Irish guy were remote. But it had just happened. The guy was bumming a cigarette off me at one o'clock in the morning. It was cold and raining and we were the only two people on the long strand that runs through the city. Me and this Irish guy. We might have been the only two people on earth. I'd been out drinking but the walking had sobered me up. The other guy didn't seem too bad. He looked Irish, he was heavy-shouldered and dark-haired. More than likely his name was Seán.

'Got a cigarette?' he asked. In Germany two people walk past each other. Even on a narrow track in the middle of the forest they look the other way. Don't say a word. That's what I had been intending to do. I'd been watching him coming towards me. I hadn't been thinking anything important, only wanted to get home. Tomorrow I wouldn't need to remember that nothing spectacular had happened. Then this other Irish guy appeared out of nowhere.

'Got a cigarette?' he asked in a Dublin accent. That took me completely by surprise. Dublin was a different lifetime. He didn't even know if I understood English. Acted as if it were the most natural thing in the world. Two Irish guys, total strangers in a foreign country.

'Sure,' I said, feeling for the soft pack in my pocket. I knocked out two cigarettes and offered him one. Then I lit one for myself.

'Thanks,' the guy said and took a light. 'Man, I really need a woman. You know what I mean? You know around here where I can get a woman?' He fidgeted with his cigarette, then sucked on it like it might be his last. 'They got brothels in this place?'

We hadn't moved. In my head I replayed the moments that had just passed. The time it had taken for us to come face-to-face. If we had walked past each other, I'd be a lot nearer home now. 'You'd never find it,' I heard myself say. 'If you don't know your way around.'

'Hey, you're Irish.'

'Yeah.'

'What's got you here? You live here?'

Somehow I didn't like the finality of living here. My life here was a proviso. One day something would happen and I would be somewhere else. But I wasn't going to try to explain all this to a guy I'd never met before. 'I live here, yeah. I'm on my way home. What about you?'

'I'm in a hotel somewhere. I got lost, man. Where are we? You live around here?'

I said something vague, then changed the subject. 'You serious about this brothel thing?'

'I'm serious. I need a woman right now.'

'I'd better take you there.' If I'd been closer to home, I probably wouldn't have said this. But something prompted me. I knew where the brothel was, right near the centre of town. Business people, local council workers, even school-kids passed it on a daily basis. I sometimes went to an Asian store nearby.

I turned around and we started walking in the direction of town. Our footsteps made clacking noises on the wet pavement. Why were we silent? Two Irish guys should have had a lot to say to each other.

Anyway, I wasn't going to be the one to open up anymore. I lit another cigarette and offered him one.

'You been here long?'

'Too long.' How many times had I said that already?

'What d'you do here?' He didn't look at me. It didn't seem to matter too much to him.

'Translations mostly,' I said.

'Nice number. The money's good, I bet.'

'It's okay. More than I would make back home.'

'You married?'

I hesitated. The question was harmless. The type of thing Irish people all over the world asked, without thinking. German people would consider it an invasion of their privacy. But it was good to be reminded I wasn't German. I knew things were rubbing off on me. Things that were barely noticeable. 'Yeah.'

'Then you don't do these places, do you?'

'No, I don't.'

'Thanks for taking me.'

We walked on in silence. He was right, I had no need. My wife and I had a good relationship. We tried not to be an ordinary couple. We did things just to be different. Such as not being married. It saved a lot of explaining to tell people we were. What did it matter to them anyway? Right now she was with her study group in Prague. She'd phoned me before I went out, sounded upbeat about everything. Even though it was freezing over there, she was fascinated by the narrow streets crammed with history. She was looking for something to bring me back. Wished I was there with her. That kind of thing. Maybe that's why I was feeling sorry for myself, walking home in the rain. I didn't really know. In fact, I didn't really want any of these questions in my head right now. As I said, before this guy had come along, all I wanted was to get home to bed. Now I was going with him in the opposite direction. He still hadn't told me his name.

This place is on the edge of the Ruhr. Friedrich Engels lived here, maybe he was born here. I'm not sure. This big strand, or Allee as they call it, was named after him. The place has an overhead train, rattles across the valley on a monorail making screeching noises. But it's unique and so the city is proud of it. Unfortunately its last run is about midnight. And I wasn't taking this guy on any cultural trail. His needs were pretty straightforward.

It was odd that he wasn't telling me anything about himself. It bugged me. How did a guy walk up to a complete stranger and tell him he needed a woman? If I had been that desperate, I would never have admitted it to anyone. Maybe I wouldn't even have admitted it to myself.

We crossed at the traffic lights near the theatre and took a right. This is what got to me about Germany. Feeling guilty jaywalking in the middle of the night. I even caught myself checking if there was a police car nearby. It explained a lot of things about the psyche, the history, the way people could look right through you as if you didn't exist. Nobody could beat that. We walked down a small side-street, past a few shops and restaurants and came right to the place. A red light dangled in the doorway.

'Here we are. This is where I leave you.'

'Thanks. You saved my life.'

'That bad?'

'Don't ask. You sure you won't come in with me?'

I wish he hadn't asked. I wish he had just disappeared under the red light. What did it take to say no? Some kind of grunt or dismissive laugh. That's all it took. But something stopped me. My feet connected with the ground as if they had a mind of their own. Those few minutes that it took for me to walk away passed and I was still there. 'C'mon,' the Irish guy said, and it was too late.

On the other side of the door there was an indoor courtyard. The lighting was weird, the heat in the place overpowering. The women were sitting around, waiting. He went up and talked to one of them, then they went off somewhere. That was the last I saw of him. I stood there on my own. Nobody moved. I could feel their eyes on me. Maybe they were amused. They probably knew I should be at home in bed, doing the right thing. But I wasn't. I was here. I started to look at them, one after the other. The young blonde wearing a short purple negligee, the fat one who rolled her boobs and gave me a broad smile, the one in black leather stared right back at me. 'Take those few steps,' the look said. That triggered it. She kept her eyes on me as I walked in her direction.

'You want to go upstairs?' She stood up and let the full impact of her thigh-highs hit me. Then she turned and walked towards a door, knowing I would follow her.

The place we were in now was more like a cubicle. I sat on the edge of the bed. I had to decide first what I wanted. I didn't know. I found myself here because some sexed-up Irish guy had bumped into me. Because my wife, who wasn't my wife, was having a fun time elsewhere. And because the city's monorail train didn't run through the night. None of these reasons seemed to have anything to do with what I wanted.

I knew she wasn't impressed but we agreed a price and I paid. Then she took out a condom, ripped open the packet and dropped it on the pillow. I hadn't thought about the condom. It waited there while she started working me, automatically. I knew this wasn't going to do anything for me. Things started to come into my head, things that made it difficult to concentrate. I could feel she was losing patience with me.

'You don't like me,' she said.

I didn't like the way she said it. I looked at her, but nothing good came to mind. 'It takes time,' I said. It sounded plausible, something she might understand.

She forced a smile and went on. I wished she would try something else but she probably hadn't been paid enough. There was contempt in the way she looked at me. 'Your prick is like jelly,' she hissed and let it collapse. She cleaned her fingers off on the bed-sheet. 'You don't like me. You go now.'

I looked at her, ready to argue about my money.

'Get out! You waste my time, you not need a woman.'

I wasn't sure if this was real, but it was loud. I pulled on my clothes, then she pushed me out of the door into the stairway. I was about to defend myself until I heard footsteps rushing down from above. In the shadows I could make out a heavy shape looming over me. Whatever it was, I knew it was not interested in my side of the story. The closer it came, the clearer I realised my only chance was to get out as quickly as I could. Two steps above me, she caught hold of him. 'He go now,' she said. 'He pay. Everything okay.'

I found a door that let me out onto a backstreet, its solid thud behind me came as a relief. Part of me began to wonder if it had been a setup, how quickly she had got angry, the big guy waiting on the stairs. I tried to rationalise. It was three in the morning. I had planned to be in bed a long time ago.

From deep in my pocket I drew a cigarette from the pack. The lighter hissed. It reminded me of an old TV commercial. The one where the guy, collar turned up like Bogart, is all alone lighting up his cigarette. *You're never alone with a Strand,* a voice-over says. I buttoned up, took a long drag. The smoke raking the back of my throat tasted good.

HAWK

Gemma drove her blue Fiesta across the schoolyard to the back of the main building where there was a make-shift car park for the teachers. She hadn't touched breakfast. She'd hardly slept for the past three nights. Sky News and the History Channel kept her going. But it would be over soon. The ministerial car would roll off back to wherever the Department of Education was nowadays and St. Enda's would get on with being an ordinary secondary school again.

She gathered her things off the passenger seat and got out of the car. It was an undecided February morning, a frail sun struggling against thick swabs of cloud. She noticed Aidan was in ahead of her, his dark green Nissan tucked in the corner. He and Sister Agnes were the welcoming party, Sister Agnes all for tea and tennis, Aidan big into Gaelic. He'd often been in a tackle with the Minister's brother. That was something for them to talk about. Everybody had some kind of reference point with the Minister.

She pulled the heavy fire door and walked into the back corridor.

Inside she felt the cold. At the far end of the hall she could hear the rumble of the ancient furnace. It took hours to heat the place up. She tiptoed past Aidan's office. If she ran into him, she'd have to listen to his plan of action all over again. Where the Minister would be where and when, and who would be next to be introduced to him. All the staff knew it off by heart. In her sleepless nights Gemma had gone over her own plan, replaying it like a loop in her mind. Then she looked at the picture of her father on her bedside table, his immaculate crisp, dark green uniform, his smile. And she repeated to herself: *there was no going back.*

The computer room was on the first floor on the south of the building. Gemma threw her bag onto the console desk and relaxed into her swivel chair. She was twenty-eight and this would be her last year at St. Enda's. She wanted to take a year off, go somewhere she would only ever go once in her whole life. Lots of people her age did it. Africa, India, who knows. She was scared she was in a rut. If she didn't take her chance now she might never do it. She'd meet someone, they'd get a year or two out of it, then settle down together. She was too young for that.

She reached down and pressed the main button. Instantly the room came alive with a chorus of state-of-the art computers. This was where she would meet the Minister. Sister Agnes and Aidan would bring him here. The official speeches would be over. All that remained was for him to see the computer room.

Gemma shifted on the swivel chair. Her outfit was annoying her. She undid the buttons of her jacket and hitched up the skirt. The staff had had a near standoff with Sister Agnes. The Minister had let it be known that it could be a dress-down affair. But Sister Agnes made no secret of her opinion of the Minister. She dismissed the idea that he had any real understanding of the pressures on those at the 'chalk face'. She insisted St. Enda's would put on the full show.

'Miss Dowling.' The caretaker's voice startled her. 'All set?'

'I'm nervous as hell, Joe. Couldn't sleep a wink last night.' Gemma smiled at him. 'You look very smart.'

'Orders from the Chief. No going against them, you know what I mean. Anything you want me to do, Miss?'

'I think we're grand. I just need to make sure they're all working.'

'Do you think the Minister knows much about computers, Miss?'

'None of my business what he knows, Joe. What about yourself now?'

'Not a clue, Miss. The young lad has one. Does all his school projects on it. You can find anything you want on it he tells me. But it's way over my head, you know what I mean.'

'You'd be well able for it. If you have the time some afternoon, I'll give you a crash course.' Gemma buttoned up her jacket and came out from behind the desk. 'Here, take a look at this. Tell me something you'd like to find out, something that happened years ago maybe.'

'What kind of thing, Miss?'

'Anything you want.'

Joe bit on the inside of his lip. 'What year Bobby Charlton captained ManU in the European Cup. The year they won it. There's a good one for you.'

'So you see this. You click on this. Put in ManU Bobby Charlton. Then click search.' They both watched the screen flicker and change. '25,900 results, Joe. Everything you'd ever want to find on Bobby Charlton right there. We haven't got time now, but it's in there somewhere.'

'It was in nineteen sixty-eight, Miss.' Joe laughed. 'I was only checking on you.'

'You're a fly-man, Joe. You don't need me to show you anything.'

Joe was pleased with himself. 'Will you be down to see the Minister arriving, Miss?'

'I still have a couple of things to do. And by the time I get the class settled in, he'll be here anyway. We have to make it look like we have some idea what we're doing with these computers, after all the money we got for them.'

'A pilot project for what is it again, if you don't mind me asking.' Joe was still slow to leave.

'For historical archives. It's called *HAWK*. So the youngsters can learn history themselves. They won't need me to teach them anymore. I might as well pack up and go home now.'

'Beats me, so it does,' he said. 'At least I'll still have a job.'

'Aye, Joe. A truer word you never said.'

Gemma waited till the caretaker left, then ran Quickcheck. Everything showed up ready to go, all the kids had to do was key in *HAWK*. The programme would open up on twenty stations, each with its individual project to work on. She pressed enter on her own computer. A large silver hawk flew in a direct line across the screen, its broad wings flapping, its beads of eyes focused on hers. When it settled on its perch above the search box, she typed in the Minister's name.

'And here we are, Minister, in our state-of-the-art computer room.' Sister Agnes' voice was purposely loud. Everyone made motions to rise.

'Don't let me disturb you,' the Minister told them. 'Please go on with whatever you're doing. I won't be in your way for long.' He was less impressive than he looked on television. Smaller build. His voice was thin, not forceful.

'Miss Dowling is our History and Computer teacher,' Sister Agnes went on. 'We all rely on her expertise.'

The Minister approached Gemma's desk and offered his hand. 'Nice to meet you, Miss Dowling.'

Gemma shook the Minister's hand. 'And you, Minister.'

'Are you happy with the new computers? Do they meet your needs?'

'Most certainly. We're in a league of our own now, Minister.'

'And the programme *HAWK*. What exactly does it entail? What can the pupils do with it that makes it so new?'

'Basically it's a history archive programme which allows the pupils to tap into all available archives on the web, to cross-reference and validate the accuracy of the information.' Gemma knew that it sounded textbook. 'The exciting part and the advantage for the pupils is that the programme enables them to create their own archives. They can collate information from a variety of sources. The *HAWK* programme will accept it only when it has validated the accuracy of the information. It disallows inaccuracy.'

'Sounds very clever to me,' the Minister said. He pulled in a chair in front of her screen and sat down. 'Can you show me how it works? What do I have to do?'

Gemma pulled her chair in beside the Minister. 'You can key in your name, Minister, and see what comes up.'

'I think I've a pretty good idea of my own history.' The Minister smiled at her, the way she had seen him do so often on television.

'Then take my name,' she told the Minister.

'D-o-w-l-i-n-g.' The Minister spelt it out as he typed it in. 'First name?'

'Pat,' Gemma replied.

'P-a-t. We have a daughter Pat.' The picture of a young man in a dark green uniform appeared on the screen. Gemma kept her eyes on the Minister while he silently read the text beneath the picture. She knew it by heart. 'Constable Pat Dowling, shot Londonderry, January 1972. Married with one daughter aged four months.' She watched for anything that the Minister's face might betray.

The Minister turned to look at her. 'This is your father?'

'Yes.'

'I'm very sorry.'

'Why do I have difficulty believing that, Minister?' Gemma wished her voice would sound more angry, but it didn't. The anger she had rehearsed so many times was missing.

'Miss Dowling, I think we've heard quite enough.' Sister Agnes stepped towards her.

'It's alright, Sister. Miss Dowling has the right to her feelings.'

'I never knew my father. He was only twenty-one when he was shot. Much the same age as you were at the time, Minister.' Gemma felt the force coming back to her words.

'Minister, I think we should leave now. I apologise for Miss Dowling's behaviour. Mister Gallagher, will you look after Miss Dowling, please.'

Gemma stood at the window in Aidan's office watching the cars drive away.

'Why did you do it, Gemma? Sister Agnes will never forgive you. She'll crucify you.'

She knew Aidan was trying to be easy on her. 'She won't get the chance, Aidan. I'm leaving.'

'Oh, thanks for letting me know.' She had caught him off guard. 'But what was the purpose of it? What were you trying to prove?'

'To prove?' Gemma turned around from the window to face Aidan. He was a caring sort of person. No match for Sister Agnes. He would be one of the people she would miss. 'The programme has nothing to do with proof. It's about facts, Aidan. Historical facts. It validates their accuracy. That's all it does. It doesn't prove anything.' The way he looked at her, she knew she hadn't got through to him. 'You know Aidan, he wasn't the monster I always imagined him to be. I couldn't even hate him as much as I thought I would.' She paused. 'Do you know what struck me most? The smell of his aftershave. It was too much. Sitting there beside him, I found it overpowering. I wanted to say it to him but I had to keep reminding myself, this is the Minister. Funny, isn't it? Can I go back to my class now?'

'Yes, of course, of course you can, if you think you're alright.'

'I am, thanks Aidan. I'm alright.'

Aidan's phone rang. His eyes automatically checked the display and he didn't pick up. Before she closed the door behind her, Gemma heard it click to answer and the cackle of Sister Agnes' voice.

WINTER SUN

'Sir, I have a history to tell you.' The Cuban waiter stood at our table, his hands clenched behind his back. 'I am not waiter really. I open my first bottle of wine twelve days ago. And I make big mess.'

We stared at him, wondering what it was that made him tell us this.

'I study physics, five years, you see. Then I get job, how you say?' He made a brush gesture.

'Sweeping the streets?'

'Yes, yes. I love physics. But I have no work. Here I say to boss, I cook. Boss say I need waiter. I say him I am good waiter.'

We were tucked away for a week of winter sun. Everything was closed in our part of Fuerte, except the fish restaurant in the old harbour. We drove over in the evening to watch the sun sink into the bay. Each sunset got points out of ten. But nobody clapped, not like they do down on Mallory.

Maeve, Sandra's sister, was getting over her break-up with Connor.

It had dragged on too long. She didn't want to talk about it anymore, just put it behind her. She went crazy about the cats, fed them our fish-leftovers and watered-down milk. Sometimes so many of them turned up it got out of hand.

'My boss never smile,' Ruben said. 'He always very serious. But good boss. He not see when I open my first bottle of wine. I turn my back like this and I make big mess. Now it is better.'

We wanted to ask him if he had a villa in Cuba where we could holiday next. But then he told us his story and we were glad we hadn't. The other waiter was called Juan Carlos.

'Like the King of Spain,' he said.

'Where is your kingdom?' I asked. But he didn't understand. They stood waiting to clear away the plates the minute we had finished.

Normally Sandra and I holidayed on our own. But right now Maeve needed us. And it was okay. I took off whenever I could to the other side of the island, past the wind park, where the waves were rough like our Atlantic waves. I climbed the mountain that every evening brandished like a shield of flame in the intensity of the sun. It was an ancient portal towering over the miles of sand dunes.

There was something final about the way Ruben told us his wife had left him. 'She abandon me.' His five-year-old daughter he had to leave back in Cuba. 'My heart break.'

We looked at one another, there was no easy reply. She could come to him when she was old enough to decide for herself?

'In thirteen years? When she is eighteen?' There was a flash of anger as if we had said the wrong thing. 'But now I have new wife,' he said eventually and smiled towards the back of the restaurant.

Maeve didn't want anyone new. Sometimes after enough wine she thought she wanted Connor back. Other times she was glad it was finally over. I supposed she and Sandra had long conversations about him. But maybe I was wrong and they were only lapping up the sun. Filling in the spaces between the deserted beach bars.

'The man of your dreams just walked by,' I said to Maeve when she came out with the sliced lemon. We were on the terrace enjoying our g't's.

'What did he look like?' She made a show of looking around for him.

'Like Sting.'

Anyone like Sting would make her happy. Then he passed by again and she said he didn't look like Sting at all. The cats played around our sun-beds, just out of reach. They never came close enough to be touched. Maeve longed to touch. To coax one onto her lap. The grey one or the black one. But they wouldn't let her.

Our last sunset was an eight. Maeve said an eight-and-a-half. In its wake a cold breeze swept into the harbour. Ruben was waiting at the door for us as we hurried into the restaurant.

'Sir, I have question,' he said as he led us to our table. The three of us managed to smile. 'You have eat Cuban?'

'No,' we replied in unison.

'Then you come to my house to eat.'

For a moment we were lost. 'Tomorrow is our last evening,' Maeve told him.

Her words startled Ruben. 'I start work tomorrow eleven thirty. I must be here all day, boss say.'

I felt embarrassed, sorry we were leaving.

'Then next time,' Sandra said. 'We will come back. Will you be here?'

'I don't know. But next time. Okay.'

Ruben came back ten minutes later with a number scribbled on a wine label, Viña Berceo, the one he always recommended. 'Sir, you call me, when you come back next year. We eat Cuban together.'

I fumbled for words. 'What do Cubans eat?' It was pathetic, I knew. But Ruben explained to us and seemed to be happy.

'Next year,' he repeated and left.

'Sir, this is Lis, my new wife.' Lis gave us a shy smile. 'Next year Lis and I make Cuban food for you.'

We nodded and laughed. Ruben poured the Rioja with the usual ceremony. Tinny Elton John music sounded over the speakers. The blades of the wind park stood still in the sand-hills. Near the Supermercado a German couple waited in a glare of headlights. In the distance Costa Calma was a neon nightmare.

SAND

Halfway down the steps to the beach, I notice the couple below making love in the shelter of the large rocks. Her long, tanned body spreads over his, her arms pressing him down as she moves on top. Sandra walks on without seeing them. I hesitate, watch the woman's breasts dip close to his chest. Then I hear snatches of their voices, come to my senses. I turn quickly and follow Sandra.

She is waiting for me to catch up because there is a man sitting alone in the middle of the beach. Something is strange about him. We walk across the sand and he rises, makes a slow retreat to the bottom of the cliff. We pretend to ignore him but can feel his eyes on us as he moves in an arc behind us. Then he seems to hop up the steps and disappears. Neither of us says anything about him. We spread the towels out and strip off, lie down naked in the heat of the sun trapped in the cove. Lines of little pebbles trickle into the drag of the receding waves.

It is the type of picture-postcard place one dreams of. And we stumbled upon it. Sandra wanted me to turn back when the road down became narrower. But I insisted we were alright, kept my eyes off the sheer drop. Then we came to the dirt track. Walking down she felt better. The village was just below us, chiselled into the cliff, held together by a maze of narrow paths. In the harbour we found a room with a small balcony overlooking the two tavernas for the local fishermen. The one-man fishing boats come in and go out in slow ritual. Nothing much else seems to happen here. This is what we want. We paid for a week and were left to do as we please. We can hear the fishermen working at their nets, talking about things that have no bearing on us.

At first we didn't know about the beach right outside the village. We found it today when we were exploring. A simple wooden sign points the way along a path that disappears through a natural arch in the cliff. Then a series of steps leads the way down.

Sandra stirs. 'Are we going into the water? I'm easy. But don't make me go in on my own.'
  'Let's go then.'
  Sandra is a strong swimmer. She swims far out; I don't move much from the spot. I manage to stay afloat while I wait for her to come back. The water is pleasant. I focus on the rays of the sun sparkling across the surface onto my face, imagine a mystical point where everything meets. And I am part of it. It makes some kind of sense. Like a Zen moment. I can hear Sandra splashing nearby. If I stand still, I can feel the sand under my feet.

The thing that happened to us most people would not believe. But it's all true. The first phone-call felt like a hoax, only I knew it wasn't. I recognised the voice immediately, saw the face of the woman we had met at the Cohen concert. In an odd way she was interesting. But all her talk about the spiritual experience was a bit over the top. We should never have met up with her again.

'You and I are soul mates, Ian,' she whispered into the phone, the voice slithering down my spine. 'We understand each other. There's something you want to tell me, isn't there? Something you are hiding from everyone else. But we can't hide anything from each other.'

It was heavy stuff. I told her not to call again. But the calls kept coming. When I refused to take them, Sandra answered. Then it got worse.

'What's all this about, Ian? What are you hiding? She says you have something to tell me, but you can't.'

'She's crazy, Sandra. Don't listen to her. Don't answer the phone.'

'For god's sake, we can't just not answer our own phone. What are you afraid of?'

For a long time I managed to pretend I had nothing to hide. It just didn't seem possible that someone who was practically a stranger could read me, and know what was going on. Okay, I'd heard about the sixth sense thing, half-believed in it myself. Now it was happening to me, it was weird.

How could she have known about Ellen and me? We only met in places where we were certain we would not be recognised. Nobody we knew had ever seen us together. Sandra knew more about me than anyone; sometimes she knew what was happening with me even before I did. And she hadn't noticed a thing.

'She says when I find out what's going on I should come to her. She will help me. What's this all about, Ian? Tell me the truth.'

We are both realists. We didn't want to ditch our marriage. There had been other women before. It was a weakness in my make-up or a fault line in our relationship. But so far we always seemed to come out the other side. We told ourselves we grew through not running away from it, through facing up to it. That's what we were hoping for.

Coming out of the water, I catch sight of the person who was on the beach before. He is watching us from the rocks. Or is it the couple below he is spying on? I don't mention it to Sandra. She races out of the water before me and grabs her beach towel.

'This is heaven. A week of this and the whole world will look different. This is exactly what we need, isn't it?' She looks at me and repeats. 'Isn't it, Ian?'

'Yes.' I glance up at the rocks, then reach for her hand, draw her down beside me. I lean over and touch her cheek. 'Do you love me?'

'Yes. You don't deserve it but you know I do.'

'I know I don't deserve it. That's what makes it special. Anyway, I don't want to have to deserve it.'

Perhaps it's an illusion. But that's what sun holidays are for. People buy the illusion, and we are no different. Sandra packed her bags and left when I told her about Ellen. 'Time to make up your mind,' she said. 'You've had it both ways long enough. But I can't do this anymore, Ian. This time I need to know from now on it's only you and me. There's no room for anyone else.'

In the short winter days without her life was drip-fed. Because I asked her to, Sandra came back. Later she told me it had been an act. The last thing she had really wanted to do was leave me. There is something Siamese about us. We both know that.

'He's back again,' Sandra says.

I stare at him but he pretends not to be looking at us. He sits on the rocks, gazing off out to sea. His hand is in his trouser pocket, rubbing. When he glances over at us, I try to hold his eyes but he turns away again. The rubbing goes on. Then suddenly he gets up and hurries back up the steps, swinging around once to see if we are looking.

'Creepy,' Sandra says. 'I've read about weirdos like him. They chop people up and dump the pieces.'

'He looks more like the village idiot to me. It's how he gets his kicks.'

'It's pretty disgusting anyway,' Sandra insists. 'I'm getting dressed, it's getting chilly.' She starts picking up her things. 'What about that French woman in Cork? They still haven't got who did it, after all these years. The number of women murdered or who disappear every year, where the police never solve it. It's mind-boggling.'

This is all we need, this kind of scenario to worry about for the next few days. 'We're talking about a mindless idiot,' I repeat. 'Not Fred West and his wife. Don't blow it out of all proportion.'

'All I'm saying is we could have done without him right now, Ian. Maybe he was watching us the whole time.'

'If he was, fine. I hope he had a good time.'

'I'm quite sure he did. I just hope we won't run into him again.'

I detect a hint of annoyance in Sandra's voice, directed at me. 'I'm pretty sure we won't.' I don't know if I believe this but I say it anyway.

On the way back we pass a sign that points out along the cliff. *Taverna Stavros. Nearly 800 metres.*

'Shall we try this?' I suggest.

'You want to go there now? Look at that sign. God knows how old it is.' Sandra is still annoyed. All she wants is to get back. 'The place might not even be there anymore. Probably toppled off the cliff.'

'Just to have a look. If it's any good, we can go back later.'

Sandra breathes a deep sigh. 'No use arguing with you, is there? Go on.'

After eight hundred metres we see nothing, but we keep going. Eventually we come to a shack that's straight out of a Hopper painting. It looks deserted but there is the smell of cooking.

'Definitely fish,' Sandra says.

'Top marks. Irish stew would be a bit off.' I don't mean it the way it sounds. It just comes out wrong. Sandra ignores me. She walks around to the back.

'Oh sorry,' I hear her say. 'I didn't mean to disturb you. We saw your sign on the road. Is this the taverna?'

Round the back a heavy canvas awning is hung out over a makeshift kitchen. Pots are steaming and bubbling on an assortment of camp-gas rings. A young woman standing among them stares at the two of us.

'It's okay,' she says. 'You gave me a surprise. Usually people don't come till late. But it's alright. What do you want? A drink? Or would you like to eat?' She's wearing a headscarf and a jeans overall. She looks tired but she smiles. 'Stavros can get you something to drink.' She calls out his name. 'I have to keep an eye on these.'

Stavros appears from inside. He's muscular and gruff, makes no pretence about us interrupting things. 'Where are you from?'

'From Ireland,' I say. It's okay to be Irish in Greece. There is an affinity between us. Maybe it has to do with the sea.

'Ireland? You come here all the way from Ireland?' He seems to warm to us. 'You need to drink. The generator is broken. Nothing works. Regine is cooking on the gas stoves. We get so many guests tonight. But sit down. What would you like? Retsina, ouzo?'

He brings ouzo, long glasses and a jug of water. For a while Regine is busy with the pots, then she joins us. She is from Germany. One night Stavros took her out fishing with him. They stayed out all night, swam under the moonlight. 'That was nine years ago,' she says. 'Next year we are hoping we can take over one of the tavernas in the harbour.' We both nod as if we understand, as if life is the same everywhere, the same trials, the same hopes. As if it is more than just the sea that we have in common.

'I will try one more time.' Stavros rises from the table, swots a mosquito with the cloth that hung from his trouser belt. 'Baltimore,' he turns suddenly. 'That is in Ireland, isn't it? Yes! I was there many, many years ago. Guinness. We drank Guinness all the time. I remember Teresa.' He looks wickedly at Regine. 'She could drink Guinness. She said she was a nurse.' We hear him laughing as he goes inside again.

It is Regine who breaks the silence. 'If you want to eat, you must pick your fish now,' she tells us. 'Stavros was fishing today. It will be ready for you when you come back this evening. We will have a lot of people here, but we will make a place for you. Just say a time.'

Sandra looks over at me. I know she wants to say we don't want to be of any trouble, besides it will be too dark later.

'We have lights if Stavros gets the generator to work.' Regine is reading Sandra's thoughts. 'Or I give you a torchlight.'

'Sounds good,' I say, helped by the buzz of the ouzo. 'Where's the fish?'

It is stacked in boxes under a tarpaulin. The tails are still kicking, the eyes bulging. Exotic shapes and colours compared to what we know. I hardly listen to Regine explain the differences. Sandra seems more interested. I let her pick two for us. I'm thinking of Ellen, I wonder how she is coping. I told myself it was the right way. That's rubbish. Right does not come into it, there is only this way or that. I knew she would be hurt. I knew all of us would get hurt.

Then there is a bang and Sandra jumps.

'It's the generator,' Regine's face lights up. 'It's working.'

YESTERDAY'S NEWS

The young woman was face-down in the water. Of course one immediately thinks of suicide. The newspaper says a corporation worker jumped in and rescued her. A passing driver took them to a nearby hospital, where she remains critical.

He looks at his watch. Ellen is late. She said she would come for breakfast. It's odd because being punctual is a big thing for her. He folds the newspaper and drops it onto the armchair. Then it crosses his mind Ellen might want to sit there and he tucks the newspaper into the bookshelf.

The sky is heavy with low cloud, leaves frame-freezed against the greyness. He's counted the spoons into the coffee machine, remembering details like the line of shoes in her front hall, the space created between them for his own; the small tray of chocolate-coated waffles set on a wicker table. Candles poised for lighting. The first time he was there, he was afraid their lives would clash.

The image of the drowning woman returns to him. What is it like to be dragged back into this world if you have decided to leave? She must have thought about it, have come to terms with what she was about to do.

Yesterday when Ellen rang, she was parked outside his front door. The surprise was perfect. He didn't bother to ask how she had found him. She had a knack of walking into his life. The first time she appeared he could feel something was about to happen, but he managed to avoid it. Months later, when she turned up again, he was caught off guard. After that, his life never went back to the way it had been before.

'You're such a baby,' she had told him in St. Ives. The room wasn't ready. The cleaners could walk in on top of them she said. No way they were going to make love. She placated him with her finger on his lips. He sulked. The narrow streets got tangled up in it. Most of it was façade anyway. In the restaurant a waiter eventually took their order. Then they waited. Ellen told him she had known all along what they were getting into. None of it had been a surprise for her. 'Why you chose me I don't know. Or was it the other way round? Maybe I was the one.' She shifted the knife on the right. 'Who knows anymore? I knew there would be chaos.' The waiter brought the starters. Small portions on large white plates.

He checks again that everything is on the table, rearranges the blue napkins. At the sound of the doorbell he jumps. Suddenly he is walking along the hall, unsure of himself, wondering if it will be obvious that she has spent the night with someone else.

'Hi! Sorry I'm late. Still haven't caught up on Irish time.' As she slips past him in the narrow hall he feels the touch of her breasts against him. It triggers needs he has almost forgotten. She knows how to do this to him, the same way he knows she can do it to others.

'How does anyone find you in this mumbo-jumbo?' she is saying.

Outside the wheelie bins are lined up for emptying. He closes the door and turns to her. 'What do you mean?'

'All the houses look the same. You need to make things a little easier for people.'

'People?' Anyway, yesterday she didn't have a problem.

He follows her into the kitchen where a single green candle flickers on the table. It jars with the napkins but Ellen won't say anything. She turns and angles her face towards his, allows herself that second of hesitation. A rock-breaker in the distance hammers staccato as their lips touch.

'Poor Ian.' Her fingers trace a line across his cheek. She lets her fingertips rest on his lips, then pulls them away.

'Cut the pity-crap, Ellen. It's not you.'

'It's not *my* pity we need to talk about.' She walks over and sits down at the table. 'Feel this place. It oozes with pity. You have to get out of here. Christ, why do Irish mothers have to screw everything up?' She stares at him, waits for him to speak. It's hard to pinpoint which direction the rock-breaker is coming from.

'Straight into it as usual. Not much changed, has it?' He turns his back to her and reaches for the coffee pot.

'You started it.'

Ian decides not to reply to this. The coffee smell drifts in the air. 'Did you have a good night?' he asks as he half-fills her cup.

'Do you really want to know?'

'I probably don't,' he lies. 'Doesn't really make much difference who you are fucking at the moment.'

'I don't fuck.' The way she spits out the words appeals to him. 'That's your department.' Her eyes lock on his, ready to release bolts of contempt. 'Is that what it was, Ian? Did we fuck? Was that all?'

'Of course we fucked. We enjoyed it, remember?' Had that been all, the chaos would not have happened. The noise of the rock-breaker stops. 'Anyway, have you a better word for it?'

'Fucking's fine with me.' For a moment she poises the white cup at her lips and stares into the garden. Then she swings around. 'We had our chance, we didn't take it. No, correction, *you* didn't take it. The cage was wide open, Ian. What held you back?' She is dangling a strip of salmon on her fork. 'And now, are you anymore ready? I don't think so. You want to know how my night was? Spectacular. How about yours?'

The noise of the bins being emptied outside disturbs his concentration. Last week he complained about his bin being dragged halfway through the estate. 'We don't get paid to keep people happy, mate.' The way they looked at him, he knew what they thought.

He wishes they hadn't got so tangled up again, after all she has come back, for whatever reason he isn't sure. 'We're good for each other,' she always told him. A kind of a mantra.

'I had a strange dream,' he tells her.

'Try me.'

The bin lorry has reached the corner. 'I was somewhere in France, standing outside a bakery, looking at all the cakes and sweet things. But I've no money. Suddenly I feel someone tapping my shoulder. When I turn around, this woman hands me a bag of sweets. Before I can say anything, she disappears into the crowd. Leaves me wondering why me.'

'That's easy.'

'Sorry?'

'Ian please, don't act so innocent. You must know it's about you, about the signals you send out. Maybe it's not even a conscious thing you do. I picked them up. Other women pick them up. We all come running with our little bags of sweeties for you. Sweeties, sweeties!' She dangles the blue napkin in the air.

'Stop it, Ellen. Just stop it!'

'Oh, have we touched on a sore spot? How many bags of sweeties will it take to make it go away, Ian? Have you any idea? Or maybe you don't want it to go away. We all need our little hang-ups, don't we?'

'Cut it out. You didn't go to all the trouble of finding me here just to go all psycho on me now.'

'You asked for it. Anyway, let me be good at something.' She reaches for bread, fidgets with a slice on her plate. 'We used to talk every day, remember? Fuck the cost. We knew everything about each other. I miss that. I wanted to see how you are.'

'So, can you spot the difference?'

'Nothing's changed. How much longer are you going to go on doing this to yourself?'

In September they rented a house somewhere near Killarney. He picked her up off the late flight in Shannon. It rained all the way down. He told himself they needed time together, it didn't matter where. But the everyday things caused complications. The absurdity of pushing a trolley around Costcutter; the frustration of damp fires; Ellen's need to take in everything new. The real world impinged on them. After the week nothing was certain anymore.

'I don't know. Three years, five years? How long does it take? These life changes. You're the expert, Ellen. You should know. You've read all the books.'

One day he built a fire in a corner of the garden, watched the flames eat through the pages of the books she had given him. He thought this way he could break the hold she had on him. She laughed at him when he told her what he had done.

'What are you freeing yourself from, Ian? I have no power over you.'

'What's his name?'
   'Does it matter?'
   'What does he do then?'
   'He's a doctor.'
   'A real one?'
   'An anaesthetist.'

'So how did you two meet?'

'Does it matter?'

'And you're sticking to your story that it's nothing?'

She doesn't look at him. She dabs her lips with the blue napkin, then drops it on the plate. 'On a scale of one-to-ten he's a five, maybe a six.' As she speaks, she walks over to the patio door. 'Probably more a five. Do these things open?' She releases the catch and slides back the door. 'You were an eight, maybe a nine. Not bad,' she says as she steps out onto the patio. The candle flickers in the draught. 'The gardens they give people here aren't big enough to swing a cat in. You don't have a cat, I know. You're not into animals. Pity! They can be such good company.' From the garden she asks, 'who did your wall?'

'I did it.' He's surprised that she has noticed.

'I like the colour.'

'The grey was doing my head in. A few cans of paint was all it took. Blue breeze blocks seem less obscene.' He leans against the patio door, notices the paleness of her hand as she touches the wall.

'True,' she says and turns to face him. 'Do you keep a score on your women, Ian? Was I a five or a six, maybe an eight or a nine?' He wants to answer but she doesn't let him. 'It's okay. Don't get alarmed. I don't think I really want to know. Where's my Brooder?'

'He's in the other room.'

She comes back in, slides the patio door shut behind her.

It's the only picture on the wall. The other paintings are still in a pile in the corner. She told him it reminded her of him. He had to stop brooding she said, had to get himself out of it.

'I thought of you the minute I saw this. I told you. You're back in that same place, aren't you? But it's no use raking over the past, Ian. You'll never work it out.' Her eyes fall on the edge of the newspaper in the bookshelf. She pulls it out, glances at the headline and drops it on the armchair again. 'I'd better go.'

'You could stay.' He wants to walk towards her. 'Keep us company for a while.'

'No, Ian. I have to go. I don't want to be part of your prison anymore. We almost had you out. But now the two of you are stuck here together. We failed miserably, didn't we?'

When she leaves he blows out the candle, clears the table, dumps the napkins in the bin. Then he picks up the newspaper. There's a story about a fire in one of the new estates. A man trapped in his bedroom, overcome by smoke. The fire had probably started downstairs in the kitchen. He was unconscious when they got to him. The medics tried to resuscitate him in the back of the ambulance. But he didn't make it.

NEW YEAR'S DAY

Till was angry with himself because he'd come to blows with his da again. On New Year's Eve. They'd been drinking cider and Bull all day. Then when his brothers left, the da laid into him. The same old crap about breaking his mother's heart, for running away, getting lifted and bringing the guards in on top of them. How she couldn't take anymore of it and just wasted away. All a load of balls as far as Till was concerned. And he told him so. That's when the da smashed the bottle on the table and went for him. Till f'd him out of it and left him in a heap in the corner. The place was a wreck. His brothers would be after him as soon as they found the da. They'd go for Till first and then ask the questions. But he wasn't hanging around for that shit anymore.

It was dark and freezing. He had only the waist-length leather jacket they'd got him, the same stuff they hawked at the fairs in Ennis and Wexford, no questions asked. Came in bulky brown boxes. He kept walking, looking around every now and then for car lights, rubbed his hands together and blew hot breath onto them. His da was the one broke the mother's heart. Dragged her around the country till she was a nervous wreck. Then dumped her in that kip. Not much love lost between the two of them. He remembered them getting all nicety-nice with each other on a Friday night, only to go on the tear again and end up worse than before. Not much love lost between his da and himself either. Going back thinking they could make things up, because of the time of year. All bullshit. There was no making up between them to be done anymore.

He was hoping a car would come along and he would get a lift. Though maybe he wasn't safe on the road, they would be looking for him everywhere. But they'd never know where he was, he'd been walking for a good couple of hours now. If nothing else, he'd find a hayshed. That would do, unless there were dogs. He didn't know exactly where he was, somewhere between Letterkenny and 'Bofey. He didn't like towns. There was always trouble waiting for him when he hit a town. He used fields and backstreets, made his way round them.

He saw car lights in the distance, clawing their way through the night. His blood rushed. He looked at the ditch, deep and dark, probably icy and wet. He could freeze there. He decided he'd take his chance. He stood by the road in the glare of the headlights and stuck out his thumb.

The car passed him at speed, then the driver slammed on the brakes. They made an awful screeching as the car came to a halt. Till ran towards it, came up level with it the moment the passenger door was thrown open.

'Get in fast for crissakes. It must be freezing out there.'

Till climbed into the passenger seat and pulled the door shut.

'You're out late,' the driver said as the car moved off again.

Till caught the smell of drink from him. 'Thanks for the lift, mister,' he said, without looking at the driver.

'I nearly didn't see you. Wear something bright at night. Did you never hear of that?'

'I did alright.'

'But you like doing things your way.'

'I s'pose,' Till muttered.

'Where you going?'

'Anywhere, mister. Anywhere you're going'll do me.'

'Stop mistering me for crissakes. My name's Ian. What's yours?'

'Till, mister.'

'Would you cut out the mister bit, I told you.'

Till didn't reply. He didn't want to cause any trouble. He settled back into the warmth of the big seat.

'I'm heading for Galway. That any good to you?'

'That's good for me.' Till caught the mister just in time. He was heading far enough away now for any of them to catch up with him.

'What's got you out at this hour of the morning? Your chances would have been zero if I hadn't come along.'

'I dunno.'

'You dunno?'

'I dunno what to say.' Till stared at the road ahead. The big car was crossing over and back on the white line of the road. There was no traffic but the road was full of twists and bends.

'You're as bad as meself,' the driver said. 'You don't know whether you're coming or going.'

'You said it, mister.' Till glanced at the driver, afraid he might get angry. But he didn't notice. 'Can I ask you something, Ian?' He forced the Ian.

'Fire away.'

'D'ye think you're a bit drunk?'

'Between you and me, I'm shit drunk. Are you getting worried?'

'I'm worried you're gonna get the two of us killed.'

'Well, I made it this far.'

Till noticed he wasn't straying as far over the markings anymore since they'd started talking. But the bends were getting worse. 'You're lucky you didn't get stopped.'

'I'm lucky because I haven't a clue how I got this far. All I remember is driving off in a mad fit. The rest is a blank. Not good, eh? Do you know your way to Galway, Till?'

Till hesitated. He knew all the roads, it was the towns he had to think about. 'It's a straight run down the coast.'

'Well, tell me, can you drive, Till?'

'I can.'

'Do you think you can drive a car like this, Till?'

'What make is it?'

'Volvo. They're big brutes of cars, built like tanks.'

'I never drove one of these. But I'd be better off driving it than you.'

Ian laughed. 'Okay, Till, I'll pull over, you take the wheel. I can grab a sleep.' Ian pulled the car over and put on the handbrake. He left the motor running. 'I'd better take a piss while I'm at it. Sit in there and get the feel of her.'

Till climbed over into the driver's seat. He sank his hands into the soft leather of the steering wheel and held it tight. The feel of the wheel was so light, so natural, like in the TV ads. He felt for the lever at the side of the driver's seat and eased the seat closer to the pedals. Then he pressed down on the clutch and ran through the gears. Everything smooth. Finally he put his foot on the gas pedal and revved the engine. It was rearing to go.

'You'll manage alright, will ye?' Ian's voice came from behind.

'No bother.' He heard Ian stretch out in the back with a deep sigh.

'Just follow the signs for Galway. Wake me up when we get that far, if I don't wake up before myself. I'll take it from there.'

'Sound as a bell, Ian.'

'Put on your seatbelt. I never let anyone in the car without a seatbelt.'

Till drew the belt across and clicked it in. He released the handbrake and let the car roll back out onto the road. He shot a look in the rear-view mirror but he saw no sign of Ian. As the big Volvo sailed easily along, he noticed there were stars all over the place, flashing and blinking into the cold night.

Till was twenty-three. His birthday was coming up at the end of the month, always too close to New Year and Christmas. Nobody made a big thing of it. He'd been driving vans since he was fourteen. Heavy, red diesel vans that always made a helluva racket. Driving this big Volvo was a cinch. He wouldn't have minded some music, but was afraid to waken Ian. He heard him snoring. He wondered why someone like Ian was out driving on New Year's Eve night, totally out of his head. Families always got into rows at this time of year. Any row he ever had was mostly with family. They couldn't leave him alone. All he wanted now was to put the miles between him and them, and this time keep it that way.

    He knew Galway. They held a mart there couple of times a year. He could see the hill where they parked all the vans and the trailer boxes, the baker's where they got the iced buns. Or was that Sligo? He thought he knew Galway, but he could be wrong. The only place he really knew was Kilkelly, because of the accident. The guy speeding like a madman ploughed into the side of them just after the da pulled out. They were only crawling. The red Hiace was knocked clean off the road. The da got done for it because of the few drinks he'd had. But it was the madman's fault. To this day he still got angry when he thought how the da was summonsed for it.

    There was a junction ahead where he had to turn right. As he swung round he caught sight of the moon. A very thin slice, metallic bright. He'd have to watch the road coming up through Barnesmore. There could be ice. He doubted Ian would have made it through the Gap. He wouldn't have felt safe beside him.

    Till reckoned it would be another hour before Sligo. It wouldn't be daylight by then. His plan had been to stay at the da's for a week or two. Give it a go until the cold spell broke. But that was no good now. He had an older brother somewhere near Ballinrobe. They got on alright. But the wife suffered from moods. One day when the brother was out on a job, she cornered Till, started talking sweet to him. The next thing she was all over him, unbuttoning his shirt and his trousers. They ended up in bed. She was mad for it. Told him not to worry. He did what she wanted. Let her think everything was alright. Then, when she was asleep, he got away. Raided her purse on the way out. No idea what she'd told the brother.

Till felt like a racer taking the twists and turns through the Gap. He tried the brakes gently, just to check the road. No bother. A mate of Till's had brought him into the flashy new BMW showrooms in Letterkenny. They'd clowned around talking big time to the dealer. All figures and technicals, as if they had a clue. Got to sit into one of the three-one-six convertibles. Mad the money they cost. But it made you feel a whole lot different, like the icing on the cake was all yours.

The tail bit after Barnesmore was the last winding stretch. Till took the car through the bends, then shifted into top and sat back easy as the shadows of Donegal town came up on either side. Donegal was dead. He took a left coming into the square. When they got the new road finished it'd be even deader. He heard they had a big new disco all the farmers' sons went to and tore the livin' daylights out of each other. He'd worked on farms around Donegal. He knew the people they were talking about.

On the far side of Donegal he felt the tiredness creep over him. He fiddled around and found the switch for the window. Everything electric. The window zipped down an inch, letting in the cold air. It snapped him awake again. He wondered if he played his cards right, could he get a bed out of Ian. Around five o'clock they'd be in Galway. He didn't know anybody in Galway.

There was something about this Ian guy. The way he handed him the car keys. Crashed out on the backseat. Okay, the guy could have been a goner at the bottom of the Gap by now. But Till wasn't pulling any fast ones this time. The road in front of him from here on was straight nearly all way. All he had to do was follow it.

'You still alright?' Ian's voice startled Till. He'd no idea how much time had passed.

'Sure.'

'You must be tired.' Till heard him getting up. 'Where are we?'

'Near Sligo.' There hadn't been any signs for a while. He wasn't really sure.

'Pull over. You better get some sleep. Sounds like you need it. Better let me take over.'

'I'm alright.' Till knew he wasn't, but he was stubborn.

'Pull over,' Ian insisted. 'You get the head down.'

Till switched gears and slowed down, pulled the car over. Doors opened, they both got out at the same time. The ice in the wind cut into his cheeks. They passed each other without a word. Till resisted the urge to bolt. To slam the door and walk off. The old Till. The don't-tell-me-what-to-do Till. He grabbed the door steady and walked around it. Got himself into the back and pulled the door shut. He did up the zip on the jacket and spread out on the seats. The smooth rhythm of the big motor soothed him. He wanted to hold on to something in his head, but in a couple of minutes he was sound asleep.

*

Till opened his eyes and saw trees outside the window. Bare branches, a palm tree shaking in the wind. A telegraph pole and wires against a soft grey sky. He heard the noise of the wind, dogs barking, the way dogs in the countryside barked at each other. He started up. He was in bed, a big double bed that took up most of the room. His shoes and socks, trousers and jacket were thrown around on the floor. He sat still and listened, but he heard nothing. Nothing to give him a clue where he was. He forced himself to think, then slowly remembered waking, going into the house, the guy Ian showed him the room. He collapsed into the bed he was in now. His watch showed three-thirty. He must have slept right through. He needed a piss. He got out of bed, picked up his trousers and pulled them on quickly. Outside in the hall he checked

New Year's Day

the doors and found the bathroom. A big, white-tiled bathroom that was freezing cold. There were pictures on the walls, strange colours, nothing he could make out that made any sense. A weird kind of room for a bathroom. He washed and looked at himself in the mirror. For somebody who'd been in a punch-up with his da he looked alright. The da could throw a vicious punch. But he hadn't got close enough to do him any harm. Till had grabbed his wrist, wrung the bottle out of his hand and pushed him away. It all came back to him. The da hadn't made any moves to get up again. The drink had him beat.

Till examined the fancy bottles on the bathroom shelf. He took the cap off one and put his nose to it. Woman's stuff, probably the real thing, not the fakes you could spot a mile off. He had a flashback of buying stuff for his ma. When he was a kid. Paid for it with money of his own. Fancy box and all. The ma was all teary that he'd done it. The box sat there for ages. She never used it. Then she forgot about it. Years later he and his brother were selling the stuff, swearing it was the real thing, god's truth missus.

Till wondered what he should do. He could go back and wait in the bedroom until the Ian guy came for him. He didn't feel comfortable sneaking around his house. On the other hand, he was thirsty and hungry. He opened the bathroom door and walked out into the hall. He couldn't remember what way he'd come in. The hall had a corner, then led on to a porch and on the right he saw a door, probably into the living room. He was about to touch the handle when he heard Ian's voice. He was talking loudly, the way people talk when they are on the phone.

'Yeah, yeah, I know. That's what most people think. I didn't know you thought like everybody else.'

Till stood at the door, waiting to hear more.

'Don't be ridiculous! He's still asleep in the other room. I'm just up myself. We were completely knackered, the two of us.'

It felt odd to hear yourself being talked about. Maybe it wasn't the right thing to do, listening at the door.

'I don't care. For me he was a fuckin' godsend. Who else would have been out there hitching a lift at that hour of the morning? At New Year? He was meant to be there. Otherwise I mightn't be here right now.'

Till felt awkward. If there was any family they might catch him listening at the door. But somehow there was an empty feel to the house.

'I'll think about it. You know me.' There was the hint of a laugh in Ian's voice. It reminded Till of him asking if he thought he could drive the Volvo. He wasn't serious. A Volvo was like any other car. He knew that. Till heard a chair being moved.

'Yeah, yeah. I'll be careful. Listen, sorry for what happened. Are we alright then? Okay. Talk to you.'

He decided to knock on the door, rather than wait for Ian to find him there.

'Come in, come on in!' Ian called out.

Till opened the door and walked into the room.

'You're alive, good. Bet you're hungry too.'

'Sorta,' Till answered. The room was all windows. A fire was started in a big grate but it hadn't caught yet. Ian was looking at him as if he expected him to say some more.

'You sleep alright?'

'Out like a light. Don't remember how I got to bed. Slept right through.' Ian was standing behind a chair. The phone was lying on a newspaper. There were breakfast things scattered on the table.

'Are you a coffee or a tea man?'

'Tea,' Till mumbled.

'Fried egg, bacon?'

'The works. Can I get some water?'

'Grab a mug. Help yourself.' Ian pointed to the kitchen. 'The tap water's good. I'll cook us up some breakfast. See if you can do something with that fire. The pilot on the heating must have gone out. There's no heat. But I'm not going out to see about it in this weather.'

Till took a mug with the name Sandra on it. He wondered if it was a real name. The water was icy cold. Tasted good. He drank down a whole mug quickly, then refilled the mug and took it with him over to the fire.

'Can I use a bit out of your newspaper, mister?' It came out before he could stop himself. Ian was staring at him, about to say something, but didn't. 'Sorry. I mean Ian. Can I take a page from your newspaper to get the fire going?'

'Sure you can.' Ian was cutting open a pack of bacon. The fat was sparking in the pan.

Till lifted the phone off the paper and took out the centre page. He held it up in front of the fire to block the air flow. The paper was sucked in by the draught up the chimney. Till held on to it and soon he could hear the flames and the crackling of the wood. He looked over into the kitchen. 'Old Indian trick.'

They sat at the big table close to the window. Outside dusk was closing in. Till gulped his tea.

'You never told me what had you out on the road in the middle of the night.' He could feel Ian's eyes on him. He didn't like it. 'What were you running away from?'

Till felt a tightness in his stomach. He didn't care for people asking him questions. Wasn't any of their business. 'I wasn't running away. I didn't do nothin' to nobody.'

'I'm not saying you did. Not saying you did anything. Just curious. You don't have to tell me. Good thing for me you were there anyway.'

Till caught up a large piece of bacon and stuck it into his mouth. He chewed on it for a minute then swallowed it down. 'I had a row with me aul fella. He came at me with a bottle. He likes cutting me up.' Till rolled up his sleeve. 'You see. That's what I got from him the time before.'

'Jesus! 'Nice guy your father.'

Till rolled the sleeve down again. 'You have to be able to give as good as you get.'

'You mean that's what you did to him too?'

Till didn't like the sound of Ian's voice. 'I dunno. Don't think so. Don't think I did him any hurt. Can I have more tea?'

'Sure. I'll make some more.' Ian rose to go into the kitchen.

'I don't want to give you any bother.'

'It's no bother. Water's boiled. Just throw in a teabag. No bother.'

Till felt he shouldn't have said those things to Ian. He looked around at the big room, wondering what a guy with all this thought about him. About a stranger sitting at his table, showing him his scars, not knowing what he'd done. It would have been better for him to say nothing. He looked out at the trees shaking. Dark clouds, heavy with rain bore down on them. Far in the distance he could see low hills, other houses tacked onto them. The wind kept at it. A bitter cold January south-westerly.

'So what's the plan then, Till?' Ian came back with the tea and more toast. There was an edge to his voice. 'Where you heading after this?'

'Dunno. Anywhere s'pose.'

'There's an awful lot of dunnos about you, Till.'

'Must be. Dunno where I am, do I? So dunno where it is I'm likely to be heading then.'

'Galway, Till. We're just outside town. Do you have anybody you know around Galway?'

Till shuffled his feet under the table to ease the agitation building up inside him. He felt Ian's eyes on him. 'Could I stay here? I'll leave in the morning. I won't give you any bother.' Till could feel Ian wasn't the same guy anymore, the guy who handed over the car keys, let him drive his big Volvo.

'Listen, Till. Tell you what we're going to do. We'll drive into town. I'll take you to a hostel there. There are a couple of good hostels. I'll pay. How about that? You'll be better off in town.'

'I don't like towns,' Till said. 'I'd rather stay here. I'll go into the room and sleep. You can lock me in if you like.'

'I've somebody coming later on, Till.'

'Sandra?' Till said.

'Yeah. How did you know that?'

Till held up the mug. He could see a flush of redness in Ian's face.

Ian rose and went over to the fire. He took a few logs from a log box and set them into the fire. 'When you're finished, I'll drive you in,

Till. I need to be back out again before seven. I'd say we should have no trouble getting a place for you in one of the hostels.'

Till got up from the table. 'My jacket's in the room. I'll go get it.'

'Take your time,' Ian said. 'There's no rush.'

'Might as well go now.'

'Whatever you think, Till. Ready when you are.'

Till was annoyed. You were a goner, mister, without me. With your big car and your big house and your fake Sandra. They'd be no good to you now if it weren't for me. Go ahead, throw me out. Out of the corner of his eye he saw Ian watching him, expecting something from him. But he didn't say any more. He walked out of the room and closed the door behind him.

The road leading into Galway was empty. New bungalows, Santa Claus and reindeer figures in long gardens down to the road. Somebody had done a deal on trampolines, big blue ones for the kids. But it was too cold for them now. It would be dark again soon. The thought of Galway made Till nervous. He wasn't sure anymore that was where they held the mart. And hostels, he'd never been to one. What kind of people stayed there? Not many like himself he thought. He watched the road and saw a petrol station coming up on the left. 'Can we pull over?' he said to Ian.

'What?'

'I want to get out.'

'Get out? What for? We're not there yet. We're in the middle of nowhere.'

'Just let me out at the Statoil. I'll be alright.'

Ian slowed the car down and pulled onto the forecourt of the Statoil. 'For god's sake, what are you going to do here? There's nothing here, Till.' Ian stared at Till, his face twisted in a strange way. 'Let me take you into town, to the hostel. You'll be alright there.'

There was no way he could make him understand. He'd felt safe at Ian's house. 'I'll be alright,' Till said and opened the door.

'Alright where? It's freezing outside. Where are you going to go?'

'I'm not going into Galway.'

'I can't just drop you here, Till, and drive off. Shut the bloody door.'

'I can't.' Till shot a look at Ian. Something in Ian still cared, but not enough to silence the fear that had crawled under his skin. 'Thanks for the lift,' he said and got out.

'Here, take this.' Ian was taking money out of his wallet.

Till shook his head.

'For crissakes, take it, Till.'

'You might need it yourself, mister.'

Till closed the door. He took a few steps away from the car, watched it swing around and head back the way it had come. Then he pulled his jacket tight, zipped it up and started walking.

THIS COULD BE HEAVEN

It all starts in Monroe's. This time of year they keep a fire burning, and I am freezing; the winds that get twisted around the corners of Dominick Street are fierce. She is standing right where I would like to be, holding her hands to the flames. She gives me a sideways look and goes up to the bar, starts arguing with Tony. I'm not interested in what's going on between her and Tony. I get her place at the fire and turn away. It's dark and cold outside. All I want is some warmth.

When she comes back, she pushes in beside me. 'Tony's a jerk,' she says by way of introduction. I look at her and move a little to the side. I know Tony's okay. 'He won't give me anymore drink,' she goes on, as if I need to know this. 'He takes all my money, leaves me bust, then expects me to beg. Screw him.'

I'm not really sure who she's talking to. She looks more like a Radisson type. She's checking the tables, looking for somebody. But most of the tables are empty. When she's finished, she turns her attention to me. 'Do I know you? You look familiar.' She's pretty good-looking, well-dressed, neat make-up. Some jewellery, not much, but expensive stuff.

'I don't think so.'

'You know Eddie? I think I saw you with Eddie.' She takes another look around. 'He's not in yet.'

Maybe I know Eddie. I'm not sure. But I think I've slipped her mind already. She goes to the bar again and this time Tony gives her a drink. He doesn't ring it up.

'I knew Tony was alright,' she says when she gets back. 'You've nothing to drink. What's wrong with you?'

'It's okay. I only came in to get warmed up.'

'Hey, c'mon, sit down with me. Here, this one's close to the fire.' We sit down facing each other. I'm wondering what it is about her.

'Are you sure I haven't seen you with Eddie?'

'Who's Eddie? Do I know him?'

'Everybody knows Eddie.' She's taking her time with her drink. 'Eddie's father like only owns about half the bars in Galway. He wouldn't be one of my biggest fans. Not ever. But that doesn't bother Eddie.'

Something tells me not to ask what the father has against her. Right now it could be the wrong way to go. I have the feeling if she wants to, she will let me know.

'You know Tony's gay? He likes good-looking women, as long as there's a bar between us and him. We scare him if we get too close. Don't know why. Personally I've never done him any harm.'

That Tony is gay is an open secret. A gay barman is a bonus. I don't need to answer. I can tell her mind is shifting. As she holds her glass, I notice how perfect her nail-polish is. TV-commercial perfect. Everything about her is right. But there is something. And I'm trying to think of some question to ask but nothing is coming to me. 'I'll get you a drink,' I say. 'What is it?'

'Would you?' She perks up. 'Vodka martini. You're sweet. Hey, what's your name?'

'Ian.'

'Nice to meet you, Ian. I'm Denise.'

This is where it starts to get complicated.

'Do you know who you're with?' Tony asks me. He's just set the vodka martini in front of me on the bar. Tony knows I don't, but he's not for telling me. 'Watch yourself.' That's all he says. I'm drinking tap water with blackcurrant and ice. I only wanted to get warm.

'What did Tony say?' Denise tips her old glass into the full one. 'Did he tell you to watch yourself?'

'Yeah. What's it all about?'

'Tony's got a whole fantasy thing going about me. He warns everyone. I think Eddie puts him up to it. The two of them go way back. Anyway, thanks for the drink. You can go now, if you like. That's if you're worried about what Tony says.'

'Can I finish my water first?'

'Sorry.'

We stare into the fire. I can hear the wind outside. It's Wednesday, and it's a lousy night. Even the tourists have stayed away.

'There's Eddie.' Denise gets all excited. 'Hi Eddie! Over here!'

Eddie walks over and stares at her. Doesn't say anything. He stands there, takes a look at me, then goes straight to the bar. He pulls up a stool and turns his back on us.

'He's a bastard,' Denise says. 'Don't worry about him, Mister Big Cheese.'

At this point I should go home. What am I doing out anyway? I am still trying to get used to living on my own. Tonight I needed to get out. Bumping into Denise is the last thing I expected. But now I want to know where this is going.

'I've got to go over to him. I've got to talk to him,' Denise says. But she's not moving. 'He's mad at me. Don't worry, it's nothing to do with you. I screwed up, that's all. Thanks for the drink, Ian. You're sweet.'

You know I feel kind of sad that it's all over so soon. And that puzzles me. All I know is Denise is getting up, swings her coat over her arm and is on her way to the bar. I move my chair around, so I can keep up with what happens.

Denise throws her coat over a high-stool and slips on to the one beside Eddie. I like the way she does it. Eddie doesn't want to know. His body is rigid. From behind the bar Tony is keeping an eye on them. Then she starts talking to Eddie. She moves closer. Her whole body is leaning into his. It's not difficult to make out what her body is telling him. Suddenly Eddie barks at her. It all happens in a matter of seconds. Denise starts up, her arm flashes and she slaps Eddie hard across the face. Before he can react, she grabs her coat and is walking back over to me.

'C'mon Ian. We're getting out of here. This place stinks.'

I know whatever I do it's going to be the wrong thing. I don't even want to leave right now. But I don't have time to argue. Denise is on her way out, she's holding the swing door open for me. Outside the rain is pelting down. The cars splash through the overflow. Denise has taken off towards Spanish Arch. Then she stops at the line of cars parked on the canal. She hooks up her leg, reaches back and takes off a shoe. With the heel she starts hammering the taillights of one of the cars.

'Jesus, what are you doing?' I grab her and try to pull her away.

'That's for Mister Eddie Bullshit. He's no right to treat me the way he does.' She's making a real mess of the left taillight of Eddie's '08 BMW. 'He deserves this. He deserves everything he gets. That's why I whacked him.' She gives the lamp one last thump before I get her away. 'There. That'll give him something to think about.' She hooks the shoe back on. Bits of expensive plastic are lying on the ground.

'C'mon Ian, we're going to a party.' When we get to the bridge, Denise takes a sharp look around and hurries across. I wait and get drenched by a passing car. 'Ian, get a move on,' Denise screams. 'I'm getting soaked.'

A light clicks on inside my head. I could turn right now and go home. There is nothing to stop me. But before it gets that far, I dash across in front of the next car. Denise hooks my arm and hurries me along beside her. 'Murray's having one of his bashes,' she tells me. 'They're great, you know. Everyone gets smashed. There'll be loads of stuff. I so need to get smashed right now. How about you, Ian? Want to get smashed?'

Nimmo's is in darkness. The rain splashes off the new paving stones as if it has a point to make. 'I don't do smashed anymore,' I answer.

'Jesus, how do you survive?' There is an almost-hint of sympathy in her voice.

'Good question,' I say and wonder what it would be like to get smashed again.

Down in the harbour there is a maze of new apartments. We stop at one and Denise starts banging the intercom on a security gate. A voice crackles, a buzzer sounds and the gate clicks open. I follow her down a tight corridor. I'm beginning to feel claustrophobic already. We come to a door Denise recognises. Whoever is standing behind it opens it the minute she knocks.

'Ger, hi. Meet Ian. He's cool. Where's Murray?'

Ger opens the door wider and lets us in. As soon as we are inside Denise takes off, tells me to get myself a drink. The room I'm in is dimly lit but I can make out some people sprawled on the floor. Maybe they're on cushions or mattresses. Some of them are backed up against the wall. When my eyes adjust, I can see it's mostly guys. I don't like staring but it's hard not to. Anyway, no one seems to be bothered about me. I can hear an argument going on in the other room. Murray is not happy about people crashing his party.

'Who are these people? Who let them in?'

'They're cool, Murray. No one's causing any trouble. Everything's cool. Here, try this.'

This could be heaven, this could be hell. Right here. I catch sight of Denise coming from the other room. She doesn't seem bothered about any of the people around her. She comes straight for me.

'Ian, what's happening? You get something to drink?'

'I'm going. This isn't my scene.'

'Mine neither,' Denise surprises me. 'There's nothing happening tonight. Murray is in one of his tissies. I've just got to get my coat. Wait for me.'

I'm standing at the door where we came in. It feels like a long time. It crosses my mind that back then we used to laugh when we got high. We laughed at the simplest things. One person started, then infected the rest of us. That's why we did it. No one's laughing here. There's a guy across from me flat-out on the floor. He looks like he could be dead, except every now and then he twitches. No one's interested in him. I wonder if he needs help.

Denise is having difficulty with her coat. 'Where's your car?' she asks when we get outside.

'Near the fire station. Where I always park.'

'Jesus, you are so weird, Ian. I have to get to Terry's. Can you drop me there?'

'You need to get home. That's the only place I'm dropping you right now.' I'm annoyed. The rain has stopped but it's still miserable. It's a long time since Monroe's fire seemed like a good idea.

'Please Ian. Take me to Terry's. You don't have to wait. Just drop me there and you can leave. Please.'

'I'm going home. I should have gone long ago. You can get a taxi.'

'Taxis cost money. I don't have any. Please Ian. One last time. I won't ask anymore of you.'

'Haven't you had enough? You're freaked out already. What's this Terry guy got that you need so badly?'

'I need to talk to Terry. He owes me.'

I've no way out of it. I don't want to leave her stranded and she doesn't want to go home. It's early morning. Whoever Terry is, unless he runs an all-night drop-in centre, he is not going to be pleased. But I give in. 'Where does he live?'

'Off The Circular. I'll take you.' I almost laugh at her. She slips her arm through mine as if everything is okay again.

It's a steep hill up to The Circular. When we get to the top, Denise directs me off left into a housing estate I didn't know was there. Everything is quiet, normal. Cars in sloped driveways, pencil-point lighting from consecutive doorbells. Denise points to a house that looks like all the others. 'That's Terry's. You can drop me here. Thanks, Ian. You're sweet.'

Something stops me from driving off. Something is keeping me there. I wait as she rings the bell. Nothing happens. She rings again, then starts banging the door with her fists. I can hear her screaming. First a light goes on upstairs, then a curtain draws. A few minutes later the front door opens and Denise rushes in. It's all over. But there's something in my head. I'm turning the car when the door opens again. I catch it in the rear-view mirror. Somebody shoves her out of the door and she stumbles to her knees, then crumples in a heap on the drive. I back the car up as near as I can and swing open the passenger door.

'Get in,' I say. 'Get in!'

Denise looks at me as if she has forgotten who I am. Then she lifts herself off the ground and falls into the passenger seat. 'Ian, take me home, please. I want to go home.'

Denise lives in an ivy-covered two-storey on Taylor's. Lots of trees and privacy. The BMW in the drive has a banged-up taillight. I notice it but I don't mention it. Neither does Denise.

'I owe you, Ian,' she says. She holds the door to steady herself. She looks a mess but she smiles. 'Thanks for waiting.'

The city has a clean feel to it in the early morning, when the rain stops and people have not started moving. Sitting at a traffic light, wondering if I should drive through, I get to think. This time of the morning I like.

THE WAY THINGS HAPPEN

His Story:

    I still prefer the old Róisín Dubh with its low stage and folk-club atmosphere. This new Róisín feels too all-over-the-place. But if there is anyone who can dispel this feeling, then it's John Spillane. It's hard to make out if John is being himself or if he switches persona when he goes onstage. Whatever, right now he's doing a great job. 'The Cherry Trees'. *Well done everyone.* Yes John. Well done everyone, just for being alive.

    After 'Hey Dreamer' I get up to go to the bar. John is doing one more song before the break. As I pass her table, I notice her long black hair. It sparkles. 'Like your hair,' I say. I don't know why I come out with it like that. She smiles at me. I smile back and go on to the bar, order my pint and wait for the break. 'One half down, one to go,' John says. 'Fair play to me.'

Her Story:

He has already started his set when we get there. But that's how it is when you're on holiday. Relaxing and relaxing, and then rushing about last minute to make it to a show that someone says you absolutely cannot miss. We've just returned from Aran—me and the others from the course—and I look a mess, my hair still wild from the ferry ride. I was tired and looking forward to an easy night-in; but then there was the taxi driver telling us we have to see this guy John Spillane.

'He's great craic,' he said. I'm still getting used to that word, *craic*. There is so much about Ireland that I am still getting used to. 'He does this song about a whale.' His laugh quickly turned into a hacking cough until he finally caught his breath. 'Sure, it's the funniest thing I've ever heard. And then there's the one about the Dunnes Stores girl. If you do one thing while you're here in Galway, go see his show.'

And so here we are in the Róisín Dubh watching John Spillane. He's certainly got charisma, and he's funny. 'So far, so good,' is his punch line. I can't help but laugh every time he says it. And then there are his digressions in between songs that seem to get more fanciful as he goes along. All I can think about is how I don't want to leave in three days.

Just before the break I catch myself looking around, for what or who I don't know. And that's when I see him. 'Nice hair,' he says. I smile. There is something about him. Charming and wicked and kind of sad, all at the same time. I turn around and watch him walk to the bar. I think about following him but decide not to.

His Story:

Returning from the bar, I haven't really planned to say anything more to her. Still a bit puzzled about myself. Of course, I could decide to *not* take the same way back. Well, maybe my subconscious has its own plans. As I come closer to her table, she looks around. Then at the same moment we both say 'Hi!' It makes us laugh, together.

'You've really got beautiful hair.' I'm not just saying it, because she does. It's long and flowing and has a sparkle, the sparkle that got me the first time. Everything is easy, the conversation I mean. Her name is Amy. She is with a group of Americans attending a writing course at the university. They've just got back from Aran and are celebrating the end of their course. I'm a writer and I love Aran.

Her Story:

At the end of the first set the other girls get up to grab a smoke. That's when I find myself looking around again. Through the rush of bodies heading toward the bar I see him. It is his striking white hair. 'Silver-blonde,' he later corrects me. I look away, telling myself not to be so obvious. But a moment later I turn back around and there he is, right in front of me. I smile stupidly. I can't stop. But it feels good. Sometimes stupid is good.

One of us says hello and we start talking about why I'm here in Ireland. I tell him about the writing course and it turns out he is a writer too. I stare at his lips as he speaks, watching the way they stretch with every syllable. He tells me that he has only just got back to writing, that he put it on hold for a while.

'For how long?'

'Too long,' he says, shaking his head.

It's obvious he doesn't want to talk about it so I change the subject. 'So does John Spillane really have a whale song?'

He smiles, his grey-blue eyes lighting up. 'Not only does he have a whale song, but it's a killer of a whale song: *Orca! Killer whale!*'

I laugh at the way he hisses the words. 'I can't wait.' Then the other girls come back. I turn and give them a welcome-back smile, though what I really want to say is to go away.

His Story:

I'm not sure exactly what to do now. I'm on my own and she is with her group. I don't want to gatecrash, make things too obvious. So I just kind of wave a goodbye and go back to my seat, hoping we'll get the chance later to talk again. Anyway, John is back onstage, swinging his guitar over his shoulder.

Her Story:
When the second set starts I keep thinking about him, replaying the conversation in my head. Everything seemed to fall into place with him so naturally. The conversation. Eye contact. Body language. Everything. Part of me wonders if this is routine for him. But in truth I don't care. It feels good and at the moment I need that.

His Story:
On my way out we get talking again. She tells me I'm cute. I'm not sure whether I like that or not. I hope she means it in a good way. I give her my telephone number and we agree to meet in the Róisín the next evening at seven. I give her the number in case anything goes wrong. Very forward-thinking of me. They have their last day to get through tomorrow. Something tells me she would rather be spending it with me. Who knows? Maybe that's me being big-headed. I'm not really, I don't think. It feels good to have a date. Totally out-of-the-blue. I go home feeling a lot happier than when I left.

Her Story:
I take my time putting on my jacket and getting my purse together, all the while looking around. The other girls are becoming impatient and want to go. I know that waiting behind for someone who has likely already left is a foolish idea, but I tell them to go on without me. I wait for a few minutes and then go up to the bar.
'I thought you left,' I hear someone say. I turn around in surprise. 'Not yet.' I smile. I swear I've never smiled so much in my life. We go back to the table and talk. He starts telling me about himself, how everything fell apart on him and that he's trying to figure things out. 'Not fuckin' easy,' he says. 'I could do with some of that John Spillane

mindset, some of those cherry trees.'

I've been there so many times I don't need him to explain. 'It's not always a bad thing,' I say. 'When things fall apart it can lead to new things, if you open yourself up to them.' I tell him how the trip to Ireland is about my trying to find peace after my father died.

'Has it worked?' he asks.

'Not so far.' Then I make a comment about how we are in deep already, maybe too deep for the atmosphere we're in. That's when he asks if I want to go home with him. I want to, of course I do, but I know he has had a few beers and don't want it to be from that. And so I suggest we meet the next evening. 'If you want to, that is.'

His Story:

Right now there are a lot of things about my life I don't like. My marriage gone down the drain, my job that I've been doing for too long, and I'm pretty sick of myself also. What a score! Her popping-up out of nowhere is a breath of fresh air. All the way from the States to the Róisín for me to tell her that I like her hair.

What do I do until seven? Some cleaning-up, that's for sure. Hanging out in the Róisín or in some half-empty restaurant is not how I want to spend the evening. I want her back here, just the two of us. Enough said.

I get through the day, thinking about her a lot of the time. Then at around six-fifteen I drive to the Róisín and wait for her at the bar. And wait for her at the bar. I wait for about forty-five minutes, becoming more miserable with every five minutes she doesn't show up. Eventually I tuck in my tail and leave, silently cursing my luck.

Her Story:

Our speaker today is good but I tune out, thinking about the night before and meeting Ian later. In truth it's been a while since I've had a date and I've nearly forgotten what it feels like. The nervousness, excitement, anticipation.

At the break I take a walk through the campus and along the river. I think about what I told him about my father, how strange it is that I mentioned it at all. I haven't said a word to anyone on the course. Even back at school only a few people know and only because they wondered why I missed so many classes the week of his funeral. So why have I told him? I'm still thinking about it when I get back to the apartment.

As I'm getting ready there's a commotion with one of the girls in my apartment. Now they are looking to me because I am older than them. And so, like it or not, I get tangled up in it.

I'm already late when I finally get myself out of the apartment. I did a quick job getting ready and then slipped out. I know I should feel guilty about leaving, but in truth I'm relieved.

His Story:

I would rather not go home. I know I will only get more depressed there on my own. But there isn't anywhere else I want to go. So I drive back, feeling a bit foolish for letting myself be taken in. All the kinds of feelings that go through your mind when you get stood up. I pull up outside the house. As I'm locking the car, I hear the phone in the hall ringing. It's right there on the table behind the door. I rush to open the front door. But these double security locks take time to open. By the time I get inside, the ringing has stopped.

Her Story:

It seems to take forever for my taxi to arrive. The driver wants to get out, to open the door for me but I quickly hop inside. 'To the Róisín Dubh, please,' I say before he has a chance.

'No bother,' he says and then starts asking me the usual questions—what part of the States I'm from and why I'm there. I'm not in the mood to talk though. I just want him to get me there. But the traffic is backed up.

'Roadworks, there's roadworks everywhere.'

I look at my watch. Twenty-five minutes late. I wonder if he'll wait. I turn and look at all the backed-up traffic, telling myself to relax. But it isn't working. I lean forward. 'Excuse me. Is there another way we can go?'

'We can try,' he says, then shakes his head. 'It might not be any better. Sure this will clear in a minute.'

I look at my watch every couple of minutes until we finally get there, more than fifteen minutes later. I jump out of the taxi and run to the door, my heart thumping. I take a deep breath and smooth my hair and skirt. Then I open the door. I look around, something in me feeling hopeful. But he isn't there. I wait ten minutes and then call from a payphone across the road. With a shaky voice I leave a message, part of me feeling bad for being so late, the other part wondering if he ever came at all.

His Story:

She has left a message on the answer machine that she got there late and that she is sorry about that. And now I'm not there, so everything is a waste. I need to ring the Róisín fast, reach her before she leaves again. I dig out the phone book and find the number. From my description—the girl with the sparkly black hair—the barman knows who I'm talking about and hands her the phone.

'Stay there,' I say. 'I'll be there as soon as I can. Don't go away.' Driving in to town again I sing to myself, *Well done everyone!*

Her Story:

I sit at the bar, keeping a close eye on the door, and order wine. I will give it until the end of the glass before resolving myself to giving up and going back to the apartment. Drinking as slowly as I can, I get more depressed with each sip. I tell myself that if he doesn't come then it's not meant-to-be. Actually, I don't believe in meant-to-be. But I say it each time I check the door. Each time I take a sip of wine. *If he doesn't come then it's not meant-to-be.* I stare into the glass, wondering how long I can make the rest of the wine last. Will it be long enough? I check the door one more time and then I down the last of the wine in one quick gulp, deciding that it is enough. It is enough now. But just like that, the way some things happen, the bartender is standing in front of me, holding out the phone.

'Hello,' I say, the sweet taste of the wine lingering in my mouth.

His Story:

When I get there, she's sitting on a high-stool at the bar. The barman gives us that happy-end look, but we decide not to hang around for the credits. We drive off into the sunset, stopping en route to pick up dinner-for-two at Joyce's. And that is the way things happen.

MY PERFECT UNCLE

'Well fuck me pink, Neph! What are you doing here?' Uncle Roy's words can be heard loud and clear over the speakers. 'Oh, Christ! Forgot that was still on.' There is good-humoured laughter from the crowd, pockets of applause.

'Watch yourself,' I say as he trips over the microphone cable and stumbles into my arms. 'What am *I* doing here?' I mumble into his shoulder. 'What are *you* doing here?'

'Neph, I live here.'

'Mogan?'

'El Palmito, up the valley.' He looks fit with his perfect suntan. I remember him taller; now he is about a head shorter than me. 'Didn't you do well!' He yanks me to him again. 'So what's the story? On your holliers?'

'I'm here to take you back.'

'Dead or alive?' His lips curl in a John Wayne imitation.

'You're no good to us dead.'

'Didn't know I was much good to anybody, dead or alive.'

He means it to be funny but it doesn't work that way. 'Take two,' I say. 'We enjoyed your show.'

'Still floggin' it,' he says. 'You gotta make a livin'. This is still the best way I know how.'

'Do you need a hand?'

'I'm grand. I'll be done here in a few minutes.'

'Come over when you're ready.' Amy waves as I point to the table.

'Be right over. Nice lady.'

'That was short and sweet,' Amy says. 'I love the way you men bear-hug. There's something so primeval about it.'

'What's that supposed to mean?'

'It's just the way you pound into each other like …' She flicks back strands of her long hair. 'Oh, forget it. Give me more wine, please … before I say the wrong thing again.'

'Remember, it's more than thirty years the last time we saw each other.' I reach for the bottle and refill our glasses. 'The funny thing is Uncle Roy is smaller than me now.'

Amy cocks her head at me like a bird, takes a deep breath. 'You sound so boyish when you call him Uncle Roy. It's cute.'

'I've always called him Uncle Roy, I've never called him anything else. What do you expect me to call him?'

'It's okay,' Amy says. 'I didn't mean anything. For a grown man it has a certain charm. Anyway, here he comes.'

Uncle Roy offers Amy one of those long cigarettes that always remind me of Bogart and Bacall movies. 'What about you, Neph? You smoke?'

'I gave them up.' I scratch one thumbnail across the other, about to say something else.

Amy leans toward him for a light. 'I shouldn't smoke either, but the odd one now and again with my very occasional glass of wine won't do me any harm, will it?' Amy's shoulders shiver as she laughs at herself.

'We'll let you away with it this time,' Uncle Roy says. 'Chris, my partner, is dead against me smoking. I daren't smoke anywhere in the house.'

'A woman after my own heart,' Amy says.

'Yeah, probably.' It will take him a while to get used to the way Amy switches. 'How long are you guys staying?'

'We've got a couple more days,' I tell him.

'What you say I pick you up tomorrow and you come to our place? Meet Chris. Right now I got another gig in town. You two early-risers?'

Amy and I look at each other. 'Borderline,' Amy says, making that gesture with her right hand.

'Not crack-of-dawn freaks,' I add.

'I get up real early, like to pack in as much as I can.' He leans over towards the ashtray. 'How about twelve-thirty? Keep everybody happy. We can grab some lunch together.'

'Terrific,' Amy says.

Uncle Roy keeps his eyes on Amy as he stubs out his butt. Then he swings his attention to me. 'I gotta run. See you tomorrow. What a surprise!' He turns around to Amy before he leaves. 'Look after this guy for me, won't you?'

'Will do,' Amy says and bends across to me. 'You need looking after?'

Uncle Roy looks back when he hears Amy's laugh.

On either side of us the slopes stretch to an arc of blue sky as we motor up the highway to El Palmito. It feels that if the mountains came any closer we could be squeezed to death. Amy is in the front of the jeep, shooting pictures. At breakfast she told me there was something instantly likeable about Uncle Roy. She looked forward to seeing him again.

'He was always a hit with women,' I told her. 'But he never settled for any of them. I suppose that was a good thing in a way. He probably wouldn't have left if he'd met the right one. Be interesting to see what Chris is like.'

Amy took back the bear-hug comment. Said it didn't really fit anymore.

Uncle Roy shouts things at us over the engine noise. Something about barrancos and rock-slides. I watch the massive boulders poised above, imagine gigantic eruptions that could send them rolling down on top of us. At a sign for El Palmito he veers to the right and heads off on a dirt track up the mountain. 'Hold on tight. Gets bumpy for a while.' We bounce along with a lot of suspension noises, a dust cloud rising behind. Around us it is all lava rock and tall cacti, a sprinkle of palm trees, no houses anywhere. 'Okay in the back?' Uncle Roy shouts.

'Hangin' in there.' Up ahead the landscape is changing. Lots of greenery, large sagging palms. We drive under an arch of purple bougainvillea into a courtyard full of big-bellied clay pots stacked with flowering bushes. In the middle there is a windmill, white and red with large slatted blades. Ripples of colour drip from a wooden balcony. The red tiled conical roof makes me think of a jester's cap.

'Oh my god!' Amy says. 'Is this for real?'

The blades of the windmill are pinned against the sky. I count six of them as Uncle Roy pulls up at the wooden door. 'It's real alright, no mirage' he laughs. 'You guys hungry? I hope Chris has got some lunch for us.'

Amy and I look at each other. 'I need time to take all this in,' she says. 'Can't think of food right now.'

'Take all the time you want. Plenty of that here. But me, I'm hungry.'

The clouds move in slow shapes across the slopes of the mountain. The white exterior of the windmill glows like a beacon. 'How in god's name did you end up with this?' I can hear the echo of familiar voices. Voices I thought I had left behind.

'When we bought it, it was a ruin.' Uncle Roy swings onto the deck. 'Chris and me worked at it for years. A lot of things my old man taught me went into it. You could call it a labour of love.' He glances at me. 'I'll see where Chris is. Come in when you're ready.'

'I thought you said he and his father didn't get along.' Amy bends down to stroke one of the kittens running around at our feet.

'Maybe I picked it up wrong. Anyway, all we ever got was closed-door stuff.'

'Are you going to ask him about it?'

'There are so many things I want to ask him about. But let's take it slow. See what happens.'

Uncle Roy is waiting for us, another man standing at his side. 'Good, you guys ready? Meet Chris.'

There is a moment of hesitation, just long enough for it to sink in. 'Hi Chris,' I manage and stick out my hand. Chris ignores it and wraps his arms round me. Awkwardly I do the same.

'Oh, you're so convincing, Neph.'

'Roy, you're an asshole. Letting us walk into it like this. An' stop calling me Neph. My fuckin' name's Ian.'

The three of them are staring at me. No one says anything. Then Amy bursts out laughing. 'What's so funny, Amy?' I turn on her.

'You are. You haven't seen your favourite uncle for thirty years and this is how you act? You have a gay uncle, Ian. Congratulations. Some people would be envious.'

'You didn't warn them, Roy? That's mean of you,' Chris says.

'Just my little joke.'

Jack Nicholson, I think. Roy, you could be a stand-in for Nicholson but I don't say it. 'Now listen everybody. So I was expecting Chris to be a woman. Amy, you were too. It just seemed so …' The word won't come to me.

'Natural?' Chris says.

'Right,' I say and I know that I've walked into it. They laugh at me and this time I join in.

'Come on through, everyone,' Chris says. 'Lunch is getting cold.'

'This place is amazing.' Amy is taking in every detail as we walk through. 'I've never seen anything like this back home. Roy said it was a ruin.'

'Most of the old mills were. We came here on a holiday and saw this one. Roy fell in love with it straight away. I thought he was crazy. We wanted to get out of London, but buying a ruin, I couldn't see it. Luckily Roy did.' Chris has a soft accent that I like, somewhere south-east. Amy is waiting for him to go on. 'We got guys to build up the walls, replace the shafts. We drove around collecting old roof tiles from all over the island. That was fun. The inside is all Roy's work. The man's a wizard. Carpentry, plumbing, electrics, he can do anything.'

My favourite Uncle Roy winks at me like you-know-who. 'We'll let you have the grand tour later,' he says. 'Let's eat first.'

The deck looks out over a mix of tall cacti and palms, here and there some fir trees.

'You guys okay with rabbit, I hope.' Chris comes back with a steaming ceramic bowl. 'I made stew. You don't get rabbit that much back in Ireland, do you?'

'No we don't,' I say. 'We love it.'

Uncle Roy is filling our glasses with Rioja. 'Hey, what about the time you and me cycled to that old Celtic fort? Remember? Grianan, that was it, wasn't it? We could've got plenty of rabbits that day.' He turns to Amy. 'There's a tunnel inside the wall of the old fort. You had to crawl into it, prove yourself.' Uncle Roy turns back to me. 'Nothin' for cissies. But we did it, didn't we?'

He did it, he'd gone in as far as he could. I still remember the stench inside, much worse than what might be in there. 'We did it alright,' I say and take a stab at the stew, pick out some rabbit. 'This is good.'

Chris nods. 'Thanks. You two spent a lot of time together back then?'

'Yes and no.' Uncle Roy is in there before me. 'Neph here, sorry,

Ian was a bit of a scholar. My sister had her plan for him. Me, I was never one for the books and other people's plans for me. We did lots of nothin' together, like everybody else.' He laughs and sucks on a piece of rabbit. 'Wasn't much to do, was there? We cycled a lot. Grianan, Inch Island, Hegarty's Rock. Places you guys never heard of.' He pauses, remembering something.

'I know them,' Amy tells him. 'Think I even know the tunnel. I didn't go in though.'

'Yeah?' He smiles at Amy but his mind is on something else. 'Whatever happened that old guitar of mine? You make anything of it?'

I hold my left hand across the table and stretch my fingers. He feels the tips. 'Hey, pretty good. What kind of stuff you play?'

'Dylan, Cohen. Some Eagles.'

'Cool. Chris has his studio upstairs.'

'You have a studio in the mill?'

'Sure. We do all my backing tracks there. You know, like the ones you heard at the Zona. That's me, every note of it. I got the tracks on my iPod. Just plug in an' away I go. Chris used to do the sound stuff for Mott the Hoople. You heard of them? Chris can tell some stories.'

'Ian Hunter and Mick Ronson?' I say to Chris.

'"All the Young Dudes",' he replies.

'But "Dudes" was Bowie, wasn't it?'

'Yeah, sure, Bowie gave it to the Motts. They were about to split up and Bowie was trying to get them not to. I can still see him squatting on the studio floor playing it on the acoustic for us. Blew everybody away. "Dudes" gave the Motts a whole new life.'

'Wow! How long were you their sound man?'

'I had to get out after a couple of years. Around the time I met Roy. It all became too crazy.'

'So how did you and Roy meet?' Amy hasn't said anything since talking about the tunnel.

'Roy had a regular gig at a place called The Red Cow in Hammersmith. When was it, Roy, seventy-two, seventy-three?'

'Something like that. Sue and Bill from Liverpool ran the place. They put me on in between strippers. I had my own little circle of fans.' I notice a little bald spot as Uncle Roy leans forward to pick rabbit from the bowl.

'And I was top of the list,' Chris says. 'One evening Roy's sound guy didn't show up.'

'Enda. Enda from Omagh. Got lifted under the PTA. Anybody with an Irish-sounding name was getting nabbed left, right and centre. Real *Name of the Father* stuff. I got hauled in twice.'

'Roy asks over the mike, "Anyone here do sound?" The chance was too good to miss. He came home with me later that night.'

'An' here we are like a pair of old codgers, still makin' music together.' Uncle Roy looks around at the three of us with a broad boyish grin. 'So what's it like having a gay uncle?' he asks me, his lips slipping into that John Wayne curl again.

'Better than no uncle.' I shoot the words back at him. 'You just disappeared.'

His smile frame-freezes. 'That's not the way I thought it was going to be.' He combs his fingers through his hair, then wipes his hand on his thigh. 'But I had no idea how people at home would take to me being gay. Things were different then, Ian.'

Amy is shaking her head and mouthing 'Don't' at me. Chris is staring.

'You know we were always more than just uncle and nephew. We were real friends, buddies. You gave me my first fag, remember? There was a vacuum when you left.' I'm not sure how true this is. The drift started before he left. We both know that. But there is something there, something that needs to be said.

'Listen, Ian, my old man, I don't know how well you knew him, when I left he told me that if I walked out that door, I would never walk in it again, as long as he lived. Imagine me landing in on him with Chris. That just wasn't on.'

'So I got to be the one to sit at his deathbed. The one who closed his mouth. How old was I, fifteen, sixteen? It should have been you.' I've never said this to anyone before. But I've said enough, more than I wanted to. I get up and walk down onto the terrace, stare up at the ridges, wondering what is happening. Why has it burst out now?

When I come back, Amy is petting one of the kittens that jumped onto her lap; Chris is watching her and smiling. Uncle Roy is gone.

'He's outside in the jeep,' Chris tells me. 'Waiting for you.'

'I'm sorry. I didn't mean to spoil things. I don't know why I turned on him like that.'

Amy flicks the hair back from her face. 'It was too sudden, Ian. You could have given us all a little more time before dumping on him. But you need to deal with it now. Go see how Roy is.' The kitten wriggles on her lap.

'Roy's a big boy,' Chris says. 'He can take it.' The sun is blinding him as he looks over at me. 'These things got to happen sometimes. Go talk to him. We're okay.'

Roy is sitting behind the wheel smoking one of his cigarettes. I climb into the passenger seat beside him. 'You got one of those for me?'

He lifts a pack from the dash and knocks one out. 'They're the light ones. The strong ones were ruining my voice.' He taps his chest a few times.

I inhale slowly, waiting for the coughing. 'I'm sorry. I don't know what made me say those things. Guess something's been bugging me for a long time.'

He turns towards me, his right arm strapped over the wheel. 'I did it the only way I knew how and that was total shut-down. Anything else would have been more painful.' He takes one last pull on his cigarette and flicks it away. 'I'm not sayin' I was right. Maybe it was all wrong what I did. Who knows? I just didn't want to go back to see how people were hurtin', or to hurt them more. But you know what, until now no one ever came after me either. You're the first of the posse.' Uncle Roy ruffles my hair, then turns and starts the engine.

'Where are we going?'

'Veneguera. Got something I want you to see.'

The jeep rattles and bounces across the mountain through a landscape of scrub and cacti. For a while we shout at each other above the noise of the engine, then we go silent. So many things I still want to know, so many more pieces to the jigsaw.

Gradually the track descends into a valley that tapers to a sharp end. I can see the ocean ahead of us.

'Nearly there,' Roy shouts. He swings the jeep onto a high bank of stones and turns off the engine. 'Look to your right!'

I turn my head and I know what he means. The mountain sweeps down, falling in stages until the last sheer drop leaves a huge ridge jutting out into the ocean.

'Hegarty's Rock,' I say.

'Minus the cross.' Roy looks at me with a smile, satisfied. 'Ready to jump?'

JOHN WALSH was born in Derry in 1950. After sixteen years teaching English in Germany, in 1989 he returned to live in Connemara. He's published three collections of poetry, including his latest, *Chopping Wood with T.S. Eliot* (Salmon Poetry, 2010). He has read and performed at events in Ireland, the UK, Germany, Sweden and the USA. He is organizer and MC of the successful performance poetry event North Beach Poetry Nights in the Crane Bar, Galway, Ireland's leading monthly performance poetry event. His fiction has appeared in *Crannóg* and *Natural Bridge*. He has also been known to show up with his guitar and deliver one or two of his own songs.

Visit his website at www.johnwalshpoet.com.

*To Lizzy
With best wishes*

IN THE SHADOW OF A DREAM

Sharad Keskar

by Sharad Keskar

authorHOUSE®

AuthorHouse™
1663 Liberty Drive
Bloomington, IN 47403
www.authorhouse.com
Phone: 1-800-839-8640

© 2012 Sharad Keskar. All rights reserved.

No part of this book may be reproduced, stored in a retrieval system, or transmitted by any means without the written permission of the author.

Published by AuthorHouse 7/31/12

ISBN: 978-1-4772-1531-9 (sc)
ISBN: 978-1-4772-1532-6 (hc)
ISBN: 978-1-4772-1533-3 (e)

Any people depicted in stock imagery provided by Thinkstock are models, and such images are being used for illustrative purposes only. Certain stock imagery © Thinkstock.

This book is printed on acid-free paper.

Because of the dynamic nature of the Internet, any web addresses or links contained in this book may have changed since publication and may no longer be valid. The views expressed in this work are solely those of the author and do not necessarily reflect the views of the publisher, and the publisher hereby disclaims any responsibility for them.

To Frances
With deep affection

&

To my Parents
To whom I owe my love for English Literature

Guildenstern. *The very substance of the ambitious is merely the shadow of a dream.*

Hamlet. *A dream itself is but a shadow.*

Rosencrantz. *Truly, and I hold ambition of so airy and light a quality that it is but a shadow's shadow.*

CHAPTER ONE

He promised to marry her and to take her back with him to England after the War. But he was killed in Burma. It was 1942. She was young, trusting, and when she realised she was pregnant, the unhappy woman left her nursing post at the Military Hospital in Basirabad and decided to return to her parents in Goa. Then in panic and afraid to face them, she thought it better to wait till after her child was born. It was a difficult and painful birth; the trauma of it, and the desolation of her situation, drove her to distraction. In no fit state to travel, she took her child and boarded a train. It was the wrong train. Sick and distraught, she got down when, two hours later, it stopped at a siding. The child began to cry. Mechanically she fed him and helplessly watched the train leave. She shivered and sobbed bitterly. The only other person at the siding was a man. He moved towards her but stopped when she sprang up with a sharp cry. Wide-eyed and afraid, she pressed her child to her breast and waved a hand frantically at him. He shrugged, turned back, picked up a wheel-barrow and slowly disappeared behind a shed. The woman rocked as she began to hum a lullaby. Then a sudden calm overcame her. She wrapped her boy-child in her shawl and walked the two miles of the dusty track that led to the gate of a walled village. There, on the worn steps of the Temple to Vishnu, she abandoned her child. And in the gathering smoky darkness, ran out into the unremitting isolation of the Thar Desert...

Snaking its way through the Aravalli hills, the railway track enters the hot plains of Southern Rajasthan, where the land is too barren for cities. But small villages mottle the sandy landscape near oases and alongside shallow man-made lakes. Here living is possible, though not without the obscene contrast of privilege and poverty—often a feature of Rajput villages owned by those few landlords, related to or employed by the local Rajas. But Rajputs are an ancient people, too Hindu for envy, too proud to beg, and too steeped in feudal custom and tradition to seek change.

Railway travellers, through this area of sandstorms and heat haze, on their way to Baroda from Jaipur, could miss the ancient walled village of Fatehpur, appearing, as it does, suddenly round a bend and as suddenly disappearing behind a spur of high ground. Its yellow sandstone walls are of the same colour as the silent, barren wasteland in which it is cradled. But twice each day that dun monochrome is broken. At dawn, the procession of women, in brightly coloured tight bodices and full skirts of gaudy cotton prints, pour out of the main gate; and the village comes to life like an unexpected flash flood. They come to fetch water from the lake outside the village walls; a lake hidden from view by a series of earth dams, which hide a mango grove and fertile fields beyond.

The women carry earthen-ware pitchers or shining brass ones, balanced with easy grace on their sullen heads. Then at sunset, accompanied by children, they go out to the lake again, to bathe and wash clothes. But the trains, which daily pass by at noon and midnight, miss the glorious technicolour of these spectacles and the six hundred and fifty-nine inhabitants of Fatehpur remain a hidden people. This is not deliberate, because every afternoon, at a time when their elders snatch brief siestas, children are to be seen on the ramparts waving to the goods train as its iron wagons go clattering by. They are children of better off parents, though, even for them, such displays of spontaneous enthusiasm are stolen moments before they gather under a banyan tree to recite lessons in word and number, led by a middle-aged, bearded man, wearing a white cloth cap and whom they address as "masterji". In those same hot hours of the day, the children of the poor and destitute work in the fields and manure pits outside the village walls. From their number, the lucky hand-picked ones, armed with slings and pebbles, have the task of shooing birds away to protect the precious crops. They are hired for a pittance by caretaker-farmers who live in huts perched on stilts over fields owned by the two wealthiest landlords: Motilal, the village headman and the even richer *bunnia* or merchant, Seth Lala Murari.

The Sitasar, as the lake is called, is greatly valued. Every year on the eve of *Holi*, that riotous spring festival, the *pujari* or high priest and two assistants chant hymns and prayers by the lakeside *mandir* and make thank offerings of flowers, coconuts and incense to Lord Rama. The offerings are then taken in procession to the sound of bells and drums and thrown into the great *Holika* bonfire that has been lit outside the Maha Narayan Temple. Local legend has it that when Sita, Lord Rama's wife, was abducted by the demon Ravana, who carried her off in his flying chariot, one of her sandals fell to earth and where it landed the ground wept. The tears collected to form a pool, giving credence to the fact that the water is brackish. Then, in the twelfth century, the pool was deepened and extended into a lake by Jai Singh, one of the generals of the princely state of Dinapur. He built dams, landscaped the fields behind it and planted mango trees below the high ground. Today, that mango grove, along with the sugarcane, sorghum and maize fields are a source of Lala Murari's wealth. Beyond his fields is also a grove of *mohwa* trees and a secret distillery, where cane juice and the *mohwa* berries are used to make an intoxicating rum-like spirit. But by employing six *Bhil* tribesmen to work the stills, Murari caused much consternation in the village. For ages Fatehpuris have avoided contact with their *Bhil* neighbours for reasons of caste and because they take pride in having a temple dedicated to Vishnu, a god they consider far superior to the household gods that the *Bhils* worship with wild ritual and superstition.

Four *Bhil* settlements are within a radius of twenty miles from Fatehpur, but apart from the hamlet of Bodi, they are little more than a wretched collection of mud huts. The *panchayat*, Fatehpur's governing body, discouraged having *Bhils* in their midst by banning the sale of *daru* or spirits within the village walls. But they were helpless to prevent Murari setting up a canteen near the railway station. Murari managed to secure a licence from the State Government for his distillery and got permission to build an ice and soda-water factory. Liquor, in poor hardworking communities is an irresistible temptation, and the elders faced a losing battle. They hoped that when the State Government's impending prohibition laws came into force, Murari's business would collapse. They were to be disappointed. Murari threatened to renege on the contract that had given him a monopoly over the production of gram, ground-nuts and sesame seed. The economy of Fatehpur relied heavily on his commerce. It was blackmail and gave the village headman, Motilal, no option but to co-operate. And so, even before State Prohibition arrived, Murari had ensured for himself a growing and productive market.

Seven miles away, among the low hills on the Eastern horizon, the river Kunti, a small seasonal stream, becomes a dry course in summer and a stagnant, shallow lake in the June to August season of rains. During the building of the Sitasar dams, Jai Singh's workers discovered the spring, which had subterranean links with the Kunti, but they decided it unwise to destroy the myth of the Sitasar. Besides, they could not explain why the water in the large well outside the village, used for irrigating the fields and also fed by the Kunti, is sweet, while that of the Sitasar is both brackish and undrinkable. The mystery of the myth remains.

In the village itself, drinking water is drawn from two small wells, and a nominal annual tax, based on each householder's ability to pay, is levied for their upkeep. The wells are kept covered and padlocked and sentries, appointed by the *panchayat*, supervise the strict rationing of water. Every morning, between the hours of eight and ten, the wells are opened for the daily ration of one large pitcher-full per person. No one complains. Water is precious and made sacred by the temple authorities, who have proclaimed that anyone who took more than the allotted share will bring upon the village a curse and a punishment from the gods: the drying up of the wells.

Only women collect water, no man will be seen near a well. Single men will have some woman—mother, wife, sister, daughter or some volunteer, to collect his ration. The use of the wells follows a discriminatory practice by which higher caste women collect water before lower caste ones. But, the Government of India frowned upon such discrimination and, officially, this practice was supposed to have ended some time ago. The ruling was announced with great reluctance, but as none of the outcast villagers seemed keen to take up this new freedom, there is little evidence of change in the day to day life of the village. It comes as no surprise. In remote corners of the India, communal reforms are slow to establish. The village governing *panchayats*, who dislike outside interference, drag their feet on laws that weaken their powers or break with tradition.

Fatehpur's main gate, the *Burra Uttar Darwaza* or Great Northern Doorway, is an impressive edifice of yellow sandstone. Smaller versions of it mark the other points of the compass. Of these, the South Gate, now blocked by fallen rock and masonry, once had a watchtower. The West Gate is for the exclusive use of Fatehpur's menial workers, among them, the families of three sweepers, a potter, two cobblers and a Muslim butcher. One other Muslim family in this very Hindu community is that of Billu Khan, the Pathan watchman. "Billu" was the nickname, given by the villagers, after *billy*, the Hindi word for cat, because his eyes are a cat-like greyish green. The land beyond this gate is stony and wild with cactus and *babul*—the thorny mimosa. The main drain of the village empties its effluence here, and the stench, often overwhelming, is made worse by the fact that the near bank of the drain, outside the gate, is used as an open-air lavatory.

The East Gate looks over the vast flat plains. From its terrace one has a fine view of the distant hills. Here, before the coming of the railway, a mysterious Arab trader set up his tent outside the gate and kept a stable of four camels. For many years the village farmers hired them to carry their produce to the market in Biwara, a township less than thirty miles north of Fatehpur. But soon after the arrival of the railway, the man and his camels vanished as suddenly as they had appeared.

With the building of the railway, two-miles of unmetalled road, but with firm earth and gravel foundations, was built to lead from the East Gate to Fatehpur's railway station. That station, little more than a siding, consists of a cemented brick platform and a signal-box. Here the slow train announces its arrival at noon with long blasts of its steam whistle; but the midnight Express speeds past the sleeping village. In late October, bullock carts may be seen trundling down the road with their loads of sugarcane, maize, and terracotta pottery—wheat, sorghum and other cereals are seldom surplus to the needs of the village. Occasionally the village cobbler may be seen driving a donkey cart to collect a consignment of used car tyres, which come by arrangement from a scrap merchant in Biwara. These he cuts up for resoling sandals and shoes at half the cost of leather. More often, in its moving cloud of dust, a perky Ford Prefect can be heard on the road. It is one of the two cars owned by Motilal. The other, an old black Chevrolet, also owned by him, has never moved since its noisy, backfiring arrival three years ago, but stays jacked up on bricks under a pipal fig tree next to his large lime-washed brick house. It needs a new gear-box, but Motilal is content to do nothing about that. It remains on its plinths, lovingly polished to a gleam by his driver, Bisham Singh, a retired Indian army sergeant. It is Bisham's toy and when he is not driving his master to the station, where his son Vinod combines the job of stationmaster and signalman, he can be found tinkering with the Chevrolet aimlessly. Why he spends so much time on it remains a mystery. But as village headman, Motilal, the most powerful and fitfully benevolent member of the village council is duly respected and his cars add to his prestige. Behind his house is an oil-press, located in the centre of a sunken circular pit. It is operated by a pair of bulls, yoked under a long wooden shaft. When put to work the animals are blindfolded to prevent them getting vertigo, as they go round and round treading the same circuit. A mud and cow-dung plastered terrace surrounds the press. It is swept clean and on it cakes of the sesame seed, from which the oil has been extracted, are left to dry in the sun and stored as cattle-feed in the long low shed that runs the full length of the terrace. The walls of this shed are almost always covered with drying pats of cow dung, while on its corrugated zinc roof is a thick layer of reed and grass thatch. Under this roof, in a far corner of the shed, is a Norton motorbike that belonged to Motilal's only son, Captain Krishna Mathur. In 1941, Krishna joined the 2nd British Infantry Division as a Liaison Officer, but was reported missing after a Japanese counter attack in the Assam Hills near Kohima. He chose to join the Army against his father's wishes but with his mother's support. Normally, in a Rajput household, Motilal's objections would have prevailed, however, and this was a well-kept secret, he always deferred to his wife, Rukmini, a woman of influence and education. Her father was chief clerk to the Rajah of Mandipur and Motilal owed his appointment of village headman to him. As an only son and a good-looking young boy, Krishna was made much of and grew up to be spoilt and independent. Much of his youth was spent with his grandfather, who hired tutors to teach him English and through his considerable influence in high places, got him into the Prince's School in Rajnagar. During school holidays, he took Krishna with him on his visits to the royal palaces of Rajasthan. Krishna admired the grand portraits of Rajahs decked in Indian Cavalry uniforms, and was smitten. He wanted not only to join the army but, like the Rajput princes he met, to study in England, at Wellington College, and from there on to Sandhurst.

'Why not?' Murari said, when Motilal told him about his son's ambitions. 'You are a rich man. You can afford it? And I will be making you richer still.'

'No son of mine is crossing the black waters. England will give him wrong ideas and turn him of little use to me in my old age.'

'*Arrey*, nonsense! Listen to me. I was surprised you agreed to his future career in the army, without consulting me. I too am not happy to have an army officer as son-in-law. But I let it pass.' Murari's chubby round face broke into a sly grin. 'I see that you have allowed him take on his maternal grandfather's surname, Mathur. These sort of decisions matter to some people…not to me. But whose idea was that?'

Motilal stared. Was Murari prying? 'You sometimes talk in riddles, my friend.'

'I meant, what did your wife think about his joining the army!' Murari dodged.

'My son's a Rajput. We are a martial people. The army will do him good. And is he not a prince among…should he not have a surname befitting his status?'

'Yes. Who am I to question! I'm just a merchant.'

'No insult was intended. You and I have educated wives. So in many ways we are above old ideas and stifling traditions.'

'Indeed, but as elders among simple folk we must not break too many rules, for the sake of the community. So now that my daughter, Veena, is eight and your son is twelve, the *sagai*, the formal betrothal, should take place soon.'

Motilal's hesitated a moment. Rukmini had more than once drawn attention to the fact that while Murari had more money he was a *bunnia* and so of a lower caste, but she was also aware of their close business ties and wisely raised no serious objection to a liaison that the village community assumed was inevitable. 'Yes, most certainly, and before my son goes to the Princes College. But, one thing you must understand. By Army rules, no officer may marry before he is twenty-five. Did you know that?'

'I know. That rule is not legally binding...more to do with entitlement to married quarters. It presents no real obstacle to our plans. We can still have his *barat* when he's seventeen, eighteen. In any case, Veena will be of child-bearing age when he is twenty-five.' Murari embraced Motilal. 'Don't forget dowry my Veena will bring him and you? He'll be the richest young officer in the Indian Army.'

Motilal waved a hand. 'Then it's settled.' With a spring in his step and a sense of well-being he took his leave. It was time for the midday meal. Rukmini would be waiting for him. He folded his hands and raised them to heaven. The fates had been kind to him, and he was particularly pleased that Rukmini had supported him in the matter of not letting their son Krishna cross the *kala pani*, the black waters. 'He'll lose caste and respect in the community,' he had told her. 'We are not royalty. They are a law unto themselves. They have no one to answer to.'

In agreeing, she had saved him much embarrassment because it was known that he, like Murari, was anti-British. With a son in England he would have had much explaining to do at the village council. It suited Rukmini to give in to her husband on some occasions, and this was one of them; also, to have her beloved son away from her would have been hard for her to bear. Besides, since Motilal owed her much and her father even more, she knew she could always get her way—though it was not in her nature to take advantage of the imbalance her influence had created in a Rajput household that ought to be exemplary in the sight of the Fatehpur community. As a Rajput she was orthodox enough to know that a Hindu wife is twice blessed by the respect and obedience she gives to her husband, her lord and master. And it was the commitment she made when at their wedding they ate off the same silver *thali*, knowing full well that it was the first and last time they would eat together. From then on she had to be pleased to serve his meals, squat on the floor by his side and gently fan him and keep the flies off him, while he ate. Motilal, in turn, would feel unable to begrudge those occasions when he gave in to one used to a more sophisticated life-style than he could provide. Nor could he analyse his own feelings for Rukmini. If he was told, as he stood by her funeral pyre, that his tears proved there had existed a deep and binding love in their relationship, he would not have understood what that meant. Of one thing he was certain; no woman would take her place, not in his life, not in his home. Rajput widowers are encouraged to remarry, for a man should not be without a woman, but Motilal, Headman of Fatehpur, was not to be pressed.

Krishna was still at school when his mother died. She had succumbed to the small-pox epidemic, which had decimated the population of Fatehpur, twenty-six years ago. Motilal's heavily pocked-marked face, while it still bore the memory of being handsome, and evidence of his own lucky escape, reminded the villagers of his heroic conduct during those dreadful days. His reputation of being a hard man was revised when he strictly quarantined his home and the homes of the infected, thereby controlling the death toll. He rationed the grain and asked people distributing it, to leave a grain ration outside the homes of the stricken. The men were also told to watch, at a safe distance, those who came out to collect the food, and report any improvement in their health and situations...

Krishna's disappointment at not schooling in Britain was offset by the thought that an army career kept him away, for much of his time, from village life, which he found increasingly tedious, and though, at first, father and son were estranged by Krishna's decision to a serve in the British Indian Army, they were reconciled when he agreed to marry the girl Motilal chose for him. Veena, the eldest of Murari's three daughters was no stranger to Krishna. As children they had played together, till, aged thirteen, Krishna left Fatehpur to school in Rajnagar. A year later, so that Veena would not be educationally disadvantaged, Murari sent her to a Convent school, in Lucknow, where she stayed with an aunt until she returned to be Krishna's wife.

In their early years of marriage, the young couple moved from one military post to another and Veena soon grew to dislike army cantonment life. She found excuses to return to her father in Fatehpur and it was not long before she realised their marriage was failing. There never was passion in their relationship, nor anger, nor exchange of accusations: simply a dying fall, a fading away of commitment. Krishna had been far too ambitious to mind Veena's absences. An unhappy wife was an inconvenience, if not a hindrance, but fortunately for him, even before active service took Krishna to Burma, Veena had already moved back to her father's house—the grandest and the only two-storied building in Fatehpur.

Before leaving Krishna, Veena was determined to have a child. In a business-like way she overcame their sibling-like relationship and set about fulfilling her father's desire for a grandchild—a strategy in which she succeeded.

Murari, even more anti-British than Motilal, hated the idea of any Indian fighting for them; and he and the Anglicised Krishna were seldom long together without sharp exchanges about the British, War and national politics. Murari believed a Japanese victory would rid India of British rule, insisting, when Krishna said he would rather be ruled by the Brits than the Japs, that Japan had no long term plans to rule India. Yet, like everyone else, who knew Krishna, he too was charmed by him and when the tragic news came that Krishna was no longer missing, but had been captured and executed by the Japs; he genuinely was broken by the news. However, when there was talk of Veena's *suttee*, Murari reacted with fury. A wife's *suttee* is correctly performed on her husband's funeral pyre, and Krishna's body was never found. Besides, Veena was pregnant and he urged the priests to remind the villagers that mothers were exempt from *suttee*. This the priests did. The talking ended only after Murari left his mansion in Fatehpur and took his widowed daughter and grandson to live with him in Biwara, returning once a week, every Tuesday, for a few hours in the day, to keep an eye on his business interests...

Krishna's only contribution to the life of his village had been the setting up, ten years ago, of a shop for bicycle sales and repairs. But though he was able to locate it in the clean and spacious market square next to the temple, it made little impact. The villagers came, stood, gaped at the bicycles in wonder and then slipped away. '*Arrey* they're waiting for two things,' his father said: 'firstly, the completion of the road to Biwara, and secondly, someone to teach them how to ride a bike. The price of a bike is lot of money to them. Your customers are likely only to be Veena's brothers, and are a useless lot when it comes to outdoor activity. In any case they live in Biwara.'

But Veena had inherited her father's business acumen and on taking over her husband's legacy, she had the good sense to realise that the road linking Biwara to Fatehpur was at least a decade away, and transferred the bicycle shop to her town, permitting Chotu Ram, the village *durzee*, to move into the vacated premises at a rent that was a tenth of his income. The village tailor had another condition to meet before he took over the shop. Veena had taken to designing women's clothes, and Chotu Ram had to make and display these prominently, and a third of the sale price was to be handed to her.

With the Vishnu Temple as its hub, Fatehpur radiates from there to its perimeter walls in concentric circles. These were designed to serve as caste boundaries, which were meant to keep its lower caste inhabitants to the outer rings. But an over-spill of menial workers around the West Gate broke the scheme and a bulge in the west of the village led some pariahs, that is people without caste, to encroach into the inner circles. In time, and entirely for commercial reasons, even the protected temple area could not remain exclusively for the priestly Brahmins and warrior caste Rajputs. Lower caste *bunias* or merchants had to be allowed to set up shops and to live in their premises. Among them, Mangal Singh, the *halwai*, or sweet-maker, who took on the role of a medic, and dispensed borax eye-drops free to children suffering from mild conjunctivitis and brown fennel and dill seed placebo pills for those with minor tummy upsets.

The Maha Narayan Temple to Vishnu is raised on a square pyramid of steps. It was on these steps that Motilal's mother, Girja Devi, had found the abandoned baby six years ago…Regularly at about two o'clock in the afternoon, the old woman would draw water from the temple well, which lay under the shelter of a sacred pipal tree. There she would bathe, change into a clean white sari—as mother of the village headman she could do this at the well without raising objections—then climb the temple steps, enter the porch of the temple, ring the large bell that hangs from its central arch, fold her hands and bow her head in prayer. On that day, when the sound of the bell died down, she heard the crying of the child. Girja started, listened and, having located where the crying sounds came from, went down the temple steps and behind the main entrance. The child had been left on the lowest step. Girja Devi was a kind and wise old woman. Many young mothers-to-be had turned to her for advice and help and now she knew at once why the child had been abandoned. Girja Devi cradled the boy in her arms and rocked him till he stopped crying. She looked around and called out. 'Are you there? Come out. Don't hide. I can help you. I'll care for you and your son.' She put the child down, waited, and called out again. The boy started to cry and jerked his hands. She picked him up and the child tugged at her lose bodice. 'You must be hungry,' the old woman whispered.

On her way home, she passed the *pan* shop. The *panwalla*, a coarse, rather loud man, called out to her. '*Arrey Mataji*!' (All the villagers addressed Girja Devi with the respectful title of "Mother" or "Deviji".) 'I saw the mad woman leave that bundle there. She did not return to collect it. Is it a child? Must be her child.'

The woman stopped. 'Look, it is a beautiful boy child.'

'Chee! Chee! He'll be some untouchable *Bhil* baby; unclean and defiling to touch. Keep him away from me. Let not even his shadow fall on my person. Or I shall have to bathe seven times.' The man held up his Brahmin string, which ran across his bare chest, by his thumbs, and waved his hands, as if to ward off evil.

'Not so,' said the woman. 'Here, look at the boy. He has a light complexion and no untouchable or low caste child will have such fine features. Do you presume to teach me about caste matters? *Bhils* are almost black. You should know that, if you have eyes in your head. *Arrey*, I dangled you in my arms when you were born. And even you were not half as beautiful as this boy.'

'But Mother, there must be some bad reason for any child to be left there. I have been watching for some time. It is a wonder the *langurs* did not pick up the child?'

Langurs, the black-faced, long tailed, grey monkeys, lived and frolicked in the branches of the large, spreading banyan tree, near the Temple and under which the *panwalla* sets up his stall every morning. The woman drew nearer. '*Arrey*, speak of the monkeys with respect. They are sacred children of Hanuman. And have you not noted, when they gather together there are never more than seven? Every Brahmin knows seven is an auspicious number...' She hesitated as if in doubt. 'But long time now I have not seen that number. Don't seem to be seven left, now.'

'That's because the main colony moved to Biwara. Hast thou not seen them at the Biwara railway station? It is festooned with monkeys.'

'Biku, why would I go to Biwara?'

Biku rolled his head. 'Believe me, they have become a damn nuisance. They raid the trains and harass the train passengers. Children of Hanuman! Huh!'

'Biku, if you drove them away, some evil fate will befall you. Mark my words.'

'Mother, I don't believe in all that nonsense. My protector is goddess Lakshmi.'

'Spoken like a bunia.' The old woman shook her head, pressed the child to her breast and moved on.

But her son Motilal was unhappy. 'Mother, what have you done? See, the boy is hungry. See how he searches to be fed.'

'My dugs may be dry!' Girja Devi shouted, 'but...' Her son gestured her to keep her voice down. She took a deep breath. 'I have thought with great care. I'll not let this child die. *Hai Ram*! Padmini is full with milk. She can suckle the boy.'

'Our cook Padmini? She has her own child to feed.'

'She can spare a little. Seen how big her breasts are? Like melons. All that *ghee* she robs from us...' Girja Devi was interrupted by the sound of Motilal striking his forehead with the palm of his hand. 'Don't do that! Lately you have been showing a lot of impatience. Listen, whenever Padmini can't,' she continued, 'I'll dilute cow's milk with water that has been blessed by the temple priest. It'll be doubly sacred— *gow mata,* mother cow, is holy—and will give the boy strength. Just leave me to it... to...and since when does a man know more than a woman? My maternal instincts have never failed me.'

Motilal threw up his hands. 'Well, do what you want. Old age, they say, truly casts its spell of madness. Anyway, that child won't live. Not without his real mother.' Motilal left the room.

'See! As I said, you know nothing.' She shouted after him.

Motilal returned with frowning deeply. 'What do you mean? I can't be the village headman and be accused of knowing nothing. Mother you do...'

'*Arrey*, just you wait. The boy will live…he's *Bhagwan* Vishnu's gift to me. For too long my life has been loveless. All that's been left for me till now is to patiently await death. Evil spirits took away my grandson, Krishna. But now, great god, Harè Ram a, gives me a gift to bless my last remaining days.'

'Then, ungrateful mother, pray that the gods give you a long life, because once you've gone, I'll not have a fatherless child in the house. I can't. I am the village headman and my role is an example to all. Understand?'

'I shall call him Balaram, the child of Rama, Lord Vishnu's gift to me.'

'Make up your mind. Rama or Vishnu?'

'Fool. They are the same. Lord Rama is an *avatar* of god Vishnu.'

'And in time he will be called Bal for short. Thought of that? Bal means child. Fancy how he'll feel to be called "child" all his life. Yes, yes, it also means hair. That is even worse. But have you heard? I said I'll not foster him. He will be homeless. Better to let some low caste woman bring him up in a permanent home. I'll make enquiries when the elders meet. I'll find a mother for him. I am not headman for nothing.'

'I will not let you do that. With my dying breath, I will see to it that he goes to my brother's house.'

Motilal hooted. 'Randhir Singh?' He laughed derisively. 'Krishna called him Uncle Randy. And randy he is. You know what randy means? You'll understand when I tell you he keeps a woman in Biwara. Sujata found that out and wanted her brothers to give him a good thrashing. I saved him from that indignity. Did I not?'

'You! It was me. I told his wife, Sujata. I reminded her that I knew she did not care for my brother. I told her not to listen to empty gossip and rumour and as she didn't care why should she mind even if the rumours were true? "Why," I said, "why upset peace of a home? Apji," she calls him Apji. I said, "Apji gives you clothes and jewellery. Be content and enjoy that." She loves Bombay *halwa*. Loves sweets, that's why she's so fat. He brings her packet after packet.'

'If that boy lives, he won't thank you for it. Randhir will make him work at the oil mill, morning, noon and night. And he'll beat the boy soundly for every mistake he makes. You know, if he wasn't afraid of her brothers, he would like to beat his wife too. So he'll take it out on the boy, when he is drunk. Why do you think their son ran away? First chance he got, he went. God knows where he is. Randhir is...'

'My brother is not a bad man. It's the demon drink. It makes him do bad things. And you don't have the guts to stop Murari selling drink.'

'He spends more time in Biwara. That's where he does most of his drinking.'

'You forget. If it wasn't for Randhir we wouldn't have a railway station. And still you did not make him an elder in the *panchayat*.'

'We were happy without the station. He also wanted a post office and a *Tar*...a wire...telegraph office. We don't need all that. Fatehpur is well without the modern world knocking on our door. And Biwara is near enough if we need...I know he's your youngest brother, but you and your mother spoiled him...now Randhir is an old *saand*...a servicing bull. A violent man, who drinks and still chases women.'

'Well, then, you tell me what should I do for the boy after I'm gone?'

'Give him up, now. I'll pay a *bhil* woman to bring him up and soon she will let him beg for his bread like any orphan does. And work for whoever will hire him, like that other village orphan. That – that *musalman* boy, Asif. He's lucky to be here. Thanks to Rukmini, this is a kind village. There are villages where orphans and low-caste people are ill-treated, abused...sometimes even killed.'

'I would rather he was free than to be brought up by some low-caste woman.'

'Why not, mother? Most likely he's low-caste too.'

'Let it be. I know he's not. Look at his face. His skin is light and his features are sharp. That is not the face of a low caste child.'

Motilal bent over, and pulling the child's blanket down, started. 'Fair? Yes, much too fair. I hope he's not some Britisher's child? Half-caste.'

'Nonsense. He's no lighter than our Krishna was. Oh, what a beautiful baby he was. Remember? Moti? I used to call you "Moti" my little pearl. For your son's sake, give this child…*Hai Raam!* ' Girja Devi held the child up like an offering.

'All right! All right, mother. But let Sujata find a *dai,* a wet nurse. Another thing to remember, Sujata gets little house money from Randhir. That boy will starve.'

'I will give her my money for the boy. I will leave, in his name, all my *javery*.'

'Your jewellery?'

'Yes, even my mother's gold necklace. When I am gone, Vishnu's gift to me must live on.'

'Do you realise the boy will still be a minor after you have gone? Randhir will bully Sujata and spend all your legacy on drink. Nothing of yours will benefit the boy. He will be abandoned and become a gypsy among the *Bhils*.'

'Then you must help. See that does not happen.'

The fate of Bal went exactly as Motilal predicted. He was four when Girja Devi died. Her ashes were taken by her son to Benares, to be blessed and scattered on the River Ganges. Six months after his return the boy was handed over to the care of a childless *Bhil* woman, who once a week called at Sujata's house to sort the wheat grains before milling it into flour. But the lazy, self-indulgent Sujata was not entirely without a conscience. When Bal was six, she sought to allay her feelings of guilt.

'Bal!' she called. 'Now listen well. You are six. Old enough to herd cattle for grazing by the river. Soon it will earn you good money. Then you can help Daadi. She's been good to you. Made sacrifices for you. But she is old and poor. You owe her a lot. I've arranged to have Jaswant, the herdsman, teach you his trade. He's also old. Maybe in ten, twelve years, you can do his job.'

The boy nodded but said nothing. He understood what she said and intuitively knew he was facing another time of abandonment and hardship. Fear of the unknown gripped him and made his tiny body tremble. But he refused to plead or cry. He was not going to let Sujata or anyone else see him cry. His helplessness and dependence on adults angered him and hardened the look with which he stared back at Sujata.

'How dare you look at me like that? Where's my cane. I'll thrash the life out of you! You, you ungrateful dog!' The boy ran to the old woman as Sujata tried to jump out of bed, slipped and fell heavily on her ample bottom. The old woman covered her face and tried in vain to hide her giggling with that part of her sari which went over her head and shoulder. Like women of her tribe the sari below her waist was tied like a man's *dhoti*. It was this part of the garment the boy clung to, as he took shelter behind her.

'*Hai rey*! Bala,' cried the old woman in alarm. 'Don't pull my *dhoti*!'

'Control yourself, woman!' Sujata shouted breathlessly and, raising herself with difficulty, she sat down heavily on her *charpoy*. 'Take this fan. Fan me. What's this? Still grinning? Laughing at me? How dare you? It's not funny.'

'I do not laugh at you, my queen!' The old *Bhil* peasant woman lifted her hands in placation and drawing near the cot, fanned urgently. 'The boy made me laugh. What the boy was doing made me laugh. Another pull at my *dhoti* and I would have been naked as a *langur*. Please, don't be angry. The child means no disrespect… see he smiles. No, no, not to insult you. He is smiling because he understood what I said about my being naked as a monkey.'

'Shut your mouth! *Besharam*. Have you no shame? Speaking like that in front of the boy. Naked like a monkey, huh! And I don't care what you say. I think he is laughing at me. Give me that fan. Slap his face for me.'

'No, no my Rani, pity the poor motherless child. See those eyes…those so lovely large brown eyes of his?'

'Hush, Daadi, don't say that. You will cast the evil eye. *Nazar*. I know how much you love the boy, but always better to say something negative. Never praise. At least, not to his face. As I said, you will cast the evil eye.'

The old woman rolled her head in solemn agreement. 'I shall throw some salt and chillies into the fire, before I cook my meal. That will remove the evil eye.'

'Yes, do that as soon as you can.' Sujata stared at the boy. The boy stared back with stern disapproval. 'See, that *Daadi*. Just see!' screamed Sujata. 'That look he's giving me? Don't tell me that's not defiance.'

The old woman put on a stern expression. Shaking the boy, she turned him around and gave him a gentle push. 'Go. Go out and play. Soon you will have no time for play. Make the most of it. See those boys there. Join them. They're playing *gilly-danda*.'

'They won't let me play,' said the boy sullenly, 'and I don't know the game.'

'Go, then, watch. It's nothing. That small piece of wood, which is pointed at both ends, that's the *gilly*, which you tip with the *danda*, the big stick, and when the *gilly* jumps in the air you hit it as hard as you can...That's all there is to it. Go now.' The woman waited till the reluctant child went outside and shut the door behind him.

'You've spoiled the boy. When did you last give him a thrashing?'

'My Rani, I did, many times, at the beginning. But now I find it hard. He frightens me. Sometimes when he sits very still and watches me, I tremble. It's like seeing a murthi, an idol, a little god. He is blessed with long eyelashes and beautiful eyes...It is Lord Krishna's eyes and in their depths I sense power. Good and bad. Both. Power of a god and the curse of the devil.'

'Now, *Daadi,* you're talking rubbish. How can a little orphan have power?'

'No, no my Rani! I believe the goddess Saraswati has blessed him with wisdom. He is very clever. You should have sent him to the village school.'

'That's what Motilal said to my husband. But it meant keeping the boy here. I didn't want that. Many children here don't go to the school. And of the few that go, the schoolmaster wants to know everything about them. So inquisitive he is. There's enough rumour and gossip in the village, without adding scandal. Why do you think I wanted you to keep him? What about your village? Is there no school there?'

'Ours is no village. We don't even have a marketplace.'

'How do you know he's clever?'

'My niece, my sister's child, she...'

'Sister! You have a sister? I didn't know you had a sister.'

'My dead sister's child, my niece...her husband runs a *kabari* shop. They go to people's houses and collect paper, empty bottles... things people don't want. The *sarpanch* gave her some old school books that his son...'

'Oh, you mean Krishna's primary school books...*Arrey hah*, I told Motilal to get rid of them because of Girja Devi. His mother. Every time she saw them, she would press them to her heart and

In the Shadow of a Dream

start crying *toba toba*. But of what use keeping them? Those were ABC English school books...and so long time ago.'

'She kept them so that one day her own son would learn from them and become a sahib, like Motilal's son. But that was not to be.'

'That is what I mean. One can't learn English if you don't know English.'

'No Rani. Niece knows a little. But god has not blessed her with children.'

'I see. But what is all this to do with Balaram?'

'One day I took him with me when I went to see her and she gave him a slate for the boy to draw on. And he did. She got a shock. He had drawn pictures, my niece said, that were like the English letters in those books. So she showed them to him and he told her that when he was with Girja Devi, she let him see those books. My niece wanted to give the books to Bal, but I said no. There is no place in my hut to keep such things. But whenever we visit her, she lets him look at the books and even tells him the letters she knows. She has even started on some Hindi letters. She says she only has to show him once, and he was able to say the letters and write them, also.'

'*Arrey*, if she is so impressed, why doesn't she keep the boy?'

The old woman shook her head sadly. 'Don't talk Rani. Gomji, her husband, is a hard man. He wants nothing to do with Bal. Says he is a half-caste orphan. Anyway they are now in Ajmer. His brother arranged to get Gomji a job on the Railways. But before going, my niece felt sorry for Bal and gave him an old book and a pencil for him to draw and write. He does all funny things on it. I don't know what.'

'All this talk is a waste of time. I want the boy to do as I say. As I said, you have spoiled him. Soon he will be no good to anyone.'

'But Kanti, that's my niece. She says that it seemed as if he already knows some secret things.'

'Enough Daadi, enough of this nonsense. Forget it.' Sujata lay back on her cot. 'There, press my legs; nice and hard. Yes. Now tell me the news. When you came in this morning, you said you had some news. What was it you were going to say?'

'What about...Oh, that! Oh, that is simply...gossip. Just gossip, nothing more.'

'You were going to tell me about his…mother, his real mother. You heard some news about his mother. Rumours have been going round, but I'm always the last to know any scandal. Now, no more dodging! You are an ungrateful woman. I pay you good money, and you hide things from me. You should have told me before. As soon as you knew.'

'I didn't tell you because, maybe, there is no truth in the story I heard. Our *Bhil* women are such gossips. And they make up stories.'

'Never mind about all that. Go on. Tell me.'

'It has been a rumour among our women folk, that some six years ago. A group of our women, drawing water from the well at Bodi—that's the name of our little *Bhil* village…'

'Yes, yes, I know, I know. Go on, will you.'

'It was by the well at Bodi, that a starving, ragged, wild, distraught woman…At first the women thought she was a *churael,* that is a witch…'

'Will you get on with the story! You don't have to explain everything to me.'

'Well, this woman, she started to scream at the women, something like "where's my baby?" "What have you done with my baby?" And "give me back my boy". The women called out to Bhima, our village headman. He came. Lucky for her he is a kind man. Another man would have threatened her with his lathi and driven her away. Instead, he gave her a glass of buttermilk and listened to her story. She rattled on in some language he could not understand. Then she spoke in Hindi, but it made no sense to him. There was nothing he could do. His wife—Bhima's wife is my sister—she calmed her down; and saw to it that she had a bath and combed her hair. Bhima got interested in the woman's story. He remembered that some years ago he had been asked about a missing woman. The Bombay police had approached him about it at the time.'

Sujata shook her head gravely and clicked her tongue. 'There are many, I should say, hundreds of reports of missing peoples in Bombay and Gujarat. Of wives running from husbands; children from parents, jobless, starving men, but mostly of boys who jump on trains to Bombay and other big towns to find work. The police do nothing. They make half-hearted inquiries, then do nothing.

They don't find anyone. They just file their reports. It means nothing, unless husbands or parents turn up and make them get off their backsides and see that they do something. Mind you, if it is a missing woman they find wandering the streets, they take her to their police station, lock her up, then at night four or five of them rape her. After that they drive her back into the streets and dump her. I don't trust the police. That's why, if a young woman is missing, wise parents keep *chup*. They are afraid what the police will do. So many cases of women gang raped.' Sujata paused, contemplating the evoked situation with some excitement and heavy breathing. When she regained her composure, she said: 'Have you heard anything about a husband? If she was with child, even if she was not married…someone will know something about who the child's father is, and definitely about the where and when the child was born…'

'I don't know, No one has said anything about all that. My sister said that the mad woman's mother and father did come from Goa to collect her. It took them four days before they reached our village. By then the woman had become quite submissive. But before her parents arrived she begged my sister not to mention the baby to them, especially as the baby was missing. My sister began to respect her. She said she was educated woman.'

'A *kala memsahib*,' chuckled Sujata. 'The ones who put on airs and try to pass off as Anglo-Indians…But *kala*. You know *kala*, black? They're black as coal because a lot of them are low caste or no caste. Becoming Christians, as my husband says, for a bowl of rice.'

The old woman stared in blank astonishment. 'And,' Sujata went on, 'how can any mother not remember about having a baby? She must have really gone mad.'

'She remembered about having a baby in Basirabad Hospital.'

'Arrey, Basirabad is miles away. Near Ajmer. Can't be. And what sort of mother? Not to tell her parents, means she did not care about her child and its fate. And what about…did she say something about the child's father?'

'Nothing. Though my sister asked.'

'Sister, cousin, niece…Most confusing. Never mind.'

For a moment neither spoke. Then Sujata said: 'If she was a Goan, she'd be *kala*. Goans are dark, with curly black hair and heavy features. So I don't believe the boy could be hers. Look at him. He is quite fair and as you say, everyone talks about his fine features.'

'I don't know what the woman looked like. My sister did not say. But Rani, many Goans are beautiful, some even light coloured with grey eyes.'

'Maybe. I say only what my husband says. But if she was seen in your village, why do you connect her with Bal. He was found here, in Fatehpur, on the Temple steps. I would think this woman your sister is talking about, her child must be dead.'

The woman rolled her head. 'Most unlikely. But there has been no talk of a dead child. Nothing like that has been heard. On the other hand, this woman was seen six years ago, and our Bal was found six years ago.'

Sujata sighed. 'Still, it can't be. Not if he was born in a hospital. Arrey, why have you stop pressing. There.' Sujata drew her knees up. 'Now do my arms. And press with some force in your hands.' She raised her head and looked at the old woman. 'If you're tired, sit down and press.'

The woman sat on her haunches. 'Rani *bai*, you know, Goans are Christians. And Christians care for orphans and the poor. They have schools. If that boy is alive and if some Christian has found him, he may now be in some orphan school or convent. It is also what Bhima thinks, Bhima our headman.'

'All right, then tell me, has there been any more news since the parents came?'

The woman did not answer.

'What's the matter? Lost your tongue?'

'I am thinking. You must give an old woman time.'

'Don't bother. It is all in the past. Six years, long time in any child's life. There, you can stop now. Go, sift the rice and lentils, then call the boy in.'

'Let me just say this. This is a matter of *Kismet* and, therefore, important. Because even if Bal is her son, his destiny is to be here. I think he believed Girja Devi was his mother, and for her sake he respects you. If at times he sulks, it is because he knows you don't love him.'

'What decent woman would want to acknowledge such a thing; a fatherless boy? Not me!' Sujata yawned and sat up with strenuous effort. 'You make sure he does not know about all this *gup shup*, these rumours. Empty talk. After all, you don't know for sure whether her parents came—I'd be surprised if they did. After all, it's such a disgrace to the family, to any family.'

'Oh, yes. They came. Their daughter had another fit of hysterics when she saw them. Started crying. Asking their forgiveness. They came with someone, a Christian priest or maybe a doctor. He said she was mad, but he knew a place that would take care of her. Some place near Ranchi. Her parents agreed although, my sister said he looked a hard man. *Hi*, my Ranisahib, I may be simple peasant, but I know Ranchi is a thousand miles away in the hills of Bihar. I know, because my husband made the journey to Gaya. He was told the Lord Buddha would cure his broken back...'

'*Bus, bus,* enough. Fat lot of good it did him. People forget that the Buddha was a Hindu first. Silly Hindus convert to Buddhism, I can't see the point. There's another thing I know about Ranchi. It has a *pagal khanna,* a mad house. Once there, always there...no escape.'

'*Bus*, there it ends...Still, *Malkin,* even if Bal is her son, the poor boy will never know his mother. Even if she's alive, she is as good as dead.'

'Yes, but think about his future. This Asif, this Muslim boy...you want him to look after Bal. Do you know anything about him?'

'He's an orphan, too.'

'No, no. At least not to begin with. He was four years old when he was left with Abdul, the butcher. His father was on a *Haj* pilgrimage. From Bombay to Mecca, by dhow, you know, Arab sailing boat. On the way back, somewhere near Karachi, that boat disappeared. Nothing was found. No bodies, not even the boat!'

Daadi shut her eyes, feigned a pained expression, rocked on her haunches, and slapped her forehead with the flat of her palms. '*Hi, Bhagwan*!. God, what a tragedy! But why Abdul? Did the boy not have uncles, aunts...and why did Abdul stop caring for the boy?'

'I don't know. They are Musalmans. The boy is one of them. He is circumcised. But, I believe Abdul's childless wife hated Asif. She used to beat him mercilessly till one day he ran to Motilal for shelter, and Motilal coaxed Jaswant to take the boy on. Motilal's got a soft heart. Pretends to be hard and when he can't do something, he gets other people to do what he can't do. See how, after his mother died, he got round my husband. The result. I'm lumbered with Bal? He did not even bother to ask how I felt. Huh, men can be tyrants.'

The old woman clicked her tongue and shook her head sadly.

'What does that head shaking mean?' Sujata raised her voice. 'Speak, now! *Arrey* Daadi, are you being rude?'

'No, kind Rani, I was just thinking about Bal. What future has the boy got in this village? None. It is a sad fate for such a clever child.'

'What rot you talk sometimes. He's lucky to be alive. He's not starving. I give you enough money? And stop calling me Rani. It sounds like short for *methrani*. What the horrible *memsahibs* call women who clean their latrines.' Sujata lay back. 'Go now. Leave me alone.'

The old woman, who had been sitting on her haunches, paddled up, frog-like, to the cot. Her bony, black and spidery hands sank into Sujata's fat arms. She smiled as she began to knead Sujata's flesh as if it was dough for making chappatis.

'What is wrong with you today. Go! Do what I said.'

Daadi raised her hands penitently. She continued with her massage.

'*Bus*! I told you, enough. Anyway, it's time you went. Take the boy and go. You can sort the lentils and rice tomorrow. One more thing. Don't let Bal play with dogs. Dogs here are mad. They'll bite him. Then he'll go mad also.'

'*Malkin*, there are no dogs or cats in the village.'

'One or two wild ones have been seen. God knows where they come from. Billu, our watchman, has been told to drive them away and keep watch by the shut gate at night. They sneak in, I suppose. Can't stop them. Specially cats. I hate cats.'

'What about monkeys and rats?'

'You're joking! Monkeys are sacred. Rats too, though we kill them. *Arrey*, what's all this giggling? Get out! Go, go, before I lose my temper.'

CHAPTER TWO

Jaswant Singh, the village herdsman, was a tall, thin man with blood-shot eyes. He was seldom seen without his large, bright red turban, which consisted of many yards of thin twisted muslin, giving it a rope-like appearance. He carried a stout staff, at the top end of which were tied, like a bunch of grapes, shiny brass cattle bells. Early every morning he entered the village to collect goats, sheep and cattle, from homes that had hired his services, and would shake his staff as he went from one end of the village to the other, punctuating the jingle-jangle of the bells with full-throated farm animal calls. The bells signalled his employers to free their animals from their briars, while the calls were for the animals. They responded with excited bleats and moos and, without much coaxing, meekly followed him into the low hills beyond the River Kunti. At the rear of this procession was thirteen-year-old Asif, expertly mimicking Jaswant's calls, while the occasional knock on the ground of his bamboo staff, kept the straying animals in check.

On this particular morning, Bal and the old *Bhil* woman stood by, watching and staring with sheer wonder at the gathering and flow of animal life.

'*Arrey*! Asif!' The woman called above the noise of the melee. 'This is the boy. Here, take him with you. He is not yet seven years old but he's big for his age. Look after him. Does he need a *danda* like the one you have got?'

Asif glanced at his staff, which now he carried across his

shoulders with studied nonchalance. 'I'll make him one,' he called back, 'a small one, when we get there,' and coming up to them he took Bal's hand and drew him alongside.

'Mind, you take good care of him.'

'Don't worry, Daadi, he'll be all right. I shall be an elder brother to him.'

'Good. Then I'll keep my promise. I'll feed you; and you can sleep in my *jhoopri*, with him. Here take this. Lunch for you both; bread, pickles and an onion to share.'

Asif's mouth began to water. Daadi's lime and mango pickles were famous in the village and earned her a useful income. He also knew that she was an excellent cook, and the memory of the brinjal curry that Bal once shared with him, made his tummy rumble. Of course, Daadi did not know that Asif had tasted her cooking nor was she aware that the two village orphans were already firm friends, who had met secretly during many hot afternoons, while the adult world took a restful break from their morning labours. Bal, who had started to admire Asif's physical agility, listened avidly to his wild stories, marvelling at Asif's cheek, resourcefulness and self-confidence. Once, at their secret hide-out behind a disused shrine, under an old spreading banyan tree, they sat together, peeling and chewing sugarcane, which Asif had foraged from the fields, till the sticky, sweet juice made them retch. At another meeting at that same secret rendezvous, Asif roasted two bunches of green gram over a makeshift fire, sharing that loot with his new friend. He wouldn't say how or where he acquired his plunder and though Bal begged to be his accomplice in any future raiding expedition, he refused. 'No, you're too young. You'll get caught and then they'll catch me also. I've got a hungry mouth to feed: mine. I don't want to starve. You've got someone to feed you. I have no one. Sometimes, when I'm hungry, I have to beg for food. I hate doing that. I'm no robber. I take no more than I need.' Bal asked if Asif went to the temple, as he did, on feast days, when the priests distributed *puris* and semolina *halva*. 'Asif, it's free; and it is good and tasty.' The older boy shook his head. He explained why he couldn't. 'Most people here are Hindus. The priests give food that has been offered to their idols. I'm Muslim. That food is forbidden to us.' When Bal asked: 'What's Muslim?' Asif scratched his head and after some fruitless thought, solemnly replied: 'Muslim is not

Hindu. My name, Asif, is Muslim name.' But Bal insisted Asif went to the temple. 'When they give out food, the priests won't refuse you.' Asif shook his head again. 'They know I'm Muslim. I was not found, like you, for anyone to claim. My father left me with the butcher, Abdul. I cried. I was four, but I remember crying. I never saw my father again. Soon I realised Abdul's family were angry with my father for leaving me with them and for not returning to collect me. Abdul felt he had to give me a home, but his wife was against it. So he took me to old Hamid, our water carrier's father, who told me stories of the great prophet and taught me that Muslims must never enter Hindu temples. He did not live long and I was taken to the headman, who declared I was an orphan and made me work with Baba Jaswant Singh. I can show you the difference between a Muslim and a Hindu.' Asif felt under his shirt and undid the knot that held up his check, kilt-like *langothi*. 'Look,' he said. Bal stared intently at his penis. 'This means,' Asif said, pointing to his circumcision, 'I'm Muslim. Let me see yours.' In the dark of Asif's hideout they peered at each other's penises till an inner stirring, far beyond their comprehension, made them giggle involuntarily.

Now, recalling that encounter, Asif put his arm round Bal once more and looked at him curiously. Tales and rumours had reached him too. 'You think you're Hindu? But you're not, you know. So, what are you?'

Bal frowned. 'I don't know. Daadi is not my mother. This much I know.'

'Of course, she's not your mother. She is old. She's very black. You are not.' Asif spun his bamboo stick round his neck, and caught it neatly in both hands.

'I have no mother...how did you do that?'

'I've no mother, too. Oh, that? Easy, look!' He caught the stick again, and this time held it in front of him horizontally above the ground and jumped over it. 'But everybody has a mother. Women become mothers. They have babies. I know all about that too.' He pointed to a fallen tree trunk under the shade of a neem tree. 'Sit for a while. Jaswant is slow today. It's burning hot. We'll soon catch up.'

'Tell me, Asif. Tell me about women and babies.'

Asif shook his head. 'Not now. Some day. If people find out I told you, they'll beat me. Grown-ups are cruel. All grown-ups want some excuse to hit and beat you. Don't know why. And when they see a grown-up beating a child, they don't try to stop it. "Good, they say, that's what the boy needs." But I don't let them. I run away and hide and wait till they forget. It is not fair. They can do what they like.'

'Tell me about women. How they become mothers? I won't tell.'

'All right, I'll tell you. Not here. When we get out there, out in the grazing fields.' Asif jerked his head in Jaswant's direction. 'When he's asleep. I'll tell you. Oh, look there! There. See that bull and cow…' he giggled. 'See what the bull is doing? Men do that to women. The same thing. Then the women have babies…same like cows.' A strange, inexplicable excitement made Bal shiver. Asif smirked. He dug Bal in the ribs. 'Don't tell anyone. *Kasam*! Promise!' He held his right hand to Bal and hooked his little finger. Bal linked it with his own, tugged at it, and nodded. Asif had taught him that this ritual meant they had taken a solemn oath. 'One evening,' he whispered, 'I'll take you to Govind Singh's hut. There's a hole from which you can see inside. I'll show you what he does to his wife Gauri.'

'Govindji, who is in charge of the well at Bodi? But Gauri? I thought Gauri is his daughter. Is she not?

Asif shook his head sagely. 'She is his wife. After he's had his dinner, he…no, no, forget it. You'll make a noise and then Govind Singh will thrash us. Forget it. But you'll soon find out. It happens everywhere, all the time.'

Bal made a face and gave a philosophical shrug of his little shoulders. 'Anyway Daadi, won't let us. She says it is bad to peep. What people do in their own *jhopri*, she says, is private.' He waved his hand dismissively.

Asif glanced at him curiously. 'People say you're clever. They call you: "little man". You talk like a man, sometimes…' He yawned and stretched himself. Bal copied him. A sharp call from Jaswant made the two boys jump up.

When the herd reached the grazing grounds at the foothills north of the Kunti river, old Jaswant rested his staff against a *neem* tree, removed his turban to reveal a close cropped head of grey stubble, and with great care placed his turban at the base of the tree, rubbed his eyes, brushed his luxuriant, henna dyed moustache away from his full and sensuous lips, cleared his throat violently and spat. Then, looking about him with satisfaction, he stretched his arms and called out: 'Asif! Listen, you and the boy. Keep watch. I'm resting.' He hitched his *dhoti* above his knees, removed his white calico tunic, which he spread on a grassy patch under the tree and sat down on it, bare torso and cross-legged.

Bal started to walk up to him, but Asif pulled him back violently and placed a warning finger on his lips. 'Daadi said he'll teach me to be a herdsman,' Bal said sullenly. 'If I don't go up to him, how will I learn to…'

'I'll teach you. Remember what I said yesterday evening? How important it is not to get on the wrong side of Jaswant Singh. He never talks. Gives orders only. Yes. He doesn't teach. I learned by watching. He treats boys like animals. Make one mistake and he'll prod you with his stick. That hurts. Or, he'll pull your ears. That hurts worse. There's nothing to being a herdsman. Watch and copy. Use your eyes. Never show fear. I know how to deal with him. He can be kind, but that's when he will try to touch you in a way you won't like. Keep away. He won't chase after you if you stay away. He is old and forgetful.'

'Where's the boy?' Jaswant bawled suddenly.

Asif pressed Bal down. 'Keep low. Don't answer. Don't let him see you. If he asks again, I'll speak.' Jaswant did and Asif said: 'I'm taking him to the gram field. I need help to keep the cattle away from destroying the crops.'

'Good. You show him how.'

'I will,' Asif shouted back, 'he'll soon learn how. He's a clever boy.' Then he whispered to Bal. 'Now watch! He'll take his *goolee*, now.'

'What's *goolee*?'

Asif unwrapped his small white turban, found the end of it, undid a knot and took out a rolled up *pan* leaf. He opened the leaf to reveal a sticky looking small ball, the colour of molasses. 'It's a mixture of ground tobacco and *ganja*. *Ganja*, makes you all groggy and sleepy. I tried some once.' He spat. 'I was very sick.'

'Then why have you got it?'

'For him. When he hasn't got any, he asks me. I give it to him.'
'Why?'
'Because he likes it. I don't care. It knocks him out and gives me two, three hours peace.' Asif gave a triumphant smile and from the top pocket of his soiled and torn tunic, brought out a packet of *bidis*. 'These are for me.'
'You smoke? Where did you get that?'
'The *bidi* shop. I work there, some evenings, rolling *bidis*. I get five annas and one packet of these free. The *golee* I nicked. Worth the risk. When *baba*,' he nodded towards old Jaswant, 'doesn't get his afternoon nap, he can be big trouble. He'll call you and try to give you a *chuma*. A kiss.'
'Now you're frightening me.'
'Don't worry, I'll protect you. He's afraid of me. I shout at him: "Any funny tricks and I'll tell the whole village you're a *gandoo*!" That is someone who likes boys. He wouldn't want that.' Looking away, he added: 'Do you think he heard me?'
Bal shook his head. 'No, he's sitting very still. His eyes are shut.'
'Hindus don't like to be accused of doing dirty things to boys.' Asif, who was sitting frog-like on his haunches, scratched his chest through a hole in his tunic. Then he put a leaf brown *bidi* between his teeth and lit it with a match that needed several strikes before it flared. 'Why are you staring like that? Oh, look! He's chewing his *golee*.'
'Can I have a *bidi*?' Bal asked, tapping Asif's elbow.
Asif stubbed his *bidi* in the earth and stood up. He shook his head. 'No, Bal. I am supposed to take care of you. I promised Daadi. Smoking is bad.' He sighed. 'You know, I've said this before. You have beautiful eyes. When you look at me, like that, I could kiss you.' Asif laughed. 'Don't worry. I won't. I'm no *gandoo*.' He sat down again. 'I'm hungry. I dream of food. Also of Malti. It matters little to me, whom she marries'
'Malti? What's that about? Is she...'
'Yes, little Malti, The *Bidiwalla's* daughter.'
'The man who makes and sells the *bidis* you were smoking?'
Asif nodded. 'Once she brought me some mango pickle rolled up in a *puri*. So I pulled her and gave her a big kiss on the mouth.

Then I got scared. I thought I'll be in trouble the next day. But she didn't tell her father.'

'But she's older than you?'

'She passed by me many times as I sat rolling *bidis*. Looking angry at me and tossing her head like this, all the time. You've seen her? She's pretty. Then, when her father wasn't looking, she gave me a big kick.'

'Why?'

'That was three weeks ago. I haven't seen her since.'

'I have. I was with Daadi. She came with her mother to see Sujata maami. Yes, I remember now. There was talk about her getting married. That's why they came. My Maami gave her a present of a sari and five rupees.'

'Anyway, don't talk about that kiss. Secret, okay.' He watched Bal trying to undo the knot of his food bundle. 'What are you doing? No, not now. After, baba's goes to sleep. I'll show you a nice place. Where there is shade and a small spring. We'll eat there. Not long now.' Asif picked up a stone and flung it with unerring aim at a dwarf date palm. The stone struck it with a thud. 'That tree is dead,' he declared.

'If he sleeps now, when does he eat? He must eat during the day?'

'Don't let him hear you say "he", say "Jaswant baba" or he'll hit you—at six every morning, he has a gourd full of buttermilk and a bowl full of cooked ground maize. At six in the evening his wife gives him the same. Jaswant *Baba* tells me that it the best food in the world. That it makes you strong. He eats nothing in the middle of the day. But when he gets up from his afternoon rest, he has a drink. Fresh milk. He takes it from one of the cows. Yes, he fills his gourd—that yellow thing tied…I haven't seen it today…it's usually tied to his belt. *Baba* maybe old but he's strong. All that stolen milk…' Asif giggled. 'No one finds out. He never takes it from the same cow. But don't talk about this to anyone…or anything I tell you.'

'Is he really old? How old?'

'Seventy, eighty.'

'I'm hungry.'

'Not long…there, I told you. He's out. Asleep now. Let's go. Follow me.'

As they set out together, the bleating of sheep could be heard in the distance, and the whooping of the hoopoe bird seemed to come from nowhere. The day was fresh, and the September landscape, following the rainy season, showed patches of green among the rocks and sandy soil. The hot afternoon sun emphasized the fragility of the greenery, which in a fortnight would turn yellow again.

'You walk too fast,' Bal complained. He stopped to adjust the strap of his sandal.

Asif turned and waited. He stood like a stork on one leg, leaning on his staff and resting the sole of his left foot against his right knee. 'Leave it, the strap's broken.'

'You're barefoot! Don't you have sandals?'

'*Arrey*, yes. Can't you see? Round my neck. Yours have old tyre soles. These are leather, all leather. I wear them only when I have to. Watch out, near that *babul* tree there'll be thorns. Later today, give me your sandals. I'll get them mended. *Mochee*, the village cobbler, is my friend. I do him many favours.' He laughed. 'Don't look at me like that. Swear, I mean it, I'll prove it.'

They shared their lunch and when they had finished, Asif took the boy to the far end of a field, where by a kirkar or thorny mimosa tree were three carefully placed rocks. Asif pointed to them. Then he knelt on the ground and lifted the largest rock. A bubbling trickle of water issued. 'Nobody, not even Jaswant *babu*, knows about this spring. This is my secret. This is clean fresh spring water.' He lifted the other rocks, releasing a gush of water. 'There, make a cup of your hands like this. Tight. Scoop the water, like this. Now drink. I don't let the cattle come here. See that pool lower down, away from the river? That is where they drink. They know where to go. On their own. The new ones follow them.'

A low whistle in the distance gave Bal a start. 'What is that?'

Asif did not answer immediately. He bent down, drank deeply off the spring, then removing his small turban, wet his hands and passed them through his thick jet black hair. 'That's the 2-down, going to Bombay.'

Another low but prolonged whistle blew over the fields and a long trail of smoke above a row of dark green cactus revealed the location of the moving train. 'It would take us less than ten minutes to get there,' Asif said thoughtfully. 'It's so near. Those low *bunds*, field boundaries, are strong mud walls. You can run on them; zig-zag up to the railway.' He slumped down heavily against the gnarled roots of the acacia tree. 'Only ten minutes away from freedom,' he sighed and covered his face in his hands.

Bal stared down at him. 'Are you crying?' He sat next to Asif and putting his arm round Asif's neck, began to cry also. 'I never expected to see you cry? Why, friend, why? Asif, why? I want to be like you... happy and free.'

'I'm not happy. I pretend.' Asif picked up a pebble, studied it, and threw it with an expression of disgust. 'You can't know how much I hide...I've been beaten and abused. For years. People in the village...the butcher, old Jaswant, priests, all found some excuse to shout and hit. Even Malti's father.' He held up his wrists. 'See those white marks? I was your age. He tied my hands with a rope...hung me from a low beam and thrashed me with a cane. You wouldn't want to see my back. It still has scars. All because he accused me of taking two *paisa* from his *pan* tray. I hadn't. But now, I nick things and he knows nothing.'

'To me, you're clever. You know how to get things. And you are strong.'

'I've learned how to avoid beatings by telling lies. Oh, look, look!' The train had slowed down as it approached the small stone bridge over the river Kunti. 'It always goes slow there. So slow, I can run faster...and sometimes it stops. See that *khamba,* that tall post?'

'Lamp post?'

'No, silly. The white one. It's a train signal. That arm thing. Sometimes it is up.'

'It's down.'

'I know, but when it's up the train has to stop. I could climb on to the train and hide. Easy. Hide till it gets to Bombay.'

'Have you done that?'

'No, but one day I will. I dream of Bombay. In Bombay you get rich. There's the cinema and jobs that pay good money for work. Shops never close. At night street lamps shine bright. Tea stalls play loud music. And boys carry tea in glasses to sell. Hotels too...boys can do many jobs. You can polish shoes. You'll see what Jaswant gives me. Four annas for full day...you'll get nothing, you'll see. He'll make some excuse for no money. You're learning, he'll say...

then after one week, maybe two annas. But Bombay, is big, is rich. Shops need boys to run around, to fetch and carry. And if you work at *chaat* stalls, there is free left-over food. And then in the evening, cinema. Tickets are cheap.'

Bal stared at him with eyes full of excitement and wonder. 'What is *chaat*?'

'Oh, brother. Tasty food. Hot, sweet, sour. You can get *chaat* in Biwara. Many times now, I tasted *chaat* in Biwara. And I dream of it.'

'But *Halwai* Mangal Singh makes tasty food.'

'Sometimes only. Like for *Holi* and *Divali*. When Motilal and Murari spend money. Here in Fatehpur people eat at home. No one spends money. And Mangal only makes *puris, katchoris and samosas*. But I have had soft lentil balls soaked in yoghurt and sweet tamarin sauce, with salt, chilli and ground cumin.' Asif brushed his mouth with the back of his hand and made a lip-smacking sound.

'And you. Have you seen Bombay?'

Asif shook his head.

'Then how do you know about Bombay?'

'As I said, I've been to Biwara. The butcher took me one day. There I met Yosef. We became friends. We went to the cinema house. We had no money to buy a ticket, but we climbed up to the roof and looked through a hole in the wall. He told me about Bombay. How he worked as a shoe-shine boy. Sitting on streets outside hotels and cinemas, listening to songs on the radio. Bombay streets are full of music… and you don't have to sleep. Just walk the streets. There always something to see and do and even to eat…you can steal bananas and *chikoos* and guavas from fruit carts left overnight under sheet covers. Of course you can sleep if you want to…just curl up on pavements…Bombay has broad payments, Yosef said, and many railway stations giving you cover from the rain…also small jobs to do…and you can beg from the people who get off the trains…chase after them till they give you something.'

'And the music? Is it like our village priests beating drums?'

'No, donkey. Loud cinema music. Singing, dancing…pretty girls. I saw them that day in the cinema…' Asif hummed a tune. He danced; swinging his hips and waving his hands. 'And the girls shaking their big round...things.' He pointed to his chest. A shout from a distance put an end to his antics.

'Stop that at once or I'll give you a thrashing to remember! You're supposed to be teaching that boy herding. Get on with it.'

'*Arrey baba*, that is what I'm teaching him. Herding, I'm telling him it is not fun or games or like dancing. It's hard work. He must be ready to run with goats and the bulls and chase after them with a stick.'

Jaswant grunted, sat on his haunches, lit a *bidi* and inhaled deeply.

Bal nudged Asif. He was trembling. 'Will I really have to chase the bulls?'

'Yes, why?'

'I'm afraid of the bulls.'

The older boy waved his arm in a gesture of dismissal. Then with a sudden jerk, he pulled the boy down and pinched his cheeks affectionately. 'Come to Bombay with me. We'll get rich in the big city. We'll find jobs. Work for ourselves.'

'What job can I do?'

'You can be a tea boy. Stop shaking. Listen, when I'm gone you'll be alone in the village. Nobody wants you. I know that.'

'But Daadi...'

'Do you really like her?'

'Yes. She's black and ugly; and she has only one tooth.'

'Does she beat you?'

Bal shook his head.

After a moment's thought, Asif said. 'Anyway, she's not your mother. You don't have a mother; and many in the village believe you're a half caste. There, put your arm next to mine. Look, see, your skin is different. Lighter colour. That's why other children call you *gulabi*, "pinky".'

'But I'm not pink. My skin colour is not so different from yours.'

Asif shrugged his shoulders. ' Is *Daadi* good to you?'

'Yes.'

'She is paid to look after you. But you can do better. We can do better.'

'How?'

'If we run away, we'll be together. No grown-up to push us

around.' Asif boxed Bal's arm affectionately. They giggled and wrestled together. Then Asif pressed Bal down flat on his back and kissed him hard on his cheek. Bal pushed him away.

'I let you do that because you're not-not *gandoo*,' Bal said sullenly.

Asif laughed. 'You learn fast.' They sat facing each other, silent for a while. 'Bal, *Daadi* is not going to live long. When she goes, no one will care about you.'

'Stop fooling around! *Kaam chor*! Lazy, time-wasting thieves!' The boys started and turned round to find Jaswant glaring down at them. 'Come here! You!'

'No!' cried Asif, defiantly.

'What! You dare answer me back? You'll feel the back of my hand in a minute.'

Jaswant and Asif glared each other. Jaswant blinked. He was still groggy from the effects of the drug he had taken. 'You'll do as you're told. Now, leave the boy here with me, while you start rounding up the cattle.'

'Okay. But I'll take Bal with me. He has to learn.'

'You heard what I said.'

Asif stood where he was and the look on his face was one of uneasy desperation. 'You touch the boy and I'll tell the whole village.' Asif warned, wagging a finger. 'You know I will.'

'*Arrey, go*, go!' shouted Jaswant. 'All right, let the boy choose. Does he want to stay with me or...Bal? Come on, choose.'

The little boy was tearful. 'Asif,' he said. 'I go with Asif.'

Jaswant smiled at the boy. 'Stay here, and I'll give you some fresh milk to drink.'

Asif saw Bal hesitate. 'Here, take my stick,' he said, and taking hold of Bal's arm, led the boy away. As they left, Jaswant gave Asif a swift kick on his backside, and as the boy turned to face him, slapped the back of his head. 'Why?' Asif screamed. 'I won't work for you anymore. I'm going to Bombay. Just you see. Yes.'

Jaswant laughed. 'Idiot! The guard will catch you. You'll go to prison. I told you before. You need ticket. Ticket means money. Where will you get six rupees?'

Asif shrugged. 'Come, Bal.' When they were out of hearing, he said, 'don't you worry, the guard won't catch us. If he does, he can't get money out of us. What can he do? A slap or two? Make us get off at the next stop? Yosef told me how he got on and off, changing trains and hiding every time he saw the guard. Easy. He said that Third Class is so full of people, there's no room to move. Guards, ticket collectors... they give up, or wait till people get off. But they can't run as fast as we can.'

'Why didn't you let me stay with Jaswant? He was smiling at me.'

'Fool!' Asif looked over his shoulder. Jaswant was adjusting his turban. 'A pretty boy needs to be smart. When men smile like that, that's when to keep away from them. Don't worry about Bombay. We'll get there, soon.' Again Asif glanced back. Jaswant, now with staff in hand, began making a series of calls and cattle noises. 'Hush! C*hup*! Listen!' And as they watched, the countryside was filled with mooing, bleating and the dull sound of hooves pounding the dusty scrub land. Jaswant's calls orchestrated the animal responses till they grew increasingly musical and prolonged.

'What do we do, now?'

'I can make sounds too. I'll teach you how to click your tongue and to whistle. But now we must go right up to the railway bank and shoo the cattle that have wandered away from the herd. Come. Just remember that Jaswant baba's okay, but learn when to fear him and when to defy him. He can't run and he soon forgets. As for Bombay, we'll pick the right time, when no one suspects. I'm making plans with Yosef. He'll come too.'

'But now you've told Baba! They will know we have gone to Bombay!'

'Bombay is very big. They'll never find us. Oh! Look. See, that moving cloud? There, up in the sky. It's Abdul's pigeons. Abdul, the butcher, keeps pigeons.'

CHAPTER THREE

Boman Irani's grandfather had left Persia to find his fortune in Bombay. He set up a stall selling hot sweet tea, spiced with cardamon, mint and lemon grass, and, for an extra *paisa*, a hard rusk for dunking. The rusks, and later, teacakes, shortbread and biscuits, were supplied by a local bakery. In less than ten years he bought the bakery and when he died, left a small fortune, enabling his son to buy a Queensway corner shop in Bombay's Churchgate area. Boman's father simply called it Irani Restaurant, but in 1942, when Boman took over the business, he renamed it *The Light of Asia*, extended the kitchen, employed two cooks, and served full meals. Boman himself stood behind a long, highly polished teak wood counter on which were a line of large transparent glass jars filled with peanut brittle, mint toffees, fairy cakes, biscuits and boiled sweets. From the counter he would shout the customer's order at the kitchen behind him and wait for one of the two cooks to echo the order in acknowledgement. In front of him was a large, shining brass samovar, which he alone handled and from its tap poured boiling hot water into pots of tea.

Boman's restaurant remained open, Monday to Saturday, from six in the morning to eleven at night but, like other traders in the neighbourhood, it closed on Sundays, a day when he regularly made a trip to the Haji Ali mosque on the Mahim causeway. There he prayed and made offerings for Katija, his wife, who had died giving birth to their still-born daughter, leaving him, two years ago, at the age of forty-one, to bring up his nine-year old son.

Boman Irani, a tall, loose limbed man, wore his thick black, heavily pomaded hair, neatly parted in the middle. His long Byzantine face seldom broke into a smile, but when it did, the warmth of his good nature came through and inspired his happy clientele to recommend to their friends his restaurant for its reasonably priced fare and friendly service.

It was a Saturday when he saw three boys waiting outside his restaurant, just as he was about to open for the day. Two of them, each about 14 years old, were neatly dressed in blue shirts and shorts, clearly a uniform of sorts. But the third boy, not more than eight, was a sad sight. He was clad in a filthy, near threadbare cotton tunic and white pyjamas that hung precariously from his skinny waist and barely reached his ankles. With a slight shudder Boman regarded the waif's cracked feet. 'Oi, boys! Move on!' he said in English and Hindustani. Then he relented and with a gesture invited them to draw nearer. He remembered that his father had taught him never to be unkind to beggars. He told him how his own father had to beg when, a stowaway, he set foot on Bombay's Mazagon docks. 'Where have you come from? You're not local boys, I can see that. And why are you here?'

Yosef, almost a head taller than Asif, stared uneasily at Boman. The other boys watched him. In the four weeks they had been in Bombay, they had begun to pick up Bombay's patois of a mixture of Hindi, Gujarati and Marathi, punctuated liberally with some English words. Yosef's uncle, Abdul Raman, a projectionist at Rex Cinema in Bombay's Fort area, had managed to employ him and Asif as cinema ushers, but as he had nothing to offer Bal, he suggested the little boy should find work as a tea boy in a restaurant or hotel. He had given them the address of Boman's restaurant. Sadly, though Yosef had rehearsed what to say, he found himself tongue-tied.

'Come on, boy, speak up!'
'Abdul Rehman...you know Abdul Rehman?'
'Yes, yes. From Rex Cinema.'

Yosef stammered then blurted out. 'He's my uncle. Um...Abdul Rehman of Rex Cinema sent me ...um...and these two boys are from Fatehpur.'

Asif nudged him sharply and whispered. 'Don't say Fatehpur! He'll report us.'

'Fatehpur,' Boman said, 'never heard of it. But you look and sound Marwari.'

'Yes, but Muslim.' Suddenly Yosef's nerves disappeared. 'I'm from Biwara.'

'I know a Biwara. Beyond Baroda? That's far from Bombay. You idiots! You never learn. Bombay's streets are not paved with gold.' He took a deep breath and sighed shaking his head reprovingly. 'So, you boys are runaways.'

Yosef smiled sheepishly. 'I have my uncle here. But these two have no one.'

'There's nothing here for you. Any of you.'

'*Bhai sahib*,' Yosef said with folded hands. 'Maybe you can do with a tea-boy?'

'I don't need a tea boy. Anyway, I can see that you and this boy… have jobs. So it is for this little one?'

Yosef rolled his head. 'Hah, yes, we have jobs. Me and this one. His name Asif. I am Yosef. This is our Rex Cinema uniform. My uncle, he Cinema *chalu*.'

'Cinema *chalu*?' Boman laughed. 'What's that?'

'He fillums starting, cinema showing,' the little boy piped in, gazing up at Boman with large, melting brown eyes. 'He projection man.'

Boman gazed at the boy with amazement. 'He speaks English?'

'He clever boy.' Yosef said in Hindi. 'More clever than me. Listen once only and never forgetting. He likes to English speak. From cinema watching and he learning.'

'Yes,' Boman said in Hindi. 'But the bloody English have gone. Last week, only. Big show at Gateway of India. Goodbye Raj!' He laughed but almost at once froze as he saw the three boys stared at him solemnly. He sighed. 'Well, the boy looks bright. And he'll look a lot brighter after a good wash. Take him to dhobi ghats. Give him good wash. Now off with the lot of you, I'm busy.' As he turned a key in the door padlock, he dug into his trouser pocket. 'Here, one rupee and eight annas. Get him a new pair of pyjamas.' He unlocked the door and pulled the bolt. 'Wait. I can give him a pair of shoes, also. My son's about his size. Go to the back and wait. No-no, not that way. This way. Round the back…and wait there. I'll see you soon.'

The two older boys looked at each other. 'Yes, yes,' said the little one. 'We going and we coming.' Bal nodded his head rapidly, as if to remove any doubt.

The boys waited patiently at the back of the restaurant. They were used to waiting as well as being disappointed and were about to give up when a door opened. 'Here, take these,' Boman said, handing two items of clothing. 'There's a grey shirt and blue shorts. And these *pathani chuppals*.' He held up the sandals to Bal. 'Come on boy, take them. There, now off you go.'

'I can sing,' said the boy. He slipped on the *chuppals*, jumped up, did a little jig, stood very still, coughed and sang: "Haim forever blowin' bubbles... pretty bubbles in the hair..." He stopped as unexpectedly as he had begun and started again. "Best dem all, the lawn, the shot an' the toll..." Asif!' He ran to Asif and began to cry.

'*Bus, bus*! Enough,' shouted Boman. 'Now go. *Arrey*! Was he singing English?' He grinned. 'Yes. I know: "Bless them all, the long and the short and..." '

'He singing,' Yosef said, 'but not knowing English. But he hear songs. Close to Rex Cinema...Dancing school.'

Boman nodded. 'I know. "Victor Silvester Ballroom". Afternoon Jam session, where Anglo-Indians going.'

'I work in boarding...YMCA hostel.' The boy chimed in.

'Yes, Christian Boys' hostel.' Asif blurted triumphantly. 'Clever boy. Give job.' .

'But he got job already?' Boman frowned.

'In kitchen. Washing up. Two weeks...' Yosef demonstrated a kick. 'Get out. No job. Nothing.'

Boman threw up his hands. 'You mean he's got the sack? Temporary job. That happens in Bombay. Anyway, there's nothing I can do about it. Now off with the lot of you. Go! I'm busy.'

'Please, Sahib.' Yosef pleaded. Then he added in Hindi, 'we can't keep him with us in cinema time. We will lose our jobs. Uncle says, if you can't give job, please let him work here, just one, two days. Then he take him to shoe factory in Palgaon. We come, take him. Please, just two days.'

'All right. Make certain you come. Otherwise I'll come to the cinema. Then you, all of you will get the sack.' Boman waved a hand. 'Okay, boy, you! Come here. Easy job. You know, easy kitchen-work. But first bath. There, give me those clothes. Yes, yes, you will get them back.'

The older boys left promising to return. 'Now boy,' Boman said. 'Do you see that stand pipe near the wall. Stand under tap. I'll get soap. Wait there.' A moment later he returned. 'You know how to wash? Good. It's not cold. The wind will dry you. Then, put these on and come inside through that door. You follow my Hindi? Good. Now,' he added in English, 'what is your name?'

'Bal. My name is Bal.'

'Why you like speaking English? Say in Hindi.'

Bal shook his head. 'I want talk English. Christian hostel, all talking English.'

'How long? How long have you been here, in Bombay? How many *din*?'

Bal hesitated and Boman repeated the question. Bal counted on this fingers, then indicated twenty-one with his hands.'

'And you can sing English songs you heard.' Boman smiled. 'Tonight. Where you sleep?' Boman helpfully folded his hands against is face and shut his eyes.

Bal pointed to the courtyard flagstones and lay down.

'All right, all right,' Boman nodded solemnly. 'I bet you've been sleeping on the pavements. Get up, get up. Now listen. I wanted to speak English. Your age. Small boy, like you. But I went to school. I was lucky.' He stared at the boy and realised that Bal was finding it hard to understand what he was saying. Boman mumbled to himself: 'Poor boy, how will you ever get to the school', then aloud: 'What are you waiting for? Take off your clothes. Don't be shy. Okay, leave that on, but take the top off. What's that?' Bal had taken a folded piece of paper from under his tunic, opened it, pressed it flat and placed it lovingly under the sandals. It was a cinema film poster. The first two words of the title read: *Tarzan and*...the rest of the title was hidden under the sandals. Bal removed his tunic, Boman pointed to a filthy oil drum lying on its side 'Throw those old clothes away, there. Yes, into that *kutchera* bin, and the pyjama too. You've got a nice shirt and shorts now. Wear that and come in.' He waited till the boy started to wash himself under the tap. Then he turned and entered the building. Twenty minutes later Boman came out to find the boy shivering in his clean clothes.

'Hey, didn't you understand what I said?'

The boy nodded.

'Then why didn't you come in?'

The boy leaned back and craning his neck pointed up. Leaning down from a third storey balcony was a boy wearing a green school-cap. He was grinning widely, and in his hands brandished a catapult. A second later a missile whizzed through the air. It missed Bal by inches, and ricocheted on the flag stones.

'Minoo! Stop that!' Boman shouted up at the balcony. 'Get inside! At once!'

'But daddyji, he was sneaking into the building. And he's wearing my clothes.'

'I gave them to him. They're old, and small for you. And, *I* told him to come in.'

'Oh, sorry, sorry, da.'

Boman looked at his wrist watch. 'Hey, Minoo, still half hour. Plenty time. Come down for breakfast.' He shook his head and muttered to himself: 'Today early school and half-day.' He turned to Bal. 'Did he hit you?'

Bal shook his head. 'Sahibji,' he said timidly. 'This your house?'

'Yes. Not house. Building. Many flats. Lot of families live here. Okay, now, go inside. Wait by the door. Don't come in. Not now. When I tell you. People coming into restaurant now.' He looked up at the balcony. 'Minoo's gone.' From behind the door he took out a broom. 'Here, take this. Don't look like that. Haven't you seen a *jharoo* before? Sweep the courtyard. You know how? Good. Not that hard. Slowly. Keep dust down. Put all rubbish, all *kutchera*, there. That same bin.' He turned to go in then faced the boy again. 'When finish, knock on this door. I'll send Minoo with a mug of hot tea and bread.' He looked up at the skies and pointed to a bulging jute sack by the door. 'If it rains, come inside and sit there. Make sure water don't get in. Pull sack in, like this.' Boman demonstrated. 'Any problems. Call me.'

'Onions?' asked the boy, pointing to the sack.

'Sack of onions, yes. Just come. This storeroom, and this door...' Boman opened the door, 'going into the kitchen, and...' pointing to the bamboo-bead curtain behind him, 'into restaurant. I will be there. When rain comes, call me. Don't forget.'

'Call? How calling?'

'Yes, say mister...No, no. *Malik*, say, *malik*. Yes, now what?' The boy pointed to a low pre-fabricated shed at the far end of the courtyard beyond the stand pipe, 'Yes, yes, lavatory. Flush. You know how?' The boy nodded hesitatingly. 'I'll show you, come.' They walked up to the shed. There was a small bucket outside next to a tall zinc tub of water. 'Fill bucket with water, and... Whoosh! But first wash your...' Boman pointed to his bottom and laughed.

It was the third week of June and it rained early that afternoon. Bal dragged the brown sack as far as he could into the storeroom and sat on it. The heavy downpour soon flooded the courtyard and the water started to flow over the threshold. Bal shouted: 'Malik! Malik!.' But Boman had anticipated the boy. Two men came out from the kitchen and pulled the sack in with the boy still seated on it. The astonished expression on his face made one of the men laugh loudly. 'So, this is the lad looking for a job? He's too small to do anything but wash pots and pans.'

'Well,' said the other man, who had been staring hard at the boy, 'there is always demand for that.' He was tall with black curly hair, liquid eyes and a large sensuous mouth. 'I'll give the boy a job, if Boman lets him go.'

'Come on D'Silva,' said the other man, 'don't build up the boy's hopes.'

'I'm serious, man. Honest! Phil, no joking. I cook. I could do with help.'

The man addressed as Phil laughed again. It was a strange laugh, more apparent from the jerking of his shoulders and less from the hissing sound he made through clenched teeth. 'Oh, come on!' he said. 'You've got a one bedroom flat. Where's the boy to sleep? I mean he can't work for you and sleep on Bombay's pavements.' Phil's large round eyes bulged as he dusted his hands and brushed his bald head. 'Bloody hell! That sack was full of dust. Dizzy, you've got dust on your trousers.'

'Yes, man.' Ronny D'Silva brushed his trousers. 'Well, the boy can sleep in the kitchen. I'll get him a cot. Say, Phil. Seen his eyes? Beautiful. God! I've never seen eyes like that!'

'Yeah, I saw them. Anyway, check with Boman. Just in case he's got plans for the lad. Mind you, he'll know. You're a great one for boys.'

'Shut up, man! Don't say that in front of the boy. And Boman will hear.'

'Na, he can't hear. Not with all that noise of rain.'

'God, I'm stuck. Forgot to bring umbrella. And I've got to be back in the office in twenty minutes.'

'It's June, man. What did'ya expect? Monsoon's late, already. Ask Boman. He'll lend you an umbrella. There, he...' The bead curtain moved and Boman entered the corridor dragging two sandbags, which he propped against the door to stop the water getting in. 'You okay, Bomi. I could lend you a hand. Come on Dizzy, shake a leg.'

Boman turned to the men. 'I can manage now. Thanks. Go back and finish your breakfast. Fresh made toast on the table. I heard. Dizzy can borrow an umbrella.'

The three men went into the restaurant dining hall, Boman, to stand proprietarily behind the counter; Phil and D'Silva back to their table. A tall, sad looking young man entered. 'Good morning!' Boman greeted him. 'Has it stopped raining?' The young man nodded sullenly and made straight for a free table. 'Sorry, gentleman, please!' Boman called out to him and pointed to the small notice displayed on the counter. It read: "All orders here before seating at tables."

'Masala scrambled eggs on toast; and tea,' the thin, sad man said mechanically.

Boman repeated the order down into the kitchen and waited for its echo. 'Good choice,' he said with an encouraging smile. 'Biku, my cook, makes the best masala scramble in all Bombay. What tea, Liptons, Brooke Bond, Lopchu?'

The thin sad man shrugged. 'Tea in a pot.'

A moment later Phil came up to the counter. 'D'Silva has to leave in ten minutes. He's offering the boy a job as top servant. He'll explain.'

After a brief consultation with Phil and D'Silva, Boman called out to Biku to man the counter and the three men returned to the storeroom. They found Bal on the floor poring over a school exercise book on a tea-chest, a thick lead pencil in his hand. On the floor next to him was an enamel mug and plate. Boman recognised both the book and pencil. 'Where did you get those?' he asked. 'Did Minoo give them? It's okay. What have you drawn?'

He bent down and saw in large illustrative lettering the word "Tarzan". Boman pursed his lips. 'Good. Where's the poster?' He had to repeat the question and make signs. Bal managed to convey that he had left it outside and that it was destroyed by the rain.

Boman turned to his friends. 'Okay, D'Silva,' said Boman, 'let's find out how the boy feels about working for you. Hey there! Bal. Come here.'

'Bal? That's no name. Bala means babe, does it not, Bomi?'

'Dizzy, the trouble with you Goans, you treat Hindustani like a foreign language. Why ask if you know what it means. The British Raj is *khatam*, finished. It's time you fellows decide to be part of India...'

'Yeah, yeah. We're all bloody Indians now. Come Bal, come here.' D'Silva offered Bal a slab of chocolate. 'Take it. It's sweet. Good stuff.'

'He won't like it,' Boman said. 'He won't know chocolate. The boy's a *dehatti*, a villager.'

'Go on, Bal, take a bite.' D'Silva unwrapped the silver paper.

Bal took a bite and spat it out. 'Ooh, *mutti, mutti*!' he said wiping his lips.

'God,' D'Silva said, 'he's calling it mud.'

The bald man called Phil burst out laughing. 'What did you expect. Use your head Dizzy. Boman told you he's a peasant, a villager from some...'

'But,' Boman interrupted, 'what is so surprising is his light skin colour. So much fairer than his friends. His face is sunburnt but when I made him bathe under the tap, his chest fair. Almost pink.'

'Could be Parsee,' D'Silva said. 'They're quite pale.'

'A Parsee villager!' Phil exclaimed. 'What rubbish you talk, man. Parsees look after their own. You'll never see a Parsee beggar. And look at that face. Bomi says he's from Baroda side. That face is not...'

'But, he's got a big nose, like Parsees have. See for yourself. Nice face, big...'

'Ronny,' Boman intervened, don't waste time. 'The boy's without a job. Are you really offering him one? If so, then I'll ask him. See, those alert, intelligent eyes? As if he understands what's being said. He knows we're talking about him. Hey boy! Do you want job?'

Bal nodded and his whole body shivered. 'There is nothing to be afraid about. This sahib, he'll give you job. Tell your friends this evening, you've got a job. And if you go with him, you can stay with him. Sleep in his house.'

'Food also, and ten rupees a month,' D'Silva added encouragingly.

Bal looked at Boman, studied D'Silva's face for a while, then back to Boman. He shook his head firmly and ran back to his place on the onion sack.

The three men stared at Bal and then at each other. Boman said: 'The boy is no fool. He knows what you are after. Young as he is, he's much too sharp.'

'Bloody Phil. I told you the boy was listening. I'm sure he heard you.'

'Yeah,' growled Phil. 'But how was I to know. He's not supposed to understand. He's only a *baccha*, a kid. You don't expect...anyway, good for the boy, I say.'

'You know,' Boman said. 'Even if the boy said yes, I would have stopped him.'

'Have a heart, Boman. Don't believe Phil. He's a bloody trouble maker.'

'What you do in private is none of my business, Ronny. But...'

'But what?'

'No don't misunderstand me. Nothing to do with you. There's something strange, something special, about this boy.' Boman walked to the tea-chest and picked up the exercise book. 'You see that Phil? He did that. From memory.'

Phil whistled.

'Boman held the book in front of the boy's eyes. He pointed. What's that, boy?'

'Tarzan,' Bal said.

'See what I mean? The boy's had no schooling. He couldn't have had. I'll prove it' Boman turned the page and wrote the letter "E". And what's that, boy?'

The boy stared. Then answered correctly.

'See what I mean, Phil? He can't have been to school, and no village school will teach English. Let me tell the schoolmaster. He'll be interested. Right time too.' He moved the bead curtain and peeped into the restaurant. 'Yes, he's finished marking. That's what he does. Has breakfast, a cup of coffee and marks his school books.

Phil peeped over Boman's shoulders. 'You're talking about Sam Dustoor? I once asked him why he doesn't mark his pupils' books at home. He joked: "Because," he said, "I'm bloody inefficient", and that when he goes home he gets lost in his books and forgets about school—and what books, man. He's got big, big library.'

'Also grand house in the Bombay Fort area,' added Boman.

'Hey, now, he's a Parsee and a clever bloke. He can tell you if the boy is Parsee or Gujarati. Always chooses to sit in that corner.'

'I keep it reserved for him. Comes here regularly for breakfast, and sometimes for dinner also. He's one of my best customers and a good friend.'

'Who are you talking about?' D'Silva asked and poked his head between the two men. 'Oh, him. Yeah, seen him many times. Talks like an Englishman.'

'What do you expect,' Boman said derisively. 'England returned. Cambridge.'

'He comes here because it's convenient.' Phil said turning away. 'Teacher. Head of English at St Thomas's High School, Flora Fountain. Near here. You know. Just across the Maidan. Posh school. Bomi, your son, Minoo, goes there?'

'Phil,' D'Silva thumped Phil's back. 'All Church schools in Bombay are good schools. My nephew goes to posh Catholic school, in Santa Cruz. St Anslem's.'

'But Dizzy, with all respect, this is the tops, if not *the* top school in Bombay. Very high fees, and long, long waiting list.'

'Bomi managed to get Minoo in.'

'Because Dizzy, Sam and Bomi are obviously old friends.'

'*Arrey*, it's not that simple. Minoo still had to pass the entrance test.'

D'Silva made a face. Then he waved a dismissive hand. 'I must be going. Bye. The rain has stopped, but I'll borrow an umbrella, Bomi, just in case.'

'There on the stand behind the counter. Bring it back. The umbrella. I thought Bensons was closed on Saturdays, being a British company.'.

'Yeah. It's a British company,' Phil drawled. I always envied

In the Shadow of a Dream

Dizzy. Saturday for me is like any working day. Bloody native firms. Squeeze the blood out of you.'

Boman grinned. 'Mr Philip Green, the chances of you going "home" are zero. You better get used to "native" bosses.'

'Choke it, Bomi,' Phil retorted angrily. 'If we weren't friends, I'd sock you one. One day, you'll see, I'll get to England. Wait till my papers come from Seychelles. Yes they will. Proof, my grandfather was British citizen. Then I'll be laughing. So, Dizzy, wipe that smile off your face.'

'See, he can't take a joke. Anyway, shows how little you know, Phil. American firms have Saturdays off. We get half day, like the schools. Bomi, this chap, Sam, does he really come here for dinner? Is the fellow a bachelor?'

'No! Looks younger than he is. Sam is in his late forties. His wife left him some years ago—nineteen thirty-nine or forty. He won't talk about it. That big house is the family house. He inherited a lot of money. Property also, I think.'

'So I'm right about the big library.' Phil yawned.'

'Handsome guy. Could've married again,' D'Silva said. 'I really must be going. Coming, Phil?'

'Yeah, let's go.'

Boman waved the couple off, returned behind the counter, where he made another pot of coffee and took it across to where Sam Dustoor was sitting.

'This is fresh, no charge.' Boman smiled. 'I'll take that pot back. It's gone cold.'

'That's kind. Thank you.' Sam Dustoor looked at his watch.

'Do you have a little spare time, Master sahib, please.' Boman asked.

'Yes, about twenty-five minutes. Just finished marking this little pile here. How can I help?'

'There's a boy here, I want you to see.'

'Oh, dear. I see enough boys. Well, where is he?'

The cook from the kitchen placed two steaming plates of fried eggs on toast on the counter and called out "Table number four". Boman turned. 'One moment, sir,' he said and took the plates to a couple seated in the centre of the room. Both were men, and from the sound of their conversation, British. The one wearing a white dog-collar was doing most of the talking, while his attentive listener, in a beige cotton suit, answered with grunts. 'Anything else, Padre sahib,' Boman asked.

The priest looked up. 'Not for me, thank you. What about you, James?'

'Eh, salt and pepper, och no, it's on the table. Great. Thank you.'

Boman gave a nod to Sam and went through the bead curtain. A moment later he returned with Bal. 'This is the boy, master sahib.'

'Fascinating,' Sam said. 'A charming, intelligent looking lad. What's he? Seven, eight, can't be more?'

Bal took an instant liking to Sam Dustoor. He gazed at him intently, smiled and pointing to him asked. 'Job? I working.Yes, yes.'

Boman shook his head and held the boy back. 'No, no job,' he said firmly. 'Here, take this book. Show it to Masterji. Now, sir. I saw that poster. But he didn't copy it. The poster was destroyed in the rain.'

'Drawn from memory? That's special.' Sam studied it. 'Indeed! Outstanding for his age. He's pointing to my pencil. Yes, you can hold it. It's a red and blue pencil. One moment. I'll show you.' Sam opened his brief case and took out a blank sheet of paper. He drew a blue horizontal line, turned the pencil round and drew a red one below it. The effect on the boy amazed both men. He clapped his hands and uttered a squeal of joy.

Boman tapped the exercise book. 'He drew that word "Tarzan", with no idea…'

'Tarzan,' the boy nodded, pointing to the book.

'And when I wrote this, the letter "E", he sounded it…'

'You're saying,' Sam said, 'he remembers shapes and sounds and can reproduce them. But can he link sound to letters. If I write a block T…

Bal picked up the pencil and drew a red "T".

'Remarkable!' Sam said. 'The boy's a mimic. One moment.' He took the pencil from Bal and drew a large "A". 'There, here's a test for you. This is A and this is - is…wait. That was a red A, I'll now do a blue B. Here, now you do it.'

Bal took the pencil. He not only copied the letters recognisably, chose the right colours and sounded them, a little prolonged, yet fairly correctly.

The two men looked at each other. 'This is amazing.' Sam said. He glanced at his watch. 'Where did you find the boy? Never mind. I have to go now.'

'Thank you masterji. Bal, give Mr Dustoor back his pencil.'

'That's all right. Keep it.' He smiled at the boy, who went up to him and took his hand. 'No, no you stay here. With Boman. Go to Boman.'

'*Challay challoo*! Go.' Boman chivvied the boy to the storeroom and waited till he was out of sight. Then he turned to Sam Dastur. 'The boy is an orphan.'

'Hm. He ought to be in a school and if I didn't know better, I'd say he's Parsee, but not *passé*, if you get my meaning.' He laughed helpfully, but the joke fell flat. 'But he's not, though he could pass as one. At a wild guess, I'd say, one of his parents was European. Very likely English.'

'Then he will be an Anglo-Indian.'

'In today's sense of the word. Well, no one is pure. We're all mixed. And matters like that must not affect our judgement. Right, I'll be off.'

Sam Dustoor stopped at the street door and called back. 'I say, Boman, you've got me all curious. About the boy. I'll be back tomorrow. After lunch? Your flat?'

It was four in the afternoon when they met at Boman's flat. Sam apologised for being later than he planned. 'But I've spent a fruitful afternoon. I've got good news for the boy. Now, as you know, as a member of the teaching staff I have the privilege of a place in my school. But our boys start at eleven and they have to pass a test, an entrance examination—as in Minoo's case. The boy will need grounding in primary education. I've had a useful chat with the Reverend Jack Jones, Head of St Peter's Kindergarten School. It's in the Byculla area. St Peter's also has an orphanage. Jones is prepared to place him there and in the school. What? Just a pot of tea, thanks.'

The tea was brought in by a tall, neatly dressed servant, wearing a black pill-box cap. He placed the tray on the table, bowed, waited a moment, and then left the room.

'I see you still have Ajmeri working for you.'

'Yes, after all that fuss he decided to stay. Good chap, but a hot head. I told him I'd double his salary if he also worked in the restaurant. But no. He is too proud.'

'You mean, he thinks serving at tables beneath his dignity. Keep tempting him. He'll change his mind one day. Now back to our boy. You know, Bomi, while I don't want any trouble over this, I'm sticking my neck out, because I like the boy enough to want to help. I'm curious to see what schooling will do for him. But, you know, sometimes the sparks of infant genius disappear with time. My young brother, Jimmy, who is in California, was such a case. He took to the violin when he was not yet five. Extremely talented. My father took him to Boston. Today he's a salesman. That, as the Americans say, is how the cookie crumbles. But I ramble. Remind me. You did say the boy's an orphan? And you're sure of that?'

'Yes. Yesterday, when his friends came for him, I checked again.'

'Is the boy still here with you?'

'Yes. I told them to leave the boy with me. That if I can't find him a job, I will keep him, giving him small jobs to do for me. There was a bit of *jhagadra*.'

'You mean an argument?'

'Yes. The other orphan, Asif, was rather protective. But when Yosef, the older one, told him, if he was a true friend of the boy, he must trust someone his uncle knows. Asif then calmed down. I learned a bit more about the boy. As a babe he was left on temple steps in Fatehpur village. He was found and cared for by two women.'

'You know of this village?'

'Nothing. But I will talk to Yosef's uncle. Make sure the story is true. Boys tell lies. So it's good to get an elder's okay. Sorry, masterji, for all this trouble.'

'Don't apologise. It's a challenge and about education. It's what I do. As I said, I like the boy. If it works out well, I'll go all the way. I'll get Taraporevala, the lawyer who did my divorce, to make a trip to the village. Make a deal with these women. If I can legally adopt him, I will. I've got no one.'

'There won't be a problem, of that I'm sure.'

'Yes, but I can see you have something else on your mind.'

'Mastersahib, forgive my asking. But some of my friends…they say, why you not marry again?'

'Well...I hope you didn't say too much.'

'No, no. Be sure of that. My lips are *bund*, closed, sealed.'

Sam shrugged. 'Marry again? I'd rather have my books. They are faithful friends. Besides, now I'm too old and set in my ways.' He smiled. 'Bomi, about the boy. You know, he could be Parsee. In looks I mean. He'll fit in. Also he's nameless. So when he gets to my school...incidentally Mark Evans...

'Headmaster Sahib?'

'Yes. Should have said this earlier...we had a little chat, about the boy, yesterday, after school. He was intrigued. Even said if the boy showed promise, he'd waive the fees. But you know money is not a ...I'll register him as Sam Dustoor junior.'

'You're a good and kind man, Dustoorji. God will bless you.'

'Well, Bomi, you've played your part. Tell me, what made the boys come to you? Was it by chance?'

'Chance? No, no, not chance. The fellow that one of the boys calls his uncle, he worked for me. Three years. Then I got him job at Rex Cinema. He now manager.'

'There, you see, Boman. You are a better man than I am Gunga Din.'

'Gunga Din. Who's this Gunga Din?'

'Never mind, Boman. Take it from me you are a good man.'

'Only, since my *bibi* Kaju died. Before that I was bad man.'

'Why do you say that? The year before she died, Kaju told me how good and kind you were, always, and how concerned she was about you being alone.'

'Believe me Master Sahib, I was a hard man. This city of beggars, Bombay, it makes people hard. When I was in school, boys gave me hard time. Because of my name. Boman Irani, that is Boman from Iran, but boys they call me *Bombeel*, that is Bombay duck...why you laugh? Yes, now, I also laugh. But not then.'

'Well, you and I have learned not to live in the past.'

Boman rolled his head. 'Will you now partake of some sweets? I have ordered some hot *jelabis* for your delection.'

'That's kind, Bomi, but I really must be leaving. I'm going to the flicks. Six-thirty, at the Eros Cinema.'

'But that is not far. Just end of this road. There's lot of time.'

Sam shook his head. 'I'm going with friends and I promised to meet them earlier.'

CHAPTER FOUR

'Dusty. Is that you?' Sam Dustoor turned from the bookshelves in the sitting-room and leaning heavily on his stick, limped to the sofa and sank into its yielding depths.

A tall and shapely young man entered the room. 'You are supposed to be resting,' he said disapprovingly. 'You know what doc said? Why aren't you in bed?'

'I was looking for a book. I know you've been fetching books for me, but you weren't here and I thought I knew where it was. But I can't find it. I could've sworn it was on that shelf there, behind me, third row.'

'It could be anywhere. There are bookshelves in every room of this house. What's the title,' Dusty scanned the shelf behind Sam. 'There's a gap here, in this row.'

'Eh? Oh dear, but of course, I remember now. Help me up.'

'No. You stay there. Tell me and I'll get it for you.'

'I got it out after he left, the day before yesterday. It's there, on the coffee table. Lawrence's *The Seven Pillars*. I thought I'd give it to Dr Mehta. Unless you want it? I know he hasn't got a copy.'

'No, Papa, give it to him.'

'Papa? How wonderful! I have a beautiful son through no effort on my part.'

Dusty held out a hand towards Sam. 'There, let me help you back to your room. No, leave the book. I'll remember. Now lean on me. You must do as Mehta says. He knows what he's talking about.

All that red wine and port! I hadn't the heart to stop you last night. It was your birthday, after all.'

'But now a period of enforced abstinence? Well, I'll submit to that. Four guests, you and me, six of us, and all my units have gone in one evening. Absurd! But not half as ridiculous as getting a doctor to sign a certificate to say one needs alcohol for one's health's sake.' Sam sat on the edge of his bed. 'When you're twenty-one get Mehta to certify you too.'

'By then I may not need a drink permit.'

'Why? Surely you don't believe that in the next five years the Government will see sense and cancel the prohibition laws? We'll see. That's if I'm still around.'

'Don't. You promised. Give me time. I need time to repay your kindness.'

'I'm sorry. It slipped out. Tell me, how did the meeting go with Asif and Yosef?'

'Asif is now an usher in the Metro Cinema. We were able to have a chat over a cup of tea at the Soda Fountain. Yosef has gone back to Biwara.'

'You know, Yosef lied about Ali being his uncle.'

'Yes. But no harm done. The cinema was always in his blood and those years he spent here has taught him something about the cinema business. He's taking over the local flea-pit in Biwara as both manager and projectionist…why d'you laugh?'

'Bomi told me it was the first English word you said. I haven't forgotten.'

'Gosh! You mean, projectionist?'

'Yes. You ought to see him sometime. Boman. Minoo too. You really ought.'

'Can't stand Minoo. He's too physical. Can't finish a sentence without grabbing my hand or putting his arm round my shoulder.'

'You can be hard, dear boy. It's not just Minoo. With others too. People say how indifferent, distant, and independent you can be. Yes, all that. I'm not saying you lack kindness, but I too have sensed a coolness…no, that's harsh. I mean a certain economy of emotion! That was put awkwardly. But you're bright enough to know what I mean. I can live with it. We're very alike, you and I. Maybe why we get on.'

'There's so much I want to do. Friendship and friends take up time.'

'Living is more than being clever. And what about a healthy interest in girls?'

'That will come. Right now I haven't time, but I've read the books you gave me, Stopes, Ellis…since you were embarrassed to talk about sex. Actually they did some of that in school. In the final year, well sort of…'

Sam laughed. 'You could say that again, "sort of". More botany than biology.'

'I knew all that stuff before then. Asif's teachings may have been raw in tooth and claw, but it was straight to the jaw. His curiosity knew no bounds.'

'That's it. It's what I wanted to say. The apt word I can think of is "controlled". It's time you took account of yourself. You are very controlled. I supposed you had to be from a very early age?'

'That and the French philosopher you made me read some time ago. To avoid pain, avoid attachments.'

'More Buddhist than French. Never mind. I think I know who you mean. But that's not all he would have said, surely. Anyway, we've been together long enough for you to relax. To be less controlled.'

Dusty compressed his lips. 'No. I mean, yes…look who's talking! But I need time. You must give me time. I know I'm being selfish. I want to know all that you know. So, stay off the drink.'

'Dusty dear boy, you don't need me. I enjoy my drink, I may as well…'

'You may as well do what Dr Mehta says. Please. And don't say I can manage without you, that I don't need you. I need your advice!' The young man took a sharp breath, and for a moment neither spoke. Then Dusty said: 'He's getting married next month.'

'Who? What on earth are you talking about?'

'Yosef. Yosef's wedding. Asif would like me to go with him. For the wedding. I told him I can't. I don't want to see him again. We've been out of touch for years and I find we've nothing in common.'

'You're not entirely to blame.'

'There's a lot I needed to shed and a lot to take on. I suppose I'm being a snob?'

'I'm as much responsible for that. More. Not being a snob wasn't going to help or change Asif's situation. I had to break your links with the past. It would've affected you adversely. You do understand. I couldn't help you and also your friends.'

'They understood. I'm sure of that. Asif wished me all the luck in the world. That hurt. I mean his generosity shamed me. But he's a free spirit and, since he misses the grazing wastelands, he'll return to Fatehpur soon. He told me, he feels there's every chance to be the village herdsman...since Jaswant is no longer around.'

'What about the enemies he's created by absconding with you... Heavens! That was years ago. How time flies.'

'I don't think anyone missed us, or missed enough to really care. And as we have learned from Taraporevala, all who were concerned are dead. Sujata, Daadi...even the village headman.'

'Still you ought to know that I couldn't help. Not all of you. It would have been too much for me; and they being Muslims didn't make it any easier. Don't ask why. It's just one of those things. There's a purity and sternness in their religion, which make one hesitant, even uneasy.'

'Asif will land on his feet. There's always nearby Biwara and Yosef's friendship, to fall back on.'

'And you do know the trouble I've had, just taking you on?'

Dusty nodded and smiled. He always found Sam's single-mindedness endearing.

'Thank God,' Sam went on, 'there was only my brother Dinshaw and a spinster aunt to contend with. But nothing was going to stop me helping you.'

'You've done more than enough. You don't need to do more. You've taken early retirement. Now relax and indulge yourself. Travel. Give yourself a good time.'

'I am having a good time. You've been good for me, Dusty. I so wanted to make you my heir.'

'Honest, papa. I mean what I say. There is nothing more for you to do. Nothing more I want from you. I am where I want to be. I don't need to be a semi-millionaire. Your family has every right to their property.'

'But Dusty, I want to be certain that you know I'm tied by my father's will. His property and money came to me on condition it goes to Dinshaw after my…Why won't you let me use the dreaded word?'

'Because I'm not ready for it.'

'Still, the will doesn't apply to my current bank account. I've been putting my salary and my pension into it. All that will be yours. Enough to see you through University. Jones promised …'

'No. No more Jones. I've done my bit. I became a Christian because he pressed me to. I was eight and I felt the weight of obligation. He's another one for hugging and petting. Pa, you know, what I mean?'

'Sit down Dusty. Draw that chair. I'll lie back and stretch, if I may. The trouble with you Dusty, my boy, is that you're far too attractive. I had hoped that with the passing years, you would have grown to be less so.'

'But *you*, you didn't make a…I can't think of the right word.'

Sam laughed. 'I'm no saint, but sexual desire has never been an abiding interest. Sheer laziness on my part. Why do you think my wife left me? Sex, dear old chap, as Henry James wrote somewhere, is overrated.'

'You're far too refined. It's what I like about you. You have surrounded yourself with beautiful things and rare and precious books. People come second. That's how I would like to be, pa.'

'Then begin by calling me Sam. It's far too early to make up your mind. My style of living comes when you've had a few setbacks in life, and I wouldn't wish those on you. I hope you may meet someone who'll make you think differently. Don't look at me as if I'm some curiosity. Make no mistake. I did and do find you attractive. But it's always been your obvious intelligence and phenomenal memory that fascinates me…I also knew at once you would not have stayed with me if I'd made a pass.'

'That's the word I was looking for!'

'And, I was going on to say, you had, even nine years ago, an uncanny instinct to see and avoid that kind of sexual attention.'

'Much of that wisdom I owe to Asif. I realise now that he may have learned it the hard way. I was lucky, as a boy, to get the care and attention of women.'

'Anyway, it's against the law. I had my social status to consider. I wasn't going to expose myself to a crime for which I could be blackmailed.'

Dusty took a deep breath. 'Sam, you're the best and the most beautiful man in the world. You deserve to be loved.'

'I am. Loved I mean. By you, I hope and, if you must know, Muriel Sharp. You remember Miss Sharp?'

'My physics teacher? Yes. That was sudden; her leaving, I mean.'

'She retired too. Muriel's my age, though you may not believe it. She lives in Scotland. The Isle of Bute. We write to each other, fairly regularly. I'm surprised you did not ask, because you noted the foreign stamps.'

'I try to emulate your English reserve.'

Sam chuckled. 'Did you know, India is full of Anglophiles. Actually, the whole Parsee community decided to adopt the English style of Western culture.'

'I know. Wasn't the first Indian member of the British Parliament a Parsee?'

'Yes, but that does not mean they had a slavish attitude towards the British Raj. Many champions of Indian Independence were Parsees.'

'Why didn't you marry her? I hope I wasn't in the way?'

Sam gaped. 'You gave me a start. Me? Marry? What are you talking about?'

'Sorry. Muriel Sharp. She's not married, is she? Miss?'

Sam laughed. 'No, no. It's wasn't and isn't that kind of friendship.'

'Don't you want to see her?'

'We like writing. Very platonic and literary. That is too good to lose.'

'But I don't see the point. All that time and effort? Such a waste...unless you plan to publish the letters, one day.'

'You're much too sharp and clever for your age. I've thought of that. It could make fascinating reading: *Letters of a Parsee Gentleman to an English Lady*. But there won't be sufficient time for that enterprise. She has promised to do me a big favour.' Sam slowly and painfully sat up. 'You see, I want to be cremated. The thought of being consigned to a Tower of Silence gives me the shivers. I've never been a good Parsee. Cambridge, and travels in Italy, changed all that. And I've spent many years in a Church school. I know more about Christianity than most practising Christians. Muriel's promised she'd see to it. So when the last days are approaching, I'll go to her. You must see that I get there—I am a British citizen. But if, for any or whatever reason I can't make it on my own, promise you'll get me there. It means a lot to me. I've friends at the High Commission. They'll see that you get a visitor's permit. She'll keep the ashes or you can bring them back. I don't care what either of you choose to do with them. Promise?'

Dusty sighed. 'Yes, I promise. But you're being morbid.'

'Morbid? I like that. Your use of the English language is excellent. It's a mystery how quickly you pick up, keep and use words.'

'I got a Distinction in English, thanks to your tuition.'

'You've been a good lad. I'd hoped you'd turn out to be Parsee. Not that it matters, now. My aunt Gul was certain you were not and disapproved of any attempt I might make to legally adopt you. You should know, she couldn't have stopped me if it gave you any advantage.' He clicked his tongue and looked around him. 'All this goes to Dinshaw. He doesn't deserve any of it. No, not one bit…'

'I know you fought for me. No wall is thick enough for your aunt's voice.'

Sam laughed. 'Bless you. I feel better already. We could go out tonight.'

'You'll stick to doctor's orders. The self-prescriber has a fool for his doctor.'

Sam laughed again. 'That from a saw about lawyers.'

'But pa, sorry Sam, you don't have to go all the way to Scotland to be cremated. Turn Christian or Hindu. That'll solve the cremation problem. Or is it that you don't wish to hurt the feelings of your brother Dinshaw and your Aunt Gul?'

'Hindu, yes. But I'm not sure about Christians. Cremation is against their teaching. At least for the present. No, it has nothing to do with Dinshaw or my aunt. You may consider all this an unnecessary fuss about nothing. Once dead, it matters little how the body is disposed. It's a matter of aesthetics. I would like to spend my last days with a friend. Muriel—since you're increasingly preoccupied with your own life, and rightly so. Did you know, after she retired, Muriel toured Central and South India? She clicked away—Muriel's an excellent photographer—and wants me to look at the results; and help select the ones to go with my text of a book she would like to publish.'

'It would make a fine book. You write well. You make history exciting. So don't hesitate. Make arrangements to go to Scotland as soon as you can. Don't worry about me.' Dusty waved a brown envelope. 'I picked the post up as I came in and glanced at its contents.' He waved the brown envelope again. 'A call up from the Indian Army Selection Board.'

Sam started and winced with the spasm. 'The Army? Dusty, how could you? I've been hoping you'd take up an academic career, or something in the arts line.'

'For my present qualifications the Army offers the highest salary prospects.'

'Also the highest dangers.'

'You don't believe India and Pakistan will go to war?'

'Yes, I do. Mark my words. It's inevitable. But I see you've made up your mind. From the age of ten there's been no mistaking that look. When you stick your chin out like that, it's a declaration of Independence.' Sam laughed. 'I won't argue with you. It may, at least, prevent you from going to England. I mean immediately.'

'England!'

'Bal, sorry, you prefer to be called Dusty.'

'Please, I've never liked Bal and I want to forget it.'

'Sorry. How did you apply for the Army? What name did you put on the form?'

'As at school. Sam Dustoor. In any case, I need the school certificate for my age. It would have been neat to follow the American way. Sam Dustoor Jnr.'

'They'll think you're Parsee. You'll have some explaining to do.'

'I've done that already.'

'It turns out you are not, as I hoped, a Parsee after all. Aunt Gul's been proved right. You're English. Or rather, half English and half Goan.'

Dusty shrugged. 'I suspected something like that. Asif was the first to draw my attention to it by pointing to my skin colour. I didn't want to believe it. And no one in Fatehpur knew for certain. How did you, after all these years of - of complete and utter silence…how did you find out? Who was…Was my mother English or Goan?'

'Don't give it another thought.'

'But I would like to know.'

'Your father's name was Jenkins, Sergeant William Jenkins. Killed in Burma. He was a Welshman and he had a brother. A younger brother. Your mother was Goan. Sorry, let me start from the beginning. Four days ago, I received a mysterious letter from Calcutta; from one Clifford Jenkins. He claims to be your father's brother and so your uncle. I…'

'It's a hoax. Don't answer the letter.'

'How he was able to trace you is a complex story. I'll come to that later. First the letter. There, it's on my bedside table; and my glasses. We'll read it together. Sit by me.' Sam opened the letter. 'There you see: signed Clifford Jenkins.'

'May I see the envelope? Thank you. It is postmarked Calcutta. Shucks! What on earth is an Englishman doing in Calcutta?'

'These glasses are no good. I need a new pair. Here, read it yourself.'

'No, Sam. Just tell me. Just tell me what all this is about.'

'He flew from England to Calcutta, and then journeyed on to Kohima to find his brother's grave. Then back to his brother's regimental headquarters, in England, for further enquiries. They had some of his things, that is, his brother William's; chief among them a wallet containing some Burmese currency and two snapshots; one, of a woman in a nurse's uniform, and the other of William with the same woman. He's in uniform but she's now in mufti, wearing a loud print frock. He goes on to describe her as "pretty but black". But more to the point, inside his brother's battered silver cigarette case, he found a letter, an unfinished letter from William, addressed to a Nurse Molly D'Silva, the Military Hospital, Basirabad.'

'Gosh! But where's the connection with me? Is Molly…'

'Patience. Basirabad is a few miles from Ajmer and a military cantonment. Ajmer has or had one of the biggest Railway and Engine Works, with a work force largely of Goans and Anglo-Indians. Now, D'Silva? That should ring a bell?'

'You don't mean Phil? Sorry the other one. What is D'Silva's first name?'

'Denzil…I can't think how this Clifford chappie got to D'Silva, but from D'Silva he got on to the Revd Jack Jones and the St Peter's Orphanage. Jones tells me, he has seen D'Silva, who in turn confirmed having a sister, and that she was a nurse during the war, and who disappeared nearly seventeen years ago. That'll be 1940. D'Silva? Having a pretty sister? The mind boggles.'

'Your mind? Have a heart, think of me. D'Silva! My uncle!'

'He, I mean Clifford, says in his letter that he plans to come to Bombay to meet D'Silva. And, of course, he'd like to see you. D'Silva's heard from him and, last week, wanted to come over here, but I suggested he waited till he's met Clifford and to first check whether the girl in the photograph is indeed his sister.'

'Poppy, do we have to go through all this?'

'Laddie, I don't want this to upset you, but if it's true, we're obliged to do the charitable and decent thing. William Jenkins could be your father. I know it's a bit awkward. Surely you'd like to know who your…'

'No, I don't. All these years I've been alone. I want no emotional ties, apart from the one with you. Not Jones and certainly not D'Silva; and I don't want to drag in a forgotten past. I'm not going to be unhappy again. I hate pain.'

'You can't escape pain. No one can. Anyway, Dusty, I couldn't say no. I've said he or rather they could come. Besides, as your guardian, I need to know for sure. It may all turn out to be a mistake or a coincidence. After all, D'Silva saw nothing in you to trigger any memory of his sister. Although, now he says he did.'

'Sam, I'm not at all keen about D'Silva. He's…how can I put it…he's a…'

'I'll save you the trouble. I know. But if it turns out you're his nephew, he'll be sensible and behave responsibly. And you must agree to let me invite Clifford. The poor man's spent time and money to learn about what happened to his dead brother, and if you really are William's son and therefore his nephew, he deserves to know. You do see that. In three or four years you'll be a free man, free to make your own decisions. Right? Now, I gather that he, Clifford, is a doctor, a doctor of medicine. He lives in London with a wife and two girls of school going age. Look on the bright side. He may invite you to visit him in England. As William's son, you'll be able to…'

'Thank God I'm trying for the army. I'll have a good excuse to stay put in India.'

'You'll get in. One can assume you will. It's in you. And you'll pass with flying colours…probably win the Sword of Honour or

Gold Medal or whatever is given to the best cadet in the Military Academy. You're a born winner.' Sam pointed to a row of silver trophies behind a glass fronted shelf.

'Thank God,' Dusty mumbled, as he looked absently at the shelf. 'Four? I thought I had five.' He slid the glass panel and picked up one of the cups and studied it.

'Four out of six is more than enough,' Sam said. 'In fact it's a record. In all the years I've been at St Thomas's, I don't remember any boy winning four in a single year on its Annual Sports Day. You made me feel terribly proud. It was a decent of you to let poor Rustom win the two hundred yards hurdle. He was the favourite till you almost ruined his chances.'

'He won it fair and square. But these are just for the flat races. I was no good at the other field events. Long jump for instance and Discus.'

'You collected a number of runners up silver medals, too. You couldn't have won the Sportsman of the year shield, two years running, if you were not good at the field events you took part in. There, look on the second shelf.'

'Gosh! When did you arrange all this?'

'Some days now. The carpenter took an unconscionably long time to make the shelves. That's my favourite, the one you're holding.'

Dusty looked down at the cup. It read: "First prize. School Cross-country Race". He laughed. 'Hardly cross country. From the Gateway of India to Colaba point. Of course, as I told you, I had an unfair advantage.'

'You mean, for a village boy, it was a piece of cake?'

'Five to six miles was the usual daily tramp, not counting chasing after cattle.'

'Well, you were streets ahead of the others and scarcely out of breath. I was proud and grateful. You justified all my investment in time and money.'

Dusty put the cup back and looked pensively out through the open curtains of the window. Then he turned and studied Sam. His gentle smirk betrayed a combination of mischief and smugness.

'Sorry, Dusty, I didn't mean to embarrass you.'

In the Shadow of a Dream

'I'll be miles away from Bombay, you know, way up in the Himalayan foothills.'

'The right place for a cold hearted sod.' Sam mumbled, good-humouredly.

A month passed, and a week later Dusty was asked to attend the Army Selection Board in Poona. Sam saw him off at the Victoria Terminus Station. 'You're looking terribly smart in your blue blazer,' he said.

Dusty blew on his nails and polished them against his collar.

'It's good to be confident, but remember, people don't like cocky youngsters. You'll find it plain sailing, yes, but try to hide some of your genius. Let others have the pleasure of discovering it.'

Dusty raised a placating hand and nodded. He loosened his tie. 'I hope, Poona will be cooler. Oh, before I forget, thanks for sending me off First Class. I do hate crowds. God, haven't I changed from that barefooted village boy you rescued, or rather, I should say, championed.'

'Yes, but I might not have befriended you if you were indeed just barefooted. You were clean, sandal-shod, when I first saw you. Dear old Boman, he was no fool. And I'm no saintly missionary. But you've drifted. A penny for your thoughts, dear boy.'

'Sam, tell me I don't look Anglo-Indian. Punjabis can be light skinned. And Russy, I mean Rustom. Remember Rustom? He was shades lighter than me.'

'I'm not sure, now. It's strange how a nudge can influence one's thinking! If you remember, I thought you were Parsee. Let's not dwell on this.'

They studied each other for a while. Then Sam said: 'You haven't asked.'

'Because as far as I'm concerned, no news is good news.'

'Actually, I've had news. This morning. Before we set out. Not from Goa but London, which explains the long silence. You'll be happy to know it *is* good news. I'm happy too. Funny,' Sam chuckled, 'how the thought of your absence from me made my heart grow fonder.'

'You do have a look of Henry Fonda.'

'Ha, ha. Now that's not worthy of you.' Sam glanced at his watch, then stopped a fat, middle-aged man, who wore a white cotton suit and pith helmet. 'Excuse me, is there a delay in departure?'

The man stared at Sam. With officious gestures he tucked a green and red flag under one arm, removed a whistle from his mouth and beamed a bureaucratic smile. 'My name is Deshpande. I ham train guard.'

'Sam gave a nod and offered his hand, which Deshpande shook with great vigour. 'You see, gentleman, there's been hold-up. Train will now depart in haff hour. But it is electric train, gentleman, and so it will make up time. Worry not.'

Sam thanked him and turned to Dusty. He felt in the inside pocket of his jacket and took out a letter which he unfolded. 'Since we have time, Dusty, read this.'

Dusty took the letter, glanced at it and returned it. 'Tell me the good bits, Sam.'

'It's all good. I wouldn't have mentioned it otherwise; not when you're going for a crucial interview. Although, noting your calm and absolute control, I needn't have worried. Such maturity in one so young! You know how to protect yourself. That is good. Good for you.'

Dusty took the letter again. It read. "Dear Mr Dustoor. From my last letter you would have expected to hear from me sooner. Forgive me, but although inquiries in Goa confirmed my belief that your young ward is indeed my nephew and that his mother may indeed be Dom D'Silva's sister…" 'So he's Dom not Denzil?'

'Yes. I knew the initial was D. There, I must have known a Denzil. Read on.'

Dusty nodded and read on: "may indeed be Dom D'Silva's sister, I have decided not to make the trip to Bombay and to let matters lie. Upsetting the status quo would, as you wisely stated solve nothing. I was curious, even keen, (in the circumstances, who wouldn't be), but having met Dom—he was in Goa to help with my inquiries—certain facts remain unanswered. Also, having met the rather large D'Silva clan, I got the impression that many of the D'Silvas may wish to settle in England. That would put some strain on my family. So, as I would rather not be involved in sponsoring or supporting applications to the Home Office, my South London address is for you alone. For Dusty too, should he wish to use it. From what you have said that seems unlikely and I'll respect the young man's sensitivities. You have rehabilitated the boy and deserve his undivided loyalty, but I hope he won't mind if you send me a photograph of him."

Dusty handed the letter back to Sam, but before he could speak, the stocky, pith helmeted guard returned. 'Please to board the train, gentlemen. It is about to depart. I am about to blow the whistle and wave the green flag.'

Sam nodded and Dusty climbed into the compartment, shut the door behind him, lowered the window and leaned out. They shook hands and boxed each other's chins in a coy show of affection. 'Good luck,' Sam said, and turning round, saw the plump Mr Deshpande spring up into the Guards Van with unexpected agility.

'Keep up the regime,' Dusty said. 'I haven't seen you looking so well for ages.'

Sam grinned. 'From now on you're on your own. Write.'

'You're joking. I'll be back in four days.'

'I'm getting myself a Red Irish Setter.'

'I was being selfish. I know how much you missed Bonny.'

'We both loved that Golden Retriever. So you approve?'

'Yes. Bonny's death shook me. I didn't want to go through all that again; but you should've insisted. Still, "I bid you beware/ Of giving your heart to a dog to tear."'

'Ah! Kipling.' Sam smiled. With a plangent moan the train lurched forward. There was a metallic clang as the couplings engaged, jerked and lunged. Sam held up a grey felt bag, 'in case you've forgotten to pack yours. Best razor I could find.'

'Thanks. Take care, the train's picking up...I did shave this morning.'

'Next time get closer to the razor,' Sam teased.

Dusty compressed his lips. 'I do care, Sam. In my own way, I really do.'

'I know,' Sam shouted, as the train picked up speed. 'Look out of the window when you go over the Ghats, the views are worth it.' He waited and waved till the train drew out of sight.

CHAPTER FIVE

'Sorry young man, but that's my berth. Yours is the bunk above.' The uniformed Sikh scarcely moved his lips, or so it seemed, for the general demeanour of his face was taut. Dusty put it down to his beard. It was neat and tightly tucked inside a hair net that went round his chin from under his turban. 'No offence meant.'

'None taken,' Dusty assured him. He took in the Ashoka lions on the Sikh's olive green shoulder lapels and added: 'Sir!'

'Don't tell me you're a brother officer. What, subaltern or a gentleman cadet?'

'The last. I'll move my stuff in a minute and, when it's time to turn in, I'll climb into my bunk. Till then I'll sit by this window, if I may?'

'By all means. Most welcome. So, it's to the Military Academy at Tejpore? Your first term, I guess.'

'Yes sir.'

'Good. You'll do well. I see you've been to a top school. St Thomas's?'

Dusty glanced down at the badge on his blue blazer and smiled. 'Yes.'

'The name's Amarjit. Major Amarjit Singh Grewal, Army Education Corp. You'll be seeing me. I'm an Instructor at the Academy. Geography, map reading, that's my subject.' His already stretched eyebrows moved a little. 'You are?'

'Sorry, Dustoor, Sam Dustoor.'

'Parsee? Not many Parsees in the Army.'

In the Shadow of a Dream

'Not many Parsees in India.'

The Major frowned. 'I thought, maybe you are Anglo-Indian. And what are you aiming for? Arms or Services?' He consulted his watch and sat down facing the door which opened on to the station platform.

'Arms. The infantry, if I fail to get the Armoured Corps.' Dusty said evenly.

'Armoured Corps, Cavalry? Tough. Only the ten best cadets get in. Well, no harm trying.'

'Indeed, sir. I was warned. But I have strong hopes.'

'And your worthy father's name, if I may ask?'

Dusty hesitated a moment. 'Sam Dustoor.' He smiled. 'I'm Sam Dustoor Junior.'

'How very American.'

'Well,' Dusty quickly recovered, 'Dustoor Senior has a brother in America.'

'And is there a military tradition in your family? I mean, was your father...' he broke off to spring at the door. 'Hey! This is First Class. Are you *andha*, blind? *Jao, jao!*' He gestured wildly then sat down again. 'Sorry, but these damned coolies, oh they're such crooks, you know. Just as train is about to move, they push luggage in, and then you can't get rid of the passenger and his stuff till the next stop.' He again consulted his watch. 'Good. Soon we'll be moving. Next stop, one hour away.' The door handle rattled and the door was pushed open. 'Hey, First Class! Bloody fool!'

'Get out of the way!' A voice from outside boomed. 'I know it's First Class, I've got a reservation, just couldn't locate the damn compartment! Ah! it's you, Jiti.'

'Sorry, Colonel Sahib, let me give you a hand. I've been saving your berth.'

Dusty sprang to help. Grabbing a steel trunk by the handle he pulled it in, and as he did so, a tall man in a red striped blazer leapt in, shut the door, and leaned out of the window. 'Here, coolie!' He roared. 'Take it. Come on! Come on, man! Don't pretend you haven't got change.' The train picked up speed. '*Jaldi*, blast you!' He chortled. 'There goes a fiver. Still, I made it in the nick of time.'

'Yes, sir. You have but Dhillon missed the boat.' Major Amarjit laughed.

The new-comer faced his companions. 'I see, Dhillon hasn't made it.' He mopped his brow and brushed his thin moustache. 'Typical of Monty. Bad form.'

'Actually sir, Captain Dhillon will board the train at Saharanpur. Next stop. But you won't have to use the upper bunk. First come, first served.'

The Colonel grunted.

'This is a five berther,' the Major went on, 'and there's only the four of us.'

'Thank God. I hate climbing up on to those things,' said the Colonel, then in an undertone he asked: 'And who's the whippersnapper?'

'A new cadet. Joining the Academy. Dustoor, this is Colonel…'

'Chaudhary,' filled in Dusty, 'pleased to meet you. Your name's on the trunk.'

'Well observed, young man. But it's not my trunk. I'm Colonel Dhanraj…'

'Chief Instructor,' piped in the Major. 'Why the grin, Dustoor?'

'Sorry, as P G Wodehouse would put it, I feel like a lion in a den of Daniels.'

'Cheeky,' growled the Colonel. 'A word of advice, young man. This is your first term. So you keep a low profile. Cheek will only get you punishments. Watch it.'

'The Sergeant-Major'll put him right, sir,' grinned the Major.

The Colonel nodded. 'But Jiti, I thought this compartment was reserved for us. That's you, me, and Dhillon.' He rubbed his chin with the back of his hand.

'Sir,' Dusty regarded the Colonel with equanimity well beyond his years. 'Let me explain. The Guard put me here. My reserved berth was in the coupé next door—the one with two berths. He asked if I'd be kind enough to surrender it to two ladies. VIPs I gather. One is the wife of General Sen Gupta.'

The two officers sat up, looked at each other, and speaking almost simultaneously said. 'That'll be Minnie! You did say Sen Gupta?'

Dusty nodded.

After a pause the Major said: 'So, you've already met the Commandant's wife.'

'Yes, sir. The Guard confirmed that and the lady herself thanked me.'

'Don't let that go to your head, young man,' warned Colonel Dhanraj. 'And when we arrive at Tejpore in the morning, it would be for the best to pretend you did not meet any of us. Particularly Min...I mean, the Commandant's wife. Get that?'

'That's as it should to be,' added the Major. 'Have you come prepared?'

'Prepared?' Dusty frowned. Prepared for what?'

'For what, SIR! It's January. Tejpore can be biting cold. Have you got a coat?'

'Apart from this blazer I've got a woollen scarf. But I was given to understand I will be issued with winter uniform and a great coat.' Dusty noted the Colonel had turned away and was busy spreading a blanket on the spare berth.

'Oh, yes. But that'll take some time. He's from Bombay, sir. These fellows forget how cold it can be up here, in the north. You're going to be an officer. Cadets, like officer's uniforms, are tailored. As I said it will take some time. Till then you'll wear a band with your cadet number, on your sleeve.'

'I'll lend him a trench-coat before we get to Tejpore.' The Colonel said, as he lay full length on the birth. 'Return it, after you get your stuff. Give it to your batman, I mean orderly, he'll know how to get it to me.' He sat up with a swift movement and started to untie his shoelaces. 'Don't look lost, young lad. One of the first things you do, after you're allotted your room in the barracks, is to employ an orderly—actually, they are civilians, just chaps who shine your boots and check your kit. Usually one between two or three cadets, to spread the cost of his salary.' He suddenly burst out laughing. 'This is not for you, young man. Shut your ears. Jiti, you know, Sen Gupta, as far as his Minnie is concerned, is in the "being skinned stage", you know.'

'Sorry, I don't get it. What d'you mean, sir?'

'Remember when Sen Gupta dined with us last month. I thought you were there. Never mind. He said, over the cheese and port, "you know Gentlemen, there are five stages in a man's love life. Like that of a fish. He is first baited, then hooked, caught, skinned, and finally cooked. Gentleman," he said, "I am in the being skinned stage."'

The Major dutifully laughed. 'Clearly sir, Minnie's been on a shopping spree with a friend. And you know who that lady friend will be? Malti, the Adjutant's wife.'

'You can't know for certain. Are you just guessing?'

'But I'll be surprised if I'm wrong, Rajan.' The colonel drew himself up, but as Amarjit quickly added "Sir", he relaxed. 'They say,' continued Amarjit, 'Malti wears the trousers. Bit unfair. That her husband's appointment was due to an HBE.'

'Her bloody effort!' Colonel Dhanraj giggled, then turned to Dusty. 'Young man, I think, you ought to climb into your bunk and turn in.'

Dusty held up a book. 'I'm reading.'

'I'm reading, Sir,' prompted the Major.

'But of course, Sir,' Dusty said. He stood up, removed his blazer and hung it on the hook by the door. He then executed an athletic spring up to the bunk, lay back and turned on the reading lamp.

'Don't read for long, I can't sleep when there's a light on,' the Colonel said.

'I was glad to do a good deed by surrendering my berth, now sir, you're making me regret it,' Dusty mumbled, as he got down from the bunk.

'That's insolence. You obviously have a lot to learn about the Army, young man. Where are you going now?'

'Sir? To the toilet. To clean my teeth, before I…or do I have to wait till…'

'Sorry, young man, do go ahead. Don't get me wrong.' Colonel Dhanraj got up and opened the bathroom door. 'Weren't you supposed to arrive yesterday? The cadets of your course would be in and safely billeted.' He looked at his watch.

'I've informed the Academy. My joining up letter gives my ETA a day late. The authorities know the reason. And officially the course starts tomorrow.'

'Indeed. Well, see you in the morning. I won't forget the trench coat.'

The train arrived at Tejpore in the early hours of the morning. A cold sun tried hard to pierce the grey, damp mist enveloping the station platform on which Dusty stood shivering.

'You'll be met,' said the Colonel as he handed Dusty a khaki trench coat.

'Thank you, sir, I'll treat it with care.'

'It's a good fit. Keep it. I mean that, and you need not mention it to anyone.'

The Colonel climbed back into the compartment just as the Major was getting out. 'You never see a coolie when you want one,' the Major said and startled Dusty with a heavy thump in the small of his back. 'You're not the only late comer.' He pointed to two figures at the far end of the platform. 'D'you always travel First Class? Last year, I was detailed to meet the cadets. Packed the lot off in a Bedford three-tonner. That's the meeting point, under the station clock. Wait there. Ah! I see they've sent the Sergeant Major to collect the stragglers. You've made a bad start to your first term in the Academy, young man.'

Dusty decided not to explain again, though he did wonder why Major Amarjit missed his explanation last night. 'That very tall man, sir. Is he the Sergeant-Major? But he's got red tabs on his collar and a red band round his peaked-cap.'

'He's an Englishman. Sergeant-Major Vallins, Grenadier Guards. Borrowed from the British Army to advise us on matters of drill and ceremonial parades. The last of his kind, I hope. As part of the drive to Indianise the army, the words of commands will soon be in Hindi. Then he'll hand over to Sergeant Gurung. Jung Bahadur Gurung MC. He is the little Gurkha chap, standing next to him. Well, best of luck, young man.' He went past the two men, who stamped to attention and saluted.

'Wasn't that terribly smart?' Colonel Dhanraj said as he walked up to Dusty. 'I overheard the major telling you about the army turning native. Yes, but you'll see our traditions are still very British. Sen Gupta is Sandhurst trained. That reminds me. Minnie. I'd better see to...'

'They've left, sir.'

'How d'you know?'

'I saw them get into the jeep that was parked on the platform.'

'Good. My jeep will be here shortly...ah, there's Amarjit with a coolie and the driver. There'll be coolies to help with your stuff.' He walked on, and keeping his voice down, but loud enough to be audible, addressed the Major. 'I say, Jiti, do you realise Captain Dhillon failed to board the train. Typically, bad form.'

'Yes, sir. Typical, as you say. He'll be on the mat this time. He's asking for it. Mind you he could be on the bus if he missed the train. Gets into town…two hours from now. So I guess he can still make it in time.' There was more talk between them but Dusty missed the banter for at that moment he felt the Sergeant-Major's pace-stick jabbed sharply into his midriff. He looked up at a pair of very stern blue eyes. 'Are you a new cadet?'

'Yes, sir.'

The pace-stick dug deeper. 'Don't "sir" me. It's yes, Sergeant-Major or "Sar". Get that? Now did you see that sign which says "Assembly point".'

'Yes, Sar…'

'That's where you should be. What's keeping you?' Roared the Sergeant-Major, 'Waiting to be kissed? Get a move on! Sharpish! Never mind your kit. It'll be taken care of. Smartly, now! BY THE LEFT, QUICK MARCH! Don't slouch! LEFT RIGHT, LEFT RIGHT!' The Sergeant Major's footsteps crunched close behind Dusty's. 'Eyes front! Look sharp! Get those legs moving! DON'T LOOK DOWN! The sweepers have been HALT. Stand still. At ease. That means, legs apart, hands behind you back.'

'I know, Sar, we marched and drilled on Founder's Day, at my school.'

Sergeant-Major Vallins eyes glared down at Dusty. 'You've got a lot to learn, me lad. You don't speak till I say you can. And that's never.' He growled as he circled round Dusty. 'Yes. I like your jacket, not what's in it.' The Gurkha joined them and handed him a clip board and pencil. Vallins tapped the board. 'Are you Mr Joshi, Mr Tiwari or Mr Dustoor?'

'Dustoor, Sir, er Sar!'

'I'll get the other two, Sar,' the Gurkha said, marching away, his small plump legs moving like clappers within his starched-stiff, bell-shaped, olive-green shorts.

'Not to worry, Jung Bahadur. Here they come.' Then Vallins whispered to Dusty. 'If you lot are the future hope of the Army, thank God we've got a Navy.'

Dusty laughed. Vallins pounced. 'Nothing to laugh about, you dozy man you.' Then looking away at the approaching cadets, he

In the Shadow of a Dream

shouted. 'Stop slouching! Swing those arms! Bahadur sahib, tell those coolies to make it *Jaldi, jaldi*! Right, you lot follow me. There, see the truck? Mount! On the double! That means run; and lift those feet, you sloppy lot, you!'

The Central Clock Tower of Clive Hall overlooked a large, pristine, tarmacked Parade Ground. Across the width of its asphalt, behind a gleaming white saluting dais, a fifty-foot high flagpole flew the Indian Union Flag from Reveille to Last Post. Built in 1926, Clive Hall, renamed Bharat Sena Hall, is flanked on either side by the East and West Wings of Wellington Barracks—a name, surprisingly left unchanged. These neatly pointed, red-brick, neo-Georgian buildings, form a stately symmetrical arrangement that is the pride of Tejpore's Military Academy and the hub of the new Military Cantonment. From 1949, to meet the need of an expanding Indian Army, new barracks were raised for the accommodation and training of young cadets. Much of the materials for the barracks were prefabricated, and sadly, because of this haste, the grandeur of the Academy's original blue print suffered. But since the authorities had placed the project into the able hands of one Pritam Singh, a precocious young architect, who admired Sir Edwin Lutyens and had studied his methods, chiefly the planned layouts for New Delhi, Pritam mapped out a network of tree-lined avenues and barracks in squares to hide much of what he considered ugly. Sunken sheds for washrooms, latrines and bicycle stands, maintained the discreet and tidy look; and not content to conceal both the Cinema and Swimming Pool in a wooded hollow, he had their corrugated tin roofs painted a discreet olive green, to blend with the pine and lush ilex, which cleverly camouflaged these plain buildings. The kitchens of the two dining-rooms had serving counters, that ran along one entire side of these large detached buildings. They were located between the Wellington barracks and the new prefabricated quarters. Behind a line of poplars, a library and science laboratory were near completion and beyond them flat areas of forest were cleared for playing fields and far into the rising foothills of the Shivalik hills, was the obstacle course, a First Aid Centre, a field hospital and the Rifle Range.

Neighbouring the Academy, the vast Victorian complex of the Institute for Forest Research, had rooms surplus to its needs. These were leased to the Academy and refurbished into lecture halls for the studies of Military History, the Sciences, Civics and Geography.

The shortage of funds thwarted Pritam Singh's ambitions and consequently won him faint praise. The disappointed architect left India, settled in the USA, and found the recognition he deserved in California.

His grandest legacy, the Great Avenue, led from the Parade Ground towards the high boundary walls and main gates. There, by the sentry box, were the Armoury and the Guard House. Outside the tall cast-iron gates, a cattle-grid not only discouraged Tejpur's nomadic sacred bulls, but also warned sentries of the approach of trucks and other vehicles.

On that cold January morning Vallins stopped the military truck on the grid and made the cadets dismount and line up in front of it. 'From here you'll march to your barracks,' he said. 'It's the shortest way. The truck will go round the back with your luggage. Now, I'll hand you over to Sergeant Gurung, and I'll see you lot on parade tomorrow morning. After you've settled in your rooms, an hour from now, you will have breakfast, then issued with bicycles. The Sergeant will then show you round. Get to know the geography of the place, because there are no excuses for being late on parade. Late comers are punished with severe drills and extra parades. Is that clear? Say, "yes, Sar-Major". What? Can't hear you! Scream it out!'

'YES, SAR-MAJOR!'

'You miserable specimens you! If you're the country's *creme de la creme,* God help us!' He stamped his highly polished jack-boots hard, took two steps forward, gently prodded Dusty in the ribs with his pace-stick. 'More I see of you, the more I begin to believe in the practice of birth control. What's your name again?'

'Dustoor.'

'Where I come from, that's what we call the backside of a she-camel. Stand still! Stop laughing! YOU THERE! Josh-Josey, Tee-Teeberry, whoever you are, WIPE THOSE SMILES OFF YOUR FACES! If you must laugh, laugh by numbers.'

'How does one laugh by numbers? Sar!' Dusty asked.

'QUIET!' Vallins shouted and turned to Bahadur.

The stocky Gurkha sprang to attention. 'Two, three, one: ha! Two, three, one: ha! Two, three, one, hee! hee' Sergeant Gurung's earnest face betrayed no levity.

A faint twitch at the corners of Vallins mouth made his thin ginger moustache quiver. Then, as he got into the truck next to the driver he smiled at Dusty, who till that moment wondered why he was being singled out for jokey criticism. The smile made him decide the Englishman had taken a liking to him. Dusty turned in time to see a tall young man in khaki with a red sash across his chest standing next to Jung Bahadur Gurung. 'This,' said the Gurkha, 'is Gentleman Cadet Sukdev Chadda. He wearing this,' he pointed to the red sash, 'so he's cadet on duty. Second termer! He look after new boys! Show you Academy.' Sergeant Gurung spoke in rapid bursts. Then he stiffened himself, hands by his sides and raised his voice. 'ATTENTION! SINGLE FILE!' 'QUICK MARCH! Left, left, left right left!'

They marched or rather shuffled along much to the dismay of Sergeant Gurung, who kept hopping around the nervous cadets, shrieking: 'Keep in step! No, in step! Halt! Squad, av'rybody, halt! You, Mr Dustoor, you go! Go! Go wait under Clock Tower.' Dusty marched on. His brisk step attuned to his thoughts. He felt, as never before, a deep excitement. At last, this was what he wanted. Here, where he would be independent, with no obligation to anyone but himself. In a response to impartial rules, within an impersonal and ordered framework of discipline, he could discover a new sort of freedom, a start to a new life. Two years, he mused, two years of toeing the line. Then a freedom, learned and earned. Not licence. A freedom, making him invisible, invulnerable; and with a salary. He would have security. Self-respect and pride he had in full measure, born of self-confidence and of capabilities to excel. He recalled Colonel Hafiz, of the Poona selection Board say: "Dustoor, you put down Dr Sam Dustoor MA., Ph.D., as your guardian. You have his name, but he is not your father? Right. But your age, confirmed by your School Certificate, unfortunately puts you three months under Entry Age bracket. However, I am recommending for this disqualification to be overlooked. I'm doing this on the basis of your IQ test results. Never, in all my time here and for that matter as long as any of my colleagues can

recall, has any one scored so highly. There may be delay, but you should receive a letter with details of training and ETA, that is, estimated time of arrival, at Tejpore. Courses start January and June. Letter will inform you when. At the end of two years training you'll be a commissioned officer with a regimental posting..."
It all came back to him, word for word. Yet this ability of total recall saddened him. It was a curse, not a blessing, to be haunted and hunted by memories he could not shed. Fat Sujata, drunken Randhir, black, kind Daadi; brave Asif, young Yosef, old Jaswant; and all life in Fatehpur was as clear as if projected on a cinema screen! And another, a nagging memory, not as clear, but an even more troubling vision of a young, tender frenetic face, pressed against his, while he choked, struggling for air till it became an old, smiling, toothless face; a gnarled fingertip dipping into a brass bowl, pushing between his lips drops of milk, while around him buzzed disembodied, angry voices. Dusty sat down on the marble steps that led up to the Great Hall and covered his ears to shut out the sounds. 'I'll learn to forget,' he told himself, then stood up as Gurung arrived with the other two.

CHAPTER SIX

A fortnight later Dusty received a letter from Sam. It enclosed a photograph of Sam and looking up soulfully at him, a Red Setter on a lead. "That's me with Rex in the garden, isn't he a handsome beast?" Sam wrote. "Soli Mehta took the snap on his Rolliflex. I tried hard to steer away from his pet subject, photography, but with no luck. Now I know so much about the damn thing, I've decided to get a camera—a Leica, no less—a typical complex of the amateur, safest to go for the best—and hope to take some good ones of you when next we're on holiday. I got your postcard of safe arrival but have had no news from you since—getting on for twelve days! (Exclamation! Explanation?) Hope all's well. I see Tejpore Academy follows the school-pattern of hols, so I'll be seeing you around Christmas. I suppose a military army regime gives you little time to relax and a good reason for not writing. But drop a line whenever you can. The house feels empty without you. Anyway, your absence has motivated me to write to Muriel more often. She believes you're my son and that you must have your mother's looks. But with typically dry English aplomb adds that a large nose is all right on a man, not a woman, and can understand why a rather "nosey" state of matrimony couldn't last. I'll put her right on important things, but won't say too much. Not yet."

Sam's letter touched Dusty's sense of guilt. "Your letter shamed me," he wrote back that same evening, "and though we do have a full timetable, I have no excuse for not writing. Forgive me old chap! Apologies by the score. 'Lights Out' is at ten thirty but I have, on an average afternoon, after compulsory games/shower, an hour before dinner at eight thirty. Less on week days 'cos dinner is formal and we have to dress up to the nines. I've got all my uniforms (speed tailoring out here) but during the day it's thick cotton dungarees, boots, canvas anklets…The morning half of our timetable is Drill, PT (i.e. physical training), field exercises and a punishing obstacle course. Academic subjects are after lunch, but we are so physically exhausted that, by then, most of the cadets nod off during lectures. Well, not all. Lecturers press on regardless. They have ranks of captains or majors according to seniority—honorary ones for the civilian staff—and because we have to salute them they are recognised by their grey suits and maroon ties. I've not had the pleasure of meeting Major Amarjit again, but Colonel Dhanraj—I've returned his trench coat—has twice taken us out, on Field Exercises. He's a bit of a wag—thanks for that word, I use it a lot. He's a stickler for correct English usage. On our first outing with him, we were given tasks of making simple diagrams and maps, for which we had to follow a rigid procedure of drawing attention to landmarks, by plotting it on our handcharts and giving it a name. For practise, we took turns. One of us began thus: 'Look to your front, six hundred yards, one o'clock, a tree by itself, call it "lonely tree".' Dhanraj pounced: 'Gentlemen, we are in no position to judge the sentiments of that tree. Lonely or not, it's not for us to say. I'd call it "lone tree".' On the last occasion, three days ago, I arrived at a briefing session without a notebook. He turned to me: 'No notebook? Who do you think you are? Napoleon?' The rest of the news is a slog, so I shan't bore you. I liked the snap. You look distinguished. The dog completes the squire-like image. I envy the corduroy jacket. Glad to hear you've rationed the alcohol intake. Don't weaken."

Dusty found an envelope and was about to address it, when he stopped to add a postscript. "Dear Sam, As letters go to our *daftar* before being taken by the mail truck to the post office in town, I'm addressing you in full: Dr Sarman Dustoor, MA., Ph.d., because it's impressive and I want to show off (you haven't told me why your father named you 'Sarman' and after whom) and I'm going to borrow your way of signing off. I like it. Yours as ever, Dusty.

PPS I'll make Saturday my letter writing day so that you'll get a regular weekly news bulletin."

In the Shadow of a Dream

But there followed a long wait before Dusty heard from Sam again. After a month he began to worry and asked to see his Company Commander, who gave him a "gate pass" to send a telegram from the town post office. It was not necessary. That same day he received Sam's telegram: "Dear Boy, Sorry for the long silence stop Literally seeing the world with jaundiced eyes stop Been in hospital stop Letter follows stop Sam." The letter, which arrived a few days later explained how Sam had a surprise visit from brother Dinshaw and aunt Gul. Dinshaw had flown from Boston earlier and had been staying with Gul in Surat. "Their unexpected advent forced me to lie. That, as you know, is a foolhardy course of action and one you've advised me never to try. To escape them, I said I had to leave for Bangalore in two days, which I was forced to do, since Dinshaw insisted on seeing me off at station. Oh, the tangled web etc... In Bangalore, at a not very reputable hotel, I must have been infected, jaundice and was forced to take a genuine holiday in Coonar, in the Nilgris (with Rex and a stout walking stick) to recover from it all—when it comes to demands on time, dogs are worse than wives or friends. The telegram, I sent on my last day at Coonar. I'm now back in Bombay, and most upset. Dinshaw has run off with my brand new book on Curzon. I was halfway through it when the barbarians landed!"

"Dear Sam," Dusty wrote back as promptly as he could, "Please don't avoid your family because of me. I don't know what's going on but I can guess they want you to have nothing further to do with me. They have a point. I would rather you forget me and got on with them, because clearly it's killing you and I'd be irresponsible not to stress that it's all so unnecessary. They are right to look upon me as a stranger or a parvenu. You have done your bit by me, as I said before and my future is now clearly laid out before me. Please, you must forget me. You've fed, clothed and educated me—more than adequately equipped me for life's journey. I knew there's nothing more I should expect from you, and why I took steps to fend for myself. You found me in a sty and put me in a palace. I'm for all that, forever grateful, and I will never forget you. Now, with me out of the picture, life with your family should be smooth sailing. Yours ay, Dusty. PS I feel like an old man talking to a novice, when it should be the other way round. D"

"Gosh! Dusty you've grown fast! Are you really just eighteen?

When you said not all the cadets nodded off during lectures, I guessed you'd be the wide awake one. It has to be you. But I have to say your letter hurt me. You're all head and no heart. In saying that, I hope I'm doing you an injustice. Yes, it would have been enough just to have helped you in life by all I did for you and left it at that—keeping a distance, surveying the result and giving myself a smug self-congratulatory pat on the back— but, did we not have a relationship? Do we not have one still? Did I not treat you like a son and, unless I've totally misjudged you, did you not respond in some filial measure? Your concern for my health, is that without affection? Dear boy, 'Yours ay', has meaning. Sam."

"Oh, Sam! I'm a child again. 'Bewitched, bothered and bewildered, am I' (a song going the rounds here) and I'm in a spin. I do care. Let me try another tack. At least do this for me. Forget your family, forget me. Think about you. Go West Old Chap, go. Leave me here, I'm doing fine. Leave Rex with Mehta. Fly to the England you've always loved. Marry Muriel and live happily ever after. Dusty"

Four days later a brown envelope arrived. In it was an autographed photograph of Denis Compton, Dusty's favourite cricketer, and on the back Dusty read: "My word! What a little giant I've created. Will do, or as they say in military circles "wilco". But I'll wait for the Summer hols before I go. I want us to be together, for one last time. As ever, Sam.

PS Sticking to cricket jargon, I'm unlikely to have a long innings, but finally, you'll get the ashes." S

At the Departure Lounge in Bombay's Santa Cruz Airport, two men held hands in a tightening grip and regarded each other with fixed smiles.: 'Sam, I refuse to break down, because you're doing what I've asked you to do, at last.' Dusty freed his hand and picked up a flat brown parcel that rested by his foot. 'This, for Muriel, an Indian miniature painting, Kangra School. Tell her I bought it in Kangra District itself.'

'Thank you, I will. It's what she'd like. Muriel will know Tejpore's in Kangra. On her trip to Dharamsala, she toured the area.' He took a deep breath. 'I've wound up. Left everything cleared and settled…We're unlikely to see each other again…'

'Nonsense. I refuse to listen to such talk. If you don't come back to India, well, as they say, if the mountain won't...'

'You once said that you don't wish to cross the *kala pani*, the black waters?'

'I know. I still feel uncomfortable about it, I don't know where that comes from.'

'Your roots, dear boy. It's a Hindu thing.'

'For no good reason. I should've set it aside, After all, officially I'm Christian.'

'It may be years before you get over that, and years before you can take time off from the army, to gad about.'

'You'll be around. And you must see to that.'

'Dusty, are you sure about the army? Think of your avid love for reading...'

'In the army I'll get more time for reading, compared with any other career. You know, the army doesn't work after lunch. Well, officers don't. Not much. You see, there's method in my madness.'

'Soli Mehta always marvels at the range of your English vocabulary.'

'Surely he knows, all credit goes to you. If not, I'll tell him next time we...'

'I've told him. Not about me, but that you're mad about encyclopaedias and dictionaries...but time is slipping away. Listen, your twenty-first birthday is not too long away. You'll hear from Taraporevala, my lawyer chappie and I don't care what the family thinks. In any event they won't know. I've left you a nest egg. You won't have to fight for it, or justify having it. That's why I wanted you to open a bank...'

'You're determined to make me a living monument to your generosity.'

'Well, I shan't have any other; and I want to be remembered.'

'The egg will remain in its nest. I intend to live on my salary.'

'Don't be too sure of that. Whichever cavalry regiment you choose, you'll need to draw on extra funds. I gather, that cavalry regiments are notoriously spendthrift and expensive. No officer seems to manage on his salary. There'll be fellow officers who are rajas and nawabs...aristocrats all. Why the Cavalry?'

'The uniforms. Chain mail on my shoulders and spurs in my

boots…this is what happens when you pick someone from the gutter and show 'em the grand life.'

'You mustn't ever say that…It's a terrible thing to say. How could you!'

'Sorry. I expect it was a joke in poor taste.'

'Yes. Anyway, the next important item. You won't be getting a salary for some time. Fifty rupees per month can't be enough, even for incidental expenses. Half that must go to your orderly. And, I don't want you to apply for a Governmental grant. Actually you can't without…well, without revealing everything. And in triplicate.' Sam laughed. 'Indian bureaucracy is…no I'll stop there. That's *my* poor joke. With immediate effect, Taraporevala has been told to make it ninety rupees. Hello! Hullo! Yes, over here.'

'Who are you talking to?'

'The chap with the camera. Don't smile, I hate smiling pictures. Don't give him your IMA address. I'll pay him now and send a copy when I get it, but not if it's a terrible one of me. He's taking another. One moment,' Sam passed a hand through his thinning grey hair. 'I think my eyes were shut then. Lord, that was the last call, I must go. Goodbye. Write.'

Dusty watched Sam raise his brief case as he went through the turnstile. 'Sam!' he called. 'Sam, marry her!'

Sam did not look back. Dusty was not sure he had heard.

CHAPTER SEVEN

Minnie, wife of General Jotender Sen Gupta, Commandant of the Tejpore Military Academy, was an aristocrat, related to the Nawab of Mandipur. After her schooling in England, she spent time in France and returned to India captivated by the culture and lifestyle of the West. In addition, she was beautiful as only Bengali women can be, and unlike most Indian women of her age, emphasised her trim figure by the alluring way she tied her plain soft silk saris. Their plainness was a feint, meant to offset her bright tight fitting blouses, many exquisitely patterned in gold lamé and tailored to display a wide band of bare flesh above her waistline. These she modestly covered with the free end of her sari which, constantly slipping off her shoulder, had to be retrieved in graceful movements that drew attention. And though she dressed like an Indian, her hair, not yet grey, was bobbed and neatly coiffured. Against that luxuriant backdrop, she wore pendant earrings that were long, French, but distinctly Fabergé inspired.

Minnie's husband, a man of supreme confidence and erect bearing, seemed taller than he was. His hard mouth, below a pencil thin moustache, conveyed a no-nonsense demeanour that was contrary to his soft, tired eyes, the result of Bridge sessions, which went on till midnight, when he was to be seen always with a glass of Scotch and soda by his side. Yet he never failed to be punctual on parade or smartly turned out. There was about him an air of enigma and his apparent indifference to his wife's beauty intrigued cadets who, to a man, drooled at the sight of her and looked forward to the occasions when she made an appearance. Chief among these was the Annual Sports Day and Pagal Gymkhanna when, as the Commandant's wife, she gave out the prizes. How the average cadet envied the prize winners for the privilege of shaking her hand!

At Tejpore, during training, stress was laid on cadets to acquire "OLQ" (officer like qualities). This meant that the prime requirements for officers, as future leaders, were education and intelligence. Consequently, almost all officer cadets came from the urban, Indian middle-classes. But, as it was also important to be physically fit, it became necessary to take in cadets at school leaving age. Competition in sports and games was encouraged. Clearly, those who were both mentally and physically adept were the most likely to achieve the aims of the Military Academy.

As always in such institutions there are exceptions: candidates with rare abilities were grateful for a unique opportunity to prove their worth, and were most likely to shine. Apart from Dusty, only three other cadets on his course had a boyhood history of regular physical exercise and endurance and when it came to athletic prowess, they had no rivals. Of these other three, two were from the hills of Garwhal, and the third, a Dogra had, like Dusty, a rural background.

The Annual Sports Day Gymkhanna, the grandest and most colourful affair of the Tejpore's social calendar, was invariably held in the third week of December, before the break up for the Christmas holidays. Large tents, decorated with pennants, flags and freshly painted white ropes, bordered the sports field. Here the neat, demarcated lanes of the racing tracks gleamed in the afternoon sun. In front of the VIP marquee, a large table displayed the trophies, silver cups, medals and shields, to be awarded. The Day began at 2 p.m. and following the prize-giving at 6 p.m. the day ended with a dinner and dance that went on till midnight.

Dusty, representing B Company in the long distance track events, had already won the Cross Country Marathon race, which, because it needed a full afternoon to plan, was held the day before. But as he was also competing in two other races, he hoped to collect at least two more trophies. He won the eight hundred metres, but in the mile, the Dogra beat him to second place.

In the Shadow of a Dream

'You must be six feet tall,' Minnie said, as she offered her hand.

Dusty held her hand lightly and bowed—all competing cadets had been rehearsed by Sergeant-Major Vallins on how to accept their awards. 'Five ten, ma'am.'

'Well, I wasn't far wrong,' Minnie said, taking the Inter-Company Marathon Race Shield from her husband and would have dropped it, had Dusty not deftly reached out to steady her hands. 'Goodness! I didn't realise it was heavy,' she said with a charming smile and studied his face. 'You look familiar. I believe we've met before, haven't we? But, of course, you're the young man who kindly...' she turn to her husband. 'Darling, this is the young man, I told you about, who surrendered...'

'I know. He's been pointed out to me. I suppose he had no choice.'

'Nonsense, Joe, he could have held out. He wasn't to know who I was.'

'My dear, you're looking at one of the sharpest boys in his course.' The General nodded towards Dusty and waved a dismissing hand. 'Next, Sar'Major.'

After dinner the Annual Ball was held at the Bharat Sena Hall, to which Officers, their wives and daughters; and prize-winning cadets, were invited to attend. General Sen Gupta and Minnie opened the Ball, watched by a line of nervous cadets in their best blue uniforms. The pair glided, a little stiffly on the General's part, to the strains of Johann Strauss's *Blue Danube*, fairly adequately played by a five-piece orchestra consisting of a tenor saxophone, a bass clarinet, a muted trumpet, the upright piano transferred from the Cadets' Café, and drums. The musicians were members of the Academy's Military Brass Band, except the pianist who, hired for the evening, was from Tejpore's *Golden Slipper* restaurant. The General tried hard not to look bored, but he need not have troubled; all eyes were on the graceful Minnie.

When he got to the middle of the floor, the General said: 'Ladies and gentlemen, do join in.' The officers led their wives on to the floor, the cadets hesitated, some of whom, having had dancing lessons from Dusty two days earlier, awaited his signal to take the dreaded leap, and having got it, timidly approached the tables, where the few ladies left still sitting appeared to regard their advance with some alarm. But, most of the cadets, realising they outnumbered the women, two to one, regrouped to remind each other of their earlier gentlemanly agreement to take turns, unaware that some women, realising that they would be on the floor without a break, made excuses, and the disappointed cadets had the added onus of having to stay and entertain them.

Dusty had assessed this situation. Wisely he withdrew himself and drawing a chair nearer to where the band was playing, sat down and wearily stretched his long legs. The band switched to the *Tennessee Waltz* and he began involuntarily tapping his feet in time to the music. The tune reminded him of Sam's valiant efforts to teach him the waltz before he left for the Poona Army Selection Board. 'Just in case,' Sam had said. 'I'm told the waltz is popular in Army circles, where everyone tries hard to copy the Brits of the Raj. So you ought to learn the waltz and ballroom etiquette too.' Sam had a record of the *Tennessee Waltz*, which was played again and again on his radio-gram. But he soon gave up. 'It's no good. It's the blind leading the blind. We'll need professional help.' And so the petite Shirley Boston of the Victor Sylvester Ballroom Dancing School, First Floor, Faircourt Mansion, Flora Fountain, Bombay, entered his life—sweet, patient Shirley Boston, the first to stir his libido, who with every new lesson danced closer and closer till he felt the softness of her shapely breasts...then, that last day, on the top stair, to give her the necessary height, a soft kiss, the lightest of touch, the first kiss in his life, making his lips tingle...even now, as he recalled it.

'Young man, I see you're not dancing?' The clipped Sandhurst accent of General Sen Gupta broke into his reverie.

Dusty jumped to his feet and clicked his heels. 'I'm not a good dancer, sir.'

'Who is? An officer and gentleman's not supposed to be. That's for spivs. There, come with me to my table. Keep Minnie company. It'll release me to play a rubber or two before the night's over.'

'I'm afraid, sir, I can only do the waltz and quick step.'

The General laughed. 'Nobody expects you to do the tango, young man. Besides, between you and me, the fox-trot and waltz are the entire repertoire of this band.' He nodded at the Gurkha, who had just put his clarinet down. '*Bahoot achcha*! Thapar sahib. Well done! *Shabash*!' Then, as if to prove the General wrong, the band broke into *Cherry Pink and Apple Blossom White*, giving the till now, not used, trumpeter his first moment of glory. Sen Gupta shrugged his shoulders and raised his brows. 'I forgot the Samba. Oh, well, just kick your heels and touch your elbows. In fact, just follow Minnie. She's so good, your antics will go unnoticed.'

They reached the General's table. 'Minnie this is Gentleman Cadet Sam Dustoor.'

'Darling, I know Sam. He received a shield, two cups and a medal this evening. I was surprised he did not compete in the field events, and even more surprised not to see him on the dance floor.'

Dusty bowed. Earlier in the evening, while he was dressing up, he had been told, in a tone of utmost confidentiality, by his Senior Under Officer, that Minnie was ten years younger than her husband. From where he stood, she looked even younger.

'Well, my dear, he's kindly agreed to be your escort. Be kind. He says he's no dancer. Come on, Malhotra, be the third man. A pity, Minnie won't bridge the gap.'

'It's such a waste of time, Darling. And when I try, well you know what happens.' Minnie studied her husband. 'I won't say more.' She turned away with a slight smile and an arrogant toss of her pretty head. 'Do sit down, Sam, and first let me introduce you to those left at our greatly depleted table...' she stopped. Captain Sunil Malhotra rose, bowed to Minnie and left with the General into the far end of the hall. 'This is Malti, Mrs Malhotra, just deserted by her hubby, and Colonel Ali Abbas—that's Mrs Abbas on the floor with Colonel Dhanraj, who...' She stopped as Captain Malhotra returned to tell Malti he would be in the adjacent Ante-room, and that when she felt bored, to join him there. He then threw a rather hostile glance, Sam thought, at him, and disappeared into the darkness beyond the drinks bar. 'As I was saying,' Minnie went on, 'Colonel Dhanraj, who I gather you met on the train early in January, leaves us and Colonel Abbas is taking over as Chief Instructor.'

'Yes, ma'am, we've heard Colonel Dhanraj's leaving Tejpore.'

'Not just Tejpore. He's leaving the Army. His father-in-law is buying him out, or whatever one needs to do to get out of the

Army. You've also met Janaki, Colonel Dhanraj's wife—when you returned the trench coat he lent you. Don't be surprised, little happens here I don't hear about. Now, are you going to ask me to dance? We missed the Samba. This is a quick step.'

Dusty stood up and bowed. 'May I have the pleasure of this dance?'

'Thank you. You certainly may.' They took a few steps, stopped, and started again.

'You dance beautifully, ma'am.'

'So would you, if you didn't hold me at arm's length, as if I were a leper; and never mind the formalities and compliments. Just relax.'

'Relax?' Dusty grinned, a little embolden. 'Relax with the Commandant's wife?'

'Precisely. I shan't eat you.'

For a while they did not speak. Dusty, concentrating hard on his steps in an effort to keep in time to the music, and succeeding. 'Well done, Sam' Her grey-green eyes rested on his face calmly. He looked away. 'You learn fast. Colonel Dhanraj, says you're a genius, gifted with a brilliant memory.'

He looked at her. 'I don't know what to say.'

'There's nothing to be embarrassed about. You are what you are. Acknowledge it, and be proud you're talented. I don't see why gifted people should be modest.'

'Modest. I keep being reminded by my instructors, even by Colonel Dhanraj, that I need to be, as they say, cut down to size.'

'What size? Your size? You should ask…no, don't. That'll be cheek and the Army doesn't tolerate cheek.'

Dusty gave a wry smile. 'My memory's showing signs of rusting.'

'Well, like all things that need maintaining, it requires exercise. And the Army is the last place for someone with…especially with your knowledge of literature. You should have gone into university education.'

'Sam—I mean, my-my father said exactly that.'

'You mean your guardian.'

'Yes. Sorry I meant to…'

'Anyway, I take all that back. I don't see why the Army should be bereft of talent. As my husband says, there's room for all types in the Army. Besides you're not just a brain, you're…' she grinned as she pinched his biceps, 'brawn also. Where does that athletic ability come from?' He looked down at the top of her head and hesitated as she looked up. 'You don't have to answer. I don't mean to be inquisitive.'

'But I'm no good at PE and swimming.'

'You'll get all the practice you need here. Ouch!'

'Sorry, did I tread…?'

'No, don't apologise. My fault entirely. My mind wandered then. You're very good. As I said, you learn quickly, and now…' She did not finish her sentence. She looked up. A girlish pleasure in her smile sent a tingle down his spine. He drew her in closer, till he heard a distinct rustle of her taffeta blouse. Her smile vanished. 'I don't know about you, but all I can feel is a brass button.'

He released her shamefacedly. The music stopped and they walked back to their table. He admired the sophistication with which she had admonished him, but realised it would be most unwise to apologise. She sat down and politely refused a drink. 'Do sit. Did no one tell you it's rude to point,' she added, looking straight at his pelvis.

'Oh, my God!' He burst out involuntarily. 'I thought it had… Oh, heavens! What am I saying. Please, ma'am, do forgive me!'

'Don't give it another thought. Fortunately we're alone. Even Malti's left.'

'Yes. Was I remiss? Should I also have asked her for a dance?'

'She would have refused. They're a young couple, and she's pregnant. Didn't you notice the way she held her shawl over her waist? Men are so innocent. I don't think my husband knows either.' She gazed at him, her eyes very grey, penetrated Dusty's discomfiture. Then she stood up with a sudden movement and collecting her blue and gold Kashmiri shawl, draped it round her shoulders. 'I have to say, you have the most extraordinary eyes. Not just beautiful, but unusually hazel and striking. I don't know what you are, but you're not Parsee; yes, despite the nose,' and she laughed. The band struck up a new tune. 'That'll be the last dance. I must find my Joe. My husband always has the first and last dance.'

Slowly Dusty stood up. He had not quite overcome his earlier embarrassment. He gazed at his feet. 'Ma'am, I don't know how to say…'

'Then don't.' She took a step towards him, and whispered. 'I can keep a secret.'

He bowed. 'Thank you, ma'am.'

'I've been married twenty years. If we were lucky I could've had a son your age.'

'That's hard to believe,' he said defensively. 'You look so young…'

'I was eighteen when I married. There, I must be going.' She turned and started to walk away. Then stopped. 'Aren't you coming? Complete you escort duty.'

'Indeed, ma'am.'

They had barely taken a few steps when they saw the General, Colonel Abbas and Colonel Dhanraj coming towards them. 'Rajan, where's Janaki?'

'She left early, ma'am, with the Malhotras and Mrs Abbas.'

'That tune, Minnie that tune, isn't that that Maori tune?' Sen Gupta asked.

'Yes, Joe.'

The General crooned "Now is the hour, when we…" and taking her by the waist, circled round her. 'Quick, it's the last dance.' He led her away, then stopped abruptly and turned to Dusty. 'Ah, young Dustoor, see you at the Grand Luncheon tomorrow, after the Passing-Out Parade and I'll remember to find and lend you that book about Colonel James Skinner. And thank you for looking after Minnie. Good lad.'

'It was an honour, sir.' Dusty saw the General raise a hand in acknowledgement and turned to face Colonel Dhanraj.

'Was it, young man?' Colonel Dhanraj hissed. 'Was it an honour?'

Dusty nodded and looked over his shoulder. 'The band will have stopped playing by the time the General gets…'

'No, they'll carry on. They expect the General to turn up. But you didn't answer my question.'

'Yes, it was, sir. I gather you're leaving the Army, sir.'

'Yes, and take what I have to say as a parting piece of advice. Mind how you go. I've been watching you closely. You have the makings of a cadet who could win the Sword of Honour. But one false or careless move…and it will slip from your grasp. Keep your head, as Kipling says. Remember it's not enough to be an officer, you've also got to be a gentleman.'

'I'm a gentleman, sir. My guardian, a most perfect gentleman, was my mentor. Have I given cause for doubt?'

'You're on a slippery slope, one of the dangers of being an attractive young man. You may not believe it, but it is because I like you I say this. Just a parting piece of advice; and between you and me: One's head can be so easily turned, so mind how you go. Tell yourself, a pretty face is not all that rare and that they are human even when they are angelic. Beautiful women also go to the lavatory.' He looked at his watch. 'Did you hear the clock strike?'

'Yes, about ten minutes ago, sir.'

'Well, it's past midnight. Join the other cadets. They're on the Parade ground, and mucking around. Do me a favour. Go out there. Call them to order. Say I sent you, and that I don't want to come there. If I have too they'll get three "putty" parades each. Have you had a "putty" parade punishment?'

'Yes sir, once.'

'What was that for? Explain.'

'Back chat. The Senior Under Officer asked if I had shaved…'

'You said yes and he said "next time get closer to the razor", I know.' The Colonel laughed. 'There's nothing original in the military. Right, tomorrow, Parade is late, but it's a big occasion and all of you need to look your best.'

'Sir.'

'Tell me, are you leaving soon after lunch? Or by the night train.'

'Actually, I'm staying the night here. I've been given permission by Chi…sorry, by Major Bedi, my Company Commander. I'm not going to Bombay.'

'You were going to say, Chindi. That's the nick name you chaps have given Bedi. You can tell me why. I won't pull you up for it. Now that I'm leaving the Army.'

'Sir *chindi* is the piece of lint rag we use, with a pull-through, to clean the barrels of our rifles, sir.'

'I know that.'

'Well it's four by two inches, in size. And Chi- , I mean Major Bedi is a shorty.'

'That's cruel. The chap won an MC in Burma. And rose from the ranks.'

'We know, sir, but boys are cruel,' Dusty said, with an air of maturity.

'About nicknames, I gather you have one. Don't look surprised. I didn't know till yesterday. Your guardian, or someone from Scotland, slipped up. I wasn't snooping. The postal clerk wanted to make sure that a letter addressed to "Dusty" Dustoor went to the right person.'

'I haven't seen my mail.'

"We've a copy of your School Certificate, so no one can accuse you of falsifying the records. But what is your real name?'

'Bal. No surname, just Bal. But I want to be Sam…in honour of my guardian, sir.'

'You should change your name. Clearly, you're not Parsee and on record you're Christian. I missed that bit earlier.'

'It's a long story, sir. I'm not a practising…I mean, a church-going one. But I'm a believing one. I find Christ a very attractive figure.'

'So did Gandhi. Right. Now join the others.'

Dusty found the cadets on the Parade ground as he was told. But most of them had already retired to the barracks. A group of twenty or so fellow athletes were hanging around the steps, and as he came down, one of them shouted: 'He's here! Guard of Honour, form ranks!' The young men formed two rows facing each other, and removing their side caps from under their shoulder lapels, hastily donned them and saluted.

Dusty stopped short of walking into this avenue of uniformed young men, aware he was in for a bit of "ragging". 'What's this about?' he asked, arms akimbo. 'Come on, lay off, chaps. If Under Officer Pritpal Singh's here, say Colonel Dhanraj wants everyone in barracks, in bed, and fresh for tomorrow's parade.'

'You lucky bastard! First take your punishment. Take it like a man.' said a voice in the darkness. 'Guard of Honour! Present arms!'

Dusty peered under the tunnel of raised hands. 'Who's that?'

'Who else?' Asked Pritpal Singh. A tall neatly turbaned head bent forward. 'Open hands only, fellows, or you'll have me to answer to. Right, Sam, begin.'

As Dusty walked through the double line of cadets, they thumped his back—some harder than necessary—to the accompaniment of catcalls and whoops—till he got to Pritpal Singh. 'Lucky devil!' Pritpal hissed. 'How close did you get to her?'

'A polite distance.' Dusty whispered back, adjusting his jacket.

'Sly bastard. OK, chaps, line up in twos! You too, Sam. No special privileges for champion athletes or especially not someone who's danced with the Commandant's wife. Remember, tomorrow I get my commission and will be wearing a subaltern's pip. I'll expect all you chaps to salute when you see me. Right! By the left, quick march!' Someone started to hum the "Colonel Boogey March", and the rest joined in, with a raucous

> *Hitler, he only had one ball,*
> *Goering, he had two but small,*
> *Himmler, was somewhat sim'lar*
> *But poor old Goebbels, had none at all:* Ta-ra-ra...

'Halt!' screamed Pritpal Singh. 'Chaps, the war's over, forgotten. Let's have the filthy version.' This was greeted with lewd laughter in the ranks. 'Keep your voices down. 'Begin. I'll cue the intro: "*Where was the engine driver when the engine burst its boiler...*" Come on, Sam you know the words. Be a sport.'

Sam cleared his throat: "*They found his bollocks...*" Sorry. Let me off this once. You'll be an officer tomorrow. Also, I believe Colonel Dhanraj is within earshot.'

'Okay Sam. Give him a cheer, fellows! He tried. Right, you lousy lot: Dismiss! Straight to your barracks! No fooling around.'

'Barracks? Do you realise you've pulled me away from mine.' Dusty laughed.

'No back chat. Or you'll get a pack parade.'

'You can't,' someone shouted from the departing band, 'it's the end of term.'

'Wrong, Tiwari. You'll see. When you get back, there'll be three pack parades in the book for you. Sneak. Open hands I said. You used a fist. We all envy Sam, but no need for that. Sorry, Sam, I saw you duck, but he got you on the mouth.'

Dusty ran his tongue over his upper lip. 'It's not too bad. Tiwari's a weakling.'

'By the way, who wrote that German version to the "Colonel Bogey"? The chap, must be a chap, deserves a *shabash*.'

'It's been around since the declaration of World War II, and according Sam…my Guardian…he believes it's by an Irishman, but as he says, who knows?'

As he changed into pyjamas, Dusty looked approvingly at the immaculately pressed uniform his orderly had laid out on the dummy and, next to it, his highly polished army boots. The sight helped to banish that strange unsettling feeling he never had to wrestle with before: love. He inspected his slightly swollen upper lip in the mirror and cursed Tiwari. Yes, she would there, with the VIPs, and not give him a second thought! With a deep sigh he went to bed. 'Get a grip, Dusty!' he scolded himself… and was soon asleep.

CHAPTER EIGHT

The "Passing Out Parade" was a grand and precise affair; and in his speech General Sen Gupta paid tribute to Sergeant-Major Vallins. He expressed regret that the Prime Minister was unable to take the salute and was extremely grateful to the Maharaja of Nawaraj for agreeing to stand-in at the last moment. "We were in Sandhurst together and now Nawaraj is Colonel-in-Chief of the Camel Corps,' he added. Then taking a step to the side, he invited the Maharaja to join him on the dais.

Nawaraj looked grand in his high collared *achkan* of red and gold brocade, white drain-pipe trousers and red turban, with its dazzling aigrette of rubies, pearls, and the large central sapphire. Behind the dais, which formed the saluting base, was the VIPs tent. High above it, from the flag-staff, flew the Indian Tricolour of saffron, white and green. Facing all this, in smartly turned out serried lines, stood four companies of the cadet battalions, patient and still, awaiting Inspection.

The day was bright but cold, as gusts of icy winds swept down from snow-capped mountains. Shawls of colourful Cashmere draped the women's shoulders; some had even covered their heads. Not Minnie, when Dusty last saw her. The merest glimpse, because he had to stand still and look steadily ahead. That was the drill. And he was unlikely to see her again. By now she would be hidden behind the dais and by those on it; the Maharaja, Sen Gupta and the new Chief Instructor, Colonel Abbas. But he saw her again when the cadets marched past the saluting base. All eyes turned left to salute the flag. She caught his eye and smiled. He was sure she did, but at the buffet luncheon, she ignored him, even though, on at least two occasions, she was within a few feet of him. He shrugged, took his cup of coffee and joined Pritpal Singh for the third time.

'What's with you, Sam? Stop moping. Haven't seen you like this. What's up?'

'Nothing…Prit-, I mean, sir. Nothing, sir.'

'Hey, come on, I was joking. Call me Pritpal, as ever. Now, why the mope?'

'Just a small worry. Haven't heard from…from home.' Dusty lied.

'Check your pigeon-hole. I thought I saw a letter for you, when I collected my…'

'Really! Gosh, I'll do that.'

'Yeah. Isn't Minnie looking smashing with those *kundun* diamond earrings…God look at that bosom. I'd be her bosom pal, any day.' He laughed.

'Pritpal? Minnie? What's her real name?'

'Menakshi, I think.'

'No, it's Meena, or Meena Rajkumari. She's a princess. Don't you know?'

Dusty and Pritpal turned round. The speaker was none other than Major Amarjit Singh. 'Young Dustoor, you must be wondering what happened to me. We last met in the train almost a year ago. Just one of those things. I've been in hospital.'

'Sir. Why? I mean what…gosh, I don't know what to say. You must think me rude. I passed you a moment ago. Saluted, but didn't recognise you. Sorry, sir.'

'Can't blame you. Next month, back again in hospital. One of those mysterious illnesses that need constant observation. Anyway,' he offered his hand to Pritpal, 'this is to welcome you to the regiment.' They shook hands. Pritpal saluted. Amarjit gave a limp nod, turned and walked away.

'He's dying. He's got a blood disease. Cancer of the blood. Very rare.'

'You mean, Leukaemia?'

'Trust you to know the right word, Sam.'

'And you for gossip and information. Always has been the case.'

'I listen. I ask. You're terribly English; stiff-upper lip, all that rot...' Pritpal broke off. He was looking past Dusty, who frowned and then spun round. 'What were you ogling at?' Dusty said.

'You've just missed her.'

'I don't believe you!'

'Honest, just went past you. Turn round. See, it was Minnie. Usually, on such occasions, she chats with the cadets. Today she's had to entertain the Rajkumari.'

'Rajkumari? The big woman next to her?'

'Yes. Nawaraj's sister. His fat, elder sister...there's a waiter approaching us, with a book on a silver salver...bet that's for you.'

'Yes, I know what it's about. James Skinner. Sen Gupta doesn't forget.'

'No, never. What a guy. With so much on his mind, he still...'

'D'you think I could slip away? If there's a letter for me I'd like to...' Dusty took the book and flipped open the cover. 'Gosh! It's brand new. And look!'

Pritpal leant forward and read: ' "To Sam. Yours to keep. Jo Sen Gupta". You know, one can go off a chap.' He laughed. 'You can go now, yes, no one's looking.'

'Well, all the very best in your future career...which reminds me. Isn't Amarjit Army Education Corps? And you're going into the Infantry. The Gurkhas?'

'He took a transfer. But years ago he was in 4th Gurkhas.'

'Gosh! That's John Masters' Regiment. John Masters? The writer?'

'Name sounds familiar. Are you saying he's a serving officer?'

Dusty shook his head. 'Not any longer. But he was. Thirty-four to forty-eight.'

'God! What a memory! What are the thirty-nine steps?'

Dusty laughed. 'I'm not a freak.'

'Keep in touch.'

'I'll try. I'm a terribly lazy correspondent.'

'If you're going into a Cavalry *Risala*, the chances of meeting up again are slim. But care 56 APO will reach me, wherever.'

'Goodbye, good luck, and thanks.'

'Thanks for what?'

'Friendship and guidance; and for giving Tiwari something to think about.'

'That will cost you a bunch of grapes.'

'Grapes!'

'Do me a favour. When you get back here. Visit Major Amarjit, on my behalf.'

The letter, postmarked Ullapool, was addressed to G.C. Dusty Dustoor. Sam had been careless. "Dear Boy, We're here, just for a night, and on our way back to Bute. Muriel drives a nippy MG and a very good driver she is too. Took your advice and got married last Friday. At Gretna Green, to make it special. I'm on the wagon, been exercising, building my strength. Muriel is more than a tonic. She's an inspiration. She's asleep now, while I worry about not having told you about the birds and bees. Muriel says I've been irresponsible. Will post a book or two. It'll be better than anything I can say. Sorry old chap. Yours aye, S. Will write at length when we're back home."

Dusty wrote back. "Don't worry about the 'the birds and the bees' or books about it. I knew it all before I was seven. Had I not mentioned Asif? A raw teacher was he, while the animals gave lucid demonstrations. Though, I must admit, watching them could have misled me about style, approach and direction. But the boys here soon straightened that out and were no less raw. 'You miss out on the tits if you do it from the back.' There's Tejpore for you. Hope that didn't shock, but I wanted to spare you the trouble of posting books on what I already know and me the embarrassment of being seen with them. Incidentally, I secretly read your copy of Stopes *Married Love* about three years ago in Bombay. Yours aye, Dusty. PS And now that you've let the cat out of the bag, Dusty will do from now on. Sams are one too many. I have rather grown to like Dusty, can't think why. D"

He was up early, showered, shaved and started packing; then stopped and looked out of the window. It gave him an eerie sensation to stare into an empty and silent campus. Nothing seemed to move; even the winds of yesterday had died down to an isolating stillness. He stepped out and stood next to his favourite chenar tree. Not a leaf moved. Hunger gripped him. He must breakfast before he went back to packing. Then he remembered that with the cadets away, the Mess kitchens would have shut. But surely, the cadets' canteen, just outside the campus, could at least provide coffee and biscuits! He was about to lock his room when he remembered the letter to Sam, and the something more he needed to add to it. He looked at the letter. There was space for what he wanted to say. He sat down and wrote. "PPS. I forgot Sports Day: Incidentally I won a shield, two cups and a medal. And many thanks for arranging a travel itinerary for my Christmas Hols. Yes, the agents have sent me bookings, and names and addresses. It must have cost you a packet! I'm very grateful, dear, dear generous Sam. I'll look forward to seeing you next year. Don't worry about Summer. Planned a hol, Kashi Kapoor and I. You remember "Cash" we called him, because he is filthy rich. Small, curly black hair, heavy glasses, a year junior to me in school. His Dad, businessman with the touch of Midas, has a large bungalow near Ajmer. He's negotiating to buy an even larger, off some Nawab chappie. It'll be our base, for touring Rajasthan. Love to you both. D" He addressed and sealed the envelope, chose the most colourful postage stamps he could find from his wallet, shut the suit case, drew the curtains, locked his room and took the short cut to the canteen by crossing the green maidan behind the Wellington Barracks.

The Military Canteen was recently established to serve the needs of married staff and their families. But cadets also shopped there. It had four departments: a general store, a haberdashery, a small café and a bicycle shop; all run by a manager and three assistants. 'D'you by any chance serve a breakfast of sorts?' Dusty asked.

The Manager, a chubby, affable Madrasi, expressed surprise at seeing Dusty still around. Dusty explained he had to wait a day to catch his train to Bangalore.

'Bangalore? Then you'll be going via Madras. You must spend some time there. As you know Madras is my home town. Wery fine place. Cheap. At station itself, there's Spencers. For eight annas only you'll get a plate full of *sambar rice*, best in all Madras.' He smiled, rolling his head to and fro. 'Are you vegetarian? No? Arrey then it is not for the likes of you.'

Dusty repeated his question.

'Sorry, sorry, please to forgive. But I'm afraid no breakfast of any sort. Not coffee even. You can purchase biskoots. But, it mean, buying whole biskoot packet. Scottish good shortbread. Scottish.'

Dusty was hungry, but after eating two biscuits he realised he wanted a hot drink more than anything else and remembered where he could get one. Stuffing the packet in his jacket, he walked down the gravel path, which circled the maidan and the married quarters and aimed for the Guard House, where, off-duty sentries were constantly brewing tea over a kerosene stove. There on one occasion, cold, wet and sheltering from the rain, they gave him a steaming mug of the brew—a mix of tea, milk, sugar and water, cooked to a broth to produce a strong, milky, very sweet tea, just as he had known it as a village lad in Fatehpur. Right now he would gladly share his biscuits with them in return for that hot drink.

Dusty turned the corner into the straight stretch that led to the main gates. There he saw her; and the vision struck him with a damascene impact. Instinctively, his hand went to his lips. Thank God! The soreness and the swelling had gone. She had a dog on a lead, a springer spaniel, which she was chiding for pulling her. So absorbed was she in the dog's conduct that he was alongside before she looked up and saw him. Her lips parted and her beautiful eyes widened. 'Good heavens! What are you doing here? I - I mean, why are you still here?' The start made her loosen her grip of the lead and the dog escaped. 'Monty! Bad dog! Come back at once! He's not quite broken in. Oh, Sam! Monty!'

The dog stopped. Turned to face them, barked and scampered on ahead.

'I'll get him back for you, Ma'am,' Dusty said, removing his jacket and dropping it by the side of the path.

'Oh, can you! That's sweet of you! Call him Monty. He's learnt that at least.' She picked up his jacket, shook the dust off it and resting it across her arm watched him chase after the dog. Dusty dodged and dashed while Monty pranced about excitedly. Then thinking Dusty was playing a game, the dog turned round, rushed, and sprang at him. Dusty caught him deftly in his hands and holding the wriggling dog firmly, took him back to its owner. 'Thank you Sam. It is Sam? Good.' She handed the jacket, which he took in his left hand, still keeping a firm grip of Monty under his right arm. 'And I've just realised why you're here. You poor boy.'

She put the leash back on Monty, and her hands brushed against his wrist, sending an electric current down his spine.

Dusty released the dog. 'You seem to know a lot about me.'

'You've no home to go to, because your Guardian's in Scotland. We talk about our cadets. Joe and I. The ones that need our attention.'

He looked at her steadily. His eyes burned. She glanced down at the dog. He had given up seeking attention and was quietly crouching on his belly by her feet.

She looked up again, a little coyly. 'So, what are you doing about your holidays?'

The dog sat up briskly, barked and began to pull on the leash. 'Better give him to me ma'am.' She did. 'He's planned a holiday for me. Sam has. I leave for Bangalore, tonight. From there to the Nilgiris. A hill-climbing holiday with Conoor as my base.'

'I know Conoor. Not far from Ooty. I was at Ooty when Joe was in Staff College. It's beautiful. The Nilgiris. But what brought you here? To this place, I mean.'

Dusty laughed. 'In search of breakfast. I hoped for a mug of tea at the Guard…'

'You poor boy! I'll give you breakfast. Mittoo, that's our cook, he's very used to producing meals at short notice. Yes?'

'Gosh, ma'am,' Dusty said clutching his empty stomach. 'Will it be all right?'

'Yes, of course. Worried about the general? Don't be. Joe's fond of youngsters. He's a real softie, at home. Besides, it's important you be fed. The General is master on the parade square, I'm mistress in the home; and I shall tell him how you rescued Monty. You must know the house? Monty! Stop it.'

'Flagstaff House? Can't miss it. I've bicycled past it many times.'

'Then let's hurry. You must be starving. The dining room's… Monty! Stop.'

'The room's being painted. You'll have to eat in the veranda.' She frowned. 'I don't mean to…don't mean to pry, but what have you done to your lip?'

'Last night…midnight, the boys were fooling around. I had to run the gauntlet.'

'What's that?'

'Oh, having to run between two rows of boys who punch you as you…'

'You mean a kind of punishment. Why? What did you do?'

'Nothing. Just a silly game.' He gazed at her. 'It was worth it.'

She looked away. 'You're hiding something from me. Never mind.'

The sentry at the gate of Flagstaff House saluted as they entered, and a boy came out and took the dog from Dusty. 'The jeep's gone, which means Joe's at the golf links.' She threw herself against the cushions of a cane settee in the veranda. 'But he always leaves a note. Do sit down, Sam.' She went to the coffee table and picked up the note, and as she bent down her sari *pallu* fell off her shoulder. She looked up to see Dusty staring straight down her blouse. She covered herself.

A tall, pock-marked servant, in white uniform, entered. 'Coffee, Memsahib?'

'*Ha*. Tell Mittoo, coffee for two. Fried eggs on toast for *babasahib*,' she said the last Hindustani word with some emphasis. It made Dusty wince. He was no boy. His feelings at the moment were mature and deeply masculine. 'Joe's sending the jeep so I could join him later. Are you all right?' She smiled. 'What is it? And don't keep saying ma'am.'

'Dare I say something?'

She shook her head. 'No, Sam. I think I know what you want to say. There are feelings that you may have…even that I may have… which must remain unspoken. Words spoken in haste can ruin things. Give it time. Time heals. I've already said I could be your mother.'

'But, I'll be twenty in a matter of months.'

'And that's how long I've been married to Joe, a year longer.'

The bearer entered with coffee and breakfast. She told him to leave it on the table.

'I've lost all appetite.'

'Now Sam, be sensible. If you don't eat, I shall feed you. I mean it. Please, for my sake, if you care. You don't want to embarrass me! There are servants about.'

'Sorry. But, actually, I wanted to impress you.'

'You have.'

'I wanted you to think well of me. And all I've done is make a fool of myself.'

'No, you haven't. If I was your age, I might have been even more foolish. There now. Sit on the sofa by me and don't let it get cold. There's no point encouraging feelings that you can do nothing about. Or lead nowhere. Is there?'

He nodded, and began to eat while she sipped her coffee and glanced casually at a magazine. A moment later she stood up. 'I've got to change into slacks, just in case I need to join Jo on the golf course.' He did not look up. 'Now, Sam, no one's worth starving for.' She sat down again, closer to him and rested a hand on his knee. 'You poor boy, you've never known a mother's love. That's sad.' She glanced over her shoulder, took his hand in hers and squeezed it; then she got up and left the room.

When she returned, smart and girlish in her clothes, he had finished eating. He stood up and bowed with a grim smile. 'Have you forgiven a foolish m—man?'

'Yes, immediately. At you age you must make mistakes, as long as they're not serious ones; and not dwell on them…to brood is to suffer. That's how I've kept- sustained our marriage, a childless one, by moving on. We have this in common now, you and I. Living in the future and shedding the past. Is that not what you've done? Or do I mean, living in the present. No matter.' She gave a slow pirouette. How do I look? Compliment me. I like compliments.'

'You look beautiful,' he said hoarsely. 'I suffer just looking at you.'

'It's a woman's privilege. To be desired is a compliment.'

'But no more.' He said abruptly, taking her by surprise. 'I was absurd. Childish. I deeply respect your husband. And I'll work hard to be immune to your charms.'

She burst out laughing. 'That was sweet! And you looked so very handsome.'

He smiled sheepishly. 'I'm sure I look like an idiot.'

'You don't, and what's more, I'd like you to keep me company. Come with me to the Club. We'll lunch there…but you've got a train to catch? The game goes beyond lunch and much of the afternoon.'

'My train's at 8.45, tonight; and I've just got to throw a few things in a suitcase.'

'Good, then you won't mind being my caddy. Ah, there's Mittoo's son with the golf-clubs, I'll tell him I don't need him today. He won't be disappointed, I know.'

'He's my caddy, darling.'

Sen Gupta stared passively at Dusty, who stood stiffly to attention. 'Relax Sam, here at the club we're all fellow officers.' Then turning to Minnie, he said, 'I'm afraid you're too late to join in the game. There's something else I wanted to say…' he led her away. 'We'll be back, young man,' he said over his shoulder, leaving Dusty with the distinct impression that the General was slightly discomforted by his presence. On their return he overheard the General saying: 'I'm fond of the boy too. But there's no escaping the fact it was a bit tactless. The only remedy now is for me to show he's here by invitation. I'll handle it.' He raised his voice. 'Young man, you know golf?'

'Sir, I know the game, but I've never played it.'

'You're a bright lad. You'll pick it up fast, but you mustn't win. When you play with generals, you play to lose.' He laughed, and thumped Dusty on the back. 'Right, come with me.'

'Joe, but he's carrying my clubs.'

'Sorry, darling. Yes, first carry Minnie's clubs into the clubhouse then meet me on the eighth. Darling you look disappointed. There'll be a chance after lunch.'

'I hate it when this happens,' Minnie said as she and Dusty walked together. 'I'll be forced to sip a Bloody Mary while Kanti regales me on how wonderful her hubby is.' He did not answer, and she looked at him inquiringly. 'Are you all right?'

'I apologise if I've made things awkward for you.'

'Don't give it another thought. Joe is always rescuing me from one *faux pas* or another. And he likes to be able to do that. Ah, here comes Gopi.' A young boy ran out of the club house towards them. 'Give him the clubs, you can then catch up with Joe. I'll show you where the Eighth is.' She put a hand on his shoulder and pointed with the other. 'There, he's waiting for you. Enjoy your spell. Joe's good company and especially for someone like you. He's an avid reader.'

The General was waiting under the shade of a tulip tree, when

Dusty ran up to join him. 'I've given my caddy *chutti*, so you can do his job. Tell me laddie, when you say you know the game but have not played it, d'you mean just read about it? What, P G Wodehouse...or some professional golfer's book?'

'Both, sir. Wodehouse and a book entitled *Golf is a Four Letter Word*.'

Sen Gupta stared at Dusty with raised eyebrows and puckered lips. 'Watch it boy. Being cheeky are you? If you are, it's a good one.'

Dusty smiled. 'I'm not joking, I assure you, sir. I'm sure I've got the title right.'

'Here grab these, and follow me. Have you caddied before?'

'Yes, for my fa - guardian...I'll have to admit having played a game or two. I just didn't want to admit to being a dabbler...'

'Good. Saves me having to explain. And you're not one who gives advice?'

'I've been known to do that, sir.'

'Well don't. I like absolute silence when I'm addressing the ball. Keep up. You're an unusual chap. I mean, different from the other cadets. Polite but not obsequious.'

'As Sergeant-Major Vallins says. "I have many seniors but no superiors!"'

'Good mimicry. You know, his contract ends in June. The Defence Ministry has drawn the line. No more British Warrant Officers after him. Pity, I rather wished for closer ties with Britain, after Independence. I'm an Anglophile. It's no secret.'

'So is my Guardian. Always has been. More than that, he's a monarchist. When he was a student in England, he joined the "Charles, King and Martyr, Society" or some such thing, and on 30th January he would join a service held before the King's statue in Trafalgar Square.'

'Indeed! There's a story about that Statue. During Cromwell's time a lot of stuff linked with the King and his Court was sold. The statue went to a chap called Rivett, on the understanding he'd melt it down and turn it into objects for sale. He appeared to do so, but in fact he hid the statue in a pit in his garden, for eleven years, revealing it after the Restoration.'

'A riveting story, sir.'

'There you go again, cheek first and politeness afterwards.

But I like it. So, your Guardian, Mr Dustoor, was educated in England?'

'Yes, Harrow, like Nehru and Churchill, sir.'

'Fascinating. I was at Wellington, probably about the same time.'

'Not likely, sir. My Guardian is sixty-two, sir.'

'I see. One forgets retirement is early in the Army. At forty nine, I should've gone by now. Instead, I'm being posted to command a Brigade. You know there's trouble brewing with China. You'll probably be sent straight to the front soon after you're commissioned. Pity, we, that's Minnie and I, won't be here to see you off.'

Dusty stopped and gaped.

'Come on lad,' the General urged, 'don't dally. The ninth's some distance from here. Don't tell me, the thought of seeing action appals you?'

Dusty shook his head. 'Everyone I get to know appears to be leaving Tejpore.'

'You're going to see a lot of changes...' Sen Gupta broke off.

After a thoughtful pause, he stopped and faced Dusty. 'Something you ought to know, Dustoor. There were two things Minnie wanted most in life. Both denied her. A brother and a son. Everything else she's had in full measure. Bear that in mind. I know that you, as a proper gentleman, won't want to misunderstand her.'

Dusty drew himself up. 'I assure you, sir, I honour and respect both of you.'

'Good lad! You'll do well in the army.' He looked at his watch and frowned. 'They should...ah, there they are.' He waved to two shadowy figures, which suddenly appeared above the horizon of the ninth green. 'That's Dhanraj and co. He doesn't need to play a losing game. But he's leaving the army. So, in spite of what I said earlier...if you could help, discreetly I mean, don't hold back.'

Dusty cringed. He always could match words with action, but now he felt he had exceeded himself and wished he had not talked about golf. Fortunately he was able to point to clubs that won the General's approval and, even more fortunately, when it became clear Dhanraj would win, the rain came down in torrents, and the match had to be called off. There was a rush for the club-house.

In the Shadow of a Dream

Dhanraj's buggy had room only for the General, and a dripping wet Dusty was left standing in the rain.

'Will you be lunching with us?' asked Sen Gupta.

Dusty raised his hands in a helpless gesture. 'Sir, I couldn't possibly, sir.'

'Stay where you are, Dustoor,' Dhanraj said, 'Chandu here will bring you a plate of sandwiches, and take you back…where? The Station or wherever. '

There was a clap of thunder. 'I wouldn't stand under a tree.' Sen Gupta laughed.

At the club-house Minnie asked after Dusty. The General squeezed her arm: 'My dear, let the boy be. Dustoor's a good lad, but I don't think he knows how to handle a mature and complicated woman like you.'

Dusty waited anxiously by his luggage outside a First Class coupè. There was no sign of the Guard who had left him there. Then minutes before the train was due to leave, the man turned up. 'Gentleman, I've good news for you,' he said with a strong Tamil accent. 'The party for this two-berth coupe have cancelled reservation. You may now choose the upper or lower berth with impunity. Get in, get in. Where's your coolie?'

'I let him go. I can manage. It's only a suit case and bed-roll.'

'Then allow me to give you a helping hand,' the Guard took hold of the suit case. 'You are indeed travelling light. Very best policy. However, it's my duty to remind you, next time, please make certain you have reservation. You are so lucky this time. No point of spending much money on ticket and not enjoying the full benefit of it?'

Dusty grimaced. 'Thank you, I will.' He offered the guard a five rupee note.

The man grasped it with practised dexterity and slipped it into the breast-pocket of his jacket. 'There really was no need for that, gentleman. It's my duty to care for…' He broke off, blew his whistle and waved the green flag. The engine driver answered the signal with a long warning whistle, followed by a blast of steam, loud puffing and a grinding wrench of the steel couplings before the train jerked forward with a creaking complaint. 'Have a good journey, Mr Dustoor. I see you are reading Emanuel Kant. A great philosopher, but not for travel reading.'

'My father would disagree with you. He says that the best time to read philosophy is on a train journey.'

'Indians waste much time on philosophy. Kant, much too complicated. Language most hard to follow. But, one must always adhere to what fathers say.'

Dusty nodded. 'But, what reading would you suggest, Mr Kumaraswami?'

'*Ai, ai Yoh*! Much to choose from. My own favourite is Kipling. When I was a boy, you could find Kipling in Railway Station, A H Wheeler bookshops.'

'I like Kipling too. But I'm happy with Kant. The language may be complicated but the ideas behind it are simple.'

'At the next station I'll send the boy from the railway book shop.'

'Not now. In the morning. See that I'm not disturbed tonight.'

Mr Kumaraswami rolled his head. 'Every consideration will be observed.'

"I am never to act otherwise than so that I could also will that my maxim should become a universal law." Dusty smiled. The Guard, he thought, could not have had the good fortune of an excellent tutor like Dr Sam Dustoor: "Laddie, the fun of Kant is the mental exercise he provides. Simplify the rigmarole and what do you get? Ask yourself: Would it be all right for everyone to act as I do? If the answer is: No. Then don't do it, because it will not be a universally moral course of action."

Dusty put the book down. He knew what he had to do, and he was determined to succeed—determined to dismiss those nagging feelings that were upsetting him; that were making him restless. "Time heals all wounds", that's what she meant. He smiled as he recalled William Powell, in *The Thin Man*, saying: "Time wounds all heels". He took a sharp breath. Was he a "heel"? He had resolved, since school days in Bombay, to grow up to be principled, strong, upright and, above all, independent; unmoved by weaknesses and what in his innate wisdom he considered, human folly. He had been weak. He had, till now, taken immense pride in himself and, with self-congratulatory approval, his ability to be indifferent. He hated dependence, had eschewed friendship and treated people as stepping stones to achievements. He realised that unhappiness and pain came from attachments to people, to things. Sujata, Daadi, Asif, Yousef, yes, even dear Sam, were all means to an end; and he had succeeded, till now. Now he was confused, ashamed. Pride, in his ability, in his prodigious mentality—no self-delusion but one affirmed by the evidence of people's astonishment when confronted by it—had taken a knock. He felt defeated, violated; and worse, helpless. Did these ridiculous aching desires mean he was in love with Minnie? He had had to fight those strange feelings which kept him awake last night, and had to summon all his mental strength not to give in to a desire to masturbate—that had nothing to do with the Reverend Jack Jones talk on the evils of masturbation to the boys at the Orphanage. He was too intelligent for that. Besides Asif told him he, Asif, often masturbated to get a good night's rest, and Asif was no weakling. No, he declined to masturbate on aesthetic grounds and because it was absurd and pointless. Wet dreams were another matter. Till last night they just happened and were loveless. Last night was different. Minnie had appeared, naked, magnificent and desirable; her breasts, bare, firm, splendid. He yearned, yearned to be drawn into their yielding tenderness. Something new had stirred within him. But why breasts? Breasts were nothing new to him. As a boy in Fatehpur village he had seen them, all shapes and sizes. He had even been repelled by the sight of some—Sujata's, fat, ponderous and heavy. Daadi's, flat and shrivelled. Yes, those images he recalled to kill the enticements and temptations of the night; and now he would exhaust himself physically, while on holiday in the hills... He picked up the book again, read till sleep overcame him. The book fell to the floor.

CHAPTER NINE

The confrontation with China came with a swiftness that found the Indian Army ill-prepared and tactically inadequate to meet their challenge. With supreme hubris, the Chinese made their point and left India to lick its wounds. What began in September 1962 was over by November. In December, at his Passing-out Parade, Dusty found himself a commissioned subaltern of the Mysore Lancers. But his last term had been a disaster. Well, almost. His performance during the last two months of his course, was disappointing and that, naturally, astonished his instructors. They had hoped to see him excel his peers, even win the Sword of Honour, or at least the Gold Medal. But after General Sen Gupta and Minnie left for New Delhi, the former on a posting as military adviser to the Indian Ministry of Defence, Dusty found it hard to maintain the high standards of his past achievements. Of course, his phenomenal memory and mastery of the English Language enabled him to win a special award for a "First" in Military History. That apart, his performance in other subjects was far less than what was expected of him. But all regrets, of what might have been, lay between him and his mentors. To the world outside Tejpore, to be ranked among the first twenty-five cadets was no mean achievement; and Dusty was given a warm welcome when he joined the Rathore Lancers, in Batiala, in the Punjab. He, himself, arrived at the Regiment, a stronger, more mature man, fully reconciled to making the best of his Army career. He had feared he would never recover from his disastrous infatuation with Minnie or from the hurt he felt, when she left, Tejpore and him, without a word. Now, all that was in the past. For now he was an object of admiration not only in the Regiment but also, in Batiala, where mothers saw in the eligible bachelor a prospect for their young daughters. Such attention he dodged with a consummate charm he did not believe he was capable of, and by taking advantage of the former, won the full respect of his Regimental Commandant, Colonel Har Prasad.

Har Prasad saw in Dusty the perfect subaltern; smart, well-turned out, intelligent; and was particularly pleased to see how well the men, under Dusty's command, took to his firm but friendly manner. The two got on so well that when the time came for Dusty go on the Young Officers' Course at Shivajipore, Har Prasad was sorry to lose him. But he had no choice. The Course was compulsory.

Shivajipore, near Poona, housed the Central Training School for young cavalry officers and the Course lasted for six months. The training timetable for these newly commissioned officers included basic training in driving and maintenance of tanks and military transport, the use of firearms, and practice in wireless communication. Mornings began with an hour at the Equitation School. This, every trainee eagerly anticipated and, though horsemanship did little to aid their career prospects, there was much pleasure and attention to be gained by it. By the end of the second month, Dusty was competent enough to join the Tent-pegging team and to take part in the Annual Summer *Pagal Gymkhana*. But he eschewed invitations to play Polo, since it meant the expense of owning and maintaining a horse.

A week-long holiday followed the Pagal Gymkana and Dusty, now an inveterate hill climber, walked the twenty-six miles to Pangal with his friend, Rajan. They used the little village as a base from which to explore the Western Ghats and in particular a hill, which, as seen from Shivajipore, had a funnel shaped summit. The approach to the hill was a gentle climb, but the "funnel" itself was thirty feet of sheer, vertical rock. 'It looks tougher than it really is, Raju,' Dusty said. 'But I'm not giving up. I'll get to the top.'

'I shan't join you at the top. Whatever you say it will be hard going and that's the understatement of the year. Don't ask me to brave it; not with that sun overhead.'

'Best time of the day, what?'

Rajan raised his jungle hat, mopped his brow and throwing his haversack under the shade of a Jujube tree, lay down and stretched himself. 'Well, good luck to you.' He pulled the jungle hat over his face and folded his arm across his chest. 'Wake me when you get back.'

'By the time I'm back, you'll be chewed up. That tree is full of black ants.'

Rajan sprang up. 'Oh! Fuck me!'

'No thanks.'

'Bastard! Go on. Give me a shout when you get to the top. I'll have my camera loaded and ready by then.'

When Dusty rejoined him, Rajan was peeing over a cactus bush. 'Raju, look what I've found. At the top, under some stones…once a carefully made cairn, I suppose.'

'Join me, you must need to go,' Rajan grinned, 'there's no one around.'

'Yup, but I must have lost most of it, sweating, to get to the top.'

'Cairn? What's a…forget it. Is that what you've found? A rusty old penknife?'

'Yeah, but curious. On one side of the handle is carved "sandy"; on the other the words "as here". Must be "was here". That makes sense if Sandy's the name of the owner. It must have been there for some time. Years perhaps.'

'You're a great collector of knick-knacks. And you're a Christian.'

'What's that got to do…'

'We Hindus are more superstitious. I'd never have picked it up.'

'You're not serious.'

'Yes. Certainly if it has writing. It could be cursed. Why was it left there? You can never know. It could bring bad luck.'

'Did you take a picture?' Dusty asked, buttoning up his dungarees.

'Yeah. Good one too. Got you at the top. Posing, as if you were on Everest. Hey, we're spending the last two nights in Poona. Aren't

In the Shadow of a Dream

we? Then how about…?' Rajan made a suggestive movement of the hips. 'I know a place. Clean, recommended.'

'No. Not interested. Truly. No need for the wink. I've already got your drift.'

'Come on man! Great fun!' Rajan giggled wickedly. 'Your first time, I know, so consider it a learning experience. I know the right woman to guide you. Poona's my home town, so I…You almost, remember, you almost said yes, when we first met at the Army Selection Board…before Tejpore…remember?'

'As I said, I'm not interested.'

'Okay, okay! Don't bite my head off. I get it. You're not still soft on that bloody woman?'

'That's all past and finito. I wish I hadn't told you about her.'

'You didn't say much. Anyway, mum's the word. You know me.'

'Yes, and stop pretending to be a man of the world. I bet it would be your first time too. You can't fool me. Admit it.'

After morning parade, on the very first day of Dusty's return to the Regiment, the Adjutant informed him that Colonel Har Prasad wanted to see him immediately after breakfast, 10 a.m. 'You're in for a roasting. On the mat.' The Adjutant grinned. 'No. Just pulling your leg. I suppose you'll go through life being everybody's darling.'

At the appointed time Dusty knocked on the Commandant's door, and on being invited in, checked his black beret and the alignment of his cap-badge, entered, stood smartly to attention and saluted. Har Prasad looked up, acknowledged the salute and smiled. 'Young man, first let me congratulate you. I've had a glowing report on your hard work and dedication, on the course. Now, everyone who completes this course is entitled to a short leave, *chutti*. But if you are willing to forgo it, I've a proposition to make. It's one to your lasting advantage. How do you feel about that?'

'Consider my leave taken, sir.'

'Good lad. You are on probation till you pass the Retention Examination. Well, it can be a mere formality and within my discretion to make it so. Now you can put that behind you. I want you to command Bravo Troop, with immediate effect. There's a vacancy. You know the men; a tough bunch of Sikhs. Your Squadron Commander, Major Bakshi, will guide you, and since you'll be Troop Leader, I'll get permission from Div HQ to let you wear your second pip. It'll earn you added respect.'

'Thank you, sir. I won't let you down.'

'I know you won't. I wouldn't go out of my way, if I had the slightest doubt.'

'Thank you, sir.'

'I wanted to hear you say that.' Har Prasad looked at Dusty steadily. The smile on his face turned into a slight frown. 'There's something else, Dustoor. Relax. Do sit down. This is an off-duty matter.' He opened a desk drawer. Took out an envelope, then he drew a chair and sat down facing Dusty. He took a deep breath and held out his hand. Dusty took it hesitantly. The Colonel gripped his firmly. 'It's sad news, I'm afraid. The letter was addressed to me, as you can see, to the Commandant. It's from someone called Muriel and came five days ago. She didn't want you to be distracted from important work. I was asked to choose the best time to tell you.'

'Oh my God! It's Sam. My Guardian.'

Har Prasad nodded. 'Her letter to me was short and formal. But there's also one for you; unopened, as you can see. Did you, or do you know this lady?'

Dusty nodded. 'Briefly, sir. She taught Geography in my school… but took early retirement.'

The Colonel stood up and went back to the chair behind his desk. 'And from her surname I assumed she's your Guardian's wife.'

'Yes, sir. Not for long. They married in Scotland, while I was in Tejpore.' Dusty opened his letter. "Dear Dusty, Sam died, suddenly but peacefully; a happy death, at home, in my arms, after tea, yesterday at 7 p.m. It was heart failure but painless. You will get this news late because I've asked your CO to save it till you get back. I saw no reason for you to be told at once, or I would have cabled you." He looked for the date of the letter. 'It'll be twelve days since he died,' he looked up. The Colonel did not answer. Dusty read on: "I realise that your course and career are of paramount importance and obviously you've kept yourself busy. Your last letter to Sam was three months ago!! He never forgot you. In that time he wrote three letters and a card to you. I know, because I pointed it out to him. He told me not to be harsh. That you were single-minded and young and that but for you we would not be together. I did thank you at the time. But right now, I am overcome by my deep loss and feel I've every right to be angry; and the better because of that anger. I think your behaviour inconsiderate and callous. This was a hard letter to write. I'm sorry if I'm harsh. But I loved that beautiful man dearly. So, please allow me this space to rage and rant. I know, one day, I'll find time to write you a happier note. Till then, and with every good wish, Muriel." Again he looked up, pale and a little shaken.

'You haven't turned the sheet,' the Colonel said. 'I see some writing on the back.'

Dusty turned the sheet. "PS. In my rage I forgot to say the most important thing. Sam was cremated, as he wished. And the ashes are with me. He did say, sometime ago that the ashes should eventually go back to India and to you. But he never talked about it again, certainly not after we married. I'm at a loss what to do. Write. There's no hurry. Of one thing I'm certain. He wants no communication with his own family. I haven't informed them. I'll leave it to you to decide what to do. M"

Dusty folded the letter and put it back in the envelope. Slowly he rose from his chair. 'I'll write to her.' He was barely audible.

'Good,' said Har Prasad. 'Then she'll know I've passed the news on to you.'

'I should've kept in touch. Do I have your permission to leave, sir?'

'Yes. And take the leave you're entitled to. More, if you need, on compassionate grounds. I just wanted to hear you say the right things. I have.'

'I won't need leave, sir. Just the afternoon off. Just time to write to Muriel.'

'Take tomorrow off too...' He looked at the calendar. "Today's Thursday. I don't want to see you on parade before Monday. Accept my condolences.'

Dusty saluted and returned to Mahijit Niwas, which was once the residence of a Maharaja and now the Officers' Mess. It was a palatial, Jacobean mansion of red and yellow sandstone. Five of its six bedrooms were refurbished to quarter unmarried or single officers but two of its grandest rooms, the dining-room and red drawing-room, retained their original splendour. In the latter, the Rathore Lancers Regimental Silver were proudly displayed on highly polished tables next to glass cabinets filled with exquisite Delft ware china and Venetian glass. Dusty entered the dining-room and called out: '*Kohee hai*? Anyone there?'

There was a sound of shuffling feet and a moment later the rotund figure of Juma, the Wine Waiter waddled in, adjusting as he did, the red, blue and gold striped band that ran diagonally across his immaculate turban. He was proud of the Regimental colours and had every reason to be so, for Juma had dedicated his life to the Rathore Lancers. His father had served the Lancers from shortly after it was founded in 1901 by Major Stephen Jacob of Lucknow, and as a boy ran errands for his hero "Stiffen Sahib" who in his legacy left him a pension for life. He married, after Stephen Jacob died, when he was fifty-two, but for some obscure reason Juma's date of birth was not recorded, so that his age remains a mystery. However, his earliest memories are of a time with of the Regiment that go back to 1925, when the Lancers moved from Poona to Karnal in the Punjab. Juma, of course was not his name. Some tipsy officer in a moment of light banter referred to him as Man Friday, and as Juma is Urdu for Friday, and as he himself raised no objection, the name stayed.

Juma bowed over an open hand, in a salutation reminiscent of the Mughal Court. "Sahib, *hookum*?" The man was a consummate actor.

Dusty ordered coffee, went upstairs to his room and sat in front of a writing table. Through the open window he stared, without seeing, at a row of flowering laburnum. He sighed, bent forward and buried his face in his hands. 'Oh Sam! Sam forgive me! Dear, dear Sam, forgive me. Forgive me for the tears I cannot shed.' He bit his lips and shook his head. 'You know I cared. In my own way I cared.' He stayed bent over his desk, till there was a discreet knock on the door. He sat up. 'Come in! Oh, it's you Juma. Yes, coffee, yes, I forgot.'

Juma placed a tray on the writing desk. 'Cup, hot coffee and biskoots,' he said. He turned to leave then hesitated. 'Is sahib well?'

'Yes'. Dusty shook his head. 'I mean no, Juma. I've had sad news.'

'I knowing,' Juma nodded solemnly. 'I putting a little brandy in coffee.'

Dusty sipped the coffee gratefully. 'You're a wonder, Juma. Thank you.'

'Sahib, rest in bed, Take good sleep.'

Dusty shook his head. 'No, Juma, sahib must write *chitty*. Letter, you know.'

'Then sahib is not in. I not disturbing. I collect *teray* tomorrow.'

After Juma left the room, Dusty covered his face with his hands and collected his thoughts, then, drawing out a note pad, began his letter to Muriel. Twice he revised it, before honing it down to this. "Dear Muriel, To lose Sam so shortly after marriage is deeply unfair. I understand your hurt and what you saw as heartless behaviour on my part. Let it comfort you to know that Sam would not have seen it that way, as I think you know. He never minded my rather odd and peculiar letter writing habit and off-hand style, nor saw in it ingratitude or unfeeling. Our relationship was unique. In the strange circumstances of the junction of our lives it had to be so. We were never father and son. We knew that could never be. I was a poor village boy, and great as his generosity was, it was motivated by curiosity and tempered by a strong element of caution. At first, the gulf between us was too much even to expect equality, let alone affection. I was simply a low object, a curiosity, an experiment. I was sent to an orphanage and only after I was presentable, mentally and physically, was Sam prepared to draw closer. It took years to bridge the gulf and although, in the last few years, we wanted to be like father and son, I knew, and I think he realised it too, any attempt to make me his legal heir would have caused immense problems with his family—his property was tied by his father's will to the family, and that was irrevocable. Also by then I wanted to go my own way and I knew I could make my own living. Yet we lived side by side, happily enjoying each other's company on, largely, a mental plane. Our proximity touched his heart and I will always remember he gave of his own money, over which his family had no sway, generously. But if he had not, that too would not have mattered to me. If it did, would I have pressed him to go to you? His money, less the funds he left in my bank account, is all yours now, as it should be. I don't envy that or you. Sam knew that though we were close and tied by mutual respect, yes even by a kind of loving, I wanted to be separate and independent, and under obligation to no one. When there arose a chance to discover my parental background, I begged him not to pursue it. Sam and I understood each other. In my own way I mourn and bless his memory. We were alike in many ways. He once said, our armorial motto could be "Look only ahead". So allow me this. I want not to look back.

"About the ashes. Here I can prove how well I knew Sam. He was an Anglophile. He loved England and he loved you. So his ashes are in the best possible place, and where he wanted to be. With regards, Dusty."

Muriel replied sooner than he expected. On a double folded notepaper, she wrote: "Dear Dusty, I thank you for your letter and apologise for my earlier rather peevish one. Your letter was well written, very mature, and politely showed me up. But may I pick up one point where I think you do Sam an injustice. (Having married Sam, I feel, I have some right to do so). To look ahead is to view from a platform. That platform is the past. The past gives experience and experience is something from which to learn and build on. Don't let this trouble you. In this world there's room for all kinds of thinking. Right or wrong, somehow we manage to live our lives with a measure of contentment, and it is not for any of us to claim the truth. Plato asked: how do we know what we think is true. There's no answer to that. The important thing is to think. Live the questions, as Rilke the poet suggests. It matters to know where we are. I couldn't be an amateur archaeologist or even a site-seer without admitting that. History is not bunk—as Henry Ford is reputed to have said, and I don't believe he meant it—history matters. Truly it does.

"Thank you for letting me keep the ashes. They will go with me to my grave. Yes, I like the idea of burial, of becoming part of this world. Sam and I, our time together, short as it was, was full of love and deeply happy. Keep in touch. With love, M."

Dusty put the letter down. It did unsettle him, not for long, because he refused to let it. There was nothing more he wanted to say or do and resolved to move on into the present. In the fortnight since he wrote to Muriel, he had fully immersed himself in the routine of Regimental life. The new responsibility of commanding B Troop kept him preoccupied. If the past mattered, it mattered emotionally and, therefore, not for him. History was for politicians and politics was not for him. It was different with Military History? Lessons learnt were for tactics, military tactics to be used and adapted by leaders in battle. Yes, he concluded, he was an existentialist. Life is like fiction, unfolding a story as one lives it. What's past is best forgotten. No use, he constantly told himself, since he first learned what it meant, to cry over spilt milk. He went to the window and stared down at the palace lawn. On a cane chair Captain Kishan Lamba sat sipping his cup of tea. He looked up and they waved to each other. Kishan mumbled something.

'What did you say, Kish? I couldn't hear?'

'I said', Kishan shouted back, 'why don't you join me?'

'I've had tea. Will join you later, in the Mess, for a drink.' Dusty turned away. He walked back to the desk. The envelope, in which Muriel's letter had arrived, lay on the floor. He picked it up and discovered he had missed an enclosed card on which she had written: "Sam's money does not matter to me either. He had arranged for an amount to go into your bank account. You'll get that when I've sorted things here. Before coming here he settled property matters, re his father's will, with Dinshaw. Thank heavens I'm spared that and from having to travel to Bombay. They are so different. Sam very English, Dinshaw so like a Yank, his Aunt—I forget her name—a very traditional Parsee!! Keep in touch only when you wish to. M"

Dusty sighed with relief. She had thrown him a lifeline. He did wonder how to acknowledge Muriel's letter without encouraging a to and fro correspondence. But the card was not without its sting. She knew more about him than he realised. It was astutely chosen. For the picture on the card was *Stalker's Castle*! And as he looked memories came flooding in; and hard as he tried he could not dismiss them. A jig-saw puzzle of Stalker's Castle was Sam's first birthday present to him. Sam would have told her. Of course, no one knew Dusty's actual date of birth. In 1948 St Peter's Orphanage opted for New Year's Day 1940, and made out a School Certificate accordingly. Three years later, New Year 1951, Sam came to collect him and to say: 'You're going to live with me from now on. Not just for a Saturday and Sunday as before, but for every day, and I've got you a birthday present.' That day, all the way to Sam's home there were questions he was dying to ask but said nothing. If he was watchful and patient, he would quickly find the answers for himself. He recalled looking up to see Sam smiling down at him and prompted by a feeling of well-being, he had put his hand into Sam's. It was not a memory he wanted to cherish because something of that moment left him with a sense of vulnerability, and he resented it. There and then he resolved to be independent and in control, but from that moment on, kindness had a face. It was Sam's, as he remembered it, smiling down at him.

He shut his eyes and bit hard on his lower lip to block the memory. But refusing to be shut out, other memories came flooding in: Sam with him in the bedroom that was to be his and showing him how to tune the small Bakelite radio on the window sill. The sound of Sam's deep, clear voice, which he strove hard to emulate and had now made his. The opening of his present, the jigsaw puzzle, and on its box cover, Stalker's Castle. The pristine joy of that moment returned, and broke him! His body shook violently. 'No, no, no,' he cried inwardly. 'I won't dwell on the past! There's nothing to gain from it.' He sprang up and determined to stem all emotion decided to go out for a run. Briskly changing into PE kit and feigning not to have heard Kishan calling to him, he went out through the gates and into Roshanara Park.

The Park was empty. He glanced at his watch. Five minutes to six and it was getting dark. Worse, it threatened rain. Already he could feel a light drizzle. Flashes of lightning were soon followed by a low rumble. He dashed for the shelter of the band stand and almost ran into a figure deep in its shadows. Dusty recognised the new Head Clerk. 'That you Lal Singh?'

The uniformed figure saluted. 'Sir, you may take my umbrella. I collecting it tomorrow from the Mess office.'

'I'll wait till the rain stops. I see you're wearing your new Daffadar stripes.'

'Yes, sir. Thank you sir.'

'You deserved promotion. Good man. Have you settled in your new quarters?'

In the Shadow of a Dream

'Yes, sir. My family arriving...wife, child, arriving yesterday... from Rotak.'

'Then you're waiting to meet someone?'

'Pritpal. Retiring Head Clerk. He's partaking meal with us. Showing me ropes...is that right...ropes, procedures. My English not so good speaking. No practice I have. My family all speaking Punjabi.'

'You write well, type well, and your spelling is good.'

'Thank you. You're most kind, sir.'

'But you can speak to me in Punjabi or Hindustani.'

'Sir, may I ask question. I see a warrant for Colonel sahib's signature. For railway ticket. To Bangalore.'

'That's at least three weeks old. Cancel it. I'm going on annual camp exercises with the Regiment. You'll have five days to settle in, before you join us.'

'You like mother and father. *Ma bap*, as my father used to say of Britishers. But if I may say, sir. Holidays are important. For family sake.'

'I have no family. No home to go to. All I have, Lal Singh, is the Regiment.'

Lal Singh's eyes looked troubled as he shook his head tentatively.

'There, it's stopped. The rain, I mean.'

'Still some drops. You will get wet, sahibji.'

Dusty put his hand out, squinted his eyes at the skies, and ran towards the Mess.

CHAPTER TEN

'Keep the receiver close to your lips. You won't be heard unless you do. Press this when you want to instruct your driver or gunner, and switch to that when you want to give orders to B Troop—i.e. your other two tanks. This third channel is the one you must always get back to, because it's your link with the CO. Got it, Dusty?'

'Yes, sir. I've got it.'

'And you, Captain Bhandari?'

'Sir. This is my fourth camp exercise with the Regiment.'

'I know you consider yourself a veteran, Bhandari, and in a way that also applies to Lieutenant Dustoor. It's his second year. But this year the Armoured Division is involved in exercises and Harry, Colonel Prasad to you youngsters, wants everything to go like clockwork. It's always worth checking on the drill, when we are in Camp and before mock battle exercises. So, I repeat: at all times, back to this channel. I knew a blithering idiot, who stayed on his troop channel. He got left behind because he missed his CO's order to advance.'

'Sir,' piped in Captain Bhandari. 'I know of a worse case.'

Major Himmat Singh, Second-in-command of Rathore Lancers, gave a tired sigh. 'And what is that, Bandy? Not another one of your tall yarns?'

'Honest, sir,' Bhandari, grinned. 'This troop leader was on the CO's channel, but thought he was on his tank channel, and he ordered his tank driver to "Halt!" Result, the whole Regiment came to a halt. Right in middle of an exercise.'

'Pull the other one, Bhandari. It's got bells on.'

'And when the Regiment came to a stop, the CO bellowed: "Who's that bloody fool?" The chap never let on. His wireless operator knew, but he also did not let on.'

'And you still don't admit it,' Himmat Singh said snidely.

Bhandari laughed. 'It wasn't me. I heard the story from Brigade Commander.'

Himmat Singh shrugged his shoulders, raised his field-glasses and looked long and steadily into the distance. They were standing on the broad deck of the tank, behind its turret. Lowering the binoculars, he glanced at his watch. 'Gentlemen, it's time for lunch. Back here in two hours. It's a fine clear day for target practice.'

Dusty sprang off the tank and landed like a panther on his feet. The two older men watched with envy. Himmat Singh patted his slight paunch. 'By Jove! What wouldn't I give to have a waist like that!' he mumbled to Bhandari.

'Dusty is showing off, sir.'

'Showing us off, you mean.'

'Dustoor needn't be so…Do it my way, Sir.' Bhandari climbed down, using the steel brackets on the side of the tank, planted a foot on a boogie wheel and jumped off with a backward leap. 'That's how we were trained to do it. No antics.'

'Still,' Himmat Singh said as he clambered down, 'I've decided to join him on his early morning runs. Where the hell is he now?'

'Off on his bike, sir. To find some time to read before lunch. He got the Technical Adjutant's convoy to bring his bike and books. Did that last year, too.'

As they walked towards the tents, the tall lanky figure of Captain Kishan Lamba approached them. Himmat laughed. 'Talk of the devil…I see you didn't realise that Kishan is our new TA.'

'I was looking for Dusty,' Lamba said.

'And how is our Technical Adjutant getting on with his new job?'

'Fine. Except I hate having to collect the post from HQ. There's a letter for him.'

'There's a turn up for the books. Dusty seldom gets mail. Unlike Bandy, here.'

Lamba grinned at Bhandari. 'Bandy gets far too many letters. Curse of the newly-weds, sir. Can't see how he keeps his mind on his work.'

'Lay off, Shorty. You're due. Soon you'll know what it's like to have a woman in your life. Hey, we've got nothing on Dustoor, in that line. Is his in a woman's hand?'

'Yes, Bandy, but that means nothing. It's from Scotland. And I've seen that hand before. More than a year ago. Too long a gap. Can't be a love letter. And it actually says "from Mrs Sam Dustoor, on the back.'

'And Dusty's not married,' Himmat Singh said, like one thinking aloud.

'Can't understand him not getting letters from girls, 'Bhandari remarked. 'A good looking chap like him. Or is he one of those?'

'Never,' Himmat Singh growled, 'and watch how you talk, Bandy. I happen to know. Har Prasad showed me the report on Dusty from the Commandant of Tejpore Military Academy.' He paused. 'But that's confidential,' he added, recalling General Sen Gupta's comment, "this young man could he a lothario, if he wasn't also a fine gentleman of firm principles."

'I know he's not,' Lamba said. 'He not interested in men or women, if you ask me. Bit of a loner.'

Muriel's letter explained that her reason for writing was to enclose Minoo's letter, which Dinshaw had redirected to her. "Do you remember Minoo? Boman's son? Or is that another friendship you've left by the wayside? I say that only to agree that you and Sam have much in common. Boman was a close friend of Sam, yet he knew nothing of Sam's decision to live in Britain, and neither Boman nor Minoo know anything about you, since you left school. I suppose men pay less attention to...oh, I give up...

"My fondness for Minoo grew slowly in the years I was at St Thomas's. He was always last to leave the classroom, ever eager to do jobs for me. His letter to Sam was posted to the only address Boman knew, and crusty old Dinshaw redirected it with some reluctance. He wrote 'Mrs Sam Dustoor' with a distinctly hesitant hand. I have written to Boman and told him the news about Sam. With love, Muriel."

Minoo's letter was formal and to the point. He began by saying that although he was aware that neither Sam nor Dusty cared for his friendship, he was writing on his father's behalf, because "Dad finds it difficult to express himself on paper", and that if either Sam or Dusty wished to know, their address was now 9 Bauhinia Terrace, in Singapore, where they had settled. Minoo elaborated: "Dad was approached by a big Parsee business firm, who made him a generous offer for the Light of Asia restaurant and the flat above. Also, in part exchange they have provided equal accommodation in Singapore, where they said "Dad's expertise would pay dividends, far more than what he was getting in Bombay. Dad's been in Singapore these past eight months."

Dusty put the letter in the inner pocket of his dungaree, and for a moment paused to reflect how Boman would take the news about Sam. He knew of their strong respect for each other. Maybe, he thought, taking on a new project in a far country will lessen the impact. He inhaled deeply and picking up the book he was reading, once again sank into its bold narrative, but not for long. Juma's respectful whisper over his shoulder reminded him that lunch was served.

At the table, Colonel Har Prasad drew a chair and sat next to him. 'You were very absorbed in that book. What's the title?'

'*The Conquest of Peru,* by Prescott.'

'I thought it might be a book of poems?'

'No sir. I've left poetry behind, and now, even fiction, however good.'

'My father was a Lecturer in Punjab University. He did recommend Prescott to me and suggested I begin with *The Conquest of Mexico.*'

'I've read that, sir.'

'I'm sure you did. But I must admit I've read neither. When I was eleven, father made me help in cataloguing his large library, in the hope I'd get hooked. It made no impact. After his death, in my teens, I was determined to read every book that was ever published. But one can't. I know you're a voracious reader, but you know, one can't know everything, however clever one is. Remember that.'

Dusty stared at his CO for a thoughtful moment. 'You disapprove of my reading?'

Har Prasad shook his head. 'How could I? I would if it adversely affected your work. It doesn't. But, what you do now and how you act, that, more than anything else, is going to leave its footprint in the sands of time.' He smiled.

'But sir, action needs to be informed if it's going to serve any good.'

'*Touché*. Anyway, forget all that, it's not why I chose to sit next to you. As you know Prime Minister Nehru died yesterday. Well, I've been called to Delhi, to join a ceremonial guard, along with an officer of my choice. I'd like you to come.'

'Whatever you say, sir. I'm at your service.'

'Good, then that's settled. We leave soon after lunch, in my jeep. I'll be taking my driver, as per regs. But you can drive.'

Later that afternoon, three officers walked towards the tanks that were lined up at the firing range. 'I see you're itching to say something,' Major Himmat Singh said.

Captain Bhandari gave a nervous laugh. 'Nothing. It's all right, sir.'

'Come on, out with it.' Himmat Singh and Kishan Lamba exchanged mischievous glances. 'Now is as good a time as any.'

'It's just that you gentlemen seem not to comment on the absence of Dusty.'

'And…?'

'I happen to know he's Harry's, I mean the CO's, blue-eyed boy. Dusty has been given a special assignment.'

'That, Bandy, is stale news. I knew about it this morning. The Colonel consulted me. He's quite a democratic sort of guy, the CO is.'

' Actually,' said Lamba, with a smug smile. 'I knew yesterday.'

'This is one-upmanship,' Himmat Singh growled. 'But that would only mean you knew about the CO having to go. You couldn't have known about Dusty.'

'True, but Dusty's an obvious choice for the job, sir.'

'Right, Bandy, let's test your OLQ. That, in case you've forgotten is, "officer-like qualities". There, now get on to the deck of the tank, the second from the left. Lamba yours is the third.' Major Himmat Singh stood between the tanks, raising his field-glasses.

'Now, in the turret you chaps have a gunner and a loader. Captain Bhandari, your target's a scrap tank, at 1,200 yards, 2 o'clock. Raise a hand when you've seen it. Look through your glasses. Good. So what will it be, shot or shell?

'Shot, sir.'

'Good. Yours Lamba is a bunker, 12 o'clock and 800 yards. Shell or shot?'

'Shell, sir,'

'Good. Bandy you first. Let's hear the orders to your gunner.'

'Right sir,' Bhandari shouted. 'Look to your front! 1,200 yards! 2 o'clock!'

'ON!' the gunner's shout from inside the turret could be heard.

'FIRE!' screamed Bhandari.

'FIRING NOW!' responded the gunner, but there was no sound from the gun.

'*Arrey*! What happened?' Bhandari stared into the turret.

'Tell him, Lamba.' The Major said.

'You forgot to order the loader to "load", Bandy.'

'Indeed, Captain Bhandari. Your poor loader must be looking up at you aghast. And the gunner having pressed the trigger, will be equally surprised.'

'Sorry, sir. I'll get it right this time.'

'Let me remind you Bhandari, if Dusty is the CO's blue-eyed boy, it's for a damn good reason. End this rivalry. We are fellow officers, bound by *esprit de corps*.'

While in Delhi, Dusty bumped into "Cash" Kapoor, an old friend of his Tejpore days, and now in the Army Supply Corps. 'And how's the ASC?' He called out.

'That you Dusty? I say Dust, I'm terribly sorry about cancelling that holiday.'

'Good Lord! Never gave it another thought…Where are your glasses?'

That's just it. I mean, why I had to cancel our holiday. Mother took me to an eye specialist chappie in Switzerland. Bloody magician. Now, I only need spectacles for reading. Hey, we could do that promised holiday. To Charbag, Kekri.?'

'I don't know. I…'

'Oh, come on Dust. It's a great place for a base. Ideal for touring Rajasthan.'

'Has that deal come through? Wasn't there some sort of hitch, about the house?'

'That's some years ago. It was the Munshi.'

'What d'you mean?'

'They didn't want to sell it while the nawab was alive. Now, the present owner, and nephew of the nawab chappie, has agreed. With effect, two months from now, it's dad's, the house I mean. Look, I'll write. But you've got to come. Say yes.'

They drove from New Delhi back to Batiala and the Ranges Camp. This time Har Prasad, told his driver, Omed Singh, to take the wheel while he sat with Dusty at the back. 'You should take up the holiday offer your friend has made,' his CO said. 'Yes I heard most of it. Your friend has a loud voice. It's good to have a break. Besides in six months you're due to a transfer. A three-year stint outside the Regiment. ERE.'

'Extra Regimental Experience?'

'Some day I'll catch you out. Anyway, when you go, the Regiment will miss you. I certainly shall. But, can't hold you back. It's good for career, promotion-wise, as Americans say. Soon you'll be wearing your third pip.' His Sikh driver smiled and glanced up at the mirror. '*Han*, Omed Singh,' Har Prasad said in Punjabi, 'Dustoor sahib will be Captain. But you watch the road.' He lowered his voice. 'When you're back, Dusty, after those three years, you'll be off again on a Field Officers Course, which is essential for the rank of Majors and above. By then the Regiment will have a new CO and I'll have retired and settled with Preeti, in Rajpur, near Dehra Dun.'

Colonel Har Prasad stroked his chin thoughtfully. Dusty studied the pale patrician face and the thinning grey hair under his beret, which swept over his ear in a short trim curl. Something about the head reminded him of Sam. He couldn't think what.

'You know, dear boy, I saved you from the clutches of General Gagan Bakshi. He was impressed by you, and wanted you to be his ADC with immediate effect.'

'How did you manage that, sir?'

In the Shadow of a Dream

'I said you hadn't taken leave for years and I had just granted you four weeks off. So, you better say yes to your friend.' He threw his head back and laughed. 'You've lost nothing. It may seem a privilege to hobnob with a general, but it's fatal when it comes to promotions and, you don't want to be checking the temperature of his bath, play a losing game of golf, or go on shopping expeditions with his wife?'

'Someone else said that, sir.'

'What, about shopping?'

'No, sir. About a losing game of golf. Sen Gupta, Commandant at Tejpore.'

'Now that's a strange coincidence. I met Minnie. Dinner. Last night...by the way, I hope you were comfortable at the Red Fort Officers' Mess?'

'Very, sir. I gather the food's a lot better than at your Senior Officers' Mess.'

'Don't you believe that. As I said, I met Minnie at this top brass dinner. When she heard I was the CO of the Rathore Lancers, she asked after you. Said she had news, important news, for you. Couldn't wait to meet you as she was catching the late train from Delhi Station, on the...in her own words...long, tiring journey to Ranchi—Sen Gupta was recently posted to Namkum, Ranchi. And I committed a terrible *faux pas*. Ranchi, I said, famed for its loony bin? "Yes", she said. "I'm President of LUCID." She gave me her card.' He took it out from his wallet and read. Ladies Union Caring for Insanity and Dementia. She said she'd write to you.'

Minnie's letter came a month later. She addressed him as her "Dearest Sam" and went on to tell him that she had met an old Portuguese nurse named Esther Lobo, who was a nurse in Basirabad Military Hospital, in 1939. "There she became a friend of another nurse, a Goan named Molly D'Silva and remembers how, on many off-duty evenings, they went to the Railway Institute, where they met and danced with British soldiers. Molly, she said, was a little careless and got herself pregnant by a soldier, who got posted to Burma before her child was born. An angry Esther wanted to write to the soldier's CO, but Molly begged her not to, saying he was a good lad. She trusted him to return and marry her, as he promised. But the soldier was killed at the beginning of the war. When Molly could no longer hide the fact of her pregnancy, she was sacked. With Esther's care and help, the child was born in the Hospital, but Molly, feeling she was being a burden to her friend, told Esther she had decided to return to Goa and to her parents. Molly left without leaving an address. Esther hoped to hear from Molly and when she did not, wondered if she would ever see her again. Some months later, Esther was detailed to accompany a shell-shocked soldier to Ranchi, where for a while he was admitted into a mental rehabilitation ward. To cut short a long story, there she saw Molly, who did not recognise her. Esther, convinced the authorities she was prepared to take full responsibility for Molly, sign papers and face any claims on the poor abandoned woman. Esther brought Molly back with her to Basirabad. Molly was a very sick and physically weak woman and in little more than a month, during a high-fever bout of malarial typhus, she died, but not till after, in a moment of sanity, she talked about being on a train to Baroda with her son; of getting off at a small station and walking towards a village, and leaving the boy on the steps of a temple. She told Esther that the village had a high wall, which surrounded a big fort-like gate. Esther thought of travelling to make inquiries about the walled village, but realised such an undertaking, for a single European woman, was fraught with problems. So she asked a Dr Ram Prakash, who knew that part of Rajasthan, to find the village, if it existed, but she got posted to Rangoon and they did not meet again till 1961. According to Ram Prakash, Fatehpur was the only walled village near Baroda. It was off the beaten track, and fitted the description she gave him. The villagers were unhelpful, saying, there were and are many motherless boys. Only two were prepared to say anything. One, an old herdsman, remembered a six-year old boy, who ran away to Bombay with some older boys, adding, with a sad shake of his head, that he would be dead by now; the other, a temple devotee. She did recall a strange child with peculiar eyes and rumours of him being an incarnation of Lord Krishna, and is believed to have returned to his water gardens in Mattura.

"Sam, I know you are that boy. Joe, my husband, who's seen your records, won't commit himself, but admits to the possibility.

I thought you should know. And if it is true, then you are, as I suspected, not a Parsee but an Anglo-Indian, with an English father. You are, indeed, as that old woman said, a genius, blessed with everything except, as I told you, a mother's love. Alas, that is now beyond reach. Molly, if she's your mother, is buried in the chapel graveyard of the Convent of St Mary & St Anne, Basirabad. But someday when you can, go there, to that grave, and lay on it a garland of flowers. You'll be blessed for that. With love, Minnie."

The letter upset Dusty and that made him furious. Why was Minnie doing this? But could he blame her? She hadn't set out to make inquiries. It happened. He would write at once; and tell her this tale of the past was just a coincidence with which he denied any link. Then he would destroy her letter. That would help him forget. He started to write, trying to be terse and with the aim of discouraging a response. How could he do that without hurting her feelings? Why reply at all? There was no good reason to invite or continue a correspondence with Minnie. But it would be rude not to reply. She was a general's wife. It would do his career no good to snub a woman of such importance. "My dear…" He stopped. He couldn't call her "Minnie", even though she had signed her letter "Minnie". "Dear Mrs Sen Gupta," I have no wish to act upon your…" He tore the sheet of paper off the pad, crumpled, discarded it, and started again. "Thank you for your letter. A welcome and pleasant surprise and so kind of you to remember me, but you must know, I have by now shed the past and moved on. I have not been without love—I have known love, a kind of love, and I do believe it may have worked out better than real parental love in important ways." He hesitated over whether he ought to tell her of Sam's death, and decided to mention it in passing. "I knew freedom, and now that he's gone, I am truly free." He stopped. His pen hovered over the sentence. It had come out spontaneously. He let it stay. "I keep shedding the past as my life and livelihood moves on. It matters little who gave birth to me. What I make of my life is the question. I'm a man of my environment, not my beginnings. I close with thanks for the time and care you spent on your long and thoughtful letter. Forgive me if I choose to do nothing about it, and please do not press me. My respects and regards to the General Sahib, Sincerely, Sam Dustoor."

Dusty joined Lieutenant Kashi Kapoor at the Moti Bagh Palace Hotel in Jodhpur, where they spent the night before driving off to Charbagh. Cash's father had placed one of his cars, a Mercedes Convertible, at their disposal. Sitting next to Pannalal, the chauffeur, was Laxman, the cook.

'Cash,' Dusty said, as they set off, 'do we really need a cook?'

'Oh yes. During the day we may manage with roadside *dhabas*, but in the evening you'll want a good dinner, substantial, properly prepared. Also, sandwiches for lunch for a change. And Laxman makes terrific sandwiches. How does that sound?'

'Wonderful, but you must let me make a contribution. I'm talking money.'

'Nonsense, Dust. Hell, what'll I do with it. Relax, man. All this is not coming out of my pocket.'

'But a six-week holiday romp is long and expensive…'

'Forget it. Okay, you can buy a meal or two. That reminds me. Four weeks is all I could wangle. But for the last two weeks you can stay in dad's flat in New Delhi.'

Dusty said nothing. His thoughts parodied Kipling's "A St Helena Lullaby". How far is Fatehpur and that little boy today? Here he was, the once poor orphan, in the company of riches. But he wasn't going to be overwhelmed into being over-grateful.

They lunched in Ajmer at a neat and clean Goan Cafe, run by a matronly woman whose husband worked as a foreman in the Carriage & Locomotive workshop. Then they set off towards Charbagh and some hours later their car entered the long, shady drive of a red-roofed, white house with a long pillared veranda. Half-way up the drive their car was stopped by a little man in a dhoti. He wore a black waistcoat, a black pill-box cap and carried a thick red book. Bending into the car he whispered to Cash. Cash nodded, turned to Dusty and said: 'We'll walk up the drive. I gather the last owner of the house is here and about to leave.' Cash told Pannalal to park at the back of the house, and Laxman to unpack stuff from the boot and get cracking with tea and dinner.

As they neared the house, Dusty stopped suddenly. 'God! What's that?'

'What's what?'

In the Shadow of a Dream

'In the veranda... It's okay. She moved. She was still and white like marble. For a moment I thought it was a statue. A Greek statue. Venus De Milo with arms.'

'And clothes. She's a beauty. That figure would look great, naked.'

'Not so loud, Cash! She's looking towards us.'

'And you! Good Lord Dusty, you look struck down.'

'Yes I am! I've never seen anyone so beautiful. Not even in books. I'll never forget that face. Not ever.'

A man came from the house, joined the woman in the veranda, put an arm round her waist and talked earnestly for a moment. Then they went into the house together.

'Lucky blighter! But he's not a bad-looker either.'

'Yes. A dark Rupert Brook type, and she, something by Raphael or Burne-Jones.'

'Dark? He's my colour. Not yours, light like a bloody Parsee. Hell! I should have guessed. That'll be Sandy. The chap dad bought the house from. He's Rajput. Sandy Thakur. I could introduce myself and you. Then you can have a good look at her.'

Dusty shook his head. 'No. I don't see what good that'll do me. Anyway, they're off. Listen.' A car engine started.

'They'll come this way,' Cash said. 'You'll get another look at her. Cross to the passenger side. Who the hell is Raf...whatever that was you said, earlier?'

'An artist. Medieval...never mind here they come.'

A car with large chromium headlights approached and as it went past the man saw them and waved. The woman, lost in thought, stared large-eyed ahead, very still, her raised chin accentuating her drooping mouth and pouting lower lip.

'God,' Dusty exclaimed, 'what a profile! Pure Raphael. Sorry, you were asking?'

'Forget it. I suppose you know all about Medieval Art. Spare me. I've already had a long lecture from you en route here; and I'm not even sure what that was about?'

'Colonel Todd's *Annals of Rajasthan*. That's why we're here.'

'Okay. I'll use my eyes. You use your head. I remember the bore of being forced to attend those long debates organised by the School Debating Society, with you in the Chair. You always were a bookworm. What a relief, for once, to see you take an interest in a woman. Give yourself a break. Think women. Hey, I remember now, not much, because we weren't in the same company and you were six months senior, but there was... what was her name? Something Min or Mun...the Commandant's wife? You danced with her, didn't you? Oh, yeah. There was talk. It looked as if you two were, you know, what I mean...' he made a rude gesture, rubbing his forefingers together. 'Jig-jig...we expected Sen Gupta to expel you.'

They reached the veranda and, as if from nowhere, the little man with the red book appeared. Folding his hands he bowed and with the meek emphasis of a clerk spoke: 'Please to forgive delay, but a room is now been arranged for the purposes of rest and sleep. *Chai* too is being prepared.' He drew a hob watch from his waistcoat and looked at it anxiously. 'It is phive p.m. Dinner will be arriving at eight.'

Cash nodded and gave a slight wave of the hand. The little man rolled his head. They sat down on the two central steps of the veranda. Behind them the setting sun reflected sharply on the window panes. Cash gave Dusty a sly nudge. 'We were, you know, talking about women in my life. Let's have your story.'

'What makes you think there were any? No use looking at me like that.'

'You know. You and Minnie. There, I even remembered her name.'

'Goes to show how misleading rumours can be. Actually Sen Gupta was good to me. Gave me a book autographed by him. And we almost played a round of golf.'

'No smoke without fire, man,' Cash said with a triumphant gleam. 'But, anyway, she was old enough to be your mother. But sexy.' Getting no answer, he waved his right hand before Dusty's eyes. 'Hey, you're not listening. You've gone all dreamy. Thinking about the woman you saw just now? She's only a dream.'

'No, she's a goddess. Women like that are worshipped.'

'The best.' Again he rubbed his forefingers. 'Each time, is like a rape.'

'Stop that. Where did you pick that up? That gesture with the fingers.'

'Pannalal, our chauffeur. He did that when he asked if we

wanted a woman. That reminds me. Have you done it, or are you still a virgin?'

'As one virgin to another. No. I mean, no I haven't done it.'

'Okay, I'll admit it. I too. So, why not during this holiday?'

'What here? In Rajasthan? Land of the purdah?'

'He'll fix it, Pannalal, a man of infinite resource. And discreet too.'

'No thanks. I don't want a dose of you know what. I'd rather...'

'Don't tell me. You'd rather read a book.'

'That's what I do all the spare time I can get. I wish you'd read too. You wouldn't pester me, then. And don't trouble your dad any further. I can do without Delhi. I'm happy to spend a quiet fortnight in my room at Mahijit Niwas.'

'Or, you may keep Pannalal and Laxman for a few days after I've gone. You can go where you like. I mean, it would be a pity to spend ten to twelve days twiddling your thumbs. It'll also do me a favour. Dad doesn't know I got only four weeks. If those chaps return early, he'll think you and I are on a filthy spree. Dad's a highly suspicious guy. Keeps a tag on me, so I don't ruin his marriage arrangements.'

'But you can't marry before twenty-five, without your CO's permission.'

'These things take time, and I'll be twenty-five next year.'

'I could do with a few days on my own. Your talk about Minnie reminded me.'

'Sometimes you can be so bloody mysterious.'

Dusty grinned. 'Basirabad is not far from Ajmer. We are ending up at Ajmer?'

'Yes, and no. Basirabad is not far. But explain, you sly...'

For an answer, Dusty gripped his friend by the back of his neck and shook him. 'Ask me no questions, and I tell you no lies.'

'Ouch, you're hurting me. God, Dust, you're so bloody strong.'

'Anyway, I'm not asking about your intended.'

'Intended? You mean Kamala? I'll show you her photograph, man.'

'And a moment ago you were talking about prostitutes.'

'That's different. Dad would never know. The marriage is a business deal.'

'What'd'yer mean, business deal?'
'Kam's family has even more money.'
'More money? No one can have more money than your dad.'
'Dust, sometimes, you can be so innocent.'

The Convent of St Mary and St Anne, Basirabad, had a graveyard of mostly white marble headstones, crosses, and angels. Dusty, carrying a bunch of red and white roses, zigzagged his way among the graves, and stared hard at the names. He stopped and stood over what at first looked like a dark brown bundle of cloth till it moved. Two grubby hands that had been shovelling earth, pulled back a cowl, revealing a Franciscan face, twinklng deep blue eyes and a forest of ginger grey facial hair. 'Oh, hello! Father?' Dusty asked, defensively. The squatting figure rose on its knees and offered a large open hand. 'Help me up, young man. I'm Brother Bonaventure.'

Dusty could not place the foreign accent. He took the hand, pulled and discovered his companion was elderly, short and tubby.

The figure laughed. 'Yes, they call me Friar Tuck,' he said. 'How can I help?'

'I am looking for the grave of Molly D'Silva.'

Brother Bonaventure scratched his bald pate and genially noted the flowers. 'Oh, now...'ave yer been 'ere afore, me lad.' Dusty shook his head. 'Will she be a one yer know?' Again Dusty shook his head. 'Will yer be knowing when she died?'

'I'm not sure. It could be 1941 or '42.'

'Ah, that will be at the far wall. Come, I'll take you there.'

'I'll find it, father.'

'No. no. Let me. The walk will do me good. A power of good.' After a few paces he stopped suddenly and held his head. 'Oh, I'll be losing me head next. Did yer say Molly D'Silva? Why, we reserved the plot next to her. For one Ester Lobo. Will yer be knowing that lady too. And a very fine lady she is too.'

The grave was a plain slab of white marble with a simple cross of grey slate on it. Below the cross, written in black, was: "Molly D'Silva, A Mother Beloved by God." Next to the grave, demarcated by pegs and white rope, a plot of grass had a T shaped piece of

In the Shadow of a Dream

box wood. On it, painted in red, the single word "reserved". Dusty placed his bouquet of flowers carefully on Molly's grave. He fell on his knees, bent forward and embraced the marble slab with outstretched hands.

Brother Bonaventure went to him and kneeling next to him, placed an arm round his shoulder. He spoke gently. 'There, there, me lad. Tell me, what this Molly meant to yer. Would she be yer mother, me lad? Would I be tinking right in saying that?'

Dusty shook his head. With a sharp intake of breath and a sudden movement, he stood up. 'I don't know. I really don't know, father. I should never have come. It was a mistake.' He turned and started to walk away.

The monk called out. 'Don't go, dear boy. Don't do this. Wait. Hear me! I'll take yer to the Military Hospital. Meet Sister Lobo!'

Dusty stopped. He turned and regarded the monk, who was standing by the grave with open hands. 'Forgive me, father, I've made a big mistake.'

'At least come into the church. I'll say a prayer for the two of yer.'

Dusty watched Father Bonaventure striding towards the church. On reaching the little porch, the monk turned round and beckoned to him again. Dusty shook his head and raised a hand in a gesture of farewell. 'Thank you, Father. Goodbye,' he said hoarsely, then walked to the car, which was parked under the shade of a mango tree. Pannalal and Laxman were sitting patiently in the front, till Laxman saw Dusty and sprang out to hold open a back door. As the car moved away Dusty heard the tolling of a bell. He looked back at the little bell tower on top of the central gable. He traced the bell-rope down to the wide step of the porch. The monk's head was covered and bowed against the rope. The tolling stirred a memory. He glanced at his watch. Yes, the Angelus at noon. He had heard it twice, when his school Cricket Eleven played St Joseph's Roman Catholic Academy, on their superb grounds in Parel, in Bombay. He began to mumble: "The Angel of the Lord declared unto Mary and she conceived by the Holy Ghost. Hail Mary, full of grace, the Lord is with thee, blessed art thou among women..."

'Yes, sahib, *hookum*?' Pannalal broke in.

'What saying, sahib?' Laxman asked.

'Nothing.' Dusty hastily said, embarrassed on realising he had been audible.

'Where to? Where sahib want to go?' Pannalal said without turning.

'Oh, yes, Panny. Could you take me to the station. Then *chhutti*. You're free. Tell Cash…I mean, Lieutenant sahib, I have decided to go back to Batiala. My regiment.'

'Here, Basirabad Station? *Yah* going Ajmer Junction?'

Dusty thought for a moment. 'Ajmer, Panny. If that's all right?'

'Back early! What the hell are you doing here?' Kishan Lamba raised his brows as he sat at the table and ordered his breakfast. 'When did you… Join me.'

'I've had breakfast. You're late.'

'Well, it's Sunday. Come, come. Sit opposite me. Don't want to shout across the room. Put that bloody book down. Now, tell me, what was it like, the holiday?'

'Hot. Sometimes insufferably hot. Not in the car. It was air-conditioned.'

'Did you get to that place I told you about? The Maharaja's of Jodhpur's Hunting Lodge; and the Lake, Sardar Sagar.'

'Yes. We covered every state except Bundi. We even got to Jaisalmer.'

'That's on the border. You know there's trouble brewing, with… you know who.'

'What? Oh, good! We'll see action at last.'

'We, not you. You're going to Bangalore. Attachment. Three years. You have a happy knack of skipping danger. That bit with China. You were in Tejpore. Now, when the Regiment's been put on alert…we go North, you go South.'

'I don't know. My posting hasn't been confirmed. Being a heavy tank Regiment, I bet you will probably see action somewhere in Rajasthan.'

'Ferozepore, Punjab. But you can take it from me. You're off to Bangs galore.'

Dusty chuckled. 'Bit hard on the Bandharis. The newly-weds.'

'Not to worry, Harry had already planned a long honeymoon for him.'

In the Shadow of a Dream

'Typical of Har Prasad. Decent chap.'

'More wise than decent. As Signal's Instructor in the Centre and School, Bandy'll do the least damage.'

'Poor Bandy. The ragging he gets. But I don't think he minds. Anyway I'll agitate like hell, to get off this peaceful posting.'

'I wouldn't if I were you. It's an important posting. Whatever action we see, will be little more than a skirmish. When you're back, you're due to get your lions, after a Field Officers' course, of course. Harry's pushing you to be the youngest Major in the Brigade. He wants to see you command a squadron before he retires, six years from now. He knows how much the men would like to see that.'

'How on earth do you collect all this gossip? And gossip it is. Even the CO can't juggle the Army List. You'll make Major before me. That's how it crumbles, as the Americans say, cookie-wise.' Dusty stood up.

'Maybe, but Harry'll oil the wheels to make certain you're next.'

'I'm going back to *Our Mutual Friend*. I'm still on holiday.'

'Dickens? That's heavy stuff. Ah! Here come my fried eggs on toast.'

Almost a year later Dusty was to recall this conversation with some regret. The trouble, which began in August 1965, was more than a skirmish. The Regiment had suffered casualties, among them Captain Kishan Lamba and Colonel Har Prasad.

Dusty visited the Colonel's wife, and promised, on his next leave to call on her at Rajpur and to take her two boys on a trek to Mussoorie and the Shivalik Hills.

It was generally assumed, within the Regiment, that the Second-in-Command, Major Himmat Singh, would take command of the 9th Rathore Lancers. It, therefore, came as a big surprise to all when Colonel Bisham Chand from Punjab Horse was appointed instead. Himmat Singh, himself, broke the news.

The Regiment was once again on its annual camp, in the flat, open countryside of West Punjab. It was a typically hot, windy

March day; and the officers were lunching under the shelter of their large marquee. 'It's a swap, gentlemen,' Himmat Singh said. 'I'm going over to Punjab Horse.' His glance took in their shocked faces and finally rested on Dusty. Dusty met his gaze with a calm that hid his disappointment.

'Strange,' remarked Captain Bandhari, 'our Regiment bears the name of Rathore Lancers, yet the latest intake of a subaltern is a South Indian.'

'Trust Bandhari to strike an irrelevant note,' chuckled Himmat Singh as he drew a chair and sat next to Dusty. 'We have two Sikh squadrons and a Jat one. Now, make something of that, Bandy, or hadn't you noticed.'

'What's the point of the swap?' Dusty whispered to Himmat Singh.

'Our masters have a peculiar logic.' Himmat whispered back. 'Never question any appointment is my parting advice to you.'

'You must be disappointed.'

'More angry than disappointed.'

'But you, you will be commanding Punjab Horse.'

'If that were the case, I would have no reason to be angry. No, this is a sideways move. I'll be 2iC to their 2iC, who takes over as CO.'

'But that's iniquitous.'

'Once again, I love your choice of words. It's a delight listening to you. Somehow it makes me feel better. But I've another bit of advice, for you in particular. Do tread with care, because you'll be treading on his toes. I mean the new CO.'

'Why in heaven's name, should his toes be in the way?'

'Bisham Chand's taken an instant dislike to you. He asked me to point you out. Yes, it's going to be a new experience for you. Till now you've impressed all who have met you. Not this chappie. He believes Har Prasad has spoiled you, that you were his blue-eyed boy and need taking down a peg or two. So keep a low profile. The less he knows about you the less he can hold against you. Get on to another course.'

'But I've just got back from a three-year spell away from the Regiment. And due a Field officer's course, ending in a promotion, as you well know.'

'I told him. He thinks you're too young for that. He'd like to

In the Shadow of a Dream

send you to Infantry School in Central India. It's a toughening course. No one in the Cavalry welcomes it. But for the athletic sort of chap you are, it's a piece of cake. He hasn't realised that.' He chuckled, and gave a confidential wink. 'It's a damn good course to have up your sleeve. COs can be so blinded by their petty hates, their moves often boomerang, and slap them in the face. This will. With this in your bag, you can be transferred to any Infantry unit as a liaison or advisory officer. And that's a cushy job and added rank.'

Dusty gave Himmat Singh an implacable look, but said nothing.

'You must think I've an axe to grind. I have. But believe you me, I'm not using you. Why should I? I gain nothing by getting you into trouble. You're able to succeed whatever you do, wherever you are. That's sweet revenge enough. Mind you there's no justice in this world. God is far too wishy-washy…goody-goody. He ought to be a tyrant. If He wants us to believe in Him, He ought to throw his weight about.'

'Maybe He wants us to leave Him alone. In which case, the last thing He'll want to do, is weight throwing, and leave us jokers to bumble along.'

'Ho, ho! Brilliant. I like "bumble". Like the bumble bee which goes crashing into things. That's wonderful. Poetry in accident-prone mode. *Wah, wah!*' He pushed his plate away and stood up. 'He won't be CO for long. Three years, most. Maybe why he was given the post. So the poor chap gets a decent pension. You have got youth on your side. I'm sure it's one reason why he can't abide you.' He held his hand out, shook Dusty's, and left the marquee with a smile.

"You know, Sam, Sam!' Only one of his fellow officers called him Sam. Dusty did not have to turn round. 'Hello, Bandy!'

'Sam, do you mind? I don't want to pull rank on you. But…'

'Pull rank! But we're both Captains.'

'Bear in mind that I am your senior by six months. I was Captain when you were still a subaltern.'

'Okay, fair enough. But why this sudden formality?'

'Stop calling me Bandy. I don't call you Dusty, and I don't like that smirk on your face when Himmat Singh pulls me up.'

'When did I last "smirk" as you call it.'

'A moment ago. Just before you and Himmat were…were gossiping.'

'Gossip! Anyway, it had nothing to do with you, if that's what…'

'Then what were you talking about?'

'I don't think I'm at liberty to tell. I'd need Himmat's permission.'

'I've tried to be friendly. But you're so bloody aloof. You've even turned down Mohini's invitation to dine at our place.'

Dusty looked up. Bhandari's sad eyes and full mobile lips gave his face a febrile look. Dusty frowned. If only he could tell him how determined he was to keep away from women—especially those who showed signs of finding him attractive. 'I'm a bore, Bandy. I've not singled you out. I live a confirmed bachelor's life.'

'I know, and books for company. So, you weren't talking about me.'

'No. It was about the new CO. I can say that much.'

Events in the Regiment evolved as if Himmat Singh said. After Dusty returned from his course at the Infantry School near Indore, he was ordered to join a Gurkha Battalion in Lansdowne, up in the Himalayan foothills. Barely a year later, an Army Corps was detailed for action on India's Eastern frontiers and the Commander, Major General Derek Brown, one of the last Anglo-Indian senior officers left in the Army, entered the Gurkha Battalion Mess and with a wide grin thumped Dusty on the back. 'Lucky dog! Somebody up there loves you. You'll miss another war.'

'But that's not what I want, Sir.'

'You mean that? I was going to have you sent back to your Regiment.'

'Sir, am I to understand then, the Rathore Lancers are to see action?'

'No, they're part of a heavy tank armoured division. We need light tanks. If any.'

'I'd rather be here, sir.'

'I can arrange that, if you so wish. Could do with a chap like you. Be my ADC. Not for long. Just so that, when later, I've good reasons for posting you back here.'

CHAPTER ELEVEN

'And how old are you now?'
  'Forty-four, sir.'
  The Brigadier looked up. 'Good Lord! I'm forty-one. You look years younger. I take pride in keeping fit. What's you secret? Squash?'
  'No sir, I'm a runner. Sorry, was. Long distance.'
  'Hmm. When did…' He turned a page in the file before him. 'I see. You've been a Major for ten years. That's rather long for…for one with excellent reports. And I gather, extremely bright. "Bit of a loner" this one says. We'll pass on that.' Brigadier Chopra grinned, shut the file and threw it into his desk drawer. 'You're here for two years, and I go by first impressions. I like what I see.' He extended his hand, shook Dusty's and grunted. 'This is your second stint as a liaison officer? Good. Welcome to Four Brigade. Our base is Pathankot, but have picquets in Dharamsala, Mcleodganj and two others on the Dhauladhar range towards Dalhousie. That's our beat. Other Army Units deployed here may want to borrow your expertise. But you will have a considerable amount of freedom. I mean regarding parades and routine.' He lifted his telephone receiver and pressed a button. A connecting door opened, and a tall, very dark officer, sporting a luxuriant moustache walked in. 'Ah! There you are. Meet our new liaison chappie. Major Sam Dustoor meet Major Vikram Dutt.'
  'Hello, Dusty.'
  'Vicky!'

'You know each other?' The Brigadier raised his brows. Dusty nodded.

'I met Dusty in Ooty,' Vikram said, 'we were on a Field officer's course together. And later in Calcutta.'

'Well, you see Dustoor, you're not the only Major stuck with ten years. I…' The telephone rang. The Brigadier lifted the receiver. 'Chopra here…'

Dusty and Vikram began a discreet retreat. The Brigadier covered the receiver: 'Stay! No secrets in this office.' A moment later he put the phone down. 'Is my jeep outside? Good. See you this evening at the reception. Vicky'll explain.' Chopra rose, donned his beret, picked up his cane and marched out of his office.

'Viks! He has a black beret. Which Cavalry Regiment was he in?'

'Trust you cavalry chaps to notice something like that. Skinners. Now, I'll fill you in on our way to the MO. It's better this way, so you can take in all the info you need as you meet it full on. The MO is Colonel R.P. Bhalla. Just Raj or RP to Majors and above. He insists. Bluff chap. Can be a bit rough during medical examinations.'

'Do I need a medical?'

'Have you had your jabs? You have. Then it's the usual stuff. Forms to fill. By the way, thanks for walking slower. How's your old wound getting on?'

'Fine.' Dusty slapped the back of his right thigh. 'It was unnecessary to spend two months in the Military Hospital and another two weeks for observation.'

'One could get lost in Calcutta's Military Hospital. Beside I think they forgot all about us. You got it in the right, I got it in the left. Bloody hand grenades. Once the pin is off…I mean there's nothing one can do in seven seconds.'

'You got the worst of it,' Dusty said. He had noted Vikram's slight limp.'

'Could've been fatal. I'll never forget that Dusty. I heard you shout to that *jawan* not to remove the pin. Then you threw yourself on me. It was a deafening…'

'The explosion? You don't have to remind me. I couldn't hear for two days.'

In the Shadow of a Dream

'Madness. One came out of active operations unscathed, only to get wounded due to a silly mistake by one of our own chaps.'

'You were Major at least four years before me, and you're that many years younger. I don't think Chopra realised that.'

Vikram stopped walking. 'That's the obstacle course. Opposite, tennis and squash courts; also the swimming pool.' He faced Dusty. 'You must be near six feet.'

Dusty shook his head. 'Actually, five nine.'

'I'm six, exact. Rare for a Bengali. What made you smile?'

'It's the second time someone over-estimated my height. A long time ago, when I was at Tejpore. A beautiful woman. She was Bengali.'

'Tejpore. You don't mean Minnie? Minnie Sen Gupta. Good grief. They've settled in Australia. About ten years now. He was terribly British.'

They started to walk again. And for a while neither spoke. Then Dusty asked. 'I say, what and where is this reception?'

'I hadn't forgotten. I'll take you there and show you the place.' A jeep drew up alongside them. 'I told Kashi Ram to drop the Brigadier and get back to us. Get in.' He tapped Kashi Ram on the shoulder, 'Black Elephant Institute.' Then to Dusty. 'It's in town. Was The Railway Club. We've spruced it up and built a dance floor that goes like a ring round a tree, a *chenar*—the Indian plane tree. Do you dance?'

'Yes. Not terribly keen. Do I have to attend?'

'Nothing's compulsory for you, but you must, this once. The Brigadier will say a word or two to welcome you. And I'd like you to meet my wife, Shalini. It is, I'm afraid, a black tie event, but that won't be a problem. I've detailed Mansingh to be your batman. Damn good chap. He'll help you settle down and see that your dinner jacket is pressed and your shoes shining like mirrors. You'll have your own jeep.'

'There's no hurry. As long as I get a lift tonight.'

'I'll see to that. It won't be me. I've got Shalini and her English friend, who, until recently, worked in a small primary school for local children in Mcleodganj. Most are Tibetan, so Shalini tells me. She helped in the school, when we were in Mcleodganj.'

'English, did you say, this friend. Is she a missionary?'

'I wouldn't know. I'll be seeing her for the first time. Anyway, she gave up, which isn't the missionary way. I'm told she lives in a remote corner off the road leading to Dalhousie. Comes to Dharamsala on a pony, but she'll have to get here by bus. Save all your questions for when you meet her tonight.' Vikram punched Dusty in the ribs and brushed his moustache above a sly grin. 'Keep the conversation light. I expected that from you when we were in hospital, all those years ago. Instead you ranted about Plato and Aristotle.'

'At the time I was reading Russell's *History of Western Philosophy*.'

'And you're going to dance. Books and literary chat is off the menu. Damn it, it's time you found yourself a wife. I'm being family; an elder brother.'

'Elder!'

'What's a few years between friends. Anyway, don't talk age. You're so bloody young looking. I'll introduce you to Nirmala, she is the daughter of...

'Don't you dare! I'll do my own foraging and, before you ask, yes, I've known a few women, not in the biblical sense...Indian women are great ones for the giggles, single ones especially. Puts me off. I suppose that's its purpose—a defence against seduction. And behind the giggler I see a mother ready to pounce on one, cram a *luddoo* in your mouth and announce we're engaged; now sign up and name the wedding day.'

'What do you mean by "in the biblical sense". Remember, I'm not a Christian.'

'You'll have to work that one out. Anyway, thanks, but no thank you. Viks, this is India. Sex outside marriage is nil, except at a price, if one goes after women who walk slowly...'

'Prostitutes? I like the way you put things. I'm impressed; always have been.'

'Don't be. Nothing I say is original. Second-hand from books, films, people.'

'That applies to all of us. But you have this fantastic memory. So, have you been to these, you know, women, and if you haven't, how do you manage?'

'You don't expect me to tell you.'

'No, but I hate to imagine.'

'At my age, what you imagine would be absurd. I'm as much

Hindu as Christian. For Hindus, marriage is a rite of passage from bachelor-hood into family life, and why for that reason there's pressure to marry soon after puberty.'

'Everything in Hinduism allows for hypocrisy. As long as you're eligible, and no one's going to believe your age, even if they did, it wouldn't go against you. Your future wife might even be grateful.' Vikram grinned wickedly. 'Your love for books has always made you a sober sort of guy. Remember our expedition together, in Cal? I'd introduced you to a nice Anglo-Indian nurse? Afterwards she told me, you talked all evening about Operation Overlord and the Normandy Landings.'

'Good listener she was, too. Sex is overrated. Masturbation faintly ludicrous, and when the desire arises, a good book is the perfect antidote.'

'Arises being the operative word,' Vikram said and they laughed,

'Also, Viks, with the passing of years, libido grows less. Damn it I'm forty-four, and aim soon to retire. I have plans.'

'Forty-four is nothing, not with your physique. Pity the girl at the butt end of your pent-up libido! But I'll agree, in India, sex life begins and ends with marriage. But I suppose in time it will change...not necessarily for the better.'

After a thoughtful pause Dusty said. 'Oh, by the way, I'm not all that proud of my "fantastic memory", inverted commas. It'll pass and go away with time. So medical books say. I've taken to reading books on medicine. Just read from cover to cover *The Oxford Textbook of Medicine*. Found an old copy in Bombay's Thieves Market, *Chor bazzar*.'

'Good Lord, if I saw that sort of book, I'd pass by on the other side.'

'So you do know the Bible. Were you trying to tempt me into a confession?'

Vikram shrugged. 'Got that from Westcott School, in Cal.' He gestured with his cane as the jeep turned up the drive of a large, white stuccoed bungalow. 'Right, here we are. The wettest bar in a dry country.' He sniggered. 'Now, don't forget, you'll be sitting with us at our reserved table. Let's go in.'

'Is there a billiards table?'

'Oh, yes. Two. And an excellent marker. He's been there forever.'

'Then Viks, when you have done with dancing and can bear to wrench an hour away from Shalini, give me a game of billiards. It's been years.'

'Will do, dear boy, will do, after I've seen you on the floor. I'm curious to know, and meant to ask: do you have a scar? You know, at the back of your thigh?'

'Not noticeably. I was lucky. Somehow, when we fell, you rolled on top of me. The bloody grenade only partially exploded, or neither of us would be here.'

'You're late, Dusty. What held you? Chopra's been wondering if you got lost.'

'No one's fault, Viks. To borrow a joke, flat battery gets you nowhere. The jeep engine died on the way. Kashi Ram had to flag down another vehicle to jump start the bloody thing. But it's not the battery, if you ask me. The dynamo isn't charging.'

'Anyway you're here, that's the important thing. Wait here. Let me tell Chops. I'll be back, unless you want to find our table and introduce yourself.'

'No, Viks, I'll wait for you.'

A moment later Vikram returned. 'All's well that ends well. Chopra's perked up when I explained. He's going to welcome you, officially, at dinner, after the toast to the President.' They moved between numbered round tables of seated guests. 'Like your jacket, Dusty, who tailored it?'

'Leach and Webborney, of Poonah. Now defunct. What's our table number?'

'Nine. There, can you see. He waved. What's the matter, Dusty, you look dazed?'

Dusty had frozen to a standstill. 'Oh my God! It can't be. It's not possible.'

'What on earth are you talking about?'

'The woman at your table...next to...I presume, that's Shalini, waving to you?'

'Yes, my wife. And that's her friend Kitty. I can see she's wacked you between the eyes. That smashing maroon dress is the talk of…I should've prepared you for this. Good grief, looking at you, it's a knock-out.'

'Viks, I saw that face twenty years ago. I swear. It's a face I've never forgotten, and it hasn't changed. It's not possible.'

'You're mistaken, Dusty. Twenty years. There must be an explanation. Come let me introduce you.'

'You know, Vicky, for the first time in my life, I feel weak. Give me a moment.' Dusty snatch a glass of whisky from the tray of a passing waiter and gulped it down.

'You poor boy! Well, she's single and you're single, so we have paired you two for the evening. Take it from there.'

'And who is sitting on the two unoccupied chairs next to her?'

'Our Adjutant, Captain Jaswal and Pritee. Recently married. Time only for each other. Come, let me introduce you to my wife and Kitty Franks.' He did, and invited Dusty to sit next to Kitty.

'Are you all, all right for drinks?' Dusty tried hard to hide a tremor in his voice.

'We've just had a Blood Mary,' said Shalini, 'and trays of whisky and soda are doing the rounds. You haven't got a drink. Catch that waiter going past you.'

Dusty raised a deprecating hand. 'I'll wait till he comes round again.' He sat down and saw Vicky whisper something to Shalini, who nodded, looked at him and smiled sweetly. She had a long thin, but pleasant face and she wore her hair in plaits, circled in a bun over the nape of her neck. The bun was rimmed by a loop of fresh, brilliant white, jasmine flowers. He turned to look at Kitty. She was looking pensively ahead of her, seemingly listening to the dance band playing a tune he was not familiar with. He stared and drank in her profile. It was flawless. Suddenly she turned and met his eyes. 'Sorry, I didn't mean to stare, but I suppose you're used to it?'

She smiled and looked away, and Dusty was intrigued.

'I suppose you're used to Indians staring?'

'No, not really,' she said. Her face broke into a radiant smile and her sherry brown eyes twinkled. All at once she was different from the woman in the car, twenty years ago. That face had a rare melancholic beauty and the blue eyes—yes, even in the fading light, the deep blueness of hers eyes had come through.

'What is that tune? You seem to know it.'

'I know it, but I'm not sure I can name it. Do you dance?'

'Yes, not very well. A bit out of practice.' He stood up and bowed. 'May I have the pleasure... Miss Kitty Franks.' She nodded to Shalini, and Dusty lead her on to the floor. 'May I call you Kitty?'

'Of course!' She smiled. Her forehead was in line with his chin and he realised she was smaller than she looked. Wondering about her age he glanced down. Her breasts were small and firm like that of a sixteen-year old girl. He placed his right hand round her waist and instantly a hand pressed against the hollow of his right shoulder, as if to fend off nearer encroachment.

'You will take me back if they play something fast and furious,' she said firmly and without looking up. He grunted and led her to the middle of the floor.

'Oh, dear,' she sighed. 'They are giving us room.'

'To take a good look at you. That's a smashing gown...dress.'

'It is. It's old. My aunt's. I didn't do much to it. Took in a bit at the top. Oh, no! Sam, the dancers are stopping to look at us.'

'It's not the gown. They're looking at your slim, svelte figure.' He laughed. 'How do you live with the fact you're the most beautiful girl in...in the world?'

'Girl? I'm not a girl,' she said with a slight frown, 'and you don't have to pay me absurd compliments.' She looked away. He waited. 'If you must know, my looks did matter once. Now, not for some time.'

'But the eye of the beholder can't deny what is clearly the case.'

She sighed. 'All the same, thank you.' For a while they dance in silence, then she whispered, 'please can we go back?'

'If you wish. Have I offended you?'

'No. Sam, not in the least.'

'But that's what people will think, if we go back to our table.'

'Yes, sorry. We'll stay together. We could go to the bar. I'll have a sherry...oh, look,' she pointed to the veranda beyond. 'Two unoccupied chairs. I'll wait there.'

But she was not there when he came out with the drinks to join her. The chairs had gone. She was further down the veranda leaning against a pillar, toying with a bougainvillaea frond. 'They've taken the chairs in,' she said.

In the Shadow of a Dream

'Yes, the band's stopped playing and people are sitting down for dinner. 'Alas, we are not together. You're with Shalini and Vikram. I'm with Chopra.'

'Why, will you be saying something?'

'I suppose so, looking a little sheepish after he welcomes me.'

'We had better go in,' she shivered. 'I forget how cold it can get in November and I've only brought a light shawl this evening.'

'I'll lend you my trench coat after this do is over.'

'That's kind, but I'll manage.'

'Please let me. Then I'll have an excuse to see you again.'

They looked into each other eyes for a moment. 'Can I say it again,' he said. 'You are the most beautiful woman in the world.'

She shrugged, and gave a light nervous laugh.

'It's not a chat up line…Kitty, it's the truth. Didn't you see people staring when we were on the dance floor?'

'It could be because of you. You're handsome, strong, graceful, and you lied to me about not being a good dancer.'

'Come on you two!' Vikram called. 'Dusty, you can escort Kitty to our table.'

Dusty raised his brows inquiringly. 'I thought…'

'I've fixed it with Chopra.' Vikram whispered. Kitty went on ahead.

'I don't get it.'

'You don't have to be on his table. Just stand up when he welcomes you.'

'Vicky, dear old chap, bless you.'

Dusty caught up with Kitty. She said. 'If I'm part of some wicked plan between you two, fill me in.'

Dusty threw his head back and laughed. Then he took her arm and led her to the table. ' "Once you have found her, never let her go." ' He crooned softly.

'Are you always so bold at first meetings?' Kitty asked as they sat down.

'No Kitty,' he smiled, 'but this is "some enchanted evening," and not our first meeting. I saw you twenty years ago. Ever since I've been in love with you.'

'Twenty years ago, I was twelve, well, thirteen.'

'I did see you, and you were as you are now. But your eyes were blue. I swear it.'

Kitty stared at him incredulously. Soup, served in cups were placed before them. Shalini, touched his arm and smiled slyly. 'Hope you're enjoying the evening?'

'Yes, Shalini, thank you. Where's Vikram, he seems to have vanished?'

'Look, behind you, speak of the devil. Knowing my husband, I bet he's excited by the prospect of you and...' She nodded towards Kitty.

He turned to find Kitty staring at him intently. 'Where was this,' she asked. 'It wasn't me, so where did you see this woman?'

'I was with a friend, on holiday, at a house his father was buying. Somewhere between Kekri and Charbagh, in Rajasthan'

'Wasn't she with someone?'

'Yes, an Indian. Good looking chap too.'

'Good heavens, Sam! That would have been Sandy!'

'Gosh! Yes! That's what my friend called him. I remember now, Sandy.'

'Then, you saw my aunt, Emma. It couldn't be anyone else. The time, the place and...yes, we were alike, in looks, very alike; only the eyes of blue separated us.'

He gazed into her eyes. 'I'm in love,' he whispered.

'And Sandy,' Kitty seemed not to have heard him, 'it's strange... but you know Sam, in some ways you remind me of him...even though he was...'

'He was...what?

'Sorry, I've already said you're handsome and graceful; a great mover, as they say these days...but I was going to say, Sandy was terribly good-looking. Sorry I...'

'You needn't apologise. I saw him, and said as much.'

'As a little girl I had a crush on him...' She compressed her lips and looked away. 'Such a dear, good man...Oh, please! I'll begin to cry. Talk about something else. I do beg of you. What are these?'

'These, "Angels on horseback", that what the menu card says. Please, I must see you again. Please, I'll die if you say, no.'

She gave a light chuckle. 'You can't mean it. Anyway, I'm staying the night with Shalini.'

'Tomorrow is Sunday.'

'Yes. I go back to my place after lunch. But I'm sure Vikram will let us meet at his place before I go. He seems terribly keen to bring us together.'

'It's kind, thoughtful of you, Sam, but you don't have to escort me. Besides, the last few miles to Fern Cottage is a pony ride.'

'Pony. And where did you leave the pony, overnight?'

'At a doctor's house in Dharamsala. Next to his dispensary. It's a long story.'

'And how do you get to Dharamsala, from here, Pathankot?'

'By bus. Here, thank you for the trench coat. It's warm and sunny, now. Sorry to deprive you of it. I hope you weren't cold last night.'

He slung the coat over his shoulder. 'May I accompany you to Dharamsala?'

'If you wish. It's quite a long journey.'

'Kitty, I can't think of a better way of spending Sunday afternoon. And it will sustain me for the three hours back, without you.'

'You're importunate, incorrigible,' she said, tossing her *dupatta* over her neck. She was wearing a white *salwar* and blue *kamiz,* and the Punjabi outfit suited her. He felt sure she would look good in a sari too, in anything. 'Well, if you must.'

He took her small suitcase as they walked to the bus station.

'You could get lost, getting back.' She said.

'I've been to many places, Kitty, and I'm proud to say I've never got lost.'

'Anyway. There are two bus stations. The bigger one is in town. This one is near, and is the one for the cantonment. So make sure you get back to this one.'

At the station she said: 'Give me the suitcase, Sam, and get yourself a ticket.'

He was some time; and when he joined her she said: 'the bus is about to leave and it's full. They're laying on an extra bus, shortly. It's worth the wait. I hate a crush.'

He followed her as she went round the back of the bus station. 'There, what do think of that view?'

'It's fabulous.'

'That's Dharamsala in the distance. Dharamsala, Pilgrim's Rest.'

'Well, it's certainly become a theological home to Tibetans.' He turned to look at her. 'Fern Cottage? I gather you live there alone?'

'Not really. It was the home of Sandy and Emma and I've inherited a cook, his wife and a gardener. Alone, in the sense that I lodge there. The house is managed by Mohan Singh for Dinesh. Dinesh was Sandy's nephew and ward. Even the servants are paid by Mohan. Sona, the Tibetan girl refugee Emma saw in Delhi and adopted, she comes over on weekends, with Ransingh, the chowkidar, and now her husband, but I'll tell you more, during the journey...I'm treated like a five star hotel guest.' She smiled. 'You're in luck today. It's seldom this clear. Do you see a white house with the red roof? There, just below the skyline. That's Mohan Singh's.'

'Yes. I see it. I assume this Mohan Singh was a close friend?'

'A great admirer of Sandy and Emma, and a friend to Dinesh. Now, look to your left. No, not up there. Just below you. That open square in a crowded bazaar area.'

'Ah, yes, next to that palatial house with a big red gate and marble arches?'

'That sprawling house belongs to a rich businessman, known as "The Seth". He's Dinesh's father-in-law and the open square, outside the walls, is the city bus station.' Suddenly she went quiet and pensively stared across the scene before her.

'Tell me about Emma and Sandy. You said we'd talk later. Where are they?'

Her eyes welled up. 'Oh Sam! They are dead!'

'Heavens! When?'

'A year, little more...' She started to cry and covered her face with her hands.

He reached out, touched her hand and said gently: 'May I.'

She nodded and he drew her against his chest. She remained still for a moment, fluttering like a bird. Then with both her hands she firmly pushed him away.

'Hush now, someone's coming. I'm sorry about making a scene.'

'I'm not. I'll cherish this moment, forever; and the trench coat that...'

She seemed not to hear, turned her wrist and looked at her

watch. 'It's time we went,' she sniffed. He offered his kerchief, she shook her head and took hers out from under her bra. He tried not to smile. 'You see, I'm an independent woman.'

They were quiet in the bus, which moved off shortly. Kitty kept her face turned away from his and looked out of the window. Dusty waited awhile, then ventured: 'Was Fern Cottage visible from where we stood?'

'No. It is beyond Mohan Singh's place and behind a ridge,' she spoke softly. 'Did I tell you that Fern Cottage was their home? Emma died there...and Sandy, the same day. They were so deeply in love. They lie side by side buried in the graveyard of an old chapel, which is now within the school premises.'

'The school where you taught?'

'Part-time teacher and not for long. When I first came here, I stayed at the Nurpur Mission, but then Miss Das, who was in charge of the Mission, resigned and left for Delhi. It all turned out ugly and when Shalini, also a part-time colleague, moved to a house in Pathankot, she left. I resigned too and went to live in Fern Cottage.'

Once again she gazed out of the window. 'Sam,' she suddenly asked, 'don't you think Pritee looked unwell when they left?'

'I scarcely noticed. They were hardly at the table much of the time.'

'Thank goodness. Jaswal is a chain smoker. I noticed you don't. Have you been a smoker?'

'I was a teenager before I could afford cigarettes. Mind you I did in my wild childhood, mostly to keep company. I didn't like it. And you, did you ever?'

'Yes, my father too. But we both gave up. I, before I came to India. He, after my grandmother Edith died.'

'And what are your plans for the future? I mean, now that you're...'

'I like the South, Cochin, Goa...there're schools I'd love to teach...' She paused. He noted how she often interrupted herself, trailing off mid-sentences. 'My father is coming over at the end of February. He'll holiday here. For a fortnight, before we go back to England.'

'Two months! Gosh, Kitty! I'll have to work fast to make you change your mind, about going back to England. When may I see you again. My week-ends are free.'

'Sam, surely you have better things to do?'

'No, and I'm going to be frank...'

'You've been nothing but that, since we met.'

'I want to marry you. I must marry you. Tell me, there's a chance. There's hope, or do I mean scope.'

She laughed. 'Oh, Sam, you can't be serious? Don't tell me you are.'

'Deadly earnest. At forty-four I may be old for you? Do I have a rival?'

'You're not too old. You don't have a rival. I've always liked older men. Whether you've the slightest chance, I really don't know. It's far too early to say. I refuse to be rushed. Sam, I hardly know you!'

'Then, get to know me. Like me enough to let me woo you and win you over? I know I can, if we spend time together. I won't ask for much, only whatever time you can spare. Let me build you an altar. Let me adore you for the rest of time. The die is cast. There's no escape.'

She studied his face. 'I do believe you're serious. I've never met anyone so bold, so determined, so confident…or is this some game you're playing?'

'You ask,' he said in Churchillian tones, 'what is your aim, I answer Marrriage.'

She giggled; took a deep breath, and shook her head.

'Do I have to win your father's consent, as well?'

'My father has never denied me anything…that been part of my/our problem.'

'Then I won't take no for an answer.'

She looked out of the window. 'I don't know what to say.'

He sat back in his seat and stretched his legs. 'Say yes. Yes, you'll marry me.'

She did not speak. He sat up and turned to her. 'Kitty, don't do this to me.'

She sighed. 'Sam, I do like you enough to want to see you again and that'll have to be sufficient for the time being. I can't promise more.'

He caught her hand firmly. 'You will find me, as plain as you see me. I'm alone. I have no family. Your consent is the only obstacle I have to contend with.'

The sincerity in the tone of his voice stirred her. She looked at him with tears in her eyes. 'Oh Sam, I've never had a greater compliment. But I wouldn't want you to waste your time. I'm not sure I want to marry again. Yes Sam, you dear sweet man. I'm divorced and there have been other men in my life.'

'I don't care. If there aren't any men now, now is where we are… where I begin.'

'True, there's no man, because I've been avoiding men. You must understand that. Because I remember what I suffered in the past.'

'Kitty, you and I don't need our pasts. We have a future, our future.'

'Sam, I feel as if I'm being smothered…rushed into committing myself…I give up. I've said you can see me.'

'Good. I've stormed the Bastille. Resistance is futile. Say you'll see me but don't say you can't promise me more. Tell me how and when we can meet. I'll arrange to hire a pony.'

'I can lend you a pony from our paddock. Can you handle one?'

'Kitty, I've been a polo player. You said "our"?'

'It's not my cottage, as I said. Dinesh owns the estate. He's in Bombay. Mohan manages it but I know he'd like to buy it. It's not just cottage and garden. There's land also.'

'When you say Dinesh, the nephew, was also Sandy's ward, do you mean he was like a son to Sandy…and to Emma I suppose?'

'Yes.'

'And now, is he single or married?'

'Married to Shanti, the only daughter of the Seth, the business tycoon who owns that sprawling house I pointed to, the one with the high walls and Mughal gate.'

'Then Dinesh is rolling in it. And Shanti, is she with him in Bombay?'

'No, she's in Pathankot, with her father in that big house. Therein lies a tale and a scandal involving a child. Dinesh denies he's the father. Poor Dinesh, I fear for him. But right now I'm selfishly thinking of myself and our little quandary. Sam, it will have to be Sundays. In broad daylight.' She laughed. 'This is India. Village India.'

'Grateful for any crumb you throw to me. Ever your grovelling, Spaniel Sam.'

'You're no spaniel. Sunday then, and as it's the first time, we'll meet at St John's. A landmark you can't miss…' She turned away and shuddered involuntarily.

'Kitty? What's wrong.'

'I don't think I'll ever get used seeing those poor coolies.'

'You should by now.'

She shook her head. 'The impossible loads they carry on their backs as they trudge uphill! I've seen one of them bent double, carrying a teak desk. He had a canvas strap tied to it and looped round his poor forehead. I think it's inhuman! Don't you?'

'One day you will employ a coolie to carry a cupboard or shelf or sack of coal and he'll thank you for hiring him. Other coolies will envy his luck.'

'I'll point to the Church as we pass it. We'll meet there on Sunday and I'll take you to the Cottage by a short but rather steep route. It avoids the Tibetan quarter.'

'Thank you.' He smiled. She had ignored his remarks about the coolies but he had not missed the defiance. The determined chin of that perfect profile was eloquent.

'There are conditions. Whatever we do, I'm going to England shortly, and when I return, I intend to take up a teaching job in Southern India.'

'I never interfere with job decisions. Always I placed a high value on work. Also I could be with you, help you settle. You see, I'm due to retire any time next year. So, I'll dog your footsteps, if you'll let me.'

'Retire? Oh, of course, retirement is early in the army.'

'It's a fine pony, Kitty; quite the size of a mule.' Dusty patted the pony's neck.

'Sandy got it for Bill Clayton, but Bill's feet still touched the ground. Bill was a missionary and Sandy's dearest friend. My father knew him too…Sam don't look at me like that.'

'Your breathtakingly beautiful. I can see why you choose to wear *salwar kameez*.'

'Talking to you is like playing chess. I never know what your next move will be. Now, when you come on Sunday, you'll probably meet Ransingh and Sona. They do spend Sunday, or part of Sunday, at the Cottage. And maybe Mohan Singh…what on earth are you doing with your fingers?'

'I'm counting the number of times left when we can meet. Not many, alas.'

'There's still much of February and the whole of March.'

'But sometime in February and March we have our Brigade Exercises. That will swallow three Sundays at least.'

She chuckled. 'For a brief moment you looked like a boy who'd dropped his ice-lolly. I can't make it any easier.' She smiled, and her eyes twinkled.

'When we are apart, I'll write love letters straight from the heart. Although I don't think I'll be good at that, so I'll end each letter with a plea and a proposal.'

'We're too old for that sort of stuff.'

'Stuff and nonsense. We ought to recapture that first fine careless rapture…'

'Honestly Sam, you're behaving…You must surely have had a crush before you met me, or even saw Emma?'

He looked at her uneasily and said nothing.

'Tell me, Sam. Was she beautiful, your first fine careless rapture? I assume she was Indian. Indian women are beautiful…I'm sure she was.'

'I can't say, Kitty. It was so long ago. I can't think, 'cos I only have eyes for you. Too dazzled by your radiant, almost cruel beauty, to think of anyone else. Blinded.'

Her chin turned petulant. 'Remind me, who said it, that "careless rapture" bit.'

'Browning. Robert of that ilk.'

'I was thinking Shelley or Keats. But you have to be right. Vikram told me about your immense reading and prodigious memory. Bear that in mind. I could be a bore.'

She was holding the reins of a patient chestnut pony. He reached out to touch her hands, hesitated, and withdrew them. 'Kitty, don't discourage me.'

'Sam, I find you increasingly attractive. One of us has to be pragmatic.'

'I'm not looking for a scholarly rival.'

'Remember, looks don't last.'

'You said, I've a good memory. I'll remember you like you are now for the rest of my life. When I was a boy, I fell in love with the Pre-Raphaelites. My father, I mean Sam, my guardian, had books of their paintings. I used to wonder if there were really such women, or were they fairy tale figments of male imagination.'

'Just that. Figments.'

'Then you and Emma are of some golden land that Burne-Jones peeped into.'

'I thought you were a down to earth sort of a chap. Forget the Pre-Raphaelites.'

'How can I? "Here's looking at you kid" as Bogart would say'

'I said you were incorrigible.'

Chapter Twelve

'Sam, I insist on calling you Sam because I don't like Dusty? Why Dusty?'
'Everyone calls me Dusty, Kitty. It's short for Dustoor.'
'I think it's unkind, cruel.'
'Is it? If I don't mind it, why is it cruel?'
'No one, particularly one as handsome as you, deserves such a tag.' She looked at him hard and long; sighed and looked away.
'Tell me why, why is it cruel?'
'Because…how can I put it…because it obviously refers to your colour.'
He shook his head. 'How can it be insulting? All or nearly everyone in India is a dusky brown. It's not a great nickname, I'll grant you that, but I've lived with it for what seems like forever.'
'How did you acquire it?'
'Orphans are named after foster parents. Dustoor is what my School certificate says. By the way the Army likes giving nicknames. I already had one.'
'But Dustoor is a Parsee name. And you're not Parsee. You're a light brown, not pale, like Parsees are. You could be Anglo-Indian.'
'These things don't count. Whatever my beginnings, what I am now matters. I'm happy to be Sam Dustoor, to honour my kind foster father. He was a teacher, and by taking his name I got free admission into one of the best schools in Bombay. He was an

authority on English History and Literature. And he made me the man I am.'

'With some help from your genes...was it a boarding school?'

'St Thomas's? No, I lived with him. Nine years, we were like father and son.'

'Alone? Was there any...you know?'

'What? Ah, I know what you're thinking about.'

'Sorry. Was it so obvious? It's just that we too had a "kind" teacher here, till we discovered he had abused several children—boys. It was what the row was about and led to accusations and the resignation of Monica Das. She was head of the Christian Mission at Nurpur, and the Tibetan School founded by Bill Clayton.'

'Sam wasn't a homosexual. He married, but his wife left him. That was before my time. Quite simply, he was a good man. These things are possible.'

'Anyway. Here's my address in England. I'll write back, I promise. And I'll give your proposal serious thought. There is no one else I'd want to marry. I know, I'm going to disappoint my father. He did think I had found someone and had hopes. But I assure you Dad hasn't a grain of prejudice in him. As you well know.'

'So, you and Ted fly the day after tomorrow.'

'No, there has had to be a change of plans. Dad is going ahead as he can't alter his flight. I'll join him a week later. Sam, there's been some terrible developments.'

'Good Lord! Can I be of any help?'

'Oh, Sam, if you can, it will be such a weight of my mind, and Dad's. I've been leading up to this bit by bit. Remember, Dinesh? Well, with the help of his servant Anthony, he caught Shanti red-handed.'

'Sorry, you've lost me. Don't be reluctant or embarrassed. Explain in clear frank terms. Shanti, I recall is Dinesh's wife, now go back and on from there.'

'Right. Their marriage, semi-arranged and celebrated with open display before the Dharamsala community, has been on the rocks for sometime.'

'Yes, I wondered about that, since you said Shanti is living with her father.'

'Shanti, fun as she can be, has been thoroughly spoiled by her doting father. Well, for sometime Dinesh has suspected her of infidelity and in Bombay, as I said, with the help of his servant, he caught her, as they say, in flagrante delicto. He has filed for divorce, but Sethji, her father, dreading the shame of publicity, has threatened to kill him if he goes ahead. The Seth—Seth Agarwal, that's his full name—is a man greatly to be feared. He has spies and henchmen all over the country. Dinesh did not climb down. He's been sacked from his job as Manager of Agarwal Hotels—it was a sinecure, the Seth's gift. Anthony was waylaid, beaten up, but he did not betray his master's whereabouts and both, he and Dinesh, have escaped; disappeared.'

'How do you know all this?'

'Because I've seen Shanti and the Seth—for some reason he's rather fond of me.'

'And who wouldn't be?'

'None of your...The man is gross, over fifty. Where was I? Yes. They lost track of Dinesh. But now, he's been discovered in a Poona ashram. Even the Seth wouldn't dare violate an ashram. But he had a spy there, disguised as a Brahmin. He reported that Dinesh had struck up a close friendship with a woman, a white disciple of the Guru or Maharishi or whatever. But the Seth's man has been flushed out, denounced as a fraud. The latest news: Dinesh has vanished again and it is rumoured that the Seth will direct his revenge elsewhere. This last bit was picked up by Ransingh. He and Sona are coming to Fern Cottage to keep watch while I'm away. My father feared this kind of reaction from the Seth. The Cottage will be vulnerable while I'm away.'

'What do you want me to do? By the way, why not bring in the police?

'We can't prove anything. Without concrete evidence the police won't question a man of the Seth's high standing. You now know Ransingh and Sona. Keep in touch with them. So that, if there are any serious developments, we can communicate and you could advise me.'

'Right. Then my first bit of advice is. Don't hang around. Go with your father.'

'It might be too late now.'

'We've got thirty-six hours. Most flights have VIP seats for last minute situations. I'll get Brigadier Chopra to help. In the circs, he'll make sure you're on the plane.'

Less than a week later, Dusty got a telephone call from Kitty. 'Thank you for your call, yesterday. Sam, I can't blame you for not leaving your number, but I'd lost the number you gave me. Luckily I had Vikram's and he gave me yours. There's still no news of Dinesh.'

'Plenty of news from this end. Grave news too. Mohan Singh has written to your father all about it in great detail, and he knows more than I do. But the upshot is that the Cottage has been torched, Sona's been killed and Ransingh arrested for murder. Apparently on learning of Sona's death, he raged about like a mad bull, caught a man he suspected was involved and axed him on the spot. You know how strong he is. All this happened two days ago. I was on exercise, and only learned all about it this morning. The police are no help as far as the fire is concerned; and have only acted on the obvious. There is no doubt that Ransingh is guilty, he's proud to admit it. But we know who must be behind the dastardly arson. Please Kitty, don't...'

'Oh, Sam! Sam! I loved Sona. She meant so much to me; and more each time we were together. I would fly back if I could, but I need a couple of weeks to straighten matters out here. It's important for both of us that I do. And, yes Sam, I will marry you. Bye Darling.'

'Yes to marriage! And we haven't even kissed...Exclamation!'

'So here's twenty by proxy, five more than the number of times we met.'

The excitement that gripped Dusty, as he hung up, was followed by the chill of a venture into the unknown. Having won his prize, he now felt unsure of himself. The joy in striving, in the heady scent of the chase, and in tasting success when it came to winning a woman with words, was behind him, now a sense of inadequacy began to eat into his complacency. He had lived life by the head and a largely solitary one, but now heart and soul knocked on the door of his inexperience. The years had flown leaving him a youth in middle-age. Not to have known maternal love or any physical intimacy with a woman, now meant a jump into the deep-end of the pool where he yet had to learn how to swim! Soon he would be with a beautiful woman! Twenty kisses! He hadn't known one

In the Shadow of a Dream

save a chaste kiss from Shirley Boston, of the Dancing School in Bombay. But that did not count, because it was the lightest of touch from her and he received it passively. What should he do? Admit it? The humiliation of it angered him. Why this sudden loss of nerve? Making love! He was not ignorant of the mechanics of it, and what could be more natural? Nature had gifted him with physical grace —people were always remarking on it—panache and energy. All that should see him through; enable him to play the consummate lover. But Kitty had known men. She would see through his act. Was it too late to learn now? She didn't have to know—a noble cause in the interest of their future happiness. But who would be his teacher. Indian women don't kiss. He had never seen them kiss—just the folding of hands and the shy giggle. Everything else he could imagine them doing, but that... Even on the cinema screens the attempted kiss was invariably a near miss... Cinema! Yes! Yes! Americans films! Yes! They were full of clinches and long lingering kisses. No need for nerves. All he had to do was copy the no-nonsense grip and heavy crashing down kiss on lips not always freely offered. It had been a long time since he had seen an English movie. Those long gone happy days in Bombay's Metro and Eros Cinemas. Could he emulate? He shuddered. The mouth to mouth slobber had never turned him on. But what a mouth! Kitty's mouth! The enticing pout of that lower lip was made for kissing. He took a deep breath. Sprang up and laughed out loudly. His natural aplomb had returned. Just as he succeeded in wooing her, he would succeed in making love, and even now he could feel his body needed no coaxing.

He met Kitty at the station. She looked even more beautiful than he remembered. As he advanced towards her, all anxieties fled. With supreme confidence he would make love to her and attribute any fumbling on his part to a new style, his style, of love making. She smiled radiantly as he stopped a few feet from her and ordered two coolies to collect her luggage. Both knew that in India one did not embrace in public, if one did not wish to attract attention, or at worst, disapproval.

The coolies were ready. Dusty pointed to a silver grey Buick. '*Uddar*,' he said and their eyes widening with awe, obediently tottered to towards it. 'Come with me Kitty, I'll need to open the boot.'

'Gosh, Dusty, I was expecting a jeep.'

'That's against army regs; no civilians and certainly no women in military vehicles. Of course, one can get round regulations, but I thought, since we're always going to be together, why not a car. Though I doubt if that jalopy can take the climb to Mcleodganj, but we'll make trips to the plains. It's air-conditioned and automatic drive. And Kitty, it's a present for you, for agreeing to be Mrs Dustoor.'

'But Dusty! I'll call you Dusty? I rather like it now.'

'Calling me anything else is confusing, I assure you. Except, of course, Sam.'

'Well, Dusty, that's no contraption. It's big and sleek and beautiful. Thank you.'

'Second-hand, I'm afraid. A sixties model.'

'It's special. Dad tried to get hold of a sixties Chev. How did you manage this?'

'An advantage of the Maharajas being of the fighting caste is their close link with the Army. I bought it off the ex-vizier of the Raja of Chandpur. Viks and I fought for it till I made an offer he couldn't refuse. The main advantage, which you'll see the moment I've got rid of the coolies, is to be able to drive you to a quiet corner of the woods, and then shower kisses on your upturned face. You promised twenty.'

She laughed. 'The upturned face needs a wash and some make up.'

'Gosh! You don't have to do anything and still look beautiful.' He held the door open for her to get into the car.

'I realise,' she said, as he got into the driving seat, 'that I must get used to you making frequent literary references.'

'True,' he said as he drove off. 'I keep reminding people, nothing I've said or say since the age of six is original. My life is a novel, and I never tell the beginning.'

'Then I am in for constant surprises. But first things first. As you know, since I can't possibly stay at the cottage, its Vikram's place now and Mohan Singh's later.'

'I've another surprise. The Station know about us. Viks, Chopra, the lot. They've allotted me a nice bungalow, four bedrooms and a wide veranda overlooking a small garden. Actually meant for a Colonel. But, they know I'm here for just another year.'

'But, I couldn't, not till we're married.'

'But we could marry as soon as Ted gets here. He is coming?'

'Oh, yes. Nothing, he said, would stop him. We'll be staying, dad and I at Bunty's place. Bunty is Mohan's wife.'

'I know Bunty. Mohan's got masses of room. His house is huge. I've been seeing him, for the sake of Dinesh. But you could stay at my place if your father's there.'

'We'd like that, but no. Bunty and Mohan will be disappointed.'

'By the way I've been attending Church regularly, since I arranged for the banns to be read. Two more to go.'

'At St John's, Mcleodganj? Sorry. Was that inconvenient?'

'Not really. It gave me an excuse to have lunch with Mohan Singh on Sundays. He thinks I don't eat enough.'

'So you've met the Reverend Amos Caleb?'

'Nice chap. Very protective about you and wondered if I was a baptised Christian, and if so why hadn't he seen me in Church. It wasn't till I told him your father would be at the wedding…'

'Aren't you going to kiss me?'

'…that he relaxed. Became positively enthusiastic.' He could feel her eyes on him. He started the car. 'We had better fix the date and tell him.'

'But you will kiss me before then,' she teased. 'It's a strange affair we're having. Getting married without an engagement or even a kiss to seal our pledge!'

'Because it must be done perfectly.' He touched his nose with his fore finger, but he kept his eyes firmly on the road. 'Just you wait, little Kitty, just you wait.'

'This is not the way to Vikram's. Or is this a start of some vile plan of yours?'

'I've recce'd the area and found a quiet nook, far from the madding crowd, but not too far.' He drove for ten minutes on the road to Kangra, then turned off onto a narrow dirt road and parked behind a craggy tor on the edge of an apricot grove.

'Gosh! This could be Devon!' she exclaimed.

'Now, that's new. You saying "Gosh"!'

'I've picked that up from you. Shows how much you have been on my mind.'

'Well, I wouldn't know about Devon. But I'll take your word for it. Is it the rocks and the wet greenery?' He turned off the engine, held out his hands and hesitated.

She understood intuitively. 'You dear, sweet darling. Where have you been all these years?' She drew near, cradled his face in her palms and kissed him, a quick gentle kiss and then a longer one. At first he froze like one assessing the sensation. But when she released herself, he took her in his arms, pulled her towards him and pressed his lips against hers. He kissed her again, this time his hands caressed and squeezed her breasts.

'A fast learner,' she said, breathlessly. 'Yes, I knew. You can't hide much from a woman,' she added as she rubbed a spot below her breasts.

'I'm sorry. Was that the gear lever?' He moved the lever forward and touched her lips. 'If there's a heaven on earth, it is this, it is this, it is this.'

'I've heard that before. Quite recently, in Delhi, at the Red Fort.'

'Do you know it in Persian?'

She shook her head. The guide told us, my father made a note of it, but I couldn't repeat it.'

'I can. *Agar fardos baru-I zamin ast, hamin ast, hamin ast.*'

'Show-off.'

He laughed.

'But the Persian sounded like twice. You said "it is this" three times.'

'Yes, because while the Persian on that marble wall is cold, your lips promise an even higher paradise.'

'Don't Dusty. I'm tired of compliments. Take me for what I am. I'm yours.'

'Would you rather I sang "Pale hands I held…"' he started to giggle.

'Oh, good! You weren't serious or soppy.'

'But I was serious. Kitty, my darling, you've brought me to life. I thought I had missed what it is like to be in love…and to be close to the warmth of a woman.'

She reached out and kissed him tenderly. He let her. 'Thank you.

Now Dusty, be good and take me to Vikram's, before we both forget ourselves. Don't look at me like that. I'm not romantic. There's a lot to say for arranged marriages. Love is blind, and why one stumbles. Ours is a kind of arranged marriage. It happened fast. In the past, like a fool I rushed into things, but I've watched how people find you and like you. I've talked to Shalini and Vikram, and dad…and I've given it much thought. I know you're a survivor; I know that you love me, and I think you'll make a good husband.'

'Just one more kiss…a small favour to ask, for all that.'

'Hush! Look in the mirror. There are cows, a boy, and a herdsman approaching.'

'Damn! Am I surrounded by cowherds. Will no one rid me of…'

'And you have a sense of humour. You're fun to be with.'

'One moment.' Dusty took out a ten rupee note from his wallet, wound down the window. An old deeply pitted, long white bearded face peered through the car window. The man took the money, smiled toothlessly, folded his hands in salutation and bowed deeply. 'And we've both got money,' Dusty started the engine, 'in the kitty.'

She laughed. 'There, we've got ourselves an ideal marriage.'

When they were back on the road, she said: 'I've got news of Dinesh. I've seen him. I didn't want to write or phone. He escaped to England—he's a British citizen, and through Sandy, partly educated in England. Dinesh came to see my father, with Alice. He met her in Goa. Together they spent time in an ashram in Poona. I'll tell you the whole story later, but Dusty, I need, and they need, your help. I'm sorry, but I have to turn to you, and Mohan Singh.'

'Mohan Singh's filled me in with some details. And of course I'll do anything, for you. Only, right now my mind's buzzing. Longing for you.' He stopped the car at a siding, within sight of Vikram's bungalow.

'There now, you've got time enough. Take me to Vikram's. I must settle down, and rest this afternoon, to get rid of some of the jet lag. Otherwise I'll be useless this evening. You're coming over for dinner, I gather. They're sweet, the Dutts. And it's Shalini,… You've not heard a word I've said! Don't deny it. That hungry look in your eyes is full of…'

'Kitty, you've got the most beautiful body in the world. I'm dying to see it.'

'You will. Oh, all right, you won't have to wait till we're married. We'll arrange it somehow. It's not impossible. Now, be sensible. We aren't in our teens anymore.'

She chuckled. 'You know, you're young looking. No one will believe your age.' She leaned across, kissed him lightly on his ear and sighed. 'It's no good me pretending. I'm trying not to be soft, but I am, despite what I said earlier.'

Dusty grinned smugly, started the car and drove up to the gates of the compound of Major Vikram Dutt's barrack-like bungalow. He blew his horn lightly and the mali, sickle in one hand, ran to open the gate.

'Gosh!' she said. 'Army cantonments are so spacious and clean.'

Vikram came out to the car. 'Hello, lovers. Come, come on in. We should've known, Kitty, this would happen. He took one look at you and he was a goner.'

Shalini was in the veranda. 'Welcome! Welcome! At last the happy couple! What happened? Was the train late? We've been wondering. Never mind, now you're here. Kitty, you must be tired. Such a long journey. Have a cup of tea, then you rest. Later I'll get Shambu to prepare two buckets of hot water for your bath.'

'Thank you Shalini, that is sweet of you, I...'

'No, Kitty, no formalities. Treat this as your home. Arrey, heard the terrible news. About the cottage, your cottage. I hope the police catch the culprit. Anyway as I say, this is home. As for you, Dusty, you look like cat who's stolen the cream. Let the girl rest, now. We'll see you this evening.'

CHAPTER THIRTEEN

'I've got a date from Caleb, Father Caleb. He insists on the Father bit.'

'Yes, he's High Church.' Kitty said, watching Dusty remove his blazer and drape it on the back of a cane chair.

'Sunday, 3 p.m. A week from today.'

'I'll send dad a telegram. I know he'll...'

'I've done that, Kitty. Yesterday, after my chat with Caleb. And he has replied. I told him to send an ordinary cable. Here it is. "Must have good reason for rush Stop Will be there Wednesday Stop Congratulations Stop Love to Kitty Stop" Here.' He gave the cable to Kitty. 'I'm sure he'll phone from Delhi, after the plane's landed.'

Kitty took the cable and glanced at it. 'You know, I had plans to go South, to the hills, and get a teaching job. But now, I don't know how long this Dinesh affair will last, or when, even if, he'll be able escape...Do you think the Seth was suspicious? I have never known him to be so cold towards me. What did you think of him?'

'Seth Agarwal? Ruthless. I know his type. They have henchmen to do their dirty work, while they legally cover themselves.'

'I could see he was impressed by you. I don't know what you said to him in, was it Hindustani? Yes, he certainly was placated. Mind you he has endearing moments.'

'Ah, I see. When he told me that you are an *avatar* of the goddess Lakshmi, since only Lakshmi can be so beautiful. That little *mandir* he has in his courtyard, I note is to Lakshmi, the goddess of wealth. So, you're susceptible to compliments, after all.'

'Oh, I could throttle you sometimes.'

'Any physical contact will be gratefully received.'

'You get far too much of that. So, he'll give Dinesh a second chance, and drop the charges against Ransingh?'

'Yes.'

'I'm sorry about the honeymoon arrangements. I know it's a shame to spend the fortnight here, but you have a lovely bungalow. It's new for me. The area too. And a Military cantonment is safe from the evil reach of Seth Agarwal, in case he forgets the goddess aspect and...'

'Right, you two?' Vikram called from the house. 'Shal and I are off to market. Lovely day for it.' He observed breezily. 'Back teatime.'

Shalini came up to them. 'It's getting hot in the veranda. You should go in. Order some nimbo pani, and relax in front of the TV. Old film starts, twenty minutes from now. Bhai Vikram, what name? The film's name?'

'I forget now. Something with Raj Kapoor.'

'Anyway, Dusty, it will give Kitty some Hindi practice, *Hai na.*' Shalini laughed. 'Now that she's making home in India. Okay, bye, bye. See you.'

They stood, waved and watched as Vikram and Shalini climbed into the tonga.

'Let's stay here a little longer. It's not too hot, and the servants tend not to come out here unless called. Dusty, does Vikram know much...about, you know?'

'Only about the fire at Fern Cottage and, of course, the wedding arrangements. But I'll have to confide in Chopra, more. Certainly about Dinesh, because, if I'm going to help, I may need to take time off. I'll be discreet. Chops is a decent chap and already he has been a great help. He's booked the Black Elephant Institute for our Wedding Dinner Reception.'

'Has he!' She squeaked with delight. 'I love the Black Elephant Institute. That why I'm so mad about you. You get things done.'

'And we get the full catering staff. It's too late for invitation cards.'

'And don't forget, Daddy will foot the bill. You've agreed.'

In the Shadow of a Dream

He nodded. 'I have no one. Viks and Chops are standing in as family. The three of us are paying for the wedding cake. Isn't that the custom, on the boy's side?'

She looked around, leaned forward and squeezed his hands. 'And I'm forgiven?'

'That goes without saying. After all, Dinesh is family, now.'

'Yes. You know, I didn't like him at first. I adored Sandy, and Dinesh wasn't very nice to Sandy. He was a hot head, going through an Indian nationalistic phase. Poor Sandy, bless him, was an unrepentant Anglophile.'

'My Sam was one too, but from what you said of Sandy, less openly so. Much of all that Anglophile stuff, as I said, rubbed off on me. But now I've every good reason to be one.' He lifted her hand and kissed it.

'You said your guardian was less open, was he ashamed to be an Anglophile?'

'Not really. His doctor, Dr Metha, said so once, and Sam said, that if a great man like Voltaire was happy to be one, he saw no shame in it.'

'But Dinesh has changed. And that's because of Alice. I told you about her. She's like a sister to me. Then there's Ransingh. Such a good, sad man. So…'

'Well, as I keep saying, there's nothing to worry about. I'll do anything for you, dear, anything, for you mean everything to me…'

'Even I know where that comes from.'

'Lionel Bart.' He started to sing. 'I'll go anywhere, for your smile, every…'

'Hush, hush! The servants. We must be serious. And get on with our plans.'

'Then start taking me for granted. I love you Kitty.'

'I know you do.'

'And you. You've never said it. Said the word.'

'What word? Marry? But I've said it.'

'That you love me!'

She gazed at him and her eyes softened.

'Don't say it Kitty, if you don't want to, or just because I asked.'

'Oh, Dusty, it's just a word. What is love? I've been in love so many times, it no longer means anything. All I know is that I want to live with you. Be your wife and spend the rest of my life with you. If all that is love, then, I love you.'

He took her hands in his. 'I've been silly. Of course, you do, and I am the luckiest man in the world.'

'I'll prove it. Take me to your bungalow, make love to me, now. I don't care.'

'No. It's only a week. I'll wait. Let's make it special. I had planned a honeymoon in a Lake Palace hotel. It was to be a surprise. Loving you in a place and manner that befits your beauty.'

'Dusty, please darling, don't go on about my looks. It makes me feel inadequate. I can't be as special as you make me out to be. I meant what I said. I don't want you to suffer. You can love me. But can we do our planning first…although, I must say, Dad will be glad to know we waited till after marriage. It'll put you up a notch or two in his estimation.'

'Well, I must be mad, to wait when I don't have to.'

'Come, let's get on, before they get back. You'll be meeting Dinesh in less than a fortnight. I've told him to bear in mind that you've got a job.'

'First, I must make notes, so that I am clear about the full story. As I said, I may have to, judiciously of course, let Chops know why and what I'm up to. I've already made notes and worked out a plan. I'll get my brief case. It's in the dining room. We may as well go there and work at the table. Easier for writing.'

They went inside. Dusty opened his brief case and took out a large exercise book. 'Right,' he said, opening the book. 'I've noted down what Mohan said and much of you've told me. This is a double check.'

She sat down next to him and leaned over. 'Gosh! What beautiful handwriting you have.' He smiled coyly. She stared into his eyes and turned away with a slight shiver. 'You have such penetrating eyes. You don't have to see me naked. Those eyes undress me every time you look at me.'

'How are we ever going to get on with this?' He pulled her hand towards him just as Shambu entered the room. Dusty quickly pretended to be reading Kitty's palm.

'Ho, ho,' Shambu said rocking his head. 'Lady has long, long life.' He was a tall skeletal man with a slight stoop and a benign face. '*Nimbo pani* all ready, sahib?'

Dusty looked at Kitty. She nodded. 'No ice.'

Shambu rocked his head with surprising vigour. 'Making wid cold bottle water.' The lime juice drink came on a tray. Shambu filled two glasses from a jug with a steady hand. Then he awaited approval. *'Bahut achcha.'* Dusty said, and Shambu slid out of the room after allowing himself a mystic smile. Dusty and Kitty looked at each other and chuckled.

'I rather like having servants around,' Kitty said.

'That reminds me. I haven't employed one. Of course, I've a batman. They call them orderlies here.'

'Leave it like that, Sam, for the time being. I love cooking. At least till after you retire and I start teaching; and if…I promised Dinesh I'll leave Dharamsala after he's seen the Seth. He wants me to be safe from the Seth's revenge, when the Seth realises we have put him off his guard and enabled Dinesh to slip through his hands. But, we know the Seth can't touch me here. Dinesh needn't know that, and not having a cook will help. It is hard to keep a low profile with servants around.'

'I will tell my man not to let any caller in while you're alone in the house. And you must bear that in mind, while I'm on parade or in the office—*daftar* as it's called. Right. Back to business. Now, why was Dinesh with Sandy and Emma?'

'Dinesh's father was married to Sandy's sister, Dolly. He died when Dinesh was five or six. The marriage had gone wrong. Dolly's husband took to drink and she was unhappy. So when she got a chance to marry again, she didn't want Dinesh around and begged Sandy's help.'

'Another fostered child,' Dusty mumbled, but Kitty heard.

'I know so little about your life before we met. You won't talk about your past.'

'As I told you, the past is past. Kitty, I'm what you see.'

'I read somewhere, that we are what we hide.'

'Not if one keeps inventing oneself…But, we really must get on…Dinesh grew up hostile to Sandy. He met and arranged his own marriage to Shanti. Excluded Sandy and Emma from the proceedings. Wanted to appear a staunch Hindu, anti-Brit and an Indian Nationalist. Oh, and he was the apple of the Seth, his father-in-law's, eye. After Sandy and Emma's death, he gets a plum job to manage Agarwal Hotels Ltd., in Bombay. Then, his servant, I forget the name...'

'Anthony...'

'Warned or hinted that Shanti was unfaithful...' Dusty looked at Kitty.

'Don't look at me like that. I won't be, for no better reason than that sex is rather low on my list of interests. Something in the genes. The Franks are a cool lot.'

'Franks, that's an unusual surname?'

'Not really. Norman, possibly. Where were we?'

'Dinesh sneaked up and caught Shanti in the act, decided on divorce; whereupon the Seth sacked him, sent an emissary, who failed to get Dinesh to change his mind.'

'Yes. That was the Munshi, the Seth's secretary. Kind of. You saw him.'

'Yes. Good. But I'm not clear about where Alice fits into all this.'

'I'll tell you what Alice told me. Dinesh learned that the Seth would rather have him bumped off than face the shame of a divorce scandal...Indians take these things as if it's a personal affront. Anyway, Anthony got beaten up—and Dinesh realising that the Seth was deadly earnest, escaped with the injured Anthony to Goa, in his car, then got rid of it, so as not to leave a trail.'

'And Alice?'

'He met Alice in Goa. At the time she was a disciple of a Hindu guru. You know, like the Beatles and their Maharishi, but hers was a serious commitment. They spent time together at the guru's ashram in Poona. Both were emotionally vulnerable, but Alice felt sure the Ashram would give enough protection from the Seth's assassins. But the Seth managed to get his spy in. The man pretended to be a Brahmin, but he was discovered. He had made some ritual mistake. I don't know what. I think he did something a Brahmin wouldn't do and was exposed. But he managed to smuggle in Shanti and she made a scene. Both were asked to leave the ashram. After that Dinesh and Alice couldn't stay on, and Alice realised that the only safe haven for them was England. Fortunately, Dinesh, like Sandy, is a British citizen, but there were certain things he had to do before they could fly to England. I won't go into the details now, but from what Alice said, it was quite an adventure for them. Dinesh knew a hotel in Poona, managed by some friend of his whom Dinesh had helped, and from whom he borrowed a car...'

'But, Kitty, how did they manage to leave the Ashram without...?'

'Oh, the Guru decided to help, and his chauffeur took them in the Guru's Rolls.'

'Rolls? Rolls Royce?'

'Yes. I gather these Gurus are rolling in it...' She laughed at the accidental pun. 'That reminds me. Didn't you say Chopra has a brother in Poona, who runs a hotel? I wondered, because Alice said that this hotel friend of Dinesh was a Chopra.'

'Chopra is quite a common Punjabi name. It would be helluva coincidence if it turned out...I'll check with Chops. It will go in Dinesh's favour if it is his brother.'

'They then drove to a Raja's palace—another friend of Dinesh—who had stored his stuff when he had to leave Bombay in a hurry. I can't recall the name, but Alice said the Palace looked like a French Chateau. From there they drove to Bombay, and left the car there, got to the airport and flew to England.'

'And in revenge the Seth got his men to set fire to Fern cottage, when he thought it was empty, with dreadful results. By the way, Kitty, why didn't we see Shanti?'

'She said she wasn't well. But I saw her in the courtyard with Manjit, the boy she claims is Dinesh's son.'

'They probably thought we'd know at once he was not; and they won't want that noised abroad.' Dusty shut his note book and put it back in his brief case, 'we'll now have to wait for Dinesh's arrival, and take it from there.'

CHAPTER FOURTEEN

Ted Franks walked out on to the veranda and gazed across the fields. The smoky morning mist had risen and settled behind the stately Dhauladhar Mountain Range, marking the distance between them and the snow-capped peaks of the Himalayas. They shone faintly against a golden sky. The orchards on his left were filled with pink and white blossom, and the air was filled with the scent of spring.

Kitty had noticed her father was silent during breakfast and wondered if his mind was wrestling over something that was troubling him, but decided to postpone asking till after she had finished packing for her trip to Goa. When she came out to join him she was still in her dressing gown. Her slippers made her approach a silent one. She stopped some distance from Ted and studied the back of his head. It was a shock to see how grey he was and how vulnerable he looked.

'Daddy,' she called out softly.

'That you,' he said without turning round.

She went up and put her arm around him and drew her face close to his. 'Daddy? Daddy, you've been crying. Why, my love?'

'Not to worry,' her father said, 'much were tears of joy. It's a beautiful morning.' He fumbled in his pocket, took out a handkerchief and blew his nose. 'I have to say, Dusty's gown fits perfectly.' He chuckled.

'But you are worried about something.'

'Not so much worried as mystified. The wedding's postponed,

and I don't see how or why you both are so relaxed in the circumstances.'

'Daddy, it seemed a bit heartless, to say nothing of it being a distraction, in the face of all this threat to Dinesh and Alice's happiness. Only the arrangements have been cancelled. Look at it positively. It's saving you money.'

'Kitty, money is the least of my worries. And what about the booking at the Black Elephant? Cancelling that must have caused problems. I was surprised to find even Brigadier Chopra is relaxed about it all.'

'The Black Elephant is a club. In fact, Dusty said that the Secretary of the Institute had to put off another party in order to fit us in and please the Brigadier. He will be relieved. But Dad, you and Dusty had a long, happy talk last night after dinner. You could have discussed your worries with him.'

'Like everyone, I'm in awe of Dusty. He has such a daunting presence and always comes across supremely confident and in control.'

'Dad, talk to me. I can't bear to see you troubled about anything.'

'Don't misunderstand me. I know it had to be done. What with all this business of Dinesh, and Shanti and the Seth. Both of you have done wonders with the Seth, and with the help of Mohan Singh, you are bound to save Ransingh's life. My worries are about your future. Are you sure, are both of you sure, this is what you want? Do you really love each other enough for a lifetime? You're always up and about and he seems quite relaxed about it. Kitty, don't look at me like that. No one would think you two are in love. The wedding has been…well, all right; but now you've taken up this short term job in this convent school in Goa.'

'Daddy. We are not youngsters. Goodness, Dusty will be forty-five this year, and I'm no chicken. There, once Ransingh is freed and Dinesh has escaped back to Alice, we'll celebrate, make up for the wedding party we did not have, and live happily ever after. As for long term plans? Well, we'll honeymoon in the South, in the Nilgiri Hills, and while there, set about starting a school for orphans, which Dusty and I will run together.'

'I feel sorry for poor Father Caleb. Now I shall book my flight back to London, to my dear Alice and Kay…'

'You're making me jealous. But daddy dear, didn't Dusty tell you. We are getting married. We couldn't let Father Caleb down. Not after he's published the banns! No the church bit is going ahead. A bit hush, hush, with you as a witness.'

'But there has to be two witnesses, as far as I remember.'

'Caleb's wife and young Joshua, his son is standing in. Tomorrow afternoon. If you two hadn't got into a philosophical discussion, Dusty would have remembered to tell you.'

Ted laughed, and gathered Kitty in his arms. 'You are always my dearest, Kitty. And there's no need to be jealous.'

'You know dad. The age difference between Dusty and me is about the same as that between you and Emma. You were more like a father to her than a brother. It is how Dusty treats me. Yes, he's relaxed, as I am, but we dearly love each other, and I am happy. Now smile, and promise me you and Alice's mother, I mean Kay…'

'Yes, Kitty. When Dinesh gets back, he and Alice, Kay and I, intend to have a joint wedding. By the way, you know Alice is due in a month or so. I'm glad you convinced Dinesh that she had to be with Kay in Ludlow and not waiting for him in some hotel in Calcutta, as was the original plan.'

CHAPTER FIFTEEN

The pleasant looking young man wore an expression of mild concern. He was the last passenger to get off the train and warily watched the *coolie* running towards him. Pointing to a brown leather suitcase, which he had dragged on to the footplate, he surveyed the platform expectantly. Dusty had no difficulty picking him out and walked up to him casually. 'You must be Dinesh Thakur,' he said. 'Follow me and try not to look…no, we'll save the handshake for later. Just relax, I'm trying not to draw attention to us. You can be sure Seth Agarwal has his men keeping a watch on the station.' He gestured to the *coolie* to hurry. '*Jaldi, jaldi.* I have a staff car and a uniformed driver, so you relax.'

Dusty marched briskly towards a mat olive-green Morris Hindustan, while Dinesh did his best to keep up with him. The uniformed soldier in the driver's seat got out and held the rear door open for him. Dinesh got in, followed by Dusty. They shook hands and Dusty introduced himself. 'Cheer up, old chap, as long as I'm around, not a hair of your head shall be harmed.' He grinned and Dinesh smiled. Dusty's bluff manner was beginning to have its calming effect on him. 'Thank you,' he said. There was no mistaking from his clipped speech and the way he moved that Dusty, though not in uniform, was an army officer; and his immaculately pressed blazer and grey flannels completed the picture.

'We'll breakfast in Mcleodganj, and go on from there on foot to Fern Cottage. You know the full story, but you may want to inspect the damage done by the fire. Mohan Singh will be there.' He sat back and studied Dinesh's face. 'I see you've cut yourself trying to shave in a moving train. Why? There was no need for it. You're not trying to impress Shanti, are you?'

Dinesh laughed and wondered what made Dusty a commanding presence. There was nothing he could pinpoint except those extraordinary brown, penetrating eyes. A woman, he concluded would be defenceless before their gaze. 'Dusty, may I call you Dusty? I know you won't mind. Kitty said so.'

'And she's right. Everyone does.'

'You seemed to recognise me immediately, although we've never met before?'

'Elementary, my dear Watson. Having seen Sandy, I assumed anyone from that family had to be reasonably good looking, and, being middle-class, above average height. Also, you looked nervously like someone who didn't wish to be recognised.'

'You mean, running scared?'

'Near enough.'

'I'm sorry, truly sorry for being such a burden. How is Kitty?'

'Well. And safe. Now that she's my responsibility.'

'Oh, how foolish of me. I'm sorry. I forgot. Congratulations.'

'No need to apologise. Alice hadn't. She sent a lovely card from all of you, which Ted brought with him. But, as it happens, a bit premature. We decided to postpone the day and concentrate on getting you back to Alice, safe and sound. Poor Ted came prepared with a very fine and amusing talk for the show. He couldn't resist telling me bits of it. He'll get his chance in Goa or maybe the Nilgiri Hills. But I can see you're tired. Why not take nap? I'll wake you up when we get there.'

An hour and forty minutes later, Dinesh was surprised to find the car parked at the Circuit House in lower Mcleodganj. 'You shouldn't have let me sleep that long, Dusty. Sorry.'

'No harm done. But now I need your help. You know these parts like the back of your hand. Where's the Dilkhush Hotel? Mind you, we've got masses of coffee and sandwiches and there's a small garden with benches; and quite deserted.'

'Why don't we do that? There are things to talk about and it'll be better here than in a noisy Hotel. Anyway the place is not as I remember, it would take some finding …somewhere there, hidden

In the Shadow of a Dream

by that large Tibetan *chorten*; that white dome-like temple with the large, painted single eye and buntings of coloured prayer flags. All that's new, and since we're walking, the best way to Fern Cottage is by a short cut, which starts there, down that descending line of deodars.

'Good, then I'll let Lal Singh go. He'll be back to pick us up here at three. Mohan Singh's giving us lunch and we won't be back before then. I've told Seth Agarwal, through his strange Munshi, that Uriah Heep of a chap, that I'll drop you at Ram Niwas at five-ish, this evening.'

'Thanks. It's not something I'm looking forward to.'

'Not to worry. I've established what we in the army call, a line of communication, through this Munshi. Strange and extremely cautious as the man is, he's agreed, after some persuasion, to keep me informed about you. As you know, Kitty and I have seen Seth Agarwal. It was like extracting teeth, getting his promise, re your welfare. Bloody awful man. Tread carefully, Dinesh young man. Take time to disarm the fellow. He's extremely suspicious. Don't do anything rash. Wait till you see a way out. Trust no one who works for him.'

'You and Kitty have been a great help. I can't thank you enough. I was worried for Kitty staying on in Pathankot.'

'That's sharp. So it's not just looks, you've also inherited the family brains. I'm told your uncle Sandy sparkled with them. Now, remember, the plans made in England didn't take into account last minute changes. But,' he added, deciding it was simpler to make no mention of Kitty being in Goa, 'Kitty is safe.'

Dusty picked up the telephone. Kitty was on the line. 'Yes, Kitty. I met Dinesh at Pathankot Station. All went well. He was a bit weepy at Fern Cottage. But we had a good chat with Mohan. He said Ransingh was quite cheerful. No, Kitty, I wasn't able to see the Seth. He was having his pre-supper nap. But it's been three days now and there hasn't been any bad news…sorry, say that again. Oh, lunch! Lunch is always a feast at Mohan Singh's. But chiefly I rang to say I had a call from the Munshi. Yes Popatlal, the secretary cum clerk of Seth Agarwal. I'm going over there. Ram Niwas, eleven thirty a.m. tomorrow, to see for myself how far Dinesh has got to establishing himself in the Seth's good books.'

'You know he's hot-headed and can be irresponsible.' Kitty interposed.

'Then the Seth must know that too, because he's obviously working on it.'

'What do you mean?'

'The Munshi told me that when I dropped Dinesh at Ram Niwas house, the Seth refused to see him. Dinesh spent the night in the Munshi's quarters because the Seth told him he'd see him in the morning. One can imagine that fat, sweaty drug baron, saying, with every other word punctuated by foul language: 'So, *bahainchoot*, at last the *bahainchoot* has returned...'

'What does banchort, or whatever, mean?'

'It means sister-fucker.'

Kitty laughed. 'But he hasn't got a sister.'

'Never mind, it's a popular Indian F word, second only to mother-fucker.'

'Go on. I was enjoying your mimicry.'

'I can't do it to order. Comes naturally or not at all. Anyway, when they did meet, I'm told they came near to blows. Certainly, the Seth swung out with his hand, Dinesh ducked, and the "Michelin Man" lost his balance and fell flat on his bottom. However, some sort of reconciliation did take place in the end.'

'Is it beeping? Well, take care. You know Punjabi, so little should escape you.'

The tall, skeletal Munshi Popatlal peered over his thin gold-rimmed glasses and, from his office window studied the incoming traffic of Pathankot's main bus station. A moment later he saw Lal Singh, in an army jeep, drive Major Dustoor right up to the side door of Ram Niwas. Dusty jumped out and knocked imperiously on the door with the knob of his cane. Bemused by Dusty's military panache, Popatlal went out to open the door. The rattle of moving bolts on the cast-iron clad, heavy wooden door woke the old Gurkha *chowkidar*, who had been sitting cross-legged and asleep in the sentry niche by the door. Popatlal opened the door with effort, regarded the Gurkha with a reproving wag of his head. Then

In the Shadow of a Dream

he bowed low to Dusty, a wide smile revealing pan stained teeth: 'Welcome, Major sahib, welcome. Punctual to the very second, as is your wont. Come in, good sir. This way. Be pleased to follow me.'

'I know the way, Munshiji.'

'You may, indeed, Major Dustoor, but it would not meet the Sethji's etiquette for you to arrive unaccompanied by me.'

'Lead on, Munshiji.' Dusty said with a dramatic flourish, adding sotto voce "you pompous old ass', and followed him downstairs into the open courtyard, then along the stone flagged columned archway. As they neared the family wing, Dusty spotted Shanti watching him from an open window. There the Munshi stopped to let him enter. It was a large room. Seated on a high winged-back chair, the grossly obese Seth was trying vainly to button his waistcoat, while his bare feet groped for the shoes under him. The atmosphere in the room was tense. Clearly, some dispute between father and daughter had not been resolved. 'Why papaji,' pouted Shanti, 'vot's wrong if I say "that's the sort of husband I should have had"? Look at this clown.' Shanti pointed to Dinesh, as Dinesh walked past her to meet Dusty.

'*Chup, beti*. Shut up, I telling you.' the Seth growled. 'No more nonsense like we had at *nashta*, breaking fast time. Before *mehman*, before guest, behave, like good Indian wife showing respect. Listen, Dinesh boy, just see. Is that Premchand who is talking to Munshi? Tell him to get coffee and cakes, for the Major...for all of us.'

'Yes, papaji,' Dinesh shook Dusty's hand warmly. 'God, I'm glad to see you. I've been going through hell.'

Dusty stood in the centre of the room and fearlessly surveyed all the occupants. He struck the side of his olive green trousers with his swagger cane. The Seth smiled at him. Dusty thought: 'You supercilious bastard. I wonder how much crime you've been responsible for.' Aloud he said: 'I haven't come for anything in particular. Just a friendly call, to see how Dinesh is getting on.'

'He is as you see.' The Seth rolled his head from side to side. 'Please take seat.' He wheezed as he spoke and dabbed his sweating face with a large handkerchief. 'So how is Kitty? You say she's teaching in Goa. What kind of marriage...' He checked himself. Dusty, was impressive in his olive green, gabardine uniform, polished Sam Browne belt and shining brass Ashoka Lions on his epaulets. 'So, you're indeed a Major.' The Seth's body rumbled and he belched. 'But I've seen you with Kitty. So how much respect she's giving you. I hope plenty.

'Kitty's well, enjoying teaching. I'll be joining her soon for a second honeymoon.' Dusty lied with impudence.

'That's great!' Shanti exclaimed gesticulating with her hands. '*Arrey*, vee never had first honeymoon, even.'

Dusty studied her. There was something strangely attractive about the fullness of her heavy figure, as there is in a Khajuraho sculpture. In the meantime the Seth shot an irate look at his daughter. 'Never mind my Shanti, Major sahib. Women, they so loving to gossip talk. So, Kitty's job is not full time? What teaching?'

'Teaching? Oh, English and Portuguese.' Dusty lied again.

'She knowing Portuguese?'

'Yes. That's how she got the job. Goans are quite keen to speak Portuguese.'

Late at night, on the telephone, Dusty entertained Kitty with an account of the meeting. 'I must say, I surprised myself. And I got a chance to be alone with Dinesh. We were in the garden. He thinks he's found an ally in the mali.'

'Not that shrivelled man with legs like dried twigs? He's a wily old chap. Do you think he can be trusted?'

'Dinesh will have to make up his mind about that. But he's convinced the mali means to help and a very good plan it is too. In fact it couldn't be simpler. He's got his little hut or rather a lean-to, right against a boundary wall. Dinesh said he was a builder before he turned gardener and that he'll loosen enough bricks to let Dinesh through and then replace them in a matter of minutes. It makes it easy for me. All I'll have to do is get one of Chopra's Gurkha drivers to wait on the other side of the wall and pick up Dinesh when he pops out. Best chap for the job will be the water-truck driver. People are used to seeing the truck moving about town. Then all we need do, is to synchronise the popping out and the picking up.'

'That's plan A. Is there a plan B?'

'Afraid not. I wasn't joking when I said that the place is a prison, a labyrinth of ups and downs and winding archways; some leading nowhere. The garden barely has a bush to cover any movement. The walls are six to eight feet high and patrolled by two Pathans—I thought there was only one but Dinesh discovered a second the other day. I've told Dinesh, if anything goes wrong, at the risk of losing his life, (which in any case is forfeit), to make a dash for it, by smashing the office window that overlooks the bus station; and shout for help till his lungs burst.'

'And what about poor Ransingh?'

'Ah, there I have good news. I went back to see the Seth—flattery catches him off his guard. I said, I hoped Dinesh and Shanti would soon settle down to a renewed family life, and as I don't intend coming again, I would deem it a great favour if he would give me a letter, signed by him and witnessed by his Munshi, dropping all the charges against Ransingh, so that the man can be freed from prison. Chopra himself had drafted the letter and I dictated it to the Munshi, who typed it out.'

'Give it to Mohan Singh. He's greatly respected by the powers that be.'

'I will, Kitty, but there's a rat at the bottom of the tankard. The Seth signed it, but next moment, dusted his hands saying he had done his bit, but that he was not to be held responsible for what may happen to Ransingh once out of prison. That put me on my guard. There was no reason for him to say it unless he has arranged foul play.'

'So what do you intend to do?'

'Hand the letter to Mohan, get Ransingh released, but tell him to wait till I collect him from prison in my car, our car. I'll drive him to his village or a station en route.'

'I'll come too. I'm fond of Ransingh. I want him to know how sorry I'm about Sona. A horrid way for anyone to die! Tell me in time so I can take time off.'

'Unwise. You mustn't be seen in Pathankot. It is a bore, but it's not long now. In less than two months we'll leave all this behind.'

CHAPTER SIXTEEN

'*Salaam*, sahib.'

'Hello, Lal Singh. Memsahiba?'

'*Jee Ha!* In kitchen, sir.'

Dusty entered the kitchen. 'Ah, there you are, my little kitten.'

'Gosh, Dusty, I didn't need a driver and two soldiers to protect me.'

'Better safe than sorry.'

'Being Sunday, the train was late. Did it go well?'

'Couldn't have gone better. When I got to the prison at 8.30, Mohan Singh was already there—I don't know how these Sikhs tie their beards and turbans so neatly, they must spend hours—anyway, there he was with Ransingh by his side. Mohan was quite in his element. He may be a "shorty" but he's also a Napoleon.'

'How was Ransingh?'

'Just as you described him. They make quite a pair. Ransingh calm, philosophical and Mohan cocky, greeting me with smiling grey eyes. I gave Ransingh your message, and told him how much you wanted to come, but that it would have meant catching a train that got in at midnight. Anyway, he said it's no place for a lady.'

'Ah, the sweet man!' Kitty sighed. 'I was worried. You've taken the whole day.'

'Yes. But it's over now. One part of the problem is solved. We managed to drive down to Saharanpur, sixty-four miles from here. Ransingh is now on the train, with his son—I picked up Vijay on the way—and saw them off on the train to Ranikhet.'

In the Shadow of a Dream

'So now, the tricky bit. Nothing must go wrong.' She shivered. 'How are you going to tell…That reminds me, I've got news too. Good news. I have had a cable from Dad. Alice has had the baby, Dinesh has a son. But, I don't think you should tell him. In the excitement of being a father, he might betray himself.'

'I'll save it till I see him on Wednesday, when I tell him about Ransingh. 'I'll phone the Munshi tomorrow. Don't breathe a word of this, but Dinesh and I have worked out a ruse. I tell the Munshi I'm coming over on Thursday to see Dinesh, when in fact I've arranged for him to be picked up on Wednesday. That gives Dinesh ample time to warn the old mali to prepare to smuggle him out.'

Dusty did just that; and the Munshi duly conveyed his message to Dinesh. But on Wednesday, at six in the evening, Kadam, the driver of the water-carrier returned to Dusty's bungalow. 'No one there, sahib, no one. Three o'clock, waited. Then I go I also phive o'clock. Nothing. Nobody.'

'Good Lord, you heard that, Kitty? I'll have to go there tomorrow.'

'Are you mad! Something terribly serious has happened. From what you've told me about Ayub, the Pathan sentry, Dinesh could have been caught, even killed.'

'But, I have to find out.'

'Find out on the phone. You'll get some idea from the Munshi. But I suppose, you won't take a blind bit of notice of anything I say. You never do. Things always have to be…always exactly as you…'

'Kitty, Kitty, get a hold of yourself. Remember, there's a soldier present.'

'I don't care. I don't want you taking risks. As Dinesh's friend, you're suspect. If you must go, arm yourself. Take a gun.'

'In peace time? I wouldn't get permission.'

The Gurkha soldier saluted. 'Take soldier with you, sahib.'

Dusty returned his salute, '*Shabash*, Kadam Bahadur. *Bahut achcha*. Okay I think about that.' He looked at his watch. 'You go to *langar*. Have your evening meal.'

He watched the soldier leave, then turned to Kitty. 'Don't worry,

I won't go. I'll phone tomorrow. It's too late now. There now, can I claim my reward?'

'Reward? Oh, that. How could you at a time like this?'

Dusty put down the telephone receiver and stared at Kitty. The look on his face was new to her. Her eyes widened with alarm. 'Dusty! What on earth is the matter?'

'He's disappeared! He's nowhere to be seen.'

'Dinesh?'

'Yes. There's complete pandemonium at Ram Niwas. Shanti's screaming, Agarwal shouting and a hastily organised search party is frantically scouring every nook and cranny of that rambling house. "What to say, esteemed Major sahib, Master Dinesh has vanished into air, as it were, thin air" to quote the Munshi.'

'What are you going to do?'

'I could go there. Appear as surprised as anyone else. They'll have to believe I had nothing to do with his disappearance...which is true.'

'No, Dusty, or before you do, please find out more. Speak to the Munshi again.'

'The Munshi is abnormally reticent. He hung up with "there is nothing more I can say except that the Seth's posh car, his Mercedes, is missing also.'

'Where was the driver? And who would dare nick Agarwal's car? And what about the mali? You said the mali had a plan to help Dinesh. He may have managed to smuggle Dinesh out of Ram Niwas...but then you can't ask...'

'Yes, it would betray the mali...his involvement. But there is no other option. I have to ask.' Dusty dialled, waited. "Munshiji, Major Dustoor. Have they checked with the mali? He may know something or seen something."' There was a hum on the line and a moment later Dusty slammed the receiver down and threw up his hands. 'It gets more strange. The mali was found dead early this morning and, this afternoon, in the pandemonium of his funeral arrangements, both Dinesh and Seth's car have vanished. The Seth is suffering a rush of apoplexy.'

Kitty frowned. Dusty shook his head and smiled enigmatically. 'Tell me?' She said.

In the Shadow of a Dream

'Kitty, I think the Munshi knows more than he's letting on.

'Dusty, what are we going to do? Poor Alice. What are we going to say to her?'

'Wait a day or two. I had phoned the Munshi to say I was coming over on Thursday. That, as you know, was to mislead him, because my man was to collect him on Wednesday. So, my turning up on Thursday would establish my having nothing to do with his disappearance. We'll wait till Saturday. Wherever Dinesh is, he'll try to get in touch, when he can.'

'And if he's dead? No one is going to tell us if he is. They would want to keep that a secret. Why would they let on?'

'I must inform Viks and Brigadier Chopra. And if there is still no news, I'll get on to the police. We should learn something in a day or two.'

And learn they did, on Saturday night, from none other than Alice herself. Dinesh was safe and sound in Ludlow, England…the cable promised full details in a letter that Ted will be posting. And the news got better with every new message from England.

'Dusty, as you know, Dad's marrying Kay, Alice's mother. I'm happy for him. Kay is a lovely person…and Dinesh is marrying Alice. It will be a double wedding.'

'Hold your horses, Kitty. Let me get the picture. I know Ted, your father. I've seen Dinesh. Alice met Dinesh in Goa, they became lovers and now she is the mother of his son, Davy. Kay and Alice are mother and daughter. Through Dinesh your father met Kay. And now that the whole group are united, there's to be a joint celebratory wedding. Is Alice younger than you?'

'Yes. Not much; and between Dad and Kay, the age difference is just a little more than between you and me. So there's nothing scandalous about that.'

'I didn't imply there was. Your father is fit, handsome, and good to be with. He's retired now, but he must have been an excellent doctor. When is the happy event?'

'A month from now. I'm going. I mean we. We must go. I want to see dad happy, O Dusty! If only you knew how heartless my mother was to him!'

'That will be Mabel? Yes, you've told me. A cold fish, I gather.

I'm glad you didn't take after her. I've never liked fish. I'm a meat and two veg man.'

'Be serious, Dusty. She wasn't all that…well, cold…but let's not go there. Let's not spoil the good news. We are going. Chops will give you leave. He'll surely let you go. Your time's all but done here.'

'These things are not done locally. Besides, I'm about to move our goods and chattels to a warehouse in Delhi. We then travel South to the Nilgiri Hills, to buy that abandoned school I told you about. We've planned it all. You were so keen to see the place. And you'll love the hills.'

'Yes, but we can do both. We'll go to Delhi. Leave our stuff—it's not much—then see this place. If you've chosen it, I'm sure to love it. Then to England, for a fortnight's break?'

'I can't.'

'O please, please, darling. Please! What d'you mean, I?'

'I mean you can go. Fly from Bombay.'

'Alone?'

'Yes. That's never been a problem. You've been gadding about here, there and everywhere alone. The supremely confident, seasoned traveller!'

'Don't you want to come with me? You haven't been to England.'

'Kitty, you're going to hate me for this. I could have gone with Sam, when he went to England and Scotland…and he wanted very much for me to keep him company.'

'Why? Why didn't you?'

Dusty chortled nervously. Then he fell silent.

'Answer me?' She went up to him and dug his ribs. 'Say something?' She kissed the corner of his mouth.

He cupped her face in his hands. 'My dearest, it means crossing "the black waters". Sorry darling, but I am serious. It is silly, I know, superstitious and a Hindu thing. But as to why, I can't say why, just accept it.'

'I've heard about this "black waters" stuff…Poppycock! And you're not Hindu.'

'Oh, all right, it's an excuse, an excuse for something…something I hate to admit. I'm pathologically afraid of flying. Please, my love, you go. Go with my blessing.'

In the Shadow of a Dream

'There's nothing to fear. We'll be together. And it will be such great fun.'

'Yes, it will, but not for me. And another thing, all of you will be cooing over the boy. Alice's child, Dinesh's son. Yes. And I'll feel self-conscious, worse, inadequate, while you get all broody.'

'At my age! I'm unlikely to want…It's no joke being a mother after thirty-four.'

'I saw the look on your face, when you broke the news that day, and I'm a bit self-conscious, you know, clearly something's wrong. Maybe because I married late.'

'There's nothing wrong. I should know. Darling, you may be a genius, but there are things you don't know and there are things within my control.'

'Now, if any impasse deserves to be defined as a conundrum, this is it.'

Kitty laughed. 'I laugh because I don't know what you mean.'

'Kitty, you have to stop dodging life. You can't flutter about from…oh, to put it plainly you've got to dig in, stay put, build a nest. You wanted to be a teacher, well, I'm giving you that opportunity. Your own school, for us to run together.'

'Oh, Dusty. You're making me nervous, unsure about what I want. Suppose I don't want to be tied down. The only commitment I want to make is for us to be together. But it makes me feel dependent. I don't like, even more because I see no alternative.'

'Aren't we a pair! Say what you like about what I don't know, I've certainly got the measure of you.'

'But it would be irresponsible to start a school and then give up. We have to think about the children we will be letting down.'

'I've thought of that, Kitty. We can put in some years, as much as we want to, then pass the baton to someone else.'

'But to whom?'

Dusty touched his nose, with a wink and a sly grin. 'Did you think I would go into such an educational project without covering our retreat? Remember Cash, the friend of my early years. I mean Captain Kapoor. We all called him Cash because he's got more money than he knows what to do with it.'

'The friend you were with on that holiday when you saw Sandy and Emma? But I thought you had lost touch with him over these many years.'

'Not quite. He left the army. Got bored with his career and bought himself out. But we didn't lose touch completely. A lot of army officers' wives are into education, and his wife, before marriage, trained as a teacher and taught in Canada. Then he heard about my school project and is not only prepared to make a sizeable donation but will buy us out should we decide to throw in the towel.'

'Very clever and business-like of you. I wish you wouldn't keep things from me. I get news about you from others before you decide to tell me. I pretend as if I know. Why didn't you tell me you were going to retire with the honorary rank of a Colonel?'

'A Lieutenant Colonel. Well, it's not something for me to be proud about. Those of my colleagues who use the Army list as their Bible, know I have been passed over many times. The boys who were with me are Commanding Regiments, two are Brigadiers and one a Major General.'

'And that's because you twice refused Staff College courses. You could have been right up there with the best of them.'

'Well, as I said we have much in common. I hate commitment, and I hate throwing one's weight about.'

'But you've got just the right personality for doing that.'

'I joined the army because it was the fastest way to be independent and not in debt to anyone. I could've climbed the career ladder, but I lacked ambition.'

'Ambition can take one to places one does not wish to go.'

'That is so perceptive. It reminds me, somewhere in one of the Gospels, Jesus says that when you were young you walked where you would, but in old age one is led to where one does not wish to go. Tell me if you feel let down by my lack of status?'

'Good Lord, no! I don't give a fig. So back to practicalities; my trip to England. All right, Dusty, on this occasion I won't press you to come. And you must forgive me for being selfish. For wanting to go now when I could go later.'

'Selfish, why say that, when you're going with my blessing?'

'Selfish because I want to go, and as it happens, it will be useful having you here. Dad will be here next week, on a special mission. I want you two to be together.'

'Yes, I think I know why. There's an official Government of India letter addressed to Dr T G R Franks, care of Brigadier Chopra.'

'Daddy knows about that letter. It's to do with Sandy and Emma. Dad's unhappy about their grave and their being buried here. He was close to both, especially Emma and has always felt that, for them, England is home. He's worked long and hard for permission to exhume and cremate and take their ashes back to Winchester.'

'I know that you too have a problem with their grave. Mohan Singh told me.'

'I can't bear to see the grave. Have you...'

'Yes. I didn't want to say it till you asked. On three out of the four occasions I've been to Fern Cottage, I've walked that wild path to the school and the chapel, and laid flowers. It's been beautifully kept, clean and swept. Besides Mohan, you've got Dinesh to thank for that. He left money and instructions for their maintenance.'

'You could have told me about your visits to the grave.'

'Well, I couldn't forget that it was Emma that brought us together.'

CHAPTER SEVENTEEN

'Ramaswami, the landlord of the school building lives in Conoor. I have paid the deposit. I know the hills well. I've been there thrice on holiday. Sam introduced me to the Nilgiri Hills. Swami was astonished by my interest. It was a school in the days of the Raj, but it has been derelict for thirty years. He imagined it would end up a pile of bricks. I told him there was a lot of building work to do, and, honest man that he is, I'll get it at a bargain price.'

'Dusty, I'll leave it all to you. As I've had occasion to say before. It's pointless trying to get you to change your mind. Well I've stayed a week longer than I meant to. I was so tempted to go back with Dad. You've got a lot to occupy your time and you don't really need me. I'll go soon after tea.'

'I've got you all you need from the travel agent. You'll be travelling in style, Two nights in the train, First Class Air conditioned, one night at the Taj in Bombay, then Air India to London.'

'Thank you, my sweet. I really don't deserve you. Kiss me now, oh sorry, I forget. Not in front of the servants.' She looked at him. He stood looking repentant. 'Don't press your luck, Dusty. I'm not always giving in. Next time you're coming with me.'

'You won't be able to telephone, so cable me in any emergency. Tell Ted to be on his guard. You know Agarwal's not the type to let Dinesh go unpunished. He's been so lucky. I had my suspicions about the mali. An old family retainer was unlikely to be disloyal. The plan was too good to be true. What callous treachery! To make Dinesh believe he was fleeing into freedom when in fact he was going straight into the arms of Ayub Khan and certain death. Hard to get round that. I bet the Seth was behind it all.'

'Let's go in Dusty.' Kitty said gesturing that it was hot. They went in. She threw herself on the sofa, picked up a fan and fanned herself. 'And didn't Munshi fool us?'

'True. If it wasn't for Alice's letter I would never have guessed.'

'Dinesh distrusted the Munshi more than anyone else in Ram Niwas. Clearly the Munshi loved Dinesh like a son and took his time planning an ingenious getaway. But, Kitty, I've worked it out.'

'I'm certain to get a blow by blow account from Dinesh. But tell me. So that I can tell you how close you've got to the truth.'

'Well, the Munshi hid Dinesh somewhere, from where he could slip away without being seen, and that could only have been via the Munshi's office. Once out, Dinesh gets into the Seth's Mercedes and drives off. He's a brilliant driver. It must have been that way, because I gather the car was found abandoned outside New Delhi airport.'

'But, Dusty, the car keys? You said the Munshi told you that the poor driver, who was thrashed within an inch of his life, held up the car keys in his defence. It stumped the Seth, and to use your language threw him into a fit of apoplexy.'

'It must mean the Munshi did some long-term planning. Sorry I said that.'

'But how, Dusty? Or are you thinking what I'm thinking? Duplicate keys?'

'Key. Just the one, so Dinesh wouldn't have to waste time fumbling. But if the Seth works it out as we did, he'll wring it out of one of the local locksmiths. I wouldn't want to be in the…unless the Munshi took the precaution of having it made elsewhere.'

'Poor, sweet, ingenious Munshi! And to think he gave me the creeps.'

'Courage and kindness doesn't have to have a charming face.'

'Don't be pompous. He gave you the creeps too.'

Dusty laughed. 'Yes. And all I've said so far is guesswork. But if we're right, the sad thing is, we'll never know how long the Munshi will keep his secret and what his fate will be when that secret is out. I've asked Mohan to keep me informed.'

'Still, the Munshi will have had his revenge for all his years of slaving for a man he deeply hated. He gave Dinesh a briefcase full of the Seth's money.'

'Kitty, please! No tears. This is ridiculous.'

'It isn't!' She rounded on him.

Dusty was taken aback. He stared at her amazed. 'Kitty, you've had a good time. You've even stayed on a week longer, and now you see the rapid progress on the house and school buildings.'

'What are you going to call this place?'

'What we agreed. The Sam Dustoor Orphanage. Come here, Kitty, look at the plans. We've got these two long buildings facing each other. This one, with a veranda running its length, will be the dormitory; and across this courtyard is the schoolroom, with a small office next to it.'

She put an arm round his waist. 'Forgive me darling. I'm such a bore. You have to be patient with me. I'm erratic, fickle and so unreliable. I feared this would happen. When push comes to shove, I'll be found wanting.'

'Where on earth did you pick up that phrase, the last bit. Anyway it's nonsense and the earlier stuff is not you in the least.'

'I feel I won't be up to it.'

'But you agreed. You were excited about the project. And I haven't shown you the best part. Our cottage. There, on the slope down from here. On the spur overlooking the whole valley. Four rooms, a veranda and a garden and you can plan it any which way you like. The garden goes way down to the little stream.'

'It's no good. I've always lacked the will to see things through. I want to teach, but as part of an organised curriculum and staff; where the onus is not on me.'

'I'm ignoring all that. Now, the dorm is for twenty-five beds only. Twenty-five is to be the maximum intake, for a start, and boys only.'

'But it's not a school. It's a home. Education or rather schooling will be second to lodging, feeding, clothing, and caring.'

'We won't be alone supervising the home bit. There'll be the two women helpers.'

In the Shadow of a Dream

'I know. You've employed one already, while I've been away. I've seen the way her eyes follow you with undiluted adoration...'

'Oh, for God's sake Kitty! You're not going to add jealousy to our problems. You know I want to do this as some sort of return for what Sam did for me. Now, just let things run their course. Think about how we can make things better and easier for us. Give me some suggestions. There's plenty of money for any suggestions you make. And we're not touching capital. In time, in less than a year, the Kapoors will be ready to take over. If you go to the edge of our back veranda, you can look down into the large bungalow they have moved in.'

'You mean...'

'No, they have bought the place, but have not moved in as yet.'

'Oh, Dusty, I feel so ashamed of myself. I should never have gone home.'

'I tell you what. Let's lay down tools. Let's spend a fortnight at Ooty together. A fortnight of fun and frolic and effing, unlimited. There.' He took her in his arms. 'You look even more beautiful when tearful.' He drew her hard against himself and pressed his lips against her. 'Oo, you're all salty.'

She giggled. 'I'm human. Not a vision; I'm not an angel. Possibly she is.'

He turned. Behind him, in the muddy courtyard outside the veranda, with hands folded in salutation, stood a woman in a blue-bordered white sari. She was very dark, slim, full-breasted. 'Ah, Aruna. This Madam. When starting next week, Madam will be in charge. Work together, Madam, you, daughter. Now Kitty, the landlord, Swamiji, advised me it is best to employ a family. Aruna's daughter, Leela there, is sixteen.'

Aruna bowed and smiled sweetly. 'Madam, most beautiful lady.'

'Thank you.' Kitty answered. 'You are beautiful too. I can't believe your daughter is sixteen. And Aruna, you don't look much older yourself.'

Aruna looked a little confused. 'I come to making tea.'

'Thank you, you do that. I'm dying for a cup of tea,' Kitty said, and the women fled barefoot across the courtyard into one of the buildings. Kitty studied Dusty's face with a mischievous expression.

'The daughter is pretty like her mother. You're collecting quite a harem. How long has she been here?'

'A few days before you arrived. Now Kitty, none of that. She is an ayah. This is India. Masters and servants don't. Well, I suppose a paymaster could exploit the …not me. Damn it, and I don't like admitting it, but I'm a snob. Like young Pip in *Great Expectations*, I am ashamed of my past…No, that too isn't excuse enough. But, why am I saying any of this…' He pulled her from the veranda into the cool of a dark room. 'Who said: "Why go out for a beef burger when you get steak in the home?" You have killed competition, my beautiful Kitty…your straight delicate nose, these red pouting lips, your chin and this slender neck…' He put his hands round her neck. She stood very still, like a terrified bird, as he gently traced each feature of her face with his forefinger, then kissed each in turn… 'and those hazel eyes…'

She pushed him away. 'But you would have preferred them blue.'

He laughed. 'You're determined to be contrary. Determined to find me lacking.'

'How old is Aroo…I can't say the name, if her daughter is really sixteen?'

'In India, marriages are arranged early. She could be your age. Maybe a year or two younger. Incidentally her husband is a mason. He works on the premises.'

'When I said she was beautiful, I meant it. She has a pleasant face. A dark coffee beauty. What race is she?'

'Tamil. From Madras. Their language sounds like marbles rolling in a tin. You'll need to pick up some of it. All I've learned so far is *ingeh wah* and *angeh poh*.'

'What's that?'

'Come here and go there.'

She fell silent, then started to cry again.

'Now, Kitty, what is it?'

'Isn't there something else about me, looks apart, that you love me for?'

'I don't know what to say.'

'That worries and scares me. What of the future, Dusty?'

'But there has to be something else about you, Kitty!'

'What? Even if I could think for you, I can't think what.'

In the Shadow of a Dream

'I missed you while you were away. I was so lonely, and when you stayed a week longer, that seemed forever. I felt alone and afraid, for the first time.'

'What, alone and afraid?'

'Yes. That's not me. I dread attachments. All my life I've fought that.'

She took his hands and rested her head on his chest. He hugged her. 'Kitty,' he sighed, 'I now see why Sandy couldn't live without Emma... But I'm no Sandy. And that frightens me. I can't handle that.'

'Then let's make life together easier and less of a challenge. I'll work hard to make the orphanage a success. Just don't expect too much. You're such a perfectionist. But I promise, I'll do my best.'

'It won't be easy for either of us. Orphans can be wild and filthy, even ungrateful. At least we won't have to do the dirty work. It's why I hired Aruna and Leela, and in India one can afford to do that. Oh, I've got a surprise. For our chowkidar we have an old friend. Guess who?'

'No, don't. Tell me!'

'Ransingh.'

'What! O Dusty, really! Ransingh! Where, where is he?'

'This afternoon. We're going to meet his train. We have a long drive after lunch.'

'Oh my sweet Dusty. Thank you, thank you so much.'

'I knew that would please you. And that's not all. Jai his son is joining him next year. Ransingh told me Jai speaks fluent English because he went to a Convent school in Kalimpong, where he both worked and studied. I gather he's quite a linguist, Hindi and English, beside Tibetan. Did you know about him?'

'I knew of him, but a lot more about Ransingh from Sona. He would sit quietly, with dreamy eyes, while she'd chat away. It is only until recently that father and son have spent time together. Jai is his son from his first wife, and must now be in his mid-twenties. During the 1962 war with China, his mother, thinking Ransingh was dead, when in truth he was in a Military Hospital, killed herself, leaving baby Jai to be brought up by village neighbours as best they could. But they were poor and glad to let Monica Das take him away with her to Kalimpong.'

'Das? The name rings a bell.'

'It should. I worked with her in the Mission School, and resigned when she left.'

'He'll be useful to have here. When we give up, I'll make sure the two can stay on.'

'So this is what you've been doing while I was away? Recruiting. What now?'

'Come with me to the schoolroom. We've discovered some desks and a teacher's table.' They picked their way across the courtyard. 'All this will be levelled and turfed for a playground.'

'What's happened to the tea?'

'In the schoolroom. I saw Aruna place it on the table. I'm afraid we have to drink out of earthenware cups. No handles. Smash the cup after you've drunk the tea. The tea'll be very sweet, but you'll begin to like it.'

She pointed back to the building from which they came. 'There can't be enough room for twenty-five beds.'

'It is being extended. They are good chaps and they work fast. You'll see them in action tomorrow.' He looked at his watch. 'We should be getting back to the hotel, it's quite late and it gets dark suddenly.'

'After I've had my tea,' she said with sullen childishness.

He laughed. 'You'll be the death of me! I'll never be able to love you enough.'

While they sipped tea in the school room, Dusty pointed: 'You see those plans on the wall, I showed this plan to Ransingh. He said we need to repair the perimeter walls and erect a bricked hut outside, at the entrance, for him, so that no one goes in or out without his knowing. He's so terribly protective of you. He's also agreed to supervise work while we are away in Ooty.'

'How long are we going to be away?'

'Three weeks? A month?'

She shook her head. 'A month's too long to be away. Not at this stage. Less.'

'We'll get back whenever you say. Happy? Then…I've got sad news to share. I've heard from Mohan Singh. It seems the Munshi has vanished without a trace.'

'Oh, that horrid, horrid man! How can Seth Agarwal live with himself!'

CHAPTER EIGHTEEN

Within a year the limit of twenty-five places, in the Sam Dustoor Orphanage, were filled. Begging letters from local charities had to be turned down. 'We should have seen this coming,' Dusty said. 'One solution, according to Ransingh, is to create a qualifying category. Suppose we say, orphans whose parents served in the army?'

'That could mean, in some years, not having a full house,' Jai said. He was a tall young man, of light tanned skin and deep-set, sharp eyes.

'That's all right. Some years it'll mean less work. We don't have to kill ourselves. I'm not trying to prove anything. Just making it easier to live with myself.' Dusty put his pen down, and pushed his chair back with a slight annoyance. Then he stood up, took a walking stick from the corner of the office and went out into the veranda. He stared into the distance. 'Just a short walk,' he said sullenly. 'Back for dinner.'

Jai watched him circle the playground with a brisk walking pace that was meant to discourage the boys from running up to greet him. 'I don't understand,' Jai said, turning to Kitty.

'Never mind Jai. Dusty's heart was never in this. His idea was to make use of his money by providing work for others. He's no missionary. He just happened to fall in love with this place. The buildings, the area, the climate in these hills.'

'So my salary is only for…this is an insult. I don't need charity. I can get a job…'

'Hush! Calm down, Jai. My money's in it too, and I haven't lost interest. And don't be unfair to Dusty. He doesn't see what he's done for Ransingh and you, and even for those boys, as charity. He sees it more like a hobby. He likes to know it's there, but not to the extent of being completely absorbed in it.'

'So, madam, then if he loses interest, he'll just up and go; and you with him, huh?'

'Then Jai, it will be even more important for you to be here.'

'But, this is an orphanage not school. The boys are not fee-paying. Where's money coming from? I have skill, but no money. No capital.'

'But the school has been endowed. You know that. You help to run the accounts. We shan't touch that money. You'll just have to be a good all round manager.'

'Sorry. I've been unfair. Mr Dustoor's manner, just now, put me in a bad mood.'

'You must not let that happen again. You're a good teacher, far better than I am, and the boys love and respect you. Be patient. Mr Dustoor hasn't been his usual self, after that accident. It was a nasty fall. The horse had to be put down. Give it time. He will be my wonderful husband again. Jai, I'm the one who waxes and wanes, not he.'

Then the fateful letter from Kitty's father arrived. "Dearest Cat, We have had the most dreadful few weeks and a terrible tragedy. Dinesh has been murdered. He was blackmailed, lured into a trap; tortured, beaten and pushed to his death. His mangled body was found on the rocks at the bottom of Beachy Head. Poor dear Alice. I have vowed to pursue this crime and will not rest till the British police and Interpol have caught and punished those responsible. Mohan is very angry too, and has said he will stand by me and do his utmost. Dinesh will be avenged. That is the ugly side. There is a beautiful side to all of this too. Dinesh was indeed lured, but he also knew what he was doing. He sacrificed himself for Alice and his son. But he had hopes of returning home after some settlement had been reached. He went out in the face of all our protests. I enclose a copy of his last letter written in a fine firm hand, as you will see, before he went to meet his end.

"Would it be asking too much for you to come over as soon as you can? Alice is so v.fond of you. Kay feels only you could boost her morale. She too is so v.desolate and angry. I close with all our loves to both, Daddy."

The copy of Dinesh's letter had fallen on the floor. Kitty picked it up and read: "Dear Alice, I write while waiting here to be contacted by those who have taken me away from you, and I've asked my friend in the garage to post this letter exactly a week from now. If I should get home before it reaches you, we'll read it together and laugh. If I don't, then it makes good sense to have written it, because if this letter gets to you before I do, it would mean I may never return to you. In which event, please do not grieve. No good Hindu believes life has an end. I'll be somewhere on earth growing up again into manhood, but alas with no memory of you and Davy, Kay, Ted and all the past I hold dear. I know this idea of mine is not true to the Hindu theology of reincarnation, but there's no certainty on earth. Even the gods, if they are part of our lives, cannot know all the right answers. You said the creator of the universe would. But creation involves the three great gods, Brahma, Vishnu and Shiva, who are not in single agreement. I suppose a Creator has to be outside and apart from his creation—like the Judeo-Christian Jehovah. Maybe, an answer lies there. But not consolation. For much as I've grown to respect Christianity, comfort can only to be found in Hinduism, because we cheat ourselves. There's nothing right or wrong about that. Farewell, with all my love, Dinesh.

For Kitty's thirty-sixth birthday present, Dusty had ordered a set of cane furniture for the veranda. The pair of two large chairs, a coffee table, and two stools arrived within a week and he was particularly pleased that the table had a lower shelf for magazines. But Kitty was not there to see it. He poured himself a whisky and came out into the veranda, moved one of the chairs nearer the table and picked up V S Naipaul's book on India, which Jai had given him before the young man set out with twenty boys on a two-day trek in the hills. Ransingh managed to coax Aruna's husband to go on the trip with them. Dusty had planned to go, but changed his mind before they set out on the long march down the valley. Three adults were enough for twenty boys, besides, the old wound on his right foot was troubling him again. That was not the only reason. He was overwhelmed with sadness and wanted pause to think. He glanced at the book before putting it down; a just published, first hard cover edition, and he wondered how Jai got hold of it. Picking up the glass of whisky, he walked up to the far end of the veranda and stared across the valley. The trekkers had set out early in the mists of the morning and would by now have reached the teak woods of Kalum, their destination. He scanned the distance in the fading light and picked out a flickering glow no bigger than a pin-head. That would be their camp-fire. The gathering pre-monsoon haze cast a rare florescent mauve light, silhouetting the trees and hills in front into the stylised shapes of a Japanese painting. He touched the meshed trellis that kept insects from flying into the house, when the lamps were lit, and felt the cool, moist air. Thinking of lamps reminded him of the next thing he had to do, install an electric generator. Good old Ransingh knew how to work and maintain one. Had he not done that for Sandy and Emma at Fern Cottage? The wind rose with a low whistle and a distinct rustle, but he knew the boys would be sheltered, for it would move up to the higher altitudes.

 He returned to his chair and put the glass of whisky down, and was about to pick up the book, when he heard a shuffle of bare feet and heavy breathing. It was Aruna. 'I put bucket of water in *gussalkhana*,' she said. He nodded, went into the bathroom, stripped, took a bath using a brass *lota*, dried himself with a large towel and wore his favourite dark blue dressing-gown. He studied himself in the mirror and thought that he looked rather young and handsome for his forty-seven years. In the bedroom he put his slippers on and entered the dining-room. He was surprised to see Aruna by the table. 'Thank you Aruna-bai, but I'm not hungry. Not now.'

 'Master must eat.'

 'Later. Fruit and a glass of milk.'

 She looked at the glass in his hand and snatched it. 'Is too much drinking I say, master. I bringing milk.' She left the room and returned a moment later with the milk and fruit in a bowl. Then she went out again and was back with a lighted oil lamp.

She held it low so that it lit her face and full bosom. Does master want book?'

'No, thank you, I will get it, later.'

'Five months now, madam gone away. Coming soon, master? When coming?'

Dusty did not answer. He brushed his hair back and picked up the glass of milk.

'Is master needing anything more? I do anything for master.'

He turned towards her. His eyes rested on her face then travelled down to her firm round breasts. Her chest was heaving. He shook his head. 'No Aruna. But now about Leela. Are you happy for her? In two weeks Leela will be married?'

'Yes, master. Master very kind and good to us. But my husband, he not care.'

Dusty frowned. 'He cares, Aru, he cares. Jai will be good for Leela. He is a good young man, and a Christian, like you and Leela.'

'He tell Leela about how he became Christian in Kalimpong. But we Catholics. Jai, he prostitute.'

Dusty chuckled. 'You mean, Protestant. Do you mind that?'

'No, no. He say to Leela, he marry in Catholic Church. St Thomas. It's okay.'

'I went to a St Thomas's School in Bombay. Many years ago. But that was Church of England. Good. Yes, okay. I will write to madam about the wedding.'

'You get *chitty* today? Madam's letter?'

Dusty nodded. 'Goodnight Aruna. Shut the door after you.' He watched her leave, then resting his elbows on the table, he bowed his head and ran his hands through his hair. Alone, deeply miserable he felt unloved and sorry for himself. With a long sigh he stood up, drank from the tall glass in one long draught, looked at the fruit, picked up the oil lamp, took it to the veranda and collected his book. Then he froze. Pressed against the trellis, waving gently in the soft breeze, a bougainvillaea frond caught the light. It took him back to that night on the veranda of the Black Elephant Institute and the vision of Kitty caressing one such frond, after their first dance. He shook his head sadly, went into the bedroom and placed the lamp on the bedside table. There it was: her dreaded letter. He stared at it, sat down on the edge of the bed and picked it up. She had enclosed two photographs. One was of Ted with, according to the caption on the back, Kay. He thought they made a handsome couple, she a smaller, softer image of Lady Clementine Churchill. The other snap was of Kitty, smiling with the supreme confidence of one who knows she can never look ugly even if she tried. She had an arm round an open-faced young woman with friendly eyes and a broad mouth. So that was Alice! He put the photographs down and read the letter for the third time:

"Darling D, I'm sorry if it seems as if I may never return. The days seem to fly. I so love to be with Alice. I could never leave her till I'm sure she is her happy self again. I know how you must miss me, but here I am with a sister I never had, a father I've always loved, a delightful little boy, and Kay, who mothers us all.

"I write this letter, begging you to help me to make my mind up. And please don't get cross. Try to understand and maybe you can help us to come to a decision that will be important for our future. I am so mixed up now. I've decided to spend some time in a convent, to find peace. The Nun in charge there is Mother Clare. Will write again as soon as I can. I love you as much as I ever did. Be patient because, dearest, I have IMPORTANT NEWS for you, but I need to make sure first. You will make up for all my absence, I know, when we're together again!! Till then, Ever your doting Kitty."

Kitty sniffed and dabbed her eyes. 'I've tried. I can't do it alone.' She stared sadly into the smiling eyes of the older woman, who looked frail and tiny in the large heavy oak chair she sat in. Kitty knelt before her and took her hands in hers. 'Help me!'

The woman leant forward and kissed her on the forehead, then she gently pushed Kitty away and stood up with some difficulty. 'Come,' she said, and her voice shook more than it did earlier. They walked to the mullion window and looked across a landscape of rolling hills. For a while they drank in the scene. 'You see that ring of trees on top of that hill?' The woman pointed with a shaking forefinger. 'You can't miss it, it's the only hill with trees on it. We would walk to it, in dull winter afternoons. Just us. She and I. It was quiet, so peaceful; and so close to God.'

Kitty frowned; a little puzzled. She studied the delicate, soft wrinkled profile next to her and wondered why she wore a wimple and the heavy long black habit, while the rest of the Order of St Mary Magdalene were more comfortably dressed in grey headscarves, short plain grey dresses and black stockings. She saw a faint smile and a tear roll down the cheek of that serene face. The woman looked away. 'You're so like her,' she said above a whisper. Then she sighed and turned to face to Kitty. 'It's never too late or wrong to change your mind. You are not meant for this life.'

'Were you ever in love?' Kitty asked, before she could check herself.

'Oh, yes. Angelically beautiful she was too. I thought we were in love. Sandy took her away from me. I didn't mind. He was right for her.'

'Sandy? Yes, of course, Sandy! Oh, Sister Clare…'

'Mother.'

'Oh, Mother Clare! I should have known. I thought I knew, but I really didn't.'

'Why should you? You were a child then.'

'So it was with Emma? Those walks on the hill?'

Mother Clare smiled. 'Yes, I loved her. Deeply, as only a woman can. I would tell myself that it cannot be wrong to love a woman. I did ask for God's forgiveness; just in case I was wrong.' She gave a light chuckle. 'How do we know what we think is true? Plato asked that question. I suppose we all do.' She looked out of the window. Her lips trembled. You are very like her.' She opened her arms. Kitty clung to her. 'Gently my child. I haven't the strength to take your weight.'

'Oh, Mother, it can't be wrong. Even Dusty said he could understand homosexual love in women, because it was close to being pure and spiritual.' She kissed the old woman thoughtfully on both cheeks. 'Thank you for loving my beautiful Aunt Emma. People say I am an image of her, but I've never thought so. Her beauty had a rare quality, unearthly…How can I put it. I suppose, for want of a better word…spiritual.'

'Indeed. That's how it was between us. Spiritual. It gave me great comfort.'

'And, Mother, when did you learn about Sandy and Emma… you know?'

'Your father told me, almost as soon as he got the sad news. But now my dear, we must put the past behind us. Do you think of him a lot?'

'Not for sometime…and not till now.'

'My dear, you mustn't deceive yourself, you're still in love with your husband…what did you say his name is…I used to be good at names…Dusty. That's a strange epithet.'

'It's from Dustoor; which is a Parsee name.'

'You must go back to him. Especially, now that your father is no longer a worry to you. Remind me. Where did you say Dusty is?'

'The Nilgiri Hills.'

'And he's still running his orphanage. That's good work. Good work for you too.'

'He's obstinate. Refuses to come to England. It makes me cross.'

'You must indulge people their little whims. Be loyal to him and worry less about loved ones here. And you are carrying his child.'

'Yes. Oh, Mother,' and Kitty broke down and sobbed.

'You love him. I don't think you'll ever get over that. You are unhappy here, and when one is unhappy, one is filled with self-pity. And then you can serve neither God nor man. Go back to him child. Go, before it's too late.'

A week later Dusty received an Air Letter from Kitty. The handwriting was large and betrayed emotion. "Dearest Love, I write in haste. Remember my important news! You are going to be a father, quite soon. I am six months pregnant, so now, my sweet, you must meet me half way. I am prepared to do the same. Here's the deal. If it's a girl, I fly back to you. But if it's a boy, you have to be brave and come over here. But whether it's boy or girl, I'm going to have the baby in a hospital here in Winchester. Please understand. I am afraid. At my age having a baby is not without risk. And it is going to be a Caesarean birth. Will write at least once a week. I promise. Love you. K.

PS I am praying for a boy, so that the family here will meet and congratulate you."

In the Shadow of a Dream

◆❖◆

Kitty gave birth to a girl in the early hours of a Tuesday morning. Later that day Ted, Kay and Alice gathered round her bed. Ted kissed her. 'Now I won't have you looking disappointed. She's an image of you, Cat, and we are all happy for you.'

'Yes,' Kay said, smiling down at Kitty. 'She's pure gold. You know, Tuesday's child is full of grace.' She gave a short, shy giggle. 'Sorry, that's a silly thing to say.'

Alice said: 'And darling. It couldn't have turned out better. Look who is here!'

They parted; and there, with a large bunch of red roses in his hand, stood Dusty.

'Dusty! So you came!' Her lips trembled.

'I wanted it to be a girl,' he said, 'Truly, I did.'

She shut her eyes and turned her head away.

'Nothing was going to stop me seeing my daughter. Thank you for your letter.'

She remained silent.

'Kitty,' Dusty raised his voice a little, to make sure she heard. 'Congratulations!'

She turned to look up at him, and burst into tears.'

He was about to step forward, but felt Ted's restraining hand. They waited. Then with sobs and tears, Kitty said. 'Oh, my darling Sam, forgive me!' Ted nudged Dusty. He went up and knelt by Kitty. 'Yes, Dusty, it's Sam. Dusty no longer.'

'That's fine by me. Sam Dustoor is the only name I have, on record.'

EPILOGUE

'I hope you don't mind.' Ted said. 'But you did take your time. A long time.'

'Mind about what?'

'Kitty's little sulk.'

'Oh, that. It didn't register immediately. Jet lag. I'll make up for lost time. I've not come here to be deterred by slight or tantrum. For that's what it was…Was it not?'

'Hardly a tantrum. Anyway, what are your plans?'

'To return to India, before my visa expires.'

'As her husband you'll be entitled to stay on, in England.'

'I couldn't. It's not what I…India's home…but I won't leave without them. I'm determined to go back with my family.'

'I wholly approve. But give her time.'

'My visa is for six months. They said I could extend it, but six should be enough.'

'As I said, I'll support you. Kay and Alice feel the same as…'

'It's been hell, living alone without Kitty. So I won't take "no" from her.'

'Good for you. Glad to hear that, and I'm certain she'll go back with you. She's been unsure of herself and unhappy too.'

They remained silent for a while. Then Ted said. 'Don't give it another thought. She won't say "no". And Dusty…'

'It's Sam. Now and always. Sorry, do go on.'

'You must believe me, when I say, we were always on your side. I told her she was wrong to stay away so long. But all is well that ends well. She's ready to go. I'm glad you came. I may even accompany the three of you to India. No, I'll come later, with Kay. She hasn't been to India, so we'll do the tourist round.'

'Oh, I gather it took a lot of time and effort to finally get the ashes here. But that's over and done with.'

'Thank you. The mills of India grind, but they grind exceeding slow.'

Sam laughed. 'Indians don't understand the impatience of the West. But, as Kafka said, somewhere, something like: impatience drove Adam and Eve out of Paradise, and impatience will prevent them returning.'

'Good man.'

'Or as they say in Indian English: Good man the *laaltan*.'

'I've heard that before. "Laaltan" for lantern. Quite an eloquent metaphor: the man with a lighted lantern, showing the way.'

Once again they were silent for a while. Then Ted took a deep breath.

'What was that for?'

'Nothing, Dus—Sam. Well, I was remembering Sandy. Dear old Sandy. He was far too idealistic. England was his idea of Utopia. Sadly, he was let down.'

'Now it's my turn to quote. Gandhi said, if ideals can be realised, they cease to be ideals and leave nothing to strive or long for. Or words to that effect, as they say in the army.' Sam chuckled. 'But something in its place can be achieved, a utopian end.'

'Sam, utopias are dead states. They lack aims and endeavours. To fling Gandhi back at you. I think he said of utopias that they debilitate. The utopian status quo is hard to maintain. Always there is someone ready to take advantage, an unearned advantage, an undeserved benefit. The few exploiting the goodwill of the majority.'

'But Sandy's love for England, I gather, had great charm.'

'Indeed, and it was impossible to argue with him. He had a disarming sense of logic that was hard gainsay. Once, we were talking about African states and the problems of their governments. "What went wrong," I asked. "India was ruled by the British, but it is a democracy." "I'll tell you what's wrong", he said, "the British were not there long enough. Another fifty years would have made all the difference." '

'He might have a point. As philosophers say, it's an incorrigible truth.'

Ted turned to face Sam and raised his brows. 'Kitty warned me about you. Your breadth of knowledge through reading.' He laughed, put an affectionate arm round Sam and squeezed him. 'Take good care of Kitty.'

Sam returned the hug. 'I'm too old to call you Dad. Yes, I will.'

'You look young enough to be my son.'

'You never know, Ted, we may be back here after a few years. A mother and daughter could make a formidable team.'

'Well, this is Kitty's house.'

'Ted, you'll receive the Queen's telegram on your hundredth birthday. But tell me, if Sandy didn't revise his feelings for England, after those thugs beat him up, what was there to prevent him returning?'

'Emma. He knew how much she loved Fern Cottage and, above all, her garden. But I suppose there was also the possibility that she could never forgive or forget that England let him down. Shall we, they're calling us in for lunch. By the way, what do you think of Davy, Alice's son?'

'He's so like Dinesh. And Alice is so devoted to him.'

'As Kay is devoted to Alice.'

'Yes.' Sam caught Ted's arm. 'Did Kitty tell you I saw Emma and Sandy, briefly?'

'She told me. Sam, I can't tell you how good it is for me to know they're here, feel they are here, in this house, in Winchester, where they first met. I brought them back. Right or wrong, for Sandy, home is England.'

The End

Lightning Source UK Ltd.
Milton Keynes UK
UKOW052009170812

197715UK00001B/20/P